Private property and the fear of social chaos

Manchester University Press

'Home, sweet home! There's no place like home!' by Thomas Nast, *Harper's Weekly*, 22 June 1878

Private property and the fear of social chaos

Aidan Beatty

MANCHESTER UNIVERSITY PRESS

Copyright © Aidan Beatty 2023

The right of Aidan Beatty to be identified as the author of this work has been asserted in accordance with the Copyright, Designs and Patents Act 1988.

Published by Manchester University Press
Oxford Road, Manchester M13 9PL

www.manchesteruniversitypress.co.uk

British Library Cataloguing-in-Publication Data

A catalogue record for this book is available from the British Library

A version of Chapter 3 was previously published as: 'Marx and Engels, Ireland, and the racial history of capitalism', in *Journal of Modern History*, Vol. 94, No. 1 (2019).

The writing of this book was financially supported by the Irish Research Council.

ISBN 978 1 5261 6570 1 hardback
ISBN 978 1 5261 9163 2 paperback

First published 2023
Paperback published 2025

The publisher has no responsibility for the persistence or accuracy of URLs for any external or third-party internet websites referred to in this book, and does not guarantee that any content on such websites is, or will remain, accurate or appropriate.

EU authorised representative for GPSR:
Easy Access System Europe – Mustamäe tee 50, 10621 Tallinn, Estonia
gpsr.requests@easproject.com

Typeset
by Cheshire Typesetting Ltd, Cuddington, Cheshire

For Keir

Contents

Acknowledgements	*page* viii
Introduction	1

Part I: Theories

1. The invention of a new world	23
2. The poet of real property	63
3. The Moor's laboratory	113

Part II: Practices

4. The failure of free society	159
5. Privatised utopias	201
6. The Iron Lady's imaginary childhood	238
Epilogue: Interplanetary settler-colonialism	286
Bibliography	310
Index	331

Acknowledgements

This project began in 2015 as I was finishing up my first book. My thanks to Leora Auslander for helping me formulate what was still a very random set of ideas into an initial plan. In 2015–16, I was a postdoctoral researcher at the Azrieli Institute at Concordia University in Montreal and I am grateful to my colleagues – Bina Freiwald, Jennifer Solomon, Csaba Nikolenyi – for their support. From 2016 to 2017, I was an Irish Research Council (IRC) postdoctoral fellow at Trinity College Dublin, which gave me time to read most of the primary source material for this book. Ciaran O'Neill was an always generous and welcoming sponsor of my IRC fellowship, from helping with the initial application through to my actual time at Trinity. I finished up the writing while teaching as an adjunct at Wayne State University in Detroit and, in my current position, at the University of Pittsburgh Honors College. It has always been enjoyable to work at Pitt with Josh Cannon, Nicola Foote, Dave Fraser, Lesha Greene, David Hornyak and Brett Say, among so many others. It is great to work at a college defined by collegiality and I am always hugely grateful for all those who supported me and welcomed me.

Research at the Harry S. Truman Library Institute in Independence, Missouri, was made possible through a grant from the Truman Library in the summer of 2017.

My friends and colleagues Chris Dingwall, Seán Donnelly, Beth Fowler, Peter Hession, Susanna Klosko, Adam Larragy, Robert Morrison and David Roediger all read parts (and sometimes all) of the manuscript and helped me avoid many embarrassing mistakes. And along the way I had some great discussions about this project with Brandon Proia.

Acknowledgements

Ironically for a book about the fear of chaos, the manuscript went through a long period of being chaotic and slapdash. Tom Dark at Manchester University Press greatly helped that process of refining the manuscript with patience, intelligence and judicious advice. Likewise, the two anonymous peer reviewers provided a very helpful series of constructive comments that helped me shape an overly rough draft into something (hopefully) more coherent.

My family on both sides of the Atlantic – Jane and TJ, Sheila, Claire, James, Hannah and Mike, Bill and Ruthe – are always wonderfully supportive.

It is impossible to imagine what writing this book would have been like without the support of my wife, Leslie. This project began just before our son Keir was born and the writing of it always took place in and around parenting. I completed the final revisions in a spare bedroom converted to an office and virtual classroom in the midst of the COVID-19 pandemic. And then Keir and I gladly moved out of that room to make way for his little sister Lena, an always joyous addition to our family. This book is dedicated to Keir.

Introduction

Private property has made us so stupid and one-sided.
                                                    Karl Marx[1]

Whiteness is the ownership of the earth forever and ever, Amen!
                                                    W.E.B. du Bois[2]

Seeing with private property

This is a book about whiteness and masculinity and about private property as a way of seeing, ordering and restructuring the world, from the seventeenth century onwards in the Anglophone Atlantic. This is a study of what people *imagine* it means to live in a world where private property is dominant, and their fears (and sometimes hopes) about living in a future world where private property has disappeared – it is a history of the culture of private property. What I am specifically interested in is private property as an ideology and how private property gave birth to a specific way of 'seeing' the world; seeing empty spaces as always awaiting privatisation and seeing subsequent challenges to privatisation as terrifying violations of male authority or of white authority.[3] The central story of this book is that the intellectual partisans of private property have always feared that their propertied social order will be destroyed by a diverse mob of dangerous enemies: wandering vagrants and beggars, Levellers, Diggers, Ranters, nomadic Native Americans, slaves and ex-slaves and escaped slaves, socialists, communists and anarchists, Jacobins, republicans, the Irish, Jews, Mormons, Quakers, fervent religious radicals in general, abolitionists, feminists or any class of publicly assertive women, upwardly mobile Black people, haughty welfare-state bureaucrats and climate change refugees. The history of private property is the history of a recurring nightmare that one or another of these *lumpen* mobs would storm the castle, take control and demolish private property. And in these fevered dreams, assaults on private property were assaults on white, male authority. In the story that this book narrates, private property and 'the mob' are two intimately interconnected categories of political thought and political action; the mob are the spectre that always haunts the propertied elite.

This book thus argues that 'the mob', broadly defined, has had a determining impact both on political thought in capitalist modernity, and on political action.

Private property and the history of the mob

This book aims to tell one important story within the very much larger story of the history of capitalism: namely, the history of the enclosure of common land, starting in England, but then radiating out from there, to Ireland and the New World; and the fears of mobs that always haunted this project. A capitalist world-system emerged out of the long sixteenth century. England and then Britain and then the United Kingdom of Great Britain and Ireland grew in strength until, in the nineteenth century, it was the dominant hegemon within that system. In the twentieth century, the United States, itself a product of the same Anglophone capitalist culture, took over as *the* dominant capitalist nation-state. This book treats the United States, Britain and Ireland as a discrete cultural entity; divided, for sure (by monarchism *versus* republicanism, by religion, by language, by the Atlantic) but also unified by a shared set of assumptions about enclosed private property as the normative bedrock of a modern society and a shared set of fears about what could happen if this social order ever broke down.

While enclosure had been under way in a looser form since the late Middle Ages, from 1545 until well into the eighteenth century, at least four thousand, and perhaps upwards of five thousand, acts of Parliament privatised land that had previously been commonage.⁴ All told, close to a quarter of the agricultural land of Britain – approximately 6 million acres – was privatised through the Enclosures.⁵ The newly privatised land, in the main, was either dedicated to small-scale and more efficient tillage farming, or turned over to large-scale sheep farming.⁶ Private property ownership, always more conditional in feudal times, became an unconditional and even absolute right.⁷ In the definition given in the second volume of William Blackstone's hugely influential *Commentaries on the Laws of England*, 'Property is that sole and despotic dominion which one man claims and exercises over the external things of the world, in total exclusion of the right of any other individual in the universe. This [is the] modern conception of property as sole and despotic dominion with a particular emphasis on exclusion'.⁸ (It is this sense of property as an absolute thing, sacrosanct and in need of state protection, that this book studies.)

Even so, resistance to the enclosures was practically instantaneous. Peter Linebaugh identifies a general history of early modern English radicalism and opposition to the enclosures, going back to Kett's Rebellion in East Anglia and the Prayer-Book Rebellion in the West Country, both in the summer of 1549.⁹ In his work with Marcus Rediker, Linebaugh has also provided a useful list of the major agrarian uprisings of the sixteenth century, giving a sense of the scale of rural discontent: the Cornish rising (1497), the Lavenham rising (1525), the Lincolnshire rebellion (1536), and then the Prayer-Book Rebellion and Kett's Rebellion in 1549. Urban risings became more common toward the end of the sixteenth century: the Ludgate Prison riot (1581), the beggars' Christmas riot (1582), the Whitsuntide riots (1584), the plaisterers' insurrection (1586), the felt-makers' riot (1591), the Southwark candle-makers' riot (1592), the Southwark butter riot (1595) and the Midlands revolt of 1607, the 'largest rebellion of the age'.¹⁰

The breakdown in censorship in England during the revolution of the 1640s allowed communitarian and anti-enclosure ideas to be more freely publicised. Where only twenty-two tracts were published in 1640, by 1642 there were close to two thousand works published in England. There were three newspapers in England in 1641 but fifty-nine in 1642 and seventy by 1648. Taverns and alehouses became meeting houses for radicals (and a major source of concern for the ruling elite). The ending of the state church's monopoly (a key demand of the Parliamentarians), not only led to the creation of hundreds of new congregations, but also helped to create a culture of religious dissent.[11] Religious debate was itself inextricably entangled with constitutional, legal, political and economic issues; dissent in one field led to dissent in the others. Within Cromwell's New Model Army, the Levellers acted as a vehicle for radical politics, even if they were not as radical as contemporaries sometimes feared.[12] The demand for common property was 'throughout the entire decade a continuous demand', though we generally only know of such demands from those who fulminated against them.[13] A well-documented exception is Gerrard Winstanley's Digger experiment in Surrey, a merging of print-communism and actual existing communism.[14] In Winstanley's brief literary career, he wrote a series of sophisticated treatises in favour of a very Christian-inflected post-private property society, and at his colony on George's Hill in Surrey he put such ideas into practice.[15] Founded on April Fool's Day 1649 and lasting only four months, Winstanley's commune was perceived as enough of a danger that it was violently suppressed by local elites. This reflected a more general pattern and it is this pattern which this book traces: the opponents and victims of the enclosures were feared as crazed mobs and the question of what to do with the 'masterless men' (and masterless women) made vagrant by the enclosures preoccupied English political thought during the long sixteenth century and into the seventeenth and beyond. By the time of the Glorious Revolution of 1688 – effectively a coup to remove the Catholic-leaning James II and replace him with William of Orange, a Dutch import – a regime appears to have been instituted in which the enclosures and private property would be unassailable.[16]

But this was never just an English story. Already at the start of the 1600s, one popular solution to the problem of the anti-private property mob was to send the excess population overseas, either to Ireland or to the New World, or, to put this differently, those who had been converted into an excess population by enclosures would be sent overseas to enclose and privatise even more territory.[17] English schemes for restructuring Ireland, removing the 'mere Irish' and settling the country with English or Scottish planters, were under way from the late sixteenth century and provided a template for New World settlement in the next century. English colonisation was predicated on the dispossession of Native Americans, whose rights to, and ownership of, the land were wished away. In places like the Virginia Territory, as staggeringly large farms became available once the natives had been dispossessed, and as indentured British and Irish workers sought to also enjoy this newfound bounty, enslavement of Black Africans became the preferred means of providing enough captive labour to work these estates. Enclosures in England, plantations in Ireland, dispossession of Native Americans and enslavement of Black Africans were all parts of the same process. The invention of the white race was itself born out of this process.[18] Enclosures in England helped to solidify the gendered idea that property ownership was part of what made a 'normal' man. Enclosures in Ireland and North America gave private property a racial component that it has never lost.

John Locke, the paragon of early English liberalism, touched on all these themes (domestic enclosure, foreign colonies, Native American dispossession, enslavement of Africans), channeling the regnant notion that America was an empty wilderness that could absorb the rural vagrants of England. Locke was unsurprisingly popular in the Thirteen Colonies, and his arguments about the legitimacy of rebelling against an unjust tyrant were strategically deployed in 1776 (such ideas had also been swirling around England in 1688 during the deposing of the 'tyrant' James II). On the eastern side of the Atlantic, after 1776, Jeffersonian ideas of popular sovereignty found ready purchase among an emergent working class who still lacked voting rights. These plebeian mobs became even more terrifying to the elite after 1789, when Jacobinism, the Terror and the guillotine seemed to show the logical outcome of allowing the lower classes to seize power. Edmund Burke, a proto-conservative statesman, amateur philosopher and Anglo-Irish landowner, racialised the French mob, labelling them 'Maroons' (escaped slaves) and 'Jews'. The 1790s saw a suppression of oppositional voices and groups and, briefly, a suspension of *habeas corpus*. That French-inspired rebels almost took over in Ireland in 1798, and that the United Irishmen made direct appeals to 'the men of no property', was all too close for comfort.[19] What we today call conservatism was a product of these fears; the fear that gangs of proles would take power and simply vote private property away. Ireland came under direct British rule at the opening of the nineteenth century, but conservative anxieties did not disappear.

The Industrial Revolution created a whole new, urban, working class, often exploited, regularly discontented. The fear of a politicised mob remained. Irish migrants had been arriving in large numbers in England well before 1847; this accelerated after the Famine that started in that year. The Famine's roots lay in both a natural disaster and long-standing patterns of land ownership in a country that had not yet fully accepted primogeniture (commonage still existed and privately held farm land tended to be divided among all sons rather than just gifted to the oldest). The Famine led to mass death as well as mass emigration. In both Britain and in the northern United States, Irish migrant workers filled important gaps in the labour market – 400,000 in Britain already in 1841 and 'the cheapest labour in Western Europe'[20] – and faced remarkably the same anti-Irish prejudices in both places. That the Chartists, one of Britain's first organised working-class groups, had a strong Irish presence and an Irish leader, Fergus O'Connor, did not help assuage nativist fears of the Irish mob.

Yet socialists could also be a cypher, a screen onto which fears were projected, and they were not always as radical as their conservative enemies feared. Nineteenth-century socialists were generally conventional in their assumptions about race and gender. Nonetheless, the *perception* that the lower orders were a danger to private property did have a determining impact on politics; Robin Blackburn has shown how abolition of slavery in Britain in 1833 was bound up with the desire, on the part of the establishment, to assuage the nascent working-class movement.[21] The Great Reform Act, the first tentative step towards broadening the right to vote, had been passed the previous year, which as Blackburn points out is not at all a coincidence.

In the United States, where slavery survived for another thirty years, slave-owners and their boosters certainly feared that the dismantling of one form of property (slaves) would lead to dangerous mobs dismantling all property. Anti-abolition and anti-communism were first cousins. For a brief period, it even seemed that these fears were well founded; during the Reconstruction that followed the American Civil War, various radicalisms not only took root but even seemed to receive Federal support. In any case, the (premature) ending of Reconstruction represented a 'counter-revolution of property';[22] the linkage between whiteness and property ownership remained and the mob were defeated. Likewise, after the Wall Street Crash of 1929, and more so after 1945, property ownership in the USA remained a marker of white hetero-normality, with Black Americans excluded from the new suburbs. Even if no real enemies existed to threaten the property order, the Keynesian vision of postwar suburbia remained an anxious one, walled in and beset by perceived dangers.

The collapse of the Keynesian consensus in the 1970s unleashed these anxieties, with Reagan and Thatcher both openly naming the nasty outsiders that threatened their imaginary worlds: Black welfare queens, the gay community, socialists on the wrong side of history, Irish terrorists, inarticulate criminal thugs, 'the enemy within', a nostalgic Britain now being 'swamped by people with a different culture'. All threatened to lay siege to what Thatcher called 'a property-owning democracy'. Such overwrought fears and fantasies, openly racist and longing for a gendered past of stoic men and compliant housewives, are perhaps only likely to increase under the climate breakdown of late capitalism.

This is not a linear or teleological story. The post-enclosures regime that slowly emerged in sixteenth- and seventeenth-century England changed and grew as it was adapted and challenged in other times and places. Yet having said that, the ideology deployed (and redeployed) to defend private property was often remarkably similar; private property was legitimated with and through whiteness and masculinity, in recurring narratives of imagined social stability and chaos. And that threatened social chaos, specifically, is the story this book recounts. In the propertied imagination, private property is a fragile thing, a socially positive institution beset by terrifying enemies. The narrative of private property as a source of harmony and social stability had to be told and retold precisely because of a simultaneously parallel narrative about the imminent disappearance of private property. Mark Neocleous has diagnosed an '*insecurity*' at the heart of the bourgeois order – the insecurity of property'. Property remains insecure *because* so few people own it. The class societies of capitalism are built on the assumption that only a fraction of the total population will become property owners and thus poverty will remain endemic and the inequality that this necessarily fuels in turn fuels insecurity.[23] It is thus unsurprising, that the social worlds described by John Locke, the conservative statesman Edmund Burke, the pro-slavery polemicist George Fitzhugh, or Margaret Thatcher, were both idyllically perfect and frighteningly under siege by a host of dangerous assailants.

Intersectional methodologies

Mark Neocleous has gone on to say that 'creating a clear distinction between the deodorized bourgeoisie and the foul-smelling masses' is a central goal in a propertied social order.[24] I would add that this is a racialised and gendered concept of understanding and seeing 'proper' societies and the proper/propertied social order. And as is perhaps clear by now, this book draws on an intersectional understanding of private property, and of race, gender and class, in which 'class' is the cultural expression of being a property owner or a propertyless worker or slave. In general terms, there are no understandings of private property that are not simultaneously racialised and gendered. More specifically, ownership of private property in the modern Anglophone Atlantic has an intimate connection with both whiteness and hegemonic masculinity.

One of the central ideas of race and gender theory is that they are studies of 'difference'; but masculinity and whiteness as discursive practices are less about 'difference' *per se* than concerned with sameness and normality, and with the order and social stability that normality supposedly brings.[25] This is why they lend themselves so neatly to pro-private property theorising, which also values order and stability. As John Adams once said, 'the moment the idea is admitted into society, that property is not as sacred as the laws of God, and that there is not a force of law and public justice to protect it, anarchy and tyranny commence'.[26] Stuart Hall once said that race is the modality through which class is lived.[27] In this work,

I contend that whiteness and masculinity are the modalities through which private property (*the* key signifier of class) is imagined and apprehended.

The acts of imagination which this book studies – and in which race and gender were so central – were acts of legitimation, as capitalist theorists constructed an image of the ideal world that capitalism promises but never really delivers; often constructing that image in conscious opposition to images of dismal, chaotic or violent non-capitalist worlds. A vision of harmonious private property required a vision of a savage order where private property did not receive its due respect. And as I argue in this book, over the last four hundred years there has never been a conception of private property, and of the class-ridden society it underpinned, that has been free of race and gender. Race, gender and class are all constructed social phenomena. But they are constructed with and through each other. Not only is it impossible to separate them out and think about or analyse them one by one, to do so misses their interconnected natures. As Ange-Marie Hancock has defined it, intersectionality is a 'holographic epistemology' that should allow us to think of the three-dimensional field in which all three (race–gender–class) are co-productive, rather than falling into the trap of engaging in an 'additive logic' that tacitly assumes that race, class and gender can be added to, or severed from, each other.[28]

Ultimately, race and gender, just like private property, are ways of seeing and organising the world. In 'The souls of white folk', an essay in his 1920 collection *Darkwater: voices from within the veil*, W.E.B. du Bois proffered the neat summation that 'whiteness is the ownership of the earth forever and ever, Amen!'[29] Which is to say, that whiteness is the self-perception that one has the inherent right to control and dominate all that one sees. A Black socialist who sought to avoid 'a mechanistic or economic deterministic view of society', du Bois understood that capitalism and racism, whose central elements are private property and white supremacy, 'were inextricably tied together'.[30] Du Bois also believed that race and gender were built relationally via the history of European imperialism and colonialism.

Du Bois' insights have been replicated in more recent scholarship. The Indigenous Australian scholar Aileen Moreton-Robinson, quoting her uncle Dennis Benjamin Morrison, has said that 'the problem with white people is they think and behave like they own everything'. In more academic language, and also recognising the role of gender and class in all this, Moreton-Robinson investigates 'the possessive logics of patriarchal white sovereignty', where sovereignty refers to both control over individual plots of land and national sovereignty. Moreton-Robinson later talks of 'the masculine capacity to possess property and to bear arms'.[31] That 'whiteness' is of a piece with property ownership and normativity is the focus of Cheryl Harris' seminal essay 'Whiteness as property': to be white is to be granted certain economic privileges and material security, to be granted 'the possibility of controlling critical aspects of one's life rather than being the object of other's domination'.[32] To be white is to see one's self as one's own stable property, rather than being threatened with becoming the property of another.

A specific way of seeing the world is also on display in 'Home, sweet home', a lithograph originally published in *Harper's Weekly* in 1878 and used as a frontispiece for this book. 'Communism' is personified as a walking death that will not just destroy private property, but will bring an inevitable destruction to the white family home and to a man's ability to provide for his children and his wife. That wife will presumably lose respect for her husband, and the only recompense will be the 'Free Love' propped up on the communist Grim Reaper's hat. To look upon communism is simultaneously to look upon the horror of propertylessness and the horror of sexual abnormality. Anti-communism thus has an inbuilt tendency to go beyond fears just about the end of private property, incorporating fears about 'free love, assaults on the family and on the church, homosexuality, the idea of white women becoming public property, and the threat of interracial sex'.[33] As Kathryn Conrad has noted, the desire to maintain and contain the heterosexual family is a simultaneous desire 'to control borders, to reproduce the nation, to ensure "stability"'.[34] I concur with this, with the caveat that 'stability' in Anglophone modernity is always a simultaneously propertied, gendered and racialised term. Race and gender are always essential to visions of both propertied 'stability' and the horror of a propertyless society.

Plan of the book

This book focuses on the central 'moments' in the history of Anglophone capitalist modernity – colonisation of the New World from 1607 onward, the enslavement of Africans after 1619, the Glorious Revolution of 1688, the emergence of liberalism, the American Revolution in 1776 (itself a channeling of that liberal ideology), the reaction to the French Revolution in 1789 and the invention of conservatism, the rise of socialism, abolition and anti-abolition, Keynesianism, neoconservatism and neoliberalism – and in each case identifies emblematic texts, theorists and political figures from those moments.

The first part is composed of three chapters and studies the writings of four of the most influential theorists of private property in Anglophone modernity.

The book starts with John Locke's conception of private property, mainly drawing from his two *Treatises of Government*. It is difficult to overemphasise the importance of Locke's way of thinking about private property; his influence can be seen in perhaps all subsequent Anglophone writings on the topic. As Christopher Pierson has said, Locke's status as a theorist of private property is only matched by that of Karl Marx.[35] Locke understood private property as a source of stability in society and as being the sole preserve of men. But he also saw it as something artificial; God created nature but man privatised it over the long course of human history. Locke imagined America as a massive cornucopia, a natural, pre-private property – and pre-civilisational – space. He believed that the 'empty' Americas, once privatised, would allow English men access to their own private property and they could there create an ideal social order; this would act as a safety valve for an England perceived as overcrowded and overrun with dangerous 'masterless men'. Moreover, in Locke's mind, Native Americans did not use the land productively and therefore had no real right to it. How he perceived the unprivatised land of the New World would have a huge influence on American and even global political culture. He also had a determining impact on the later intellectual history of private property on both sides of the Atlantic, with the emphases on male authority and an exclusion of non-white races from the rights to own property.

The second chapter investigates Edmund Burke's *Reflections on the Revolution in France* (1790), perhaps the founding text of modern conservatism. The *Reflections* was written in response to a popular pro-Jacobin speech at the Old Jewry, London, in November 1789 by the Welsh preacher and republican pamphleteer Richard Price. And Burke made much of the 'Jewish' location of Price's radical oratory. With an antisemitic tone, Burke argued that the Jacobins were 'Jews', that is to say men who made their money through usury and lacked the requisite respect for private property. He likewise labeled them 'Maroons' – escaped African slaves – and lamented the fact that women played so central and active a role in the Revolution. And, as this chapter discusses, Burke contrasted this French chaos with Britain; simultaneously, his *Reflections on the Revolution* were a reflection on a harmonious image of British social peace, where private property supposedly remained sacrosanct and the 'natural' racial and gendered order of his late-eighteenth-century world had not been inverted. Burke's political imagination was a mixture of anti-Jewish racial rhetoric, conservatism, patriarchal fear of women and a valorisation of landed property. This type of thinking, which Burke pioneered, would prove remarkably pervasive in the later history of private property; Burke has had an influence far beyond what is usually assumed.

The third chapter examines the romance of Marx and Engels for the island of Ireland, their belief that Ireland was a place where private property was not yet dominant and their related view that the Irish were a still feudal race that existed outside the coercive discipline of modern capitalism; Engels, and to a subtler degree Marx, saw the Irish as freer, more human and more masculine than the industrial proletariat of England. The chapter situates this stereotyping in the broader context of Victorian British attitudes towards the Irish, specifically the belief that the Irish were a lovable and warm, if also primitive, people; as with their writings on Jews, Indians and the Chinese, Marx and Engels accepted such racial stereotypes while also reworking them into their critique of private property. Yet in Marx and Engels' writings on Ireland there was a romance and a respect that remained absent from their analyses of Jews, Indians or other non-'white' races. And Ireland was a laboratory in which Marx and Engels could construct their ideas of primitive accumulation, the alienation and unhappiness caused by private property and the transition from feudal to capitalist property-relations. I focus here on seminal communist thinkers, to show how communism has often imagined the world in terms similar to propertied ideology, seeing empty spaces waiting for modernity, change and guidance, with a similar dependence on the vocabularies of race and gender. For Marx and Engels, the Irish were a mob threatening the property order, but they understood such terms in positive and anti-capitalist registers.

Chapters 1 through 3 are histories of liberalism, conservatism and socialism and of the seminal thinkers (Locke, Burke, Marx and Engels) of these three ideologies. All these thinkers were also inherently transatlantic and international; indeed, their 'transatlanic-ness' was a major motivation for choosing them. Locke was English, lived for long periods in the Netherlands and worked for colonial enterprises in the Carolinas; Burke was Irish, lived almost all his adult life in England, corresponded with American colonists and gave Parliamentary speeches sympathetic to them, and his most famous political tract is an intervention into French politics; Marx and Engels were German, lived most of their lives in England, but always retained strong interests in continental politics and Irish nationalism, and wrote for the *New York Tribune*. All four also combined theory with practical action, whether in the socialist movement (in Marx and Engels' case), as a Member of Parliament (Burke) or as a colonial bureaucrat (Locke).

Part II is made up of four transatlantic case studies that aim to show how the ideas of Locke, Burke, and Marx and Engels continue to reverberate on both sides of the Anglophone Atlantic. Focusing more on practical politics than on canonical texts, these four chapters show how the politics of private property operated according to logics earlier developed and popularised by Locke, Burke, and Marx and Engels.

In Chapter 4, I cross back over the Atlantic, to investigate the most extreme example of Lockean conceptions of private property: the notion that certain human beings were themselves a natural resource awaiting privatisation. George Fitzhugh was one of the most prominent ideologues of slavery in 1850s America; in just a few years he produced a slew of newspaper articles and two books – *Sociology of the south* and *Cannibals all!* – in which he not only defended the 'peculiar institution' of American chattel slavery but also went on the offensive, constructing an image of the 'free' north as being the true home of oppression and economic violence in antebellum America. And in opposition to an imaginary depiction of a chaotic and violent north, Fitzhugh constructed an even more fantastical image of a harmonious, peaceful and well-ordered south in which private property was dominant (including chattel property), slaves were happy and obedient, and white, male heads-of-household were never challenged or questioned.

Chapter 5 stays in the United States, studying housing in the Truman era, and how, after the chaos and horrors of the Great Depression and the Second World War, the Federal Housing Administration (FHA) actively promoted suburbanisation and an idealised vision of the white nuclear family. The combined effects of the Depression and the war effort meant there was a serious housing shortage in the USA after 1945. Within the Truman administration, there was often an open anger against a real estate industry that was perceived to be uncooperative in solving this crisis. Yet the eventual programme privileged privately built and privately owned single-family homes (conventionally holding three or four bedrooms, thus subtly insinuating how many children a couple should have), with mortgages generally made available only to white applicants. I place all this in the broader context of American welfare provision – which has tended to favour the inviolability of private property – its sustained racial and gendered underpinnings and its fear of being undermined by communists or Black outsiders. This chapter draws extensively on archival material from the Truman Presidential Library.

The policies of the Truman era were emblematic of the Keynesian consensus that dominated the postwar years. Chapter 6 examines the breakdown of that consensus and also explores the particular obsession with their own childhoods of late-twentieth-century Anglophone conservatives. In their autobiographies, Ronald Reagan and Barry Goldwater both waxed nostalgic about their supposedly idyllic youth in rural Illinois and the Arizona Territory, respectively.

Likewise, Margaret Thatcher, the central focus of this chapter, used her two volumes of autobiography and countless speeches and interviews to construct a rosy image of her prewar childhood as a grocer's daughter in provincial Lincolnshire. This imaginary world of a pre-Welfare State and implicitly white, pre-*Windrush* Britain served to throw into sharp contrast her dystopian view of 1970s and 1980s Britain, a land of oppressive socialism, race riots and family breakdown. A key goal of contemporary British conservatism was the creation of a 'property-owning democracy' and, in the Thatcherite imaginary, England can only be a green and pleasant land if private property is fully dominant. Thus, as with Reagan and Goldwater, constructed images of an arcadian childhood in the past and a fear of 'the enemy within' in the present helped to legitimise privatisation.

Finally, if the imaginary history of private property is long and varied, what is its present tense? If we have reached the global limits of capitalist expansion, what new property is there left to privatise? In this concluding chapter, I look at an emblematic figure of twenty-first-century capitalism – Elon Musk – and his various flights of fancy about space exploration, finding new resources off-planet and the colonisation of Mars. Just as Locke saw the New World as an escape valve for the problems of early modern England, so also, in the fantasies of late capitalism, the cosmos is an escape from the crises of climate disaster and perceived overpopulation.

This is all consciously presented as a history of the present, with a focus that speaks to present-day concerns; indigeneity and Lockean settler-colonialism, Burkean conservative fears of rapid social change, Black Marxism, racial capitalism with Fitzhugh, housing access with Truman, neoliberalism with Thatcher, ecological breakdown with Musk. Taken collectively, these seven chapters aim, not to be an exhaustive study of all of private property – that would be an impossible task, though Christopher Pierson's wide-angle study of private property's long history certainly comes close and Laura Brace has narrated the history of private property across the same time and places as the present work – but to provide a broad overview of the dominant forms of private property in capitalist modernity, as well as the dominant ways that private property has 'seen' the world. These are particular manifestations of a broader history, with the assumption that these case studies exemplify broader trends that are universal within Anglophone capitalism, not least, of course, the ever-present fear of the mob and the universal coexistence of private property, race and gender.

Notes

1 Karl Marx. 'Economic and philosophic manuscripts of 1844', in *Collected Works*, Vol. 3: 1843–1844 (London, 1975), 300.
2 W.E.B. du Bois. *Darkwater: voices from within the veil* (New York, 1969 [1920]), 30.
3 For one example of property as a way of seeing, see Desmond Fitz-Gibbon's apposite comment: 'Like all markets, the property market [in nineteenth-century Britain] was the achievement of historically specific work that combined ways of seeing with new ways of doing'. Desmond Fitz-Gibbon. *Marketable values: inventing the property market in modern Britain* (Chicago, 2018), 6–7. That 'private property' requires specific ways of seeing the world is true of many different times and places.
4 Frank A. Sharman. 'An introduction to the Enclosure Acts', *Legal History*, Vol. 10, No. 1 (1989), 47.
5 Gregory Clark, Anthony Clark. 'Common rights to land in England, 1475–1839', *The Journal of Economic History*, Vol. 61, No. 4 (2002), 1009–36. The Clarks' calculations, it should be said, are at the cautious and conservative end of the spectrum! The British Parliament's website gives the figure of 5,200 enclosure acts and 6.8 million acres: see www.parliament.uk/about/living-heritage/transformingsociety/towncountry/landscape/overview/enclosingland/, accessed 13 August 2020.
6 Immanuel Wallerstein. *The modern world-system* Vol. I: *Capitalist agriculture and the European world economy in the sixteenth century*, 2nd edition (Berkeley, CA, 2011), 25, 249–51.
7 Perry Anderson. *Lineages of the absolutist state* (London, 1979), 25–6.
8 Laura Brace. *The politics of property: labour, freedom and belonging* (Basingstoke, 2004), 1.
9 Peter Linebaugh. *The Magna Carta manifesto: liberties and commons for all* (Berkeley, CA, 2008), 53–4.
10 Peter Linebaugh, Marcus Rediker. *The many-headed hydra: sailors, slaves, commoners, and the hidden history of the revolutionary Atlantic*, 2nd edition (Boston, 2013), 19. See also: William C. Carroll,

'"The nursery of beggary": enclosure, vagrancy, and sedition in the Tudor–Stuart period' in Richard Burt, John Michael Archer, eds. *Enclosure Acts: sexuality, property, and culture in early modern England* (Ithaca, NY, 1994), 34–47.

11 John Reese. *The Leveller revolution: radical political organisation in England, 1640–1650* (London, 2016), 52, 69; Andrew Bradstock. *Radical religion in Cromwell's England: a concise history from the English Civil War to the end of the Commonwealth* (London, 2011), xiii, xv. The royalists had keenly recognised the dangers of eroding religious control. Charles I believed that religious obedience was essential for social control, observing 'where was there ever obedience where religion did not teach it?' An anti-Quaker tract echoed this: 'if there was not a minister in every parish you would quickly find cause to increase the number of constables': Bradstock, xv–xvi. 'Elites discovered in the Pandora's Box they themselves had opened that the rude multitude had a great many rude things to say': David W. Mulder. *The alchemy of revolution: Gerrard Winstanley's Occultism and Seventeenth-Century English Communism* (New York, 1990), 22.

12 In David W. Petegorsky's analysis, the Levellers were essentially radical liberals, still wedded to the sacrosanct nature of private property: *Left-wing democracy in the English Civil War: a study of the social philosophy of Gerrard Winstanley* (New York, 1972), 104, 111, 116. On 14 May 1649, the Levellers were defeated at Burford, thus ending their army revolt. 'On their return from Burford, Cromwell and Fairfax were honoured with degrees at Oxford for their distinguished service they were deemed to have rendered the State by their suppression of the Leveller revolt. A few weeks later the city merchants and financiers, recognizing that Cromwell was not the dangerous revolutionary they had feared, but, like themselves, a solid and conservative man of property who would brook no threat to its security, made their peace with the new regime.' Petegorsky, 160. Macpherson points out that 'the Levellers consistently excluded from their franchise proposals two substantial categories of men, namely, servants or wage-earners, and those in receipt of alms or beggars': C.B. Macpherson. *The political theory of possessive individualism: Hobbes to Locke* (Oxford, 1962), 107. Howell and Brewster argue, quite reasonably that the Levellers were never unified enough to have a truly shared ideology. Leveller attitudes ranged from proto-communism to radical liberalism: Roger Howell Jr, David E. Brewster. 'Reconsidering the Levellers: the evidence of the moderate' (1970) in Charles Webster, ed. *The intellectual revolution of the seventeenth century* (London, 1974), 79–100.

13 Petegorsky, *Left-wing democracy* (1972), 149. See also Carroll, 'The nursery of beggary'.
14 On the perceived need to 'counter' Winstanley's dangerous ideas, see Brace, *Politics of property* (2004), 22.
15 John Gurney. *Brave community: the Digger movement in the English Revolution* (Manchester, 2007); Christopher Hill. *The world turned upside down: radical ideas during the English Revolution* (London, 1975); Petegorsky, *Left-wing democracy* (1972); David Boulton. *Gerrard Winstanley and the republic of heaven* (Dent, 1999).
16 Steven Pincus. *1688: the first modern revolution* (New Haven, CT, 2011).
17 On the circular relationship between English colonisation in Ireland and North America, and the ways that each acted as a test case for the other, see Audrey Horning. *Ireland in the Virginia sea: colonialism in the British Atlantic* (Chapel Hill, NC, 2013).
18 Theodore Allen. *The invention of the white race*, Vol. 1: *Racial oppression and social control*, 2nd edition (London, 2012).
19 'As far as the English ruling classes might have been concerned, the 19th Century was inaugurated by the Irish Rebellion of 1798': Cedric J. Robinson. *Black Marxism: the making of the Black radical tradition*, 2nd edition (Chapel Hill, NC, 2000), 36.
20 E.P. Thompson. *The making of the English working class* (New York, 1966), 432; Robinson, *Black Marxism* (2000), 39.
21 Robin Blackburn. *The overthrow of colonial slavery, 1776–1848* (London, 1988), Ch. 11.
22 W.E.B du Bois. *Black Reconstruction in America, 1860–1880* (New York, 1992 [1935]), 580; Walter Johnson. *The broken heart of America: St Louis and the history of American violence* (New York, 2020), Ch. 5.
23 Mark Neocleous. *A critical theory of police power*, 2nd edition (London, 2021), 115.
24 Neocleous, *Critical theory of police power* (2021), 175–6.
25 For a further discussion of 'normality' as a productive way to think about whiteness and masculinity, see Julian B. Carter. *The heart of whiteness: normal sexuality and race in America, 1880–1940* (Durham, NC, 2007), 25*ff*.
26 See http://press-pubs.uchicago.edu/founders/documents/v1ch16s15.html, accessed 27 June 2022.
27 Quoted in Paul Gilroy. *The Black Atlantic: modernity and double consciousness* (Cambridge, MA, 1993), 85. Gilroy expands on this to discuss how 'race' is lived through gender, specifically the manner

in which subaltern Black identity has been expressed through an 'amplified and exaggerated masculinity' that 'self-consciously salves the misery of the disempowered and subordinated'. I would also argue that whiteness is an expression of class and is lived through a specific mode of 'respectable' masculinity. Class–race–gender exist as one.

28 Ange-Marie Hancock. *Intersectionality: an intellectual history* (Oxford, 2016), 100, 119. See also Tommy Curry's argument that racism is always built on, and with, sexist assumptions; that racism has such distorting force, it remakes gender (rather than merely intersecting with it). Thus, for example, the experience of being a Black man is not akin to that of a white man, with some racial differences. Rather, race changes the very experience of gender; race and gender produce each other: *The man-not: race, class, genre and the dilemmas of Black manhood* (Philadelphia, PA, 2017), 4, 20. See also Judith Butler, *Gender trouble: feminism and the subversion of identity*, 2nd edition (London, 2006), 18–19; David Roediger. *Class, race, and Marxism* (London, 2017), 8; Asad Haider. *Mistaken identity: race and class in the age of Trump* (London, 2018), 103–14. Rose Brewer's idea of the 'simultaneity' of race, class and gender is also highly useful: 'Theorizing race, class and gender: the new scholarship of Black feminist intellectuals and Black women's labor' in Stanlie M. James, Abena P.A. Busia, eds. *Theorizing Black feminisms: the visionary pragmatism of Black women* (London, 1993), 13–30.

29 Du Bois. *Darkwater* (1969 [1920]), 30. For the immediate background on du Bois' 'The souls of white folks' and his 'whiteness is the ownership of the earth' claim, written in the aftermath of a 1917 race riot in East St Louis, see Johnson, *Broken heart* (2020), 245–9.

30 Manning Marable. *How capitalism underdeveloped Black America: problems in race, political economy and society* (Boston, MA, 1983), 15.

31 Aileen Moreton-Robinson. *The white possessive: property, power, and indigenous sovereignty* (Minneapolis, MN: University of Minnesota Press, 2015), xi, xx. See also Sitting Bull's observation of white settlers that 'the love of possessions is a disease with them': Peter Matthiessen. *In the spirit of Crazy Horse: the story of Leonard Peltier and the FBI's war on the American Indian Movement* (New York, 1992), 9.

32 Cheryl I. Harris. 'Whiteness as property', *Harvard Law Review*, Vol. 106, No. 8 (1993), 1713.

33 Kathleen Belew. *Bring the war home: the White Power movement and paramilitary America* (Cambridge, MA, 2018), 62.

34 Kathryn Conrad. *Locked in the family cell: gender, sexuality and political agency in Irish national discourse* (Madison, WI, 2004), 3–4.
35 Christopher Pierson. *Just property, a history in the Latin West*, Vol. 1: *Wealth, virtue and the law* (Oxford, 2013), 21, 208.

Part I

Theories

1

The invention of a new world

> I don't feel that we did wrong in taking this great country away from the Indians. There were great numbers of people who needed new land, and the Indians were selfish trying to keep it for themselves.
>
> John Wayne[1]

The 'First treatise'

In the beginning was the Word; and no private property. John Locke's 'First' and 'Second treatises on government' – published anonymously in 1689 and reflective of the ideas of the Glorious Revolution of 1688 – have a landmark status in the history of the idea of private property; so much that came after Locke was operating with the set of conceptual and historiographical tools he developed to understand why private property exists and where it came from. As such, I want to reconstruct his argument closely, and then move out later in this chapter to its broader historical context and influence.

The 'First treatise' is a detailed response (and rebuttal) of the then-recently published *Patriarcha* (1680), a forthright defence of the traditional divine right of kings, including rights and privileges over a nation's property, by the avowedly pro-monarchist Robert Filmer.[2] Made up of eleven chapters, the bulk of which focus on Biblical history, Adam, the origins of propertied human society and the origins of monarchy, it generally receives less attention than the 'Second treatise', though it is essential for understanding the argument that stretches across both.

Locke begins the 'First treatise' by condemning Filmer's support for 'Slavery', an existence so 'vile and miserable' that Locke feigns shock that 'that an *Englishman*, much less a *Gentleman*, should plead for't'.[3] Locke critiques Filmer's argument that power and dominion over the Earth (i.e. private property) were bequeathed to Adam and are vested, by right, in monarchs only.[4] Where Filmer saw private property as a God-given thing, Locke sees it as a social construct.[5] Locke disputes the idea that Adam was given the world as property by God; instead, he says 'Man's *Property* in the Creatures, was founded upon the right he had, to make use of those things, that were necessary or useful to his Being'.[6] Property is thus a utilitarian phenomenon related to self-preservation; it does not exist because God wills it *per se*, but because mankind found it necessary for survival (though as discussed below, private property comes indirectly from God, in the sense that it is the necessary prerequisite for being fruitful and multiplying).

As Locke points out, primogeniture is not mentioned in the Bible and thus is not divinely ordained.[7] This has massive implications for the ownership of property and for sovereignty. Neither is inalienable and only acquirable through inheritance, and they do not come from God; they are human creations. In theory, anyone can possess private property. Thus, Locke implicitly advocates both a relatively more democratic society than Filmer and a flat, horizontal society where the right to own property is equal. The state exists to maintain property, but this means it serves to maintain material inequality.[8] We are all politically equal even as we live in a society that is economically unequal. It might even be said that Filmer's views are those of a feudal ideologue whereas Locke is advocating a modern capitalist conception of property, power and rights (even as certain aspects of Locke's understanding of property, such as his recourse to the Bible, simultaneously look back to the medieval period).[9]

Bolstering Locke's argument is the contemporary European discovery of the Americas; the existence of a vast and seemingly unprivatised space countered the idea that God had already privatised the world. Locke points how Robert Filmer believed that Noah divided the world by lot between his sons and yet America is not mentioned in Genesis: '*America* then, it seems, was left to be his that could catch it'.[10] America is an empty space awaiting owners.

In one of the proto-racial turns in the 'First treatise', Locke surveys 'the Nations of the World' and finds that 'the irrational untaught Inhabitants' who lead a natural life in the 'the Woods and Forests' are inferior to those 'Civil and Rational' urban-dwellers who live in implicity privatised 'Cities and Palaces'; the latter, of course, provide a better model of social organisation than the former.[11] This seems, again, to be a reference to the Americas and to the 'savages' there, who can be placed on a lower rung of humanity.[12] A nascent form of race played a role in how Locke understood the world and the need to export private property to those empty spaces still lacking it.[13]

Gender also played a major role in the 'First treatise', having an early, overt presence alongside power and property; Chapter II has the unblurred title 'Of paternal and regal power', telegraphing how much gender power and the power of feudal rulers overlapped, both in Filmer's politics and in Locke's counter-attack. Yet on a number of occasions Locke approaches an almost feminist position in his detailed criticisms of Filmer's Biblical hermeneutics. He critiques Filmer's claim that the Bible only demands obedience to fathers, and not mothers: 'I hope 'tis no Injury to call an half Quotation an half Reason, for God says, *Honour thy Father and Mother*; but our Author contents himself with half, leaves out *thy Mother* quite, as little serviceable to his purpose'.[14] Touching on the question of women and property, Locke again approaches a feminist perspective, suggesting that God granted Eve as much '*Dominion* over the Creatures, or *Property* in them' as he had given to Adam.[15] Or perhaps Locke was saying that Filmer's thinking leads to the possibility of female property ownership, and therefore is absurd? Locke remained ambiguous about female subservience in the Bible, saying that Adam 'too had his share in the fall' and going on to suggest that women's subjection is not a hard-and-fast requirement.[16]

Nonetheless, he does speak of 'the Woman's Lot' and the 'Curse' that has befallen womankind since Eve; the correctness of a woman's subservience to her husband is confirmed by both 'the Laws of Mankind and customs of Nature'.[17] And indeed, Locke's arguments about the origins and development of private property in the 'First treatise' focused almost exclusively on the rights of sons and the duties of fathers; he showed himself critical enough to recognise the gender biases of Filmer, but ultimately not critical enough to cut the umbilical cord linking gender to property ownership.[18] For Locke, the family predates private property; families come first and are then the mechanisms through which property is passed on through the generations.

While Locke criticises Filmer's notion that private property has a Godly ordination, he does not abandon the view that it is a social good. Rather, he sees mass private property ownership as a definite positive for a healthy society. In a despotic (or feudal?) society, a small number of elites, or even just one monarchical ruler, control all the property. Locke argued that this 'gives a Man Power over the Life of another' and 'he that is Proprietor of the whole World, may deny all the rest of Mankind Food, and so at his pleasure starve them, if they will not acknowledge his Soveraignty, and Obey his Will'. Conversely, Locke asserted that since it is an accepted truth that God wants all humanity to 'increase and multiply', it thus stands to reason that God would want all men to have access to property as the material basis for procreation and for the survival of humanity into future generations.[19] This positive defence of private property is one of the few moments in the 'First treatise' where Locke actually explicitly states what he *does* believe. There seems to be a strategic reason why he first couches his argument as a refutation of Filmer: he can say what he is opposed to but does not have to openly say what he believes. The two treatises are set up in a sort of binary opposition to each other; the first details the 'false principles' of Robert Filmer and the 'Second treatise' outlines 'the true original, extent, and end of civil government', as the frontispiece of the 1698 edition states. That the 'Second treatise' is actually a positive statement of Locke's views, rather than just a negating of Filmer. is probably a major reason why it is read more; its relative absence of obscure theological debates is another reason.

The 'Second treatise'

There is some debate as to which of the two treatises Locke wrote first,[20] even though in terms of logical progression the 'Second treatise' follows on directly from the first. Here, Locke begins by again dismissing Filmer's idea that private property has a specific divine origin and says no one family or group of humans have a greater right to the property of the Earth.[21] Locke's historiography is here presented in flattened-out terms; all societies have equal claims on the property of the Earth (provided they use that property correctly). With it now established that it is a human construct and not a divine gift, Locke can proceed to define and defend his conception of private property.

'Property' is *the* central idea in the political system Locke develops in the 'Second treatise', generally present in all the chapters but especially so in the fifth chapter, 'Of property'.[22] He starts from an assumption that man's natural form of existence is a '*State of perfect Freedom*', a state of nature in which all are at liberty, they 'order their Actions, and dispose of their Possessions, and Persons as they think fit, within the bounds of the Law of Nature, without asking leave, or depending upon the Will of any other Man'.[23] A political order comes into existence so as to protect men and their 'property', a term Locke understands as being both physical possessions and one's own individual existence (though he regularly slips back to seeing it just as material goods or land).[24] Thieves, who threaten 'property' in its narrower and more conventional sense, have thereby placed themselves outside society; they have returned to a state of nature and are at war with society. Therefore it is permissible to kill them. Similarly, 'he who makes an *attempt to enslave* me', which is to say threatens man's 'property' in the broader sense of possessions and personhood, 'thereby puts himself into a State of War with me'[25] and is presumably also a candidate for lawful execution.

Property is a natural right and the state is the artificial construct established to protect that shared natural right. 'Property' is the state's *raison d'être*: 'Government has no other end but the preservation of Property'.[26] And there is a flat equality at work here: the state 'comes to be Umpire, by settled standing Rules, indifferent, and the same to all Parties'. Hence a private property-centric civil society, according to Locke, is necessarily democratic, at least in the sense that it guarantees legal equality for all citizens.[27] Monarchies, by concentrating so much power in one person, are a threat to property, since monarchs will seek to use their position to amass property.²⁸ However, for all his seemingly democratic shades, an unspoken implication is that Locke sees only property owners (in the narrowly defined sense) as worthy of citizenship.²⁹

In the 'First treatise', Locke argued that property emerged as a function of man's need to subsist on Earth; private property was the economic form needed to fulfill God's injunction to be fruitful and multiply. Locke moves from this proposition to a definition of individually owned property.³⁰ The bounty of nature is replete with nourishment, but to be turned into food will require some work on the part of man. As an individual removes natural nourishment and makes it into something consumable, he uses his own labour (already established as a personal property) and thus the product of that labour in turn also becomes personal property and his exclusive right.³¹ Even those who lack a legally recognised private property can still experience it: 'the wild *Indian*, who knows no Inclosures' and lives in a kind of primitive communism ('is still a Tenant in common') exercises a private, individual ownership over the 'Fruit' and 'Venison' that nourish him; indeed, taking that private ownership is an unavoidable step in his own self-preservation. All men may have received the Earth in common from God, but this does not mean it should remain communal, an economic condition Locke associates with remaining 'uncultivated' and the preserve of 'the Quarrelsom [sic] and Contentious' rather than 'the *Industrial and Rational*'.³² A propertyless mob are thus contrasted with rational property owners.

Locke extends this thinking from property in 'the Fruits of the Earth, and the Beasts that subsist on it' to 'the *Earth it self*'. The principle remains the same: '[a]s much Land as a Man Tills, Plants, Improves, Cultivates, and can use the Product of, so much is his *Property*', though Locke also notes that this act of individual enclosure requires the consent 'of all his Fellow-Commoners, all Mankind'.³³ Private property may have its roots in natural law and in man's need to survive and his desire to honour Genesis 1:28 ('And God blessed them, and God said unto them, Be fruitful, and multiply, and replenish the earth, and subdue it: and have dominion over the fish of the sea, and over the fowl of the air, and over every living thing that moveth upon the earth'). But it survives as a socio-legal construct to which all members of society must give their consent.

Locke adds an important caveat, though. This conception of how nature becomes private property and the exclusive right of an individual labourer only holds 'where there is enough, and as good left in common for others'.[34] The act of appropriating a specific parcel of land would not be 'any prejudice to any other Man' provided there was still enough unclaimed land for others.[35] Locke's caveat requires the existence of a cornucopia to be true; there must still be empty spaces and boundless natural resources awaiting agricultural development, there must be enough potential private property for all mankind. Locke's way of thinking also seemingly precludes any man from owning more than he himself may utilise, since ownership of a piece of land is conferred by the ability to directly work that land.[36] Locke argues that each man can only own a finite and discrete amount of property, enough to support himself and his family and no more. And he talks of how in early human history there was enough land for all in the 'then vast Wilderness of the Earth', which he compares to the 'vacant places of *America*'.[37] That Locke was writing contemporaneously to the expansion of English rule into North America is obviously not a mere coincidence; his conceptions of private property require the existence of a vast, empty space which can be converted into an equally infinite number of privatised holdings.[38] As he wrote, 'there are still *great Tracts of Ground* to be found, which (the Inhabitants thereof not having joined with the rest of Mankind, in the consent of the Use of their common Money) *lie waste*',[39] in a clear allusion to America and those native 'Inhabitants' who are supposedly letting the entire continent go to waste.

The empty lands of places like America require English efficiency: 'For I aske whether in the wild woods and uncultivated wast of America left to Nature, without any improvement, tillage or husbandry, a thousand acres will yield the needy and wretched inhabitants as many conveniences of life as ten acres of equally fertile land doe in Devonshire where they are well cultivated?'[40] America, for Locke, was the proof that his theories of private property were correct.

> There cannot be clearer demonstration of any thing, than several nations of the *Americans* are of this, who are rich in Land, and poor

in all the Comforts of Life ... for want of improving it by labour, have not one hundredth part of the Conveniences we enjoy: And a King of a large and fruitful Territory there feeds, lodges, and is clad worse than a day Laborer in *England*.[41]

The tacit assumption here – that only those who rationally use the land can have a right to it[42] – would have huge implications for the European colonisation of the Americas. Locke, and even more so those that adapted and developed his ideas, consciously constructed a false image of Native Americans which would justify their expropriation and, ultimately, their replacement by English settlers and their privately owned farms.[43] Claims that the Native Americans or the 'Mere Irish' were savage, underdeveloped and not engaged in 'rational' wage labour were aleady floating around the Atlantic and being deployed to justify their expropriation. In Locke's writings, such claims 'are historicized and spatialized'. In the Lockean understanding, '[t]he Indians of North America, lacking the laws of private property, inhabit a premodern space, a time and place before the advent of civilization'.[44] Likewise, Locke's argument that children, along with '*Lunaticks* and *Ideots*'[45] and those in a state of slavery,[46] cannot own property signposts a later racialised assumption that 'immature' nations and races can be placed under the 'parental' supervision of superior races.[47] (This question of slaves, property and Locke will be discussed further in Chapter 4). Those who displayed 'rational industriousness' would inherit the Earth, and 'rational man had the right to make all living creatures the instruments of his satisfaction'.[48]

Locke's understanding of private property foreshadowed much that would come after him: the tacit assumption that property ownership is masculine (fathers make private property and private property makes fathers); debates over where private property came from; the diachronic conception of different nations and races existing in the present while simultaneously existing in other 'times' and spaces on the set path of the development of private property. Locke was clearly perturbed by the 'wrong' use of property, whether it was hoarding at one end of the scale or an almost criminal underdevelopment of nature at the other end. And like so many others, Locke sought to engage in and resolve all these problems of private property in acts of grand political imagination, in his case imagining America as a vast and empty space onto which English-style post-Enclosure private holdings could be projected. His dominant focus on the (male) individual and *his* right to own property effectively precluded any imagining that a communal form of property was possible.[49] Lockean property regimes rarely tolerate the existence in their midst of alternative ways of organising property; opponents of private property are never to be condoned.

These vermin will eat us up unless we enclose

In the ideas and in the conception of private property that he advocated, Locke echoed both the Enclosures under way in England from the fifteenth century onwards ('the first great phase of the English enclosure movement' when 'the privatization of England had begun')[50] and anxieties about vagrant and dissolute mobs. The overweening priority given to land ownership as something that should be both *individual* and *male* reflects both the decline of commonage lands and the privatisation of church lands, and the shift from holding land in a couple's name, as was the custom in feudal England, to the husband as the sole proprietor.[51]

Locke's language in the 'Treatises', particularly in the chapter 'Of property' in the 'Second treatise', was directly referencing the works of seventeenth-century agricultural improvers, 'for whom God's injunction in Genesis [to be fruitful and multiply] was a favorite justification in their call for enclosure and utilization of waste land'.[52] Locke, like these advocates for the restructuring of rural England, emphasised increased profits and productivity as central justifications for their work:

> Another principal defense of enclosure had to do with the view that common grazing lands and wastes generated unemployment, idleness, and vagabondage. Fear of 'masterless men' who roamed the countryside acknowledging no authority and who were 'insolent' to their social superiors – always a plague to landlord, church, and government – seems to have haunted the propertied classes throughout the ages. Enclosure would provide permanent employment for

such people, putting an end to their vagrancy, and it would place them under the watchful eye of landholder and magistrate.[53]

In the later 1690s, Locke himself prepared a paper for the Board of Trade, the committee that advised the English government on New World plantations, saying colonisation could be a last resort for the problems of unemployment and petty crime in England.[54] Likewise, both the humanist thinker Thomas More and the booster of Virginian settlement Richard Hakluyt believed that a variety of social problems could be solved via the western hemisphere. In his *Discourse of Western Planting* (1584), Hakluyt called the Americas an 'ample vent' and a 'remedy' for England's domestic problems. Hakluyt additionally believed that English colonies, not yet a reality by that date, 'could counter (or purge) overpopulation and idleness at home, while spreading the religion of Christ, limiting the dominion of Spain, generating additional revenue for the Crown, and increasing the strength of the navy'.[55] Sending the poor to the vast and supposedly empty spaces of the New World was a way to export the mob that were believed to threaten private property and domestic peace at home. The philosopher Francis Bacon delivered a paper to James I in 1606 specifically stating that, through sending these plebeian masses to the Americas, England would gain 'a double commodity, in the avoidance of [dangerous] people here, and in making use of them there'.[56] John Donne, poet and clergyman, depicted Virginia as England's spleen and liver, the place where 'ill humours of the body' could be drained, 'to breed good bloud', a common if unkind scatological metaphor. American colonies were labelled 'emunctories', excreting human waste from the body politic. Richard Hakluyt unabashedly called the transportable poor the 'offals of our people'.[57] A resurgence of plague in the 1620s and 1630s not only fuelled fears that God was punishing England for the country's sins, but also fomented worries about the 'wandering poor' laying siege to the countryside and the cities.[58] A pseudonymous commentator in 1665 claimed '[t]he poor increase like fleas and lice, and these vermin will eat us up unless we enclose'.[59] Indeed, there were anti-enclosure riots in Northamptonshire in 1607, the year the Jamestown settlement was established in Virginia.[60]

There has been a debate among historians as to whether or not Elizabethan and Stuart England actually needed an outlet for a surplus population. Barbara Arneil, in her study of Locke and colonialism, calls it a 'myth'.[61] However, between 1500 and 1700, 'the English population increased about two and a half fold'.[62] Concurrent changes in property-relations did seem to mean that more and more land was being concentrated in the hands of an emerging class of capitalist farmers; about a quarter of the land of England had been enclosed by the end of the seventeenth century.[63] Simultaneous with this was the separation of peasants from the land and the appearance of 'a growing class of semilanded and propertyless people'; perhaps as high as a twelve-fold increase in the numbers of propertyless people over the course of the sixteenth century.[64] It was 'axiomatic among statesmen and social commentators' that this *lumpen* class were bound up with the continued existence of 'unimproved waste and pasture'; therefore further enclosure would be the solution, since it would allow the poor to obtain newly privatised parcels of land.[65] Fears about these demographic shifts undoubtedly played a role in both the cultural politics of colonialism and a perceived need to fully legitimate the post-enclosures property regime at home.[66] 'New Worlds' are often a way to solve the problems of the old. Colonialism in the Americas was seen as a safety valve to export the mobbish threat to private property and, in turn, create new private property and new property owners in Virginia, the Carolinas or New England, which would serve to strengthen private property even further.[67]

Locke certainly saw English enclosures as a model for global privatisation, reflecting a view that was common in the seventeenth century and into the eighteenth.[68] In a letter of late 1661, a friend across the Irish Sea told Locke that Ireland was 'a desolate country that wants people and auditors rather than teachers. And some here are of opinion that a hundred good plowman would doe god and there country more good service than double the number of the black robe.' In other words, 100 English farmers, on presumably privately held estates, would do more good than 200 Catholic clergymen.[69] But America was always the place on which Locke laid the most emphasis. Drawing on the work of Carl Schmitt, Giorgio Agamben has recognised the manner in which Western political thought often has recourse to a 'free and juridically empty space' – the state of nature in America for Locke – that is imagined outside of the *nomos*, the law, but that this act of imagination is also inherent to how we construct the law.[70] Locke *imagined America* to be empty and devoid of private property partly so that it could serve as the hypothetical site for his ideal propertied social order. Already in the latter half of the sixteenth century, and into the Elizabethan era at century's end, colonisation of the Americas was becoming seen as a cure for all of England's social and economic ills, from inflation and the loss of markets to the problems arising from the enclosures of commonage land and a perceived surplus in the population.[71] Settlement in the New World became seen as a heroic act and a second Exodus; an overflowing population finding a new home in an 'empty' land,[72] though like the Canaanites (and much later the Palestinians), the natives were seen yet consciously ignored. At most they were part of the natural landscape, rather than modern citizens with attendant rights. Indeed, one scholar has made the cogent point that Native American 'dispossession' is the wrong term for what Locke was advocating, since he did not believe that native tribes were engaging in the kinds of rational or efficient labour that proved possession to begin with.[73]

These claims about the New World were not made in an academic vacuum.[74] Locke famously drew up the constitution of the Carolinas and drafted agrarian laws for that colony.[75] He invested in the slave-trading Royal Africa Company in 1671 and the Company of Merchant Adventurers in the Bahamas the following year.[76] Between 1696 and 1700 he was a member of the newly established Board of Trade and Plantations, charged with revising the legislation of the Virginia colony (a vast territory comprising what is today Virginia, West Virginia, Kentucky, Indiana and Illinois, and parts of Ohio and Pennsylvania). Locke was an active board member – attending 372 meetings during his four-and-a-half years – and the organising principle of his work for the Board was that 'the best government of Virginia would be one most responsible to its propertied interests'.[77] He advocated the use of heraldry and gentrified titles for the landowners of the Carolinas, such as *landgrave* (from the German for prince) and *cacique* (the Spanish word for a native chief): 'Pretentious institutions such as these hardly suited the swampy backwater of Carolina, but in the desire to impose order on an unsettled land, every detail mattered – down to assigning overblown names to ambitious men in the most rustic outpost of the British Empire'.[78] In this romanticisation of life in the New World, Locke was tracing already well-established patterns. An extensive cultural machinery was deployed to convince potential labour migrants to leave for the Americas:

> The promise of free land, as embodied in the head-right system, was tempting, but people needed to be convinced that settling would be easy. The proprietors of the American colonies began using the Garden of Eden metaphor in their pamphlets to sell their plots of land. The new world became one where nature was spontaneous and very little labour needed to be applied in order to garner the earth's fruits, but if Englishmen applied labour as they did in England, much greater returns could be made from the soil of America.[79]

Such propaganda was planted in an already rich soil, since America had long had a reputation for being a land of abundant resources.[80] Michael Drayton's 1606 poem 'Ode to the Virginian Voyage' spoke of that territory as 'Earth's only Paradise', filled with endless natural resources. In 'poetic propaganda' for the Virginia Company, Robert Rich held to a similar description:

> There is no feare of hunger here,
> for Corne much store here growes
> Much fish the Gallant Rivers yeild [sic]
> 'tis truth, without suppose.[81]

Robert Gray, an Anglican preacher and a propagandist for the Virginia Company, writing from the comfort of his home in London, sought to recruit overseas adventurers by promising them, in 1609, 'all happie and prosperous successe, which may either augment your glorie, or increase your wealth, or purchase your eternitie'.[82]

The idealised depictions of the New World found purchase in a context where 'bizarre stories' were current that 'inflamed the collective imagination of Europe' and inspired endless discussions – at elite and plebeian levels alike – of Native Americans 'who lived without property, work, masters, or kings'. Stories circulated among seventeenth-century Atlantic sailors of 'the Land of Cockaygne', a peasant utopia 'where work had been abolished, property redistributed, social distinctions leveled, health restored, and food made abundant'.[83] Such visions of an unprivatised world had to be adapted, domesticated or purged, lest they prove too attractive, and Native Americans, rather than being free people who lived without property or want, had to be reclassified as vicious savages, yet another splenetic mob who threatened the propertied order.[84] Against the idea that America was a vast commons, it instead became *terra nullius*, an empty land awaiting private owners.

This propaganda did seem to have some effect; in a 'Great Migration' lasting from 1629 to 1640 about 80,000 people left England, with around a third going to New England.[85] Though the reality of life there was obviously very different from the Edenic encomia, men could 'adventure' in the Virginia Company by buying shares at £12.10.0 apiece. Moving to Virginia at one's own expense was another way to earn a share. The sales of these shares funded the dispatching of 'shiploads of England's unemployed labourers as well as skilled specialists'. Those who travelled in this manner became servants of the Virginia Company, indentured to work for seven years as a way of paying for their transportation to the supposedly rich bounties and opportunities of the New World.[86] In theory, any man arriving in Virginia could claim fifty acres in free land, though this was denied to indentured servants who accounted for a half to two-thirds of the colony's white population across the seventeenth century.[87] Land quickly became centralised in the hands of those with money and legal know-how.[88] Locke would probably not have disapproved, since he felt that inequality was the moral result when the 'industrious and the rational on one side' competed with 'the listless and the idle on the other'.[89] And on the oversized farms that emerged, indentured labourers from Britain and Ireland proved unreliable; by 1619 the colonial powers-that-be were beginning to switch to importing African slaves as an ostensibly more pliant labour supply.

A global enclosure

Locke's ideas were a reaction, of sorts, to developments already under way in England, from the Enclosures to the fear of the plebeian mob to the deposing of the 'tyrant' James II in 1688; but in turn, Locke's ideas also helped legitimate major changes in the Americas. The claim that the Americas represented a cornucopia of natural resources just waiting for European ownership was already extant almost immediately after Columbus' arrival in 1492: 'He opened to western eyes an unexpected abundance of space, land, soil, forests, minerals, and waters, an abundance that was almost free for the taking. With that surprising windfall, civilization's growing sense of privation and limits seemed finally over.'[90] In a letter of 1493, Columbus described the native peoples of Hispaniola and Cuba as follows:

> The people of this island and of all the other islands which I have found and of which I have information, all go naked, men and women, as their mothers bore them, although some of the women cover a single place with the leaf of a plant or with a net of cotton which they make for the purpose ... In all these islands, it seems to me that all men are content with one woman, and to their chief or king they give as many as twenty. It appears to me that the women work more than do the men. I have not been able to learn if they hold private property; it seemed to me to be that all took a share in whatever any one had, especially of eatable things.

Thus the Native Americans were already coded as both sexually abnormal and abnormal in their relationship to private property. Similar sentiments were present in Amerigo Vespucci's 1504–05 work *Mundus novus*:

> They live together without king, without government, and each is his own master. They marry as many wives as they please; and son cohabits with mother, brother with sister, male cousin with female, and any man with the first woman he meets. They dissolve their marriages as often as they please, and observe no sort of law with respect to them. Beyond the fact that they have no church, no religion and are not idolaters, what more can I say? They live according to nature, and may be called Epicureans rather than Stoics. There are no merchants among their number, nor is there barter.[91]

Racial difference, radically divergent ideas about commerce and private property and supposed sexual deviance all overlap and co-produce each other.

The roughly contemporaneous invention of the printing press in the fifteenth century meant that such images of America as an as yet unprivatised land free for the taking could rapidly circulate across Europe.[92] As something of a function of this, throughout the sixteenth century the ability to hold private property began to be seen as 'an insignia of civilization'. In Spain, the philosopher and theologian Juan Ginés de Sepúlveda said that those who lack private property lacked 'even vestiges of humanity'. His contemporary Martin Luther contended 'that the possession of private property was an essential difference between men and beasts'. And in England, Thomas More proclaimed that land could be justifiably taken from 'any people [who] holdeth a piece of ground void and vacant to no good or profitable use', a supposition that was finding favour across the continent.[93]

But a major divergence was to emerge between the proponents of Spanish and English colonisation. That avatar of colonial imagination, Robinson Crusoe, condemned 'the conduct of the *Spaniards*' and 'all their barbarities practised in *America*, where they destroyed millions of these people'. The Spanish justified their ownership in the New World as the reward for military conquest, though that left open the possibility that, in the event of a counter-attack, native reconquest would also be justifiable. Conversely, an Englishman like Crusoe worked his land himself, brought order out of the chaos of American wilderness and thus had a legitimate claim to 'my little Kingdom'.[94] As long as 'efficiency' or 'profitable' use of the land could be denied the native population, so also could any indigenous claims to this property be rejected. Even here, these claims serve to cover up a harsh reality, since the effect of an imperial conquistador mission or a liberal Lockean settler-colonialism was still aboriginal dispossession, carried out through violence and deceit.[95]

On the eve of moving to the Massachusetts Bay Colony in the 1630s, where he would become the first governor, John Winthrop produced a manuscript 'justifieinge the undertakeres of the intended Plantation in New England'. As with Columbus, he cloaked his mission in religious language, claiming he would bring Christianity to the native heathens. But he quickly moved to address the charge that 'we have noe warrant to enter upon that Land which hath beene soe longe possessed by others'. His response was almost Lockean:

> That which lies common, and hath never beene replenished or subdued is free to any that possesse and improve it: For God hath given to the sonnes of men a double right to the earth; theire is a naturall right, and a Civill Right. The first right was naturall when men held the earth in common every man sowing and feeding where he pleased: then as men and theire Cattell encreased they appropriated certaine parcells of Grownde by inclosing and peculiar manuerance, and this in time gatte them a Civill right ... As for the Natives in New England, they inclose noe Land, neither have any setled habytation, nor any tame Cattell to improve the Land by, and soe have noe other but a Naturall Right to those Countries, soe as if we leave them sufficient for their use, we may lawfully take the rest, there being more than enough for them and us.[96]

Just over a generation later, the colonial-born Puritan Cotton Mather was still speaking of Massachusetts as a Biblical 'wilderness', in which the Puritans were 'Israel' surrounded by the Native Americans of 'Amalek'.[97]

John Smith in Virginia similarly looked to not only seize Indian land, but to claim he had a moral right to do so. Smith projected that the Indians' land was underused, justifying English seizure of it and the establishment of plantations there. The Powhatan Indians, he wrote, had 'more land than all the people in Christendom can manure, and yet more to spare than all the natives of those Countries can use and culturate [cultivate]'. Smith hoped to create in Virginia a society wherein 'every man may be a master and owner of his own labour and land'. Native American occupancy was an obstacle to this vision of a propertied and self-sufficient masculinity. When the Pamunkey Indians (a branch of the Powhatan Confederacy) attacked settlements in Virginia in March 1622, this 'provided the English with the pretext for their first move toward engrossing Indian land'. Colonists willing to settle along the ersatz border with the Pamunkey received fifty acres on which to build, another twenty-five if they stayed for a year. By the mid-1660s, the Pamunkey had been almost fully dispossessed, reduced to a 5,000-acre parcel of Virginia. By the end of the seventeenth century, Native Americans had effectively disappeared from eastern

Virginia, due to the combined effects of disease, violence and the introduction of alcohol by the English. 'With this diminution of Indians in the tidewater, the English could now impose their scheme of land tenure on the seized land.'[98] Virginia by this date was 'valuable real estate'.[99]

This remained the dominant thinking (and practice) regarding Native Americans and agricultural land after 1776; that efficient white male farmers were the legitimate owners of the land, that an ideal society could be created there and that Native Americans would have to move or be pushed aside. By the close of the eighteenth century, preachers like John Bulkley, Ezra Stiles and John Witherspoon were all employing Lockean thinking 'to justify the American's right of property with regard to both the English, and the Amerindians'.[100] The massive growth in the white American population – 5,000 in 1630, 112,000 in 1670, half a million in the 1720s, over 2 million in 1776[101] – was facilitated by this racialised privatisation; land was emptied of Native Americans and filled up with white homesteaders and speculators. Daniel Boone's memoirs, published in 1784, presented the American West as a 'paradise'. According to one historian of American Republicanism, 'Boone's West was the heart of America, where every man could rise and build a thriving, educated community'.[102] As Boone's language suggests here, this was a deeply patriarchal vision: '[p]rojecting fantasies of white male household authority onto areas of settlement was not a particularly new idea'.[103] Whiteness, masculinity and private property were at work simultaneously in these visions.

Thomas Jefferson's writings on Indians 'are filled with a straightforward assertion that the natives are to be given a simple choice – to be "extirpate[d] from the earth" or to remove themselves out of the Americans' way'.[104] Conversely, the Jeffersonian ideal of small independent farmers, itself operating according to a Lockean logic, had a 'sanctifying function'[105] for American capitalism; the expectation that all of the seized property of the continent would be distributed in 'comparatively small quantities' held out the promise (if never the realisation) of a democratising and egalitarian impulse. 'Thomas Jefferson was keenly aware of this',[106] as a twentieth-century socialist critic of his would later say. For men such as

Jefferson, 'the ideal citizen was an independent property-holder',[107] which tacitly excluded Native Americans (as well as enslaved African Americans, women and the poor) from their imagined community. President John Adams also connected property ownership with true citizenship when he opined that '[s]uch is the frailty of the human heart, that very few men, who have no property, have any judgement of their own'.[108] Adams was suggesting that only the propertied (i.e. the white and the male) could be full voting participants in the American democracy. All others should be blocked from full propertied citizenship.

From the British and Dutch-financed Louisiana Purchase of 1803 onwards, the Federal government 'purchased, fought and annexed its way from the Mississippi Valley to the Rio Grande, infringing [on] Spain's imperial claims, sweeping aside the Mexican Republic, and dispossessing dozens of indigenous societies'.[109] The United States expanded into the 'real-estate-in-waiting' of the interior.[110] The War of 1812 'destroyed Indians' power in much of the Old Northwest' from Ohio to Minnesota, after which the appropriated land was sold to white settlers (including the family of Abraham Lincoln).[111] Donald Worster talks of how, when Americans looked to the West in the mid-nineteenth-century, they saw a landscape 'not yet owned as private property'; ontologically wild and unprivatised, but teleologically privatisable and available for white settlement.[112] A million acres a year of land were sold in the 1820s, 57 million acres annually between 1830 and 1837 (due to the gold rush), 'and finally by the end of the century more than 250 million acres of the continent had become private property'.[113] The 1823 *Johnson v. M'Intosh* Supreme Court decision made it illegal for Native Americans to sell land directly to whites, denying them the right of free sale that was standard for Euro-Americans. 'Indian lands could only be transferred – by treaty or by sale – directly to the United States of America, whose General Land Office then surveyed and sold them at auction.'[114] This appropriation was always accompanied by (indeed, required) the expropriation and dehumanisation of Native Americans, who were denied American citizenship until 1924.[115] Settler-colonialism first dispossessed natives of their land, then constructed those natives as an aboriginal mob, a racialised threat to this newly privatised property.

Horatio Seymour, the unsuccessful 1868 Democratic candidate for president, once observed that:

> [e]very human being born upon our continent, or who comes here from any quarter of the world, whether savage or civilized, can go to our courts for protection – except those who belong to the tribes who once owned this country ... The worse criminals from Europe, Asia, or Africa can appeal to the laws and courts for their rights of person and property – all save our native Indians, who, above all, should be protected from wrong.[116]

When the Cherokee chief John Ross was removed from his nation's lands in Oklahoma in 1836, he used a letter to Congress to declare 'our property may be plundered before our eyes; violence may be committed on our persons; even our lives may be taken away, and there is none to regard our complaints. We are denationalized; we are disenfranchised. We are deprived of membership in the human family!'[117] The 1859 report to Congress of US Indian Affairs Commissioner Charles E. Mix spoke of Native American 'possession of large bodies of land in common' as the root cause of their 'habits of indolence and profligacy'. Such views would have found favour with the ethnologist J.W. Powell (1834–1902) of the Smithsonian Institute, who informed Congress that citizenship 'is incompatible with kinship [i.e. Native American] society'.[118] The Federal government fought a century-long series of Indian wars, from Fallen Timbers in Ohio in 1794 to Wounded Knee in South Dakota in 1890; the common thread was the desire to free up land for white settlement. By 1900, Native Americans only numbered between 220,000 and 300,000 across the entire territory of the United States, the result of a massive demographic calamity, a combination of disease, depredation, dispossession and deportation.[119] Lockean thinking about native (mis)use of land was a regular presence here, as it was also globally, expressing a general desire to impose white Anglo ownership on a planetary scale.

A common claim in the US press after the Treaty of Guadalupe Hidalgo in 1848 was that Mexicans did not deserve Mexico, as they were too wasteful of its resource-rich bounties, and thus the US had been rightful in annexing large sections of these otherwise unspent 'treasures'.[120] California's Alien Land Acts of

1913 and 1920 specifically prohibited land ownership by Asians and their American-born children;[121] racial outsiders were to be barred from the privilege of land ownership, ideally to be only accorded by white-skin privilege.

Aileen Moreton-Robinson has shown how colonial racism is predicated on a 'logic of dispossession', evident from the United States and Canada to Hawai'i, Australia and New Zealand/ Aotearoa.[122] In Canada, First Nations had lost access to most lands east of the Great Lakes by the 1830s; in the Canadian southern prairies, 'native title was extinguished in the 1870s'. As early as 1788, white British settlers in New South Wales declared the territory *terra nullius*, 'a status that sought to claim that Aboriginal people had no property rights in the land'. It was to become an 'unquestioned assumption' that the British had the sole legal right to occupy the entirety of the island continent, leading to a 'white Australia' policy being implemented by the end of the nineteenth century.[123] Further south in New Zealand/Aotearoa, the Treaty of Waitingi (1840) was supposed to guarantee Indigenous rights and land ownership, 'but this was disregarded, as the Maori were systematically dispossessed of their land, sometimes by military force, between the 1840s and 1860s'. Xhosa and Zulu peoples in South Africa were similarly dispossessed.[124] Expropriation of common lands 'from the Scottish highlands to the Irish *rundale*'[125] was also justified with claims of inefficient use. Ottoman Palestine was classified as a 'pathological landscape' and 'as a swampy wasteland inhabited by an unproductive people'. David Ben-Gurion proclaimed in 1924 that '[w]e do not recognize the right of Arabs to rule the country, since Palestine is still undeveloped and awaits its builders'.[126] French colonial figures borrowed John Locke's ideas to legitimate their rule in the emergent 'Third World', most infamously in Algeria.[127] Dispossession was not an unbroken nor a singular narrative; resistance was recurrent and native peoples were never passive victims.[128] Nonetheless, dispossession and then privatisation were still the general and overwhelming trend. Addressing issues of democracy and the ways in which the *possibility* of property ownership are held open for white settlers (even if that is never fully realised in actuality), Manu Karuka has gestured at how white settlement of the American interior helped legitimate itself: 'a sort of democratic possibility, a shared claim to ownership that could simultaneously allow for and preserve hierarchy and social differences within the community, while delineating boundaries and borders for who was included'.[129]

Privatisation of land across North America and the Caribbean also served to end the dreams of a propertyless New World utopia.[130] The idea that the Native Americans were wasting the resources of the New World and therefore that colonists had the right to appropriate this property, with the assumption that they would work it more efficiently, was (and is) as widespread as it is inaccurate:

> in fact the land was well worked by the native peoples, albeit very differently than the settler way. Among other things, the natives cleared fields to plant crops and regularly burned forests to clear the underbrush but keep the taller trees in place, in doing so making it easier to travel through forests and hunt the abundant animal life. When European settlers came, they tended to take over paths, crops, villages, and land previously worked by native peoples, taking credit for their achievements without acknowledging this.[131]

To many European observers, accustomed to monocultural planting, Native American farming was 'not an agriculture that looked very orderly', since the latter tended to plant corn with beans and squashes. This meant that 'the entire surface of the field became a dense tangle of food plants' but also created high yields per acre, discouraged weed growth and preserved soil moisture. 'Moreover, although Indians may or may not have realized it, the resulting harvest of beans and corn provided the amino acids necessary for a balanced diet of vegetable protein.'[132] Native American nomadism confused the English (who did not recognise the seasonal patterns that the itinerants followed).[133] It was also common for settlers to believe that only native women did 'legitimate work', the men idling away their time 'in hunting, fishing, and wantonly burning the woods, none of which seemed like genuinely productive activities to Europeans'.[134] And yet, the Jamestown settlement in Virginia, founded in 1607, was unable to produce enough food for its own subsistence, only surviving because of the assistance of the Powhatans.[135]

Additionally, the allegations about native backwardness or lack of development overlooked the fact that the English were arriving in the midst of a massive post-Columbian pandemic. Perhaps as much as 90 per cent of native populations were wiped out by disease. Robert Cushman of Plymouth colony, and one of the leaders of the famous *Mayflower* expedition in 1620, wrote 'I think the twentieth person is scarce left alive'. Thomas Morton observed that as he travelled near the villages of the Massachussett Indians, also in the 1620s, 'it seemed to me a new found Golgotha'. There was a second great wave of disease in 1634, after colonies were established in New England, which 'wreaked havoc among groups relatively untouched by the first. Deaths on this scale led to disarray at all levels.'[136] Dispossession could easily progress in such a situation.

Under the terms of the Homestead Act of 1862, somewhere in the region of 246 million acres of land in the western United States became available to white settlers. This could only have taken place if the original inhabitants of that territory were intentionally ignored, along with any counter-claims to be the territories' true owners. The Homestead Act, according to one historian, represents 'the most comprehensive form of wealth redistribution that has ever taken place in America'.[137] Viewed from an even broader perspective, the enclosures that took place across the North American continent represent the largest redistribution of resources in global history and perhaps the largest ever act of privatisation.[138] It was also a process of massive ecological damage. By the end of the twentieth century, somewhere in the region of 270 million acres of the American West was being leased to cattle farmers: 'Turning the land over to the industrial cultivation of domestic livestock constrains the ecosystem's ability to support wild species. After a century and a half of aggressive industrial colonization, few Indigenous species remain on the Great Plains ... only 20 percent of the region remains capable of supporting natural plant communities.'[139] Lockean thinking is at the heart of this capitalist privatisation, as summarised by Brenna Bhandar:

> the types of use and possession of land that justified ownership were determined by an ideology of improvement. Those communities who lived as rational, productive economic actors, evidenced by particular

forms of cultivation, were deemed to be proper subjects of law and history; those who did not were deemed to be in need of improvement as much as their waste lands were. Prevailing ideas about racial superiority were forged through nascent capitalist ideologies that rendered race contingent on specific forms of labor and property relations.[140]

English appropriation of Americans lands did not happen in a straight and uncomplicated narrative. In colonial Virginia, for example, there were recurring tensions between Governor Berkeley, who resisted the seizure of Indian lands, and speculators who favoured it strongly. Additionally, we cannot 'blame' Locke for English colonisation of North America and its attendant horrors of genocide and expulsion. But his ideas were part of a culture, 'a possessive rights discourse',[141] that legitimated these actions, and he can be rightly understood within that context.[142] The kinds of ideas Locke helped to develop did have a life beyond him and were used again and again to justify both expulsion and privatisation on a planetary scale.[143] Locke's ideas were ultimately interpreted within the context of what Zach Sell has recently labeled the 'global appeal of US-style settler white supremacy'.[144]

There was a symbiotic relationship between English colonialism in places like Virginia and the Carolinas and the various changes in England's domestic socio-economic structure that would later be identified as the transition to capitalism.[145] And Locke's conceptions of private property operated at this Atlantic intersection. This is not to say that Locke was an undiluted ideologue, but it is to recognise that his ideas happened within a particular historical context; 'it was John Locke, more than any other theorist,' whose work provided the 'intellectual platform for landed European expansion'.[146] 'Race', as we today understand that term, was invented in the Atlantic world. Modern conceptions of property were conceived through race, but also race was invented through property; conceived through the simultaneous dispossession of Native Americans and the repossession of that land by new 'white' owners and their Black slaves. The very concept of 'whiteness' was a product of this dispossession and repossession and a product of the process that turned English masterless 'mobs' into propertied American frontiersmen. Private property gained a racial essence it has never lost.

It is something of a commonplace to say that Locke was the preferred thinker of the American Revolution.[147] The insistence that an oppressed people have the right to overturn a tyrant, particularly when that ruler threatens their property, central claims in Jefferson's Declaration of Independence, betray an obvious Lockean inheritance. Likewise, the Declaration drew on the same British Atlantic milieu that placed Native Americans outside a propertied and gendered sense of racial normality, charging that King George 'has excited domestic insurrections amongst us, and has endeavoured to bring on the inhabitants of our frontiers, the merciless Indian Savages, whose known rule of warfare, is an undistinguished destruction of all ages, sexes and conditions'.[148] Native Americans became part of the racialised inchoate mob always seen as a threat to the propertied order, the racial order and the gender order.

Moving from Lockean liberalism to a study of conservative ideology, the next chapter focuses on another revolution; not a revolution to defend private property, but one in which anxieties were to the fore about private property's apparent looming abolition.

Notes

1 Interview with *Playboy* magazine, May 1971. Quoted in Rick Perlstein. *Nixonland: the rise of a President and the fracturing of America* (New York, 2008), 567.
2 Ellen Meiksins Wood has dismissed Filmer as a 'second-tier' thinker: *The pristine culture of capitalism: a historical essay on old regimes and modern states*, 2nd edition (London, 2015), 54.
3 John Locke. 'The first treatise of government', in Peter Laslett, ed. *Two treatises of government* (Cambridge, 1988 [1689]), 141.
4 Locke, 'First treatise' (1988 [1689]), 151.
5 Locke, 'First treatise' (1988 [1689]), 157.
6 Locke, 'First treatise' (1988 [1689]), 205.
7 Locke, 'First treatise' (1988 [1689]), 166, 222–4. Though Locke says that inheritance *is* divinely ordained, since God commands all parents to take care of their children, '[t]hat Children have such a Right is plain from the Laws of God, and that Men are convinced, that Children have such a Right is evident from the Law of the Land, both which require Parents to provide for their Children':

'First treatise', 207. For an overview of the multiple and not always complementary notions of property and inheritance in the Bible, see Richard H. Hiers. 'Transfer of property by inheritance and bequest in Biblical law and tradition', *Journal of Law and Religion*, Vol. 10, No. 121 (1993), 121–55.

8 'Because of their tacit agreement setting the value of money, men before the establishment of political society consented to the existence of property differentials. Political society was founded in order to secure and protect these differentials arising in the state of nature because no one could be supposed to enter political society with the intention of worsening his condition': Neal Wood. *John Locke and agrarian capitalism* (Berkeley, CA, 1984), 57.

9 Locke, 'First treatise' (1988 [1689]), 191; Christopher Pierson. *Just property, a history in the Latin West*, Vol. 1: *Wealth, virtue and the law* (Oxford, 2013), 21, 165.

10 Locke, 'First treatise' (1988 [1689]), 244. There can be an ambiguity to Locke's views of America. He talked of settlers as the 'People of Carolina', suggesting an empty space taken by Europeans. But he also says that 'in many parts of *America*, every little Tribe was a distinct People', which seems to recognise that America had a native population, though it is not clear whether these 'Tribes' are Native Americans or European settlers: 'First treatise', 246–7.

11 Locke, 'First treatise' (1988 [1689]), 183. Such quasi-racial sentiments could also be compared to Locke's dismissive views of the 'Barbarisme' of rural life, with cultured learning as 'a fence against the incroachments of rusticity': John Locke to G.W. [William Godolphin], [*c*. August, 1659], in John Locke; E.S. De Beer, ed. *The correspondence of John Locke,* Vol. I (Oxford, 1976), 94.

12 In the 'Second treatise', Locke used a similar language to discuss those *Indian*[s] who dwell in 'the woods of *America*' and exist in a 'State of Nature': 'Second treatise' in Laslett, *Two treatises* (1988 [1689]), 267.

13 On race as a theme in Locke, see Robin Blackburn. *The making of New World slavery: from the baroque to the modern, 1492–1800* (London, 2010), 328.

14 Locke, 'First treatise' (1988 [1689]), 145. See also his discussion of the Fifth Commandment ('Honour thy father and thy mother'): 'First treatise', 185–7.

15 Locke, 'First treatise' (1988 [1689]), 161. In the 'Second treatise', Locke rejects the idea that paternal power is the basis of political power, while still seeing politics in male terms. Rather, what he argues for seems to be a kind of impersonal political power, one that is not

based on familial ties, though he does admit that, in early societies, fathers easily became rulers; and he goes on to suggest that monarchical power emerged out of paternal power, but in a contingent manner, and has evolved into something different. He also states that, while both husband and wife have a shared interest in protecting the family's property, their different wills means that one person will have to have 'the last Determination' and 'it naturally falls to the Man's share, as the abler and the stronger'. This is a pretty weak formulation that somewhat contradicts his earlier view that might does not make right in civil society: 'Second treatise' (1988 [1689]), 314–21.

16 Locke, 'First treatise' (1988 [1689]), 172–3.
17 Locke, 'First treatise' (1988 [1689]), 174.
18 At one point, though, Locke lists a multitude of examples of children and relatives and asks why do any of them not have the same status in inheritance law as first-born sons? And he posed the great question: 'what in Nature is the difference betwixt a Wife and a Concubine?' 'First treatise' (1988 [1689]), 230–31.
19 Locke, 'First treatise' (1988 [1689]), 169–70.
20 Pierson, *Just property*, Vol. 1 (2013), 221.
21 Locke, 'Second treatise' (1988 [1689]), 267.
22 Locke called 'propriety', property in seventeenth-century English, 'the subject Matter about which Laws are made'. And for those who wanted to learn more about 'propriety', 'I have no where found more clearly explain'd than in a Book intituled *Two Treatises of Government*': letter from John Locke to Richard King, 25 August 1703. De Beer, ed. *Correspondence*, Vol. VIII, 58. See also Wood, *John Locke and agrarian capitalism* (1984), 49.
23 Locke, 'Second treatise' (1988 [1689]), 269.
24 On the fuzziness of Locke's definition of property, see C.B. Macpherson. *The political theory of possessive individualism: Hobbes to Locke* (Oxford, 1962), 198. Locke understood property as being derived from productive acts. Accordingly, he suggests that man remains the property of God, since God made man: Locke, 'Second treatise' (1988 [1689]), 270–71; though at later points he seems to think that man does own himself: 'every Man has a *Property* in his own *Person*': 'Second treatise', 287. In addition, his argument that God made man and thus still 'owns' him in some sense informs Locke's argument that murder and suicide are wrong, since both are 'theft[s]' of a life that God has created. As I go on to discuss, though, Locke sees execution as lawful in cases where a thief has stolen property; the thief's property in his self can lawfully be taken from him.

25 Locke, 'Second treatise' (1988 [1689]), 279–80.
26 Locke, 'Second treatise' (1988 [1689]), 329. Locke believed that 'Government could never legitimately deprive an individual of his property or any part of it – the reference was primarily to taxation – without his consent, which for practical purposes meant the consent of the legislature duly elected by a majority. Any legislative action impinging on man's life, liberty, and property must also be in accord with the rule of law and the law of nature and must be aimed at the "publick good", called by Locke "the Foundation and End of all Laws". Nor could a legitimate legislative regulation of property be designed to impoverish subjects': Wood, *John Locke and agrarian capitalism* (1984), 54–5. See also Andrew Fitzmaurice. *Sovereignty, property and empire, 1500–2000* (Cambridge, 2014), 121. This idea that the state exists to guard property was hardly a new idea of Locke's; in *On duties* [*De officiis*], Cicero (106–43BCE) said that the state was created to protect private property: Ellen Meiksins Wood. *Citizens to lords: a social history of Western political thought from antiquity to the Middle Ages* (London, 2008), 23.
27 Locke, 'Second treatise' (1988 [1689]), 326.
28 Locke, 'Second treatise' (1988 [1689]), 327.
29 Indeed, Locke defines citizens as property owners, though presumably he is deploying his more expansive definition of property. Yet he then talks about 'Riches and Power', which would seem to be a narrower and more conventional understanding of property; these dual definitions are used throughout. For instance, he says that taxes can invade 'the *Fundamental Law of Property*' and he condemns the raising of '*Taxes* on the Property of the People *without the Consent of the People*': 'Second treatise' (1988 [1689]), 360–3.
30 'If the world and its fruits were initially, according to Locke, a divine gift to men in common, he justified its subsequent parcelization and privatization by individual labor. The process of change he unfolded was caused by the creative, fabricating powers of men': Wood, *John Locke and agrarian capitalism* (1984), 51.
31 Locke, 'Second treatise' (1988 [1689]), 287; Pierson, *Just property*, Vol. 1 (2013), 213.
32 Locke, 'Second treatise' (1988 [1689]), 291.
33 Locke, 'Second treatise' (1988 [1689]), 290–1.
34 Locke, 'Second treatise' (1988 [1689]), 287.
35 Locke, 'Second treatise' (1988 [1689]), 291.
36 Though he later argues that money, which does not rot like food, allows for an ethical hoarding of wealth: Locke, 'Second treatise'

(1988 [1689]), 300–1. In 'For a general naturalization', an unpublished 1693 paper, Locke observed: 'The Riches of the world doe not lye now as formerly in haveing large tracts of good land which supplied abundantly the native conveniencys of Eating and drinking As plenty of Corne and large Flocks and heards. But in Trade which brings in mony and with that all things': Patrick Hyde Kelly, ed. *Locke on money*, Vol. I (Oxford, 1991), 488. 'The introduction of money by tacit consent has removed the previous natural limitation of rightful appropriation, and in so doing has invalidated the natural provision that everyone should have as much as he could make use of. Locke then proceeds to show in more detail how the introduction of money removes the limitations inherent in his initial justification of individual appropriation': Macpherson, *Political theory of possessive individualism* (1962), 203–4.

37 Locke, 'Second treatise' (1988 [1689]), 292–3.
38 'Locke based his account of natural man [man in the state of nature] on the descriptions provided by the dozens of travel books on the Americas he had in his library. Locke was not alone in his fascination with the new world. Many of his contemporaries were equally absorbed by the discoveries being made by European explorers, as evidenced by the wide circulation amongst the seventeenth-century English elite of such books as Sir Walter Raleigh's *History of the World*, or Samuel Purchas's *Pilgrims*, or Richard Hakluyt's *Principle Navigations*. Locke owned all of these works and used them, along with other accounts of the new world in his library to provide concrete evidence for the character of natural man': Barbara Arneil. *John Locke and America: the defence of English colonialism* (Oxford, 1996), 22. Walter Raleigh, 'the first Englishman to attempt colonizing New England', wrote extensively about Native Americans and described them as inhabiting a state of nature: *Locke and America*, 25.
39 Locke, 'Second treatise' (1988 [1689]), 299.
40 Locke, 'Second treatise' (1988 [1689]), 294. The perceived emptiness of America existed in sharp contrast with the supposedly crowded nature of England; see Arneil, *Locke and America* (1996), 110.
41 Locke, 'Second treatise' (1988 [1689]), 296–7.
42 Locke unambiguously stated that 'Land that is left wholly to Nature, that hath no improvement of Pasturage, Tillage, or Planting, is called, as indeed it is, *wast*; and we shall find the benefit of it amount to little more than nothing'. And he goes on to define the value derived from land in terms of the monetary value of goods produced for a market,

comparing the value of wheat produced on English farms with those from American farms: 'Second treatise' (1988 [1689]), 297–8.
43 'The idea of the noble savage can be traced in the Christian tradition to the ideal of Adam in the Garden of Eden. Many of the early descriptions which Locke would have read refer to the new world in terms of such a paradise.' America, like Eden, was assumed to be a bounty of nature, with endless resources. Locke himself presented America in such terms, though criticising the natives for not taking advantage of these natural spoils: Arneil, *Locke and America* (1996), 28.
44 Brenna Bhandar. *Colonial lives of property: law, land and racial regimes of ownership* (Durham, NC, 2018), 37–8.
45 Locke, 'Second treatise' (1988 [1689]), 307–8.
46 Locke, 'Second treatise' (1988 [1689]), 323.
47 Sinead Garrigan Mattar has dissected how, from Ireland to the Americas, 'the power-ideology of colonial regimes throughout history has continually led to an anti-primitivism, in which the native peoples of colonized states are projected as types of unregenerate savagery in order to justify the forceful imposition of the culture of the conquering nation': *Primitivism, science, and the Irish revival* (Oxford, 2004), 21. However, Locke did make attempts to seek out first-hand knowledge of the Americas' indigenes: *cf.* letter from Dr Henry Woodward to John Locke, 12 November 1675, in De Beer, ed. *Correspondence*, Vol. 1 (1976), 431–3. Locke had apparently written to Henry Woodward, an explorer who had visited the Caribbean, to ask him about the religious beliefs and customs of the native population. Locke's personal library, made up of 3,641 books, contained 275 on travel and geography, compared to 269 volumes on philosophy, and he took his understandings of North American native societies and their supposed state of nature from this extensive reading: Ann Talbot. *'The Great Ocean of Knowledge': the influence of travel literature on the work of John Locke* (Leiden, 2010), 3–4, 18–19, 21, 27, 33, 35, 122.
48 Blackburn, *Making of New World slavery* (2010), 263.
49 Locke 'reads back into primitive society the institution of individual ownership of land, taking it for granted that that was the only way land could then be cultivated. His disregard of communal ownership and labour in primitive society allows him to say that "the Condition of Humane Life, which requires Labour and Materials to work on, necessarily introduces *private Possession*".' This privileging of private property over any kind of communal property is an apt example of what C.B. Macpherson calls 'the social assumptions of his political thinking': *Political theory of possessive individualism* (1962), 202.

50 Peter Linebaugh. *The Magna Carta manifesto: liberties and commons for all* (Berkeley, CA, 2008), 47.
51 Silvia Federici. *Caliban and the witch: women, the body and primitive accumulation* (New York, 2014), 25. As part of the gendered nature of the Enclosure process, Federici also shows how witch hunts tended to match up with land privatisation; common in Essex, apparently non-existent in Ireland or the Scottish Highlands: *Caliban and the witch*, 171. Enclosures and witch hunts both sought to control 'nature', whether agricultural land or women's wombs, and both aimed at removing women from positions of economic authority.
52 Wood, *John Locke and agrarian capitalism* (1984), 57–8.
53 Wood, *John Locke and agrarian capitalism* (1984), 65. Christopher Hill has also talked about the existence of 'masterless men' in early modern England: 'victims of the rapid expansion of England's population in the sixteenth century … they existed, in the interstices of society, but undoubtedly growing in numbers by migration': Christopher Hill. *The world turned upside down: radical ideas during the English Revolution* (London, 1975), 43.
54 Arneil, *Locke and America* (1996), 72–3.
55 Sarah Hogan. *Other Englands: utopia, capital and empire in an age of transition* (Stanford, CA, 2018), 54–5. Flipping the script of 'crowded' England against 'empty' America, the New World was also desired because the plentiful, perhaps even infinite, forests of New England stood in sharp contrast to both deforested England and its attendant fuel crisis: William Cronon. *Changes in the land: Indians, colonists and the ecology of New England* (New York, 1983), 23; Federici, *Caliban and the witch* (2014), 85. 'By the end of the seventeenth century only an eighth of England remained wooded': Peter Linebaugh, Marcus Rediker. *The many-headed hydra: sailors, slaves, commoners, and the hidden history of the revolutionary Atlantic*, 2nd edition (Boston, MA, 2013), 43.
56 Eric Williams. *Capitalism and slavery* (New York, 1966 [1944]), 10. Ultimately, when that forced migration did not produce the desired numbers of obedient agricultural labourers, England turned to slavery instead: *Capitalism and slavery*, 16. This is a point I return to in Chapter 4.
57 Nancy Isenberg. *White trash: the 400-year untold history of class in America* (New York, 2016), 22.
58 Karen Ordahl Kupperman. *Indians and English: facing off in early America* (Ithaca, NY, 2000), 17.
59 Hill, *World turned upside down* (1975), 52.

60 Ned Sublette, Constance Sublette. *The American slave coast: a history of the slave-breeding industry* (Chicago, 2016), 89–90.
61 Arneil, *Locke and America* (1996), 72–3.
62 Robert Brenner. *Merchants and revolution: commercial change, political conflict, and London's overseas traders, 1550–1653* (Princeton, NJ, 1993), 43. Brenner also points out here that 'an increase of nearly the same dimensions between 1150 and 1300 to approximately the same absolute level as in 1700 had brought about the demographic crisis of the fourteenth century'.
63 Linebaugh and Rediker, *Many-headed hydra* (2013), 17.
64 Brenner, *Merchants and revolution* (1993), 40; Linebaugh and Rediker, *Many-headed hydra* (2013), 17.
65 Buchanan Sharp. 'Common rights, charities and the disorderly poor', in Geoff Eley, William Hunt, eds. *Reviving the English Revolution: reflections and elaborations on the work of Christopher Hill* (London, 1988), 108.
66 'To study modern laws of private property ownership without accounting for the significance of the colonial scene to their development is to disaffiliate the development of modern law from its deep engagements with colonial sites … There cannot be a history of private property law, as the subject of legal studies and political theory in early modern England that is not at the same time a history of land appropriation in Ireland, the Caribbean, North America, and beyond': Bhandar, *Colonial lives of property* (2018), 3. See also Hogan, *Other Englands* (2018), 52.
67 '[T]he dispossessed are displaced in order to themselves possess and produce. The imaginary resolution to England's class conflicts and moral shortcomings is clear: a land that lies somewhere across the sea might alleviate domestic instability': Hogan, *Other Englands* (2018), 55–6.
68 Laura Brace. *The politics of property: labour, freedom and belonging* (Basingstoke, 2004), 13.
69 Letter from George Percivall to John Locke, 1 December 1661, in De Beer, ed. *Correspondence*, Vol. 1 (1976), 182.
70 Giorgio Agamben; Daniel Heller-Roazen, trans. *Homo sacer: sovereign power and bare life* (Stanford, CA, 1998 [1995]), 36–7.
71 Andrew Fitzmaurice. *Humanism and America: an intellectual history of English colonisation, 1500–1625* (Cambridge, 2003), 32; Christopher Hill. *The century of revolution, 1603–1714*, 2nd edition (New York, 1980), 31.
72 Arneil, 'Locke and America' (1996), 110.

73 Fitzmaurice, *Sovereignty, property and empire* (2014), 59–60: 'Locke's moral certainty was in no way typical of the discussion of the legal status of Indians in sixteenth- and seventeenth-century England. Early modern English people often acknowledged the rights of Indians and only overcame their consciousness of those rights with considerable difficulty. Even as they reversed the force of the natural law discussion of Indian rights, they were unable fully to escape the polemical defence of indigenous rights for which that tradition had originally been employed.'

74 'As the most illustrious intellectual of the post-Restoration Whigs and an official functionary of the English state, Locke was deeply enmeshed in the administrative webs of colonial capitalism and subscribed to the new political economy that developed in response to seventeenth- century transatlantic commercial economy': Onur Ulas Ince. *Colonial capitalism and the dilemmas of liberalism* (Oxford, 2018), 44.

75 Locke's patron, the Earl of Shaftesbury, 'encouraged Colonists in Carolina to settle in towns and to devote themselves to agriculture, rather than mining', a preference Locke, of course, shared: Arneil, *Locke and America* (1996), 123–5.

76 James Tully. 'Rediscovering America: the *Two treatises* and aboriginal rights', in G.A.J. Rogers, ed. *Locke's philosophy: content and context* (Oxford, 1994), 167; Ibram X. Kendi. *Stamped from the beginning: the definitive history of racist ideas in America* (New York, 2016), 49. 'His [Locke's] writings have excited great interest amongst historians of empire not only because he made strident statements upon the status of American "Indians", but also because he made those observations in the context of his own deep professional involvement in the colonisation of Carolina to the point that he helped draft, and repeatedly revise, the constitution for that colony': Fitzmaurice, *Sovereignty, property and empire* (2014), 115–16.

77 Blackburn, *Making of New World slavery* (2010), 264–5. Locke's colonial work is akin to that of the Dutch political theorist Hugo Grotius and the Victorian liberal John Stuart Mill; all were intimately involved in colonial enterprises, even as they wrote supposedly disinterested treatises on politics, philosophy and law: Fitzmaurice, *Sovereignty, property and empire* (2014), 11. See also Ince, *Colonial capitalism* (2018), 3.

78 Isenberg, *White trash* (2016), 44–5. Countering his own arguments that land could only rightfully belong to a person who laboured it, Locke 'owned' 4,000 acres in the Carolinas (granting this land to him

also violated the King's Charter, which had stated that only inhabitants could own land, not those who remained in England): Arneil, *Locke and America* (1996), 69.
79 Arneil, *Locke and America* (1996), 74. Fitzmaurice observes that 'the Virginia Company employ[ed] propaganda more than any previous colonial enterprise': Fitzmaurice, *Humanism and America* (2003), 65.
80 Cronon, *Changes in the land* (1983), 22.
81 Linebaugh and Rediker, *Many-headed hydra* (2013), 10.
82 Hogan, *Other Englands* (2018), 1.
83 Linebaugh and Rediker, *Many-headed hydra* (2013), 24, 158. The still unknown nature of the Americas facilitated the spread of these visions: 'Although the location of Hudson Bay was known by 1610, it was only in 1682 that René-Robert La Salle travelled the whole tortuous river route from Montreal to the Mississippi mouth. Until *c*.1700 California was widely thought to be a huge island. Bering's confirmation that no land bridge connected Asia and the Americas was known only in the later 1740s. Until after 1750 it was generally assumed that a vast inland "Western Sea" lay beyond the height of land that fringed Hudson Bay': John Darwin. *After Tamerlane: the rise and fall of global empires, 1400–2000* (New York, 2008), 106. And 'as late as the 1840s geographers could not accurately place the Rocky Mountains on the continent – atlases showed mountains in Kansas, the Rockies running to 800 miles in width, and phantom rivers coursing to the Pacific': Bruce Cumings. *Dominion from sea to sea: Pacific ascendancy and American power* (New Haven, CT, 2009), 61.
84 The word 'savage' (or *saulvage*, *salvaticho* or *salvage*) entered the major European languages at this time as a synonym for Native American, stemming from the Latin *silvaticus*, a forest-dweller: Robert F. Berkhofer, Jr. *The white man's Indian: images of the American Indian from Columbus to the present* (New York, 1978), 13.
85 James Parisot. *How America became capitalist: imperial expansion and the conquest of the West* (London, 2019), 32.
86 Edmund S. Morgan. *American slavery, American freedom: the ordeal of colonial Virginia* (New York, 1975), 45–6.
87 Parisot, *How America became capitalist* (2019), 28.
88 Sublette and Sublette, *American slave coast* (2016), 137. 'Rights to individual capitalistic ownership of land did not go uncontested though. Under Charles I, after the Virginia Company lost control of the colony to the Crown in 1624, Royal Governor Sir John Harvey arrived in 1630. He was given instructions by Charles I to transform Virginia's ownership rights to something closer to a system

of subinfeudation as opposed to capitalist private ownership. He declared all preexisting patents invalid and created new ones that would require settlers to pay rents to proprietors and a quit rent to the empire. But these changes proved very short-lived, and several years later the Puritan colonialists expelled Harvey from the colony': Parisot, *How America became capitalist* (2019), 27.
89 Brace, *Politics of property* (2004), 27.
90 Donald Worster. *Shrinking the Earth: the rise and decline of American abundance* (Oxford, 2016), 14. Adriaen Van der Donck's 1655 *Description of New Netherland* said that 'the superabundance' of what is now New York, New Jersey, Delaware, Connecticut and parts of Pennsylvania and Rhode Island 'is not equaled by any other in the world' and he duly provided the colony's full list of assets: *Shrinking the Earth*, 20.
91 Both quoted in Berkhofer, *White man's Indian* (1978), 6, 7.
92 Berkhofer, *White man's Indian* (1978), 10.
93 David Stannard. *American holocaust: the conquest of the New World* (Oxford, 1992), 233.
94 Daniel Defoe; Thomas Keymer, ed. *Robinson Crusoe* (Oxford, 2007 [1719]), 116, 145.
95 'The notion that the West was something we settled, rather than conquered, pervades American storytelling and iconography; the contrast with the Spanish *Conquistadores* has never been subtle either in popular culture or in elementary and secondary education texts': James R. Grossman. 'Introduction', in James R. Grossman, ed. *The frontier in American culture* (Berkeley, CA, 1994), 1–2.
96 Stannard, *American holocaust* (1992), 235–6. Early English colonies, such as Roanoke, were devoted to resource extraction, particularly mining. The failure of these colonies precipitated a shift to settlement and a focus on agriculture. It was this shift that also caused new debates about property ownership: Arneil, *Locke and America* (1996), 69–70.
97 Quoted in Elliot Horowitz. *Reckless rites: Purim and the legacy of Jewish violence* (Princeton, NJ, 2006), 121.
98 Anthony S. Parent, Jr. *Foul means: the formation of a slave society in Virginia, 1660–1740* (Chapel Hill, NC, 2003), 16–18, 24; Steve Fraser. *The age of acquiescence: the life and death of American resistance to organized wealth and power* (New York, 2015), 70–1.
99 Gerald Horne. *The counter-revolution of 1776: slave resistance and the origins of the United States of America* (New York, 2014), 36.
100 Arneil, *Locke and America* (1996), 19–20.

101 Parisot, *How America became capitalist* (2019), 49.
102 Heather Cox Richardson. *To make men free: a history of the Republican Party* (New York, 2014), 2.
103 Honor Sachs. *Home rule: households, manhood and national expansion on the eighteenth-century Kentucky frontier* (New Haven, CT, 2015), 15–16. Family sizes were of a piece with this gendered and propertied vision of the ideal household: 'In the eighteenth century, average family sizes reached as high as seven or eight, decreasing to around four or five by the middle of the nineteenth century. Much of this decline was in rural areas, given that these populations tended to have more children, and it also appears that there is a direct correlation between declining land availability and a decrease in the fertility rate': Parisot, *How America became capitalist* (2019), 50–1.
104 Quoted in Stannard, *American holocaust* (1992), 120.
105 Bethany Moreton. *To serve God and Wal-Mart: the making of Christian free enterprise* (Cambridge, MA, 2009), 14.
106 Aneurin Bevan. *In place of fear* (London, 1952), 8.
107 Robin Blackburn. *The overthrow of colonial slavery, 1776–1848* (London, 1988), 88.
108 Brett Christophers. *The new enclosure: the appropriation of public land in neoliberal Britain* (London, 2018), 27.
109 Pekka Hämäläinen. *The Comanche empire* (New Haven, CT, 2008), 141; the Lousiania Purchase is conventionally priced at $15 million (approximately four cents an acre). Adding in payments made to Native Americans, the total cost, adjusted for inflation to 2012, was $8.5 billion: Robert Lee. 'Accounting for conquest: the price of the Louisiana Purchase of Indian country', *Journal of American History*, Vol. 103, No. 4 (2017), 921–42.
110 Zach Sell. *Trouble of the world: slavery and empire in the age of capital* (Chapel Hill, NC, 2021), 20.
111 Eric Foner. *The fiery trial: Abraham Lincoln and American slavery* (New York, 2010), 5.
112 Donald Worster. *Rivers of empire: water, aridity, and the growth of the American West* (New York, 1985), 3.
113 Cumings, *Dominion from sea to sea* (2009), 24.
114 Walter Johnson. *The broken heart of America: St Louis and the history of American violence* (New York, 2020), 47.
115 Laura Briggs. *Taking children: a history of American terror* (Berkeley, CA, 2020), 147. Johnson situates the Dawes Severalty Act (1887) in a context in which ownership of private property was understood as being synonymous with citizenship; 'only by learning how to cultivate

the land as [capitalist] owners could Indians become citizens; only by learning to be citizens could they become worthy of the land upon which they had always lived, but never truly possessed ... The Dawes Act dissolved the common holding of American Indians and pulverized their nations into 160-acre plots, assigned one at a time and on the basis of individually held parcels of private property to every Indian head of household. Because the reservation lands and other common lands, as restricted as they were, had once included land for hunting and seasonal migration, there was a great deal of unassigned land left over after severalty – as much as three-quarters of what had been Indian territory in the years leading up to 1887. The Dawes Act deemed this unassigned Indian land "surplus" and provided for its distribution to white homesteaders': Johnson, *Broken heart* (2020), 168.

116 Quoted in Peter Matthiessen. *In the spirit of Crazy Horse: the story of Leonard Peltier and the FBI's war on the American Indian Movement* (New York, 1992), xx–xxi.
117 Quoted in Sven Beckert, *Empire of cotton: a new history of global capitalism* (London, 2014), 108.
118 Both quoted in Theodore W. Allen. *The invention of the white race*, Vol. 1: *Racial oppression and social control*, 2nd edition (London, 2012), 37.
119 Cumings, *Dominion from sea to sea* (2009), 28–9.
120 David Roediger. *Class, race, and Marxism* (London, 2017), 136–7; Ronald Takaki. *Iron cages: race and culture in nineteenth-century America* (Oxford, 2000), 161.
121 Jane Dailey. *White fright: the sexual panic at the heart of America's racist history* (New York, 2020), 172.
122 Aileen Moreton-Robinson. *The white possessive: property, power, and indigenous sovereignty* (Minneapolis, MN, 2015), xiii and throughout.
123 Moreton-Robinson, *White possessive* (2015), xiii and throughout; Sell, *Trouble of the world* (2021), 17.
124 David Cannadine. *Ornamentalism: how the British saw their empire* (Oxford, 2001), 27–8. '[L]ate-Victorian land grabs in Africa, the Middle East, and Asia ... were preceded by centuries of practice with conquering territory elsewhere, such as in Ireland, North America, South Asia, Africa, Australia, and New Zealand ... Cultural notions of improvement and indigenous property; legal regimes of customary and statutory property law; economic theories of land, wealth, and taxation; and technological developments in surveying land and

cadastral mapping – all played a role in the creation of colonial land markets': Desmond Fitz-Gibbon. *Marketable values: inventing the property market in modern Britain* (Chicago, 2018), 11.

125 Linebaugh, *Magna Carta manifesto* (2008), 135. *Rundale* was the Irish equivalent of commonage farming, in which land was shared by a *clachan*, a nucleated village. It lasted until after the Famine of the 1840s. Rediker and Linebaugh believe that '[t]he English conquest of Ireland in 1596 laid the material foundation and established the model of all conquests to follow': *Many-headed hydra* (2013), 57. See also Hogan, *Other Englands* (2018), 102, 110–11.

126 Sandra M. Sufian. *Healing the land and the nation: malaria and the Zionist project in Palestine, 1920–1947* (Chicago, 2007), 58, 63. 'Unleashing the land's potential could only be done through the intervention of humans, and the Zionists at that … the land lay unattended until the arrival of the Zionists. They are seen as the only actors who could cause the land's productive forces to gush forth.' *Healing the land*, 102. See also Baruch Kimmerling. *Zionism and territory: the socio-territorial dimensions of Zionist politics* (Berkeley, CA, 1983).

127 Vijay Prashad. *The darker nations: a people's history of the Third World* (New York, 2007), 5.

128 See, for example, Pekka Hämäläinen's precise investigation of Comanche adaptability and ability to circumnavigate the colonising Spanish: *Comanche empire* (2008).

129 Manu Karuka. *Empire's tracks: indigenous nations, Chinese workers, and the transcontinental railroad* (Berkeley, CA, 2019), 5.

130 Julius S. Scott. *The common wind: Afro-American currents in the age of the Haitian revolution* (London, 2018), 7.

131 Parisot, *How America became capitalist* (2019), 37.

132 Cronon, *Changes in the land* (1983), 43–4.

133 Isenberg, *White trash* (2016), 18–19.

134 Cronon, *Changes in the land* (1983), 52. See also Syed Hussein Alatas. *The myth of the lazy native: a study of the image of the Malays, Filipinos and Javanese from the 16th to the 20th century and its function in the ideology of colonial capitalism* (London, 1977).

135 Fitzmaurice, *Humanism and America* (2003), 60. Cronon offers an interesting explanation for the failures of the American colonists: 'their myths told them that the plentiful times would never end, but their refusal to lay up stores for the winter meant that many starved to death. The pattern occurred repeatedly, whether at Sagadagoc, Plymouth, or Massachusetts: colonists came without adequate food

supplies and died. At Plymouth alone, half the Pilgrims were dead before the first winter was over': *Changes in the land* (1983), 36. See also Parisot, *How America became capitalist* (2019), 25.

136 Ordahl Kupperman, *Indians and English* (2000), 35. See also Stannard, *American holocaust* (1992), 103–9.

137 Keri Leigh Merritt. *Masterless men: poor whites and slavery in the antebellum south* (Cambridge, 2017), 38. See also Cox-Richardson, *To make men free* (2014), 33–4.

138 Sven Beckert calls the European conquest of America – the Spanish most of all – 'the world's greatest land grab': *Empire of cotton* (2014), 31. See also Ince's comment: 'The enthronement of private property as the natural and universally beneficial mode of appropriating and exploiting the earth's resources depended on the forcible marginalization of competing property systems, which was accomplished on a colossal scale by the land appropriations in the New World': *Colonial capitalism* (2018), 29. 'Enclosure was a violent and complicated process that laid the groundwork for the eventual commodification of land on a planetary scale. What was accomplished in early modern Europe by the alliance of the landed aristocracy, large manufacturers, and the "new bankocracy" was brought to the world through colonialism. In the process, countless precolonial systems of land tenure were destroyed': David Madden, Peter Marcuse. *In defence of housing: the politics of crisis* (London, 2016), 19–20.

139 Karuka, *Empire's tracks* (2019), 31–2.

140 Bhandar, *Colonial lives of property* (2018), 8. And Bhandar goes on to declare that '[t]he concept of improvement as the defining criterion for establishing a legitimate right to property finds its clearest expression in the work of John Locke': *Colonial lives of property*, 38–9.

141 Fitzmaurice, *Sovereignty, property and empire* (2014), 2.

142 Linebaugh talks of 'a combination of utopian thinking and genocidal reality that would recur in European and American history': *Magna Carta manifesto* (2008), 25. Locke would be one of the prime exemplars of this combination. James Tully has made the following apt comment: 'Three hundred years after its publication Locke's *Two Treatises of Government* continues to present one of the major political philosophies of the modern world. By this I mean it provides a set of concepts we standardly use to represent and reflect on contemporary politics': 'Rediscovering America', in Rogers, ed., *Locke's philosophy* (1994), 165.

143 Fitzmaurice, *Sovereignty, property and empire* (2014), 122.

144 Sell, *Trouble of the world* (2021), 150.

145 The border between the colonial and the metropolitan is always blurred. As I have elsewhere sought to argue, 'colonialist impulses regularly lurk in the background of modernity. Colonialism and the controlled freedom of liberal modernity are often of a piece with each other': Aidan Beatty. 'The Gaelic League and the spatial logics of Irish nationalism', *Irish Historical Studies*, Vol. 43, No. 163 (2019), 70, fn. 80.
146 Fitzmaurice, *Sovereignty, property and empire* (2014), 122.
147 'In 1969 John Dunn published an article entitled "The politics of John Locke in England and America in the 18th century", which claimed that Locke's *Two Treatises* were virtually unknown in America for the first half of the eighteenth century, while Locke's political theory, far from being the revolutionary liberal treatise needed by the signators [*sic*] of the Constitution, was very conservative indeed ... Chaudhuri Joyotpaul and George Mace also conclude that Locke's impact on the American revolutionaries was minimal': Arneil, *Locke and America* (1996), 12–13. Aside from the fact that Jefferson knew Locke's work (see Pierson, *Just property*, Vol. 1 (2013), 222), I would refute this assertion by pointing out that, whether or not Locke had a direct impact on, say, Jefferson, Hamilton or Madison, he did espouse the kinds of ideas that were already floating around the eighteenth-century British Atlantic, and which Jefferson et al. also imbibed. And in any case, it is worth remembering that Samuel Adams wrote a Lockean thesis at Harvard in 1743: Linebaugh and Rediker, *Many-headed hydra* (2013), 216. It is simply false to say that Locke was unknown in colonial America.
148 Isaac Kramnick, ed. *American political thought: a Norton anthology* (New York, 2009), 151–4. See also the discussion of Carl L. Becker's *The Declaration of Independence: a study in the history of political ideas* (New York, 1942) in Jerome Huyler. *Locke in America: the moral philosophy of the founding era* (Lawrence, KS, 1995).

2

The poet of real property

The anti-Semite has a fundamental incomprehension of the various forms of modern property: money, securities, etc. These are abstractions, entities of reason related to the abstract intelligence of the Semite. A security belongs to no one because it can belong to everyone; moreover, it is a sign of wealth, not a concrete possession. The anti-Semite can conceive only of a type of primitive ownership of land based on a veritable magical rapport, in which the thing possessed and its possessor are united by a bond of mystical participation; he is the poet of real property.

Jean-Paul Sartre[1]

A discourse on the love of our country

The end of the eighteenth century was a fortuitous time in British politics. Two important political events converged: the 1788 centenary of the Glorious Revolution, commemorating the toppling of the 'tyrant' James II, and the eruption of a contemporary revolution in France the next year. This was a seminal period for the making of the English working class, as E.P. Thompson has famously shown. The English working class moved from being a 'class-in-itself' to a 'class-for-itself' and nascent proletarian groups looked to import Jacobinism into their country. Organisations like the London Corresponding Society and the Society for Constitutional Information spread radical ideas and unnerved the ruling classes.[2] Another grouping, the Society for Commemorating the Revolution in Great Britain, linked the revolutions of 1688 and 1789, claiming the latter had the same motivations as the former and would also resolve some of the unfinished business of 1688.

On 4 November 1789, as the French National Assembly voted to seize church property, the Society for Commemorating the Revolution organised a public gathering at the Old Jewry Meeting House, a dissenting chapel in central London. Attendees at the gathering were addressed by Richard Price, a Welsh radical with republican sympathies who was also 'a prominent and respected Unitarian dissenter'.[3] Price's sermon, quickly made available as a pamphlet, began innocently with a discussion of patriotism.[4] Opening with a quote from Psalms, Price gave Biblical legitimacy to the virtues of patriotism; just as the Hebrews had prayed for the peace of Jerusalem, contemporaries should also wish the best for their 'country' (by 'country', he meant national community, not space or soil). Love of one's nation, though, should not be to think it superior to all others. Similarly, supporters of patriotism should guard against the love of one's country that can slip into domination of other countries. This 'narrow' thinking is what leads 'clans of *Indians* or tribes of *Arabs* ... to plunder and massacre'. The love of one's own country should be part of 'the principle of universal benevolence'. Or, as he said, with an obvious antisemitic contention, '[w]hat was the love of their country among the *Jews*, but a wretched partiality to themselves, and a proud contempt of all other nations?' In other words, love of one's own country, for Price, was not a simple particularistic love. It is a love of one's own that is of a piece with a love of the universal.

Price moved on from patriotism to a politico-moral discussion of what he felt were the three 'chief blessings of human nature': truth, virtue and liberty. Ideally, a nation would possess all three. Truth or knowledge (he used the two interchangeably) he defined in opposition to 'a country of barbarism', virtue was distinguished from 'a country of *gamblers*, *Atheists*, and *libertines*' and liberty 'must be distinguished from a country of slaves'. The language is careful and the politics do not seem all that controversial. Then Price advanced to his real target.

He argued that the two dangers facing a country are 'adulation and servility on one hand; and a proud licentious contempt on the other'. It was here that he started to make his political point.

He briefly spoke against this latter problem of 'licentious contempt' and reminded his audience that a sovereign is owed his 'proper respect'. But he focused greater attention on the opposite issue of excessive adulation and servility. Such postures inflame the egos of 'men in power' and reduce the citizenry to a state of 'abjectness'. According to Price, this was a particular problem in late 1780s Britain and the British would do well to remember that the king is 'more properly the *Servant* than the *Sovereign*' of the people. This was, indeed, a very Lockean idea, delineated in the 'Second treatise'; subjects owe respect to their king, but the king also owes respect to his subjects and their property, and can be rightfully deposed if that respect is not forthcoming.

For Price, the reason to celebrate the glories of the Glorious Revolution was precisely because the events of 1688 had instituted the situation where the king ruled at the behest of the people:

> By a bloodless victory, the fetters which despotism had been long preparing for us were broken; the rights of the people were asserted, a tyrant expelled, and a Sovereign of our choice appointed in his room. Security was given to our property, and our consciences were emancipated. The bounds of free enquiry were enlarged ... and that *æra* of light and liberty was introduced among us, by which we have been made an example to other kingdoms, and become the instructors of the world.

Note the possessive pronouns here: we, us, our. The Glorious Revolution may have been a century earlier, but *we* are still living in its shadow. Price did remain critical of the unfinished business of 1688 – full religious freedoms had not been guaranteed and the voting franchise was still determined by property ownership – but he now saw an opportune time for resolving this. Looking at France, he said that 'I have lived to see THIRTY MILLIONS of people, indignant and resolute, spurning at slavery, and demanding liberty with an irresistible voice; their king led in triumph, and an arbitrary monarch surrendering himself to his subjects'. The French revolutionaries were striving for the same goals as radicals like Price: a king who obeys the will of the people, security of property, universal male suffrage, full liberty. 'What an eventful period is this! I am thankful that I have lived to [see] it.' Not only that, the new politics on display would not be confined to France. Price ended with a mixture of polemic and political prophecy:

> I see the ardor for liberty catching and spreading; a general amendment beginning in human affairs; the dominion of kings changed for the dominion of laws, and the dominion of priests giving way to the dominion of reason and conscience ... Behold, the light you have struck out, after setting AMERICA free, reflected to FRANCE, and there kindled into a blaze that lays despotism in ashes, and warms and illuminates EUROPE! Tremble all ye oppressors of the world! Take warning all ye supporters of slavish governments, and slavish hierarchies![5]

Jacobinism – understood as a force for liberty by some, feared as a crazed mob by others – would come to Britain and usher in radical and, for Richard Price, necessary change.

The initial reflections

Richard Price's sermon, soon circulating in pamphlet, nourished a number of broader anxieties in Britain after 1789. The fall of the Bastille on 14 July 1789 had electrified popular opinion, in Britain, across Europe and globally. The British liberal Charles James Fox called the Revolution 'the greatest event that ever happened in the World'. Other observers were far less optimistic. According to the British *chargé d'affaires* in Vienna, the Austrian emperor experienced 'transports of passion' and swore 'the most violent Menaces of Vengeance' when told of the Revolution. The king of Sweden was reportedly suffering from insomnia as a result and 'the Empress of Russia had stamped her foot in rage'. There was a pronounced fear of 'contagion', that Revolutionary ideas, practices and even people would spread across Europe. 'There were those who pointed out that the date of the storming of the Bastille, 14 July, was the same as that on which Jerusalem fell to the First Crusade in 1099, suggesting some kind of revenge of the Infidel.' An air of irrationality often accompanied contemporary descriptions of the Revolution.[6] Radicals like Price, as tepid as their ideas might appear today, were seen in the 1780s and 1790s as dangerous importers of Jacobin violence and disorder and a terrifying threat to the property order.

One prominent person particularly disturbed by the popular purchase of Price's arguments was Edmund Burke, an Irish-born Whig liberal, a sometime writer on aesthetics and, since 1765, a Member of Parliament.[7] Burke was an arch defender of the property order that had emerged out of the Enclosures and had expressed concerns about social instability in Britain well before 1789.[8] With the start of the Revolution in 1789, he was quick to declare it a travesty, even though most of his liberal contemporaries were publicly happy at the collapse of a rotten, absolutist monarchy.

Writing in a letter of August 1789, just after the storming of the Bastille and three months before Price's *Discourse*, Burke spoke not only of his fears of French chaos but also of his understanding that the French might not yet be 'fit for liberty' because they lacked the 'fund of natural moderation to qualify them for freedom'.[9] The Jacobins were too extreme to know how to exercise a 'responsible' freedom (presumably a freedom that did not endanger property). Burke found it disquieting that so many of his fellow Whigs had revolutionary sympathies and gave a speech attacking the Revolution on 9 February 1790, which also took aim at British supporters of the Revolution.[10] Using a familiar vocabulary of Jacobin infection and contagion, he warned about 'the new and grievous malady' emanating from France, and his 'great dread and apprehension from the contagious nature of these abominable principles, and vile manners, which threaten the worst and most degrading barbarism to every adjacent Country'.[11]

Hoping to disprove Price specifically, and to dampen the spread of Jacobin-inspired ideas in Britain more generally, Burke set to work on what would become an enduring endeavour, his 1792 broadside against Jacobinism, *Reflections on the Revolution in France*, 'by far the most famous literary response to that liminal event of political modernity'.[12] The *Reflections* were both a voracious argument in favour of private property *and* a condemnation of the Jacobin mob.[13] And Burke's propertied polemic found a receptive audience; in its first seventeen days, 5,500 copies of the book were sold, a total of 12,000 in the first month. George III is said to have seen in Burke's *Reflections* 'a good book, a very good book; every gentleman ought to read it'. At 'the bastion of reaction' – Oxford University – there were debates about awarding an honorary degree to Burke, 'in consideration of his very able Representations of the True Principles of our Constitution Ecclesiastical and Civil'. *The Times* praised the book as an antidote to 'all those dark insidious minds' who would wish to 'level' the 'manly' British constitutional order. Edward Gibbon tasted in the *Reflections* 'a most admirable medicine against the French disease'. Even Pope Pius VI praised Burke.[14]

In 1789, Burke had been contacted by Charles-Jean-François Depont, a French aristocrat who hoped to secure Burke's public support for the Revolution.[15] The *Reflections* are ostensibly an extended letter written in response to this French correspondent, but in actual fact were motivated by his considerable fears of Richard Price and the Revolution Society and their ostensibly dangerous ideas. The 'epistolary discourse' of the *Reflections* follows a fluid structure, in which Burke meanders through his various objections to the Revolution: 'I beg leave to throw out my thoughts, and express my feelings, just as they arise in my mind, with very little attention to formal method'.[16] There is a free-flowing thrust to the text, and it requires some reconstruction to identify Burke's central concerns about the Jacobin mob and about the looming collapse of private property.[17]

In his extended epistolary format, he scolded his imagined French correspondent for presuming that Burke might have sympathies for the Constitutional Society or the Revolution Society. He emphatically denied that he could ever support either group. What is more, 'I never heard a man of common judgement, or the least degree of information, speak a word in praise' of such radical politics.[18] Burke named the ideas of Richard Price specifically as well as his *Discourse on the love of our country*, recalling that on a recent visit to London he had arranged to purchase a copy of the sermon: 'the whole of that publication', with its collapsing of the English and French Revolutions and what that portended for a peaceful and propertied social order, 'gave me a considerable degree of uneasiness'.[19]

He sarcastically refers to Price as 'this spiritual doctor of politics'[20] and states that '[f]ew harangues from the pulpit ... have ever breathed less of the spirit of moderation that this lecture in the Old Jewry'.[21] People like Price, Burke claims, are '[w]holly unacquainted with the world in which they are so fond of meddling'. They are inexperienced and overly excited. In addition, Price does not expound properly British political values. Rather, he speaks only 'the confused jargon' of 'Babylonian pulpits'.[22] This is a trope that resurfaces throughout the text (and throughout conservatism more broadly); radical politics cannot trace their roots back to native soil. Rather, they are always foreign and dangerous. Radical politics, a threat to private property, is a product of Babylon not of Britain. Price's ideas are nothing but 'delusive gypsey [sic] predictions'.[23] Indeed, Burke makes much of the location of Price's sermon, Old Jewry. He talks of Richard Price speaking 'from the Pisgah of his pulpit',[24] suggesting this 'Jew' is gazing longingly upon the Promised Land of Jacobin France. So, as well as being a Babylonian fomenting alien ideas, Price is a 'Jew', who disrespects private property and kings. In February 1790, as Burke was finishing the *Reflections*, he wrote in a private letter that both the Revolution Society and the newly formed French National Assembly were 'calumniators, hypocrites, sowers of sedition, and approvers of murder and all its triumphs' and had 'wicked principles' and 'black hearts'. They were 'Indian delinquents' who 'darken the air with their arrows'.[25] The sermon at Old Jewry was 'a spectacle more resembling a procession of American savages'.[26] As with Locke, as with Jefferson, so also with Burke: private property must be defended from the encroachments of a mob of racialised outsiders. Those who do not respect private property are neither proper men nor are they our racial kin. The accusations oscillate continuously between the racial and the gendered here, but with the same conservative inference: Richard Price's ideas are not only a threat to the British social order but dangerously *different* from that social order. Indeed, Burke says that Price espouses ideas that are 'unmanly and irreligious', which would shock 'the moral taste of every well-born mind'.[27] Normativity, for Burke, was clearly a simultaneously gendered, racialised and propertied thing.

The problem with Richard Price, though, is not just that he himself espouses 'foreign' and 'unmanly' radicalism. Burke is also profoundly disturbed by the broader trend that Price represents, of British citizens' desires to emulate Revolutionary France and import Jacobin ideas into Britain. Burke had little patience for claims that 1688 and 1789 drew on the same political impulses.[28] 'We ought not, on either side of the water, to suffer ourselves to be imposed upon by the counterfeit wares which some persons, by a double fraud, export to you in illicit bottoms, as raw commodities of British growth wholly alien to our soil, in order afterwards to smuggle them back again into this country.'[29] In other words, Burke was accusing Price and those like him of fabricating a false vision of the Glorious Revolution, of urging the French to emulate this imaginary version of 1688, and then of trying to (re-)import their radicalised interpretation of the proper social order back into Britain. He felt (or, more accurately, hoped) that the British people would have no truck with such radical and historically inaccurate notions.[30] He claimed 'the far greater and better part'[31] of Great Britain agreed with his anti-Jacobin politics. There is an obvious paradox here, though; the British will supposedly resist radicalism, yet Burke is clearly disturbed about the threat of radicalism finding support among the lower orders. British radicals were the 'real target' of the *Reflections*, and Burke took aim at them precisely because they were so prevalent.[32] Just as Locke and his contemporaries were animated by a fear of the 'masterless men' created by the Enclosures, so also Burke feared the Jacobin-inspired *lumpen* mobs and their possible assaults on private property.

For all his criticisms of the flights of political fancy of Price et al., Burke was also engaging in an act of suppositious political imagination. He used the *Reflections* to narrate a tale of violent societal collapse and property confiscations in post-1789 France. To construct this tale, he also needed to narrate one of peaceable social harmony and respect for private property in Britain.[33] His *Reflections on the Revolution in France* are simultaneously a series of reflections on the lack of a revolution at home.[34] And private property is central to both sets of intertwined reflections.

Where Locke used 'America' as a space in which to imagine his propertied vision, Burke used an idealised image of Britain to construct his. Burke traced British/English social harmony back to the Magna Carta of 1215, which he claimed had established a way of thinking that was then built upon by the Declaration of Rights enshrined during the Glorious Revolution. Burke shared the view of his contemporary David Hume 'that justice should be served by the stability of property over time'.[35] For Burke, a secure system of private property was 'the very basis of civil society'.[36] In 1768, three years into his parliamentary career, Burke had supported a bill advocating 'prescriptive' property rights and defining and delimiting Crown property rights. He argued that making property ownership uniform and equitable – the same kind of horizontal and nominal but shallow equality that Locke advocated – was essential for the stability of possessions, the security of liberty and the British constitution.[37] The political rights of the English were a kind of inherited property, 'derived to us from our forefathers, and to be transmitted to our posterity ... an estate specially belonging to the people of this kingdom'.[38] Political rights are thus 'a sort of family settlement', transmitted through the generations 'as a kind of mortmain for ever'.[39] Connecting property to the family gives it an aura 'of peace and permanence, and of rootedness', akin to the alleged naturalness of the nuclear family.[40] Welding property to the heteronormative family, procreation and the children who will inherit from us, it is clearly a gendered way of thinking. Understanding politics in these terms is also a key plank in Burke's idea of prescription, the idea that our actions should be limited by the rules of, and our respect for, long-standing institutions, private property foremost among them:

> In this choice of inheritance we have given to our frame of polity the image of a relation in blood; binding up the constitution of our country with our dearest domestic ties; adopting our fundamental laws into the bosom of our family affections; keeping inseparable, and cherishing with the warmth of all their combined and mutually reflected charities, our state, our hearths, our sepulchres, and our altars.[41]

The rights of the freeborn Englishman may be a kind of private property, but that does not mean that individual Englishmen can dispose of that property in any and all manners of their choosing.[42]

Freedom-as-property begets rules and order, as Englishmen seek to safeguard property and a propertied sense of freedom for their progeny. We own our property individually, but we are also duty-bound to protect that property for our children and our children's children. This restricts our freedom to dispose of property but it also means that there is a kind of familial stability to the British state and to British people's respect for private property;

the 'nation' is the machinery through which the rules of private property are both propagated through the community and preserved over time.[43] This was a specifically conservative conception of private property that differed from the Lockean or the liberal, in which property rights are freer and more open; an undiluted liberal would not agree that such limits should be placed on the property owner. Moreover, as with real inheritances, only a few would receive this inherited freedom. Women and the lower orders would never be full propertied citizens.[44] Imagining private property as a form of inheritance was an inherently gendered move, one that effectively excluded women. Christopher Pierson's quip about Cicero is equally applicable to Burke: 'as a deeply conservative thinker, he simply presumed that what was time-honoured was honourable in itself'.[45]

British freedom is not just a *type of* inherited property, though, it is also the political means that facilitates the *ownership of* property. 'By a constitutional policy, working after the pattern of nature, we receive, we hold, we transmit our government and our privileges, in the same manner in which we enjoy and transmit our property and our lives.'[46] It is this prescriptive and private-property-centric politics that Burke believed the Glorious Revolution of 1688 safeguarded. Britain was a land where politics was defined by private property, freedom was defined as a form of inheritable private property and there was no need for radical change. The Glorious Revolution was 'a parent of settlement, and not a nursery of future revolutions',[47] a closing off, not an opening up, of any debates about private property.

Your new constitution is the reverse of ours

In binary opposition to this vision of the British social order was Burke's conception of France; a chaotic and violent land in which private property, the bedrock of social peace, had been irreparably undermined. France was the opposite of post-Enclosures and post-Glorious Revolution Britain. 'Your new constitution is the reverse of ours in its principle',[48] he told his imagined French correspondent. And Burke averred that the purpose of his epistolary

Reflections was both to teach the French 'the true principles of our own domestic laws' and to remind the British of the same.[49]

> Already committed to this conception in the 1760s, Burke concluded that nothing could be more destructive to the institution of property than an arbitrary attempt on prescriptive title [i.e. an assault on private property and its inheritance]. The events of 1789 in France, beginning with the claim of the National Assembly on the corporate property of the Gallican Church, represented an assault on prescription of a kind that Burke had long feared, but on a scale that he could not have imagined in the Britain of the 1760s. In the face of such an assault, it was not merely privilege but justice itself that was threatened with extinction.[50]

In a private letter with Depont in November 1789, Burke stated his trepidations about property seizures in France. He talked of his fear that under the Revolution 'no man's possession could be safe' and 'individual property ... would be extinguished'. Burke's preferred regime for France would be one that 'endeavours to secure the freedom and property of the subject'. He thus told Depont that the French may have 'subverted monarchy' but, since freedom and property were linked in Burke's thinking, they had failed to regain their freedom.[51] The public letter of the *Reflections* picked up on this line, with Burke beginning his discussions of France by telling the reader that he could not yet congratulate the French on their revolution. He stated that, just as he could not congratulate a madman who had escaped his asylum nor a 'highwayman and murderer' who had escaped prison, so he could not congratulate the French nation on acquiring this false, unpropertied 'liberty'.[52] Burke therefore established one of the *Reflections*' recurring themes: the actions of the French are nothing but illegitimate seizures of private property – a grander form of highway robbery – and they exist outside polite society, like a madman. Indeed, he claimed that this 'convulsion in property', as well as the loss of revenues from that property, were part of the 'publick disorders' and 'national imbecility'[53] that were now on the rise in France. Burke continued to hedge his congratulations for French liberty, until he had been assured how this new freedom will be combined with the other ingredients for a stable social order: 'the discipline and obedience of armies ... the collection of an effective and well-distributed revenue ... morality and religion ... civil and social manners'. Not least of all, he was apprehensive that French liberty would not be combined 'with the solidity of property'.[54] For Burke, the freedom Britain enjoyed was linked to, and understood as, inheritable private property; and this was the true legacy of the Glorious Revolution. Therefore, France's mistake was not copying 1688 in 1789. 'You had all these advantages in your antient states; but you chose to act is if you had never been moulded into civil society, and had every thing to begin anew.'[55] France had become a country where 'the foundations of property are destroyed'.[56]

Private property, once as much a bedrock of the French social order as of the British, was now being discarded and with terrible effects for civil society; 'property is destroyed' and now 'rational liberty has no existence'[57] in France. Without private property as a linchpin for society, France would necessarily become chaotic and unstable: 'Nothing stable in the modes of holding property, or exercising function, could form a solid ground on which any parent could speculate in the education of his offspring, or in a choice for their future establishment in the world.' France would decay into a fissiparous 'Barbarism' and 'the commonwealth itself would, in a few generations, crumble away'.[58] The Revolution represented an 'outrage on all the rights of property'[59] and Burke spoke of '[t]he madness of the project of confiscation'.[60] The revolutionaries had wrecked the judiciary of the Ancien Régime, the 'great security to private property'.[61] The leaders of the Revolution had shown their ignorance that 'it is to the property of the citizen ... that the first and original faith of civil society is pledged'.[62] Burke shared the Lockean notion that the defining purpose of society and state is to safeguard property;[63] thus the French Revolution was an abnegation of any kind of ordered society or governance.

Burke, of course, was wrong in many of the details he offered up about the Revolution and about its attitudes towards private property. For sure, there was an undeniable radicalism and a desire for a massive break with the past at work in the Revolution:

> The list of corporate or ancient institutions that were suppressed in the first twenty months or so of the Revolution included the law courts, guilds, estates, the privileged position of the church,

hospitals, universities, and associations of all kinds. In every realm, the traditional hierarchies and corporate institutions that for centuries had enabled French men and women to define themselves were sacrificed in a bonfire of inherited tradition without precedent in European history.[64]

In one of the earliest acts of the National Assembly, feudalism, with all its attendant dues, taxes and seigneurial property rights, was formally abolished on 4 August 1789.[65] The legislative assault on feudalism was mirrored (but also exceeded) by peasants and their tendency to seize and burn the archival documents that detailed feudal rights and obligations.[66] Church lands were seized, becoming property of the state.[67] This willingness to break with the past distinguished the French Revolution from previous, seemingly similar, upheavals, such as those of 1688 or 1776; even class distinctions appeared to be on the chopping block, as the Revolution promoted the use of national clothing that erased 'odious distinctions' of social status.[68] Many of the most prominent leaders of the Revolution were migrants from rural to urban areas, rather than well-established members of Parisian elites.[69] And in the areas of gender and race, two of the central conceptual apparatuses through which Burke understood the Revolution, there were serious structural changes: women gained a right to inherit property; in May 1791, civic rights were extended to people of colour born of free parents, and the Jacobins abolished slavery on 4 February 1794; in September 1792 divorce by mutual consent was recognised in law.[70] The Jacobin abolition of slavery was of particular concern to Burke. Events like the Haitian revolution, led by former slaves, 'were dangerous and horrifying proof that the French doctrine of the rights of man was an egalitarian disease that acted like a solvent on empire, by leading the savages to revolt against the civilized colonists in dreadful fashion'.[71] Moreover, women did play a major, public role in the revolution. Most famously, in October 1789 women from the Faubourg Saint-Antoine and Les Halles, lower-income market districts, marched to the Palace at Versailles demanding bread. When they forced the king and his family to return to Paris, they 'rejoiced in their victory' and proudly declared that they had effected the humiliating return of 'the baker, the baker's wife, and the baker's boy',[72] as they disdainfully named the royal family. Popular antimonarchical actions mixed with inverted gender roles, horrifying conservative observers, Burke not least among them.[73]

And yet, there is a danger of accepting too readily this idea of a Year Zero, a massive and total break with the past led by a singularly united band of revolutionaries. As Antonio Gramsci once said, the representatives who dominated the Third Estate in the early years of the Revolution 'were in fact moderate reformers, who shouted very loud but actually demanded very little'.[74] Georges Lefebvre, perhaps *the* historian of the Revolution in the twentieth century, has somewhat similarly observed that 'the French Revolution was started and led to victory in its first phase by the aristocracy'.[75] Even those initially elected to the National Assembly from the 'Third Estate' (the non-aristocratic majority of the French nation), 'were for the most part mature, often rich or well-to-do'.[76] The various revolutionary clubs that sprouted up charged admission fees high enough to preclude the poor.[77] At first, such 'revolutionaries' were unsurprisingly reticent to engage in large-scale transformations in the property order. A guard organised by the National Assembly and the electors of Paris in July 1789 was charged with maintaining order and property;[78] 'indeed most of the old aristocracy held on to their lands throughout the Revolution and even the Terror'.[79] The framers of the Declaration of the Rights of Man of 1789, the programmatic text of the Revolution, insisted on defending the right of property as 'natural, imprescriptible and sacred' while all other rights were simply 'natural and imprescriptible', but not sacred.[80] There was, as the French scholar Jean-Pierre Hirsch has said, a 'remarkable consensus surrounding the idea of property', the consensus being that property rights were sacrosanct. Even *La Montagne*, the far left of the Revolution, favoured appropriation over expropriation – mandatory, compensated purchase of property by the state rather than the kind of chaotic, uncompensated seizure that Burke claimed to be observing.[81]

In a report presented to the Constitutional Committee of the National Assembly (itself a product of the Revolution), Abbé Sieyès, an influential Catholic cleric and political theorist, drew a distinction between propertied 'active citizens', who would be allowed to vote, and 'passive citizens' who would not. Sieyès, like

Burke and Locke, saw property ownership as a key ingredient for full citizenship. A majority in the National Assembly agreed with Sieyès' ideas, 'which also reflected the accumulated wisdom of the *philosophes*', though some leading revolutionaries did 'actively' oppose the Constitutional Committee's *régime censitaire* 'that relegated the poor to the status of passive citizens and excluded all but the very rich from lawmaking'; among their number was the arch-Jacobin Maximilien Robespierrre, Dominique Garat, a member of the National Assembly associated with the more moderate Girondist faction, and Henri Grégoire, a Catholic priest and supporter of universal suffrage. In any case, under this 'propertied suffrage' only about 20 per cent of the population could initially vote for the National Assembly, the rest disqualified either because of property or gender. Some localities did allow universal male voting, such as the city of Toulon in the south, because the tax rolls had not survived. Yet the poor tended to not bother voting.[82]

Even the term 'Jacobin', notwithstanding the horror with which it was soon associated, named a sundry set of people with a sometimes bewildering ideological diversity, including Orthodox Jacobins, Girondist Jacobins, Montagnard Jacobins and Feuillants. The terms 'Left' and 'Right', even the modern concept of 'ideology' itself, emerged from the French Revolution, in part as an attempt to make sense of all these ideological divisions.[83] There were two simultaneous developments hidden within the singular term 'French Revolution': a 'bourgeois revolution' – 'a relatively conscious attempt by a diverse group of the ruling capitalist strata to force through urgently needed reforms of the French state' – and a far more radical revolt by the popular masses.[84] As historian Lynn Hunt has succinctly summarised it, 'the Revolution itself was always in flux'.[85]

Burke smothered these fluid divisions and contradictions within the Revolution.[86] In his account, there is only *the* Revolution, one that apparently always posed an existential threat to private property. His goal was less to come to an accurate understanding of what was unfolding in France and more to warn of the dangers that an inchoate mob posed to the property order. Even the onset of the Terror in the middle of 1793 did not noticeably change Burke's views, because he always saw the Revolution (even at its most moderate) as a terroristic event – the terror that plebeians and women (and, worst of all, plebeian women) would involve themselves in high politics and threaten the gendered and propertied order. And he remained steadfast in his prognostications about the Revolution and about the true cause of the destruction he saw there; he believed that a slow and subtle change had taken place in the class structure of post-1789 France. The propertied, landed classes had declined and a new class of finance capitalists had arisen. With echoes of the Keynesian economist Hyman Minsky, Burke argued that a society built on finance capitalism is inherently unstable, unlike the stolid security of landed property:

> The monied interest is in its nature more ready for any adventure; and its possessors more disposed to new enterprizes of any kind. Being of a recent acquisition, it falls in more naturally with any novelties. It is therefore the kind of wealth which will be resorted to by all who wish for change. Along with the monied interest, a new description of men had grown up, with whom that interest soon formed a close and marked union; I mean the political Men of Letters. Men of Letters, fond of distinguishing themselves, are rarely averse to innovation.[87]

Burke talked of how finance destabilises landed property; 'the spirit of 'money-jobbing' is inherently speculative and fluid and as a speculative mindset took root, so also land became 'volatilized'. Being traded now for paper money, land acquires 'uncertainty in its value'.[88] France had slipped into a state of anarchy and, according to Burke, '[u]nder such a regime, no possession would seem secure, as the very notion of private property was abolished'.[89] There is a certain kind of conservative critique of finance capitalism here, but one that seeks a nostalgic return to an arcadian vision of landed stability, rather than a break with capitalism writ large. And indeed, property ownership was also shifting in Britain, as financiers and *rentiers* became more of a force in the rural economy; in language redolent of Burke, the agrarian reformer William Cobbett spoke in 1820 of the 'paper money', marriages of convenience and 'nabobs, negro-drivers, generals, admirals, governors, commissaries, contractors, pensioners, sinecurists, commissioners, loan-jobbers, lottery-dealers, bankers, stock-jobbers' who now perennially stalked the English countryside. Already by the time of Burke's *Reflections*, the effects of this change in land ownership and the class structure were being felt in England.[90]

Fundamental to Burke's politics was the belief that holders of landed property were the natural and best rulers of a society.[91] The shift in class power that he identified in Revolutionary France (and probably also feared in Britain) had two negative effects: private property no longer received its due respect, and nor did the owners of landed property. Burke believed that the ideal parliament would be 'respectably composed, in point of condition of life, *of permanent property*, of education, and of such habits as enlarge and liberalize the understanding'.[92] Only such educated property owners – 'the natural landed interests of the country'[93] – could ensure a 'steady and modern conduct'[94] in a national assembly. When Burke looked at the new National Assembly in France, he was aghast at the absence of this natural ruling elite. All he saw in the meetings of the Third Estate were 'the inferior, unlearned, mechanical, merely instrumental members' of the legal profession. 'From the very moment I read the list I saw distinctly, and very nearly as it has happened, all that was to follow.'[95] Their only attitude towards 'all property, whether secular or ecclesiastical',[96] was one of envy coupled with a desire for its destruction.[97] And with such a totalising destruction of private property and of the legislative basis of private property, France itself had become more unnatural. The French nation had 'strayed out of the high road of nature' due to the fact that the 'property of France', the propertied elite, were no longer in charge.[98] There is a kind of class determinism to Burke; the greater the proximity to property ownership, the greater the ability to exercise political authority in a responsible manner and the more normal things would be. Conversely, the lack of private property always equals a lack of responsible or mature political faculties and a freakish abnormality.

Perhaps in a reference to the rural migrants who had become the urban leaders of the Revolution, Burke believed that France was now being ruled by '*new* persons' who wield a '*new* power',[99] a concise summation of the root of all of France's problems after 1789, as he saw them. But as Burke began to think through this situation, he made a curious statement about the nature of these *arriviste* rulers. He returned to the accusation he made about Richard Price; the French revolutionaries, with their lack of respect for private property, with their grounding in finance capitalism, are 'Jews'.

Private property and civilisation

The leaders of the Revolution, seizing property and replacing gold with paper money, were, Burke said, 'like Jew brokers' who meet in 'degenerate councils' and, by trucking in 'fraudulent circulation' and 'depreciated paper', bring 'wretchedness and ruin' on their country.[100] There is an upset to the 'natural' social order here, a disturbance in the regimes of property ownership, and unnerving changes in the monetary system, all of which Burke understood in quasi-racial terms: 'The next generation of the nobility will resemble the artificers and clowns, and money-jobbers, usurers, and Jews, who will be always their fellows, sometimes their masters'.[101] Calling to mind the story of Herod, and perhaps the medieval blood libel, Burke called the Revolution 'this great history-piece of the massacre of the innocents'.[102] He mocked the English radical, Jewish convert and *déclassé* noble, Lord George Gordon, imprisoned in 1787 for defaming Marie Antoinette. Burke dismissed Gordon's plight in prison – 'let him there meditate on his Thalmud' [*sic*] – but also urges that he learn 'a conduct more becoming his birth and parts, and not so disgraceful to the antient religion to which he has become a proselyte'. Burke suggested, to his partially fictive French correspondent, that his 'new Hebrew brethren' [i.e. the French Revolutionaries] could pay a ransom to free Gordon, a ransom they could easily afford 'with the old hoards of the synagogue, and a very small poundage, on the long compound interest of the thirty pieces of silver', in a reference linking the Revolutionaries to Judas Iscariot.[103] Again, a fortuitously 'Jewish' coincidence fuelled Burke's thinking about the links between private property, normative Europeanness and Jews. Like many on the right since then, Burke criticises some of the effects of financial capitalism even as he valorises the private-propertied underpinnings of capitalism, and he labels these negative effects 'Jewish' so as to further condemn them.

Burke's anti-Jewish accusations had a particular sting to them when it came to his discussions of the seizure of church properties in the Hexagon. He asked speculative and highly leading questions about the future of France and England – 'Are the church lands to be sold to Jews and jobbers; or given to bribe new invented municipal republics into a participation in sacrilege?' – and he wondered whether 'all orders, ranks, and distinctions' will be confounded and replaced by 'universal anarchy', suggesting that the French Revolutionaries as well as the Revolution Society in England were both aiming for this.[104] He also identified the dangers that this 'Jewish' revolution will spread across the Channel. 'The Jews in Change Alley', the centre of financial trading in eighteenth-century England, may soon seek to place a mortgage on 'the see of Canterbury'.[105] Burke conflated Jewishness with finance capitalism; both are a threat to private property and the natural established order, both are led by 'new men' as opposed to the proper rulers of the landed aristocracy. And he emotively set out his fears that this racialised and dangerous new politico-economic force would come to Britain next.

Burke's talk here of the crass buying and selling of sacred property was a reference to developments then under way in France, where church lands were, indeed, being seized and sold.[106] The Revolutionaries, or at least those who came to dominate on the eve of the Terror in 1793, developed a conspicuous hostility to the church, which became 'yet another way of announcing the revolutionary break with the French and European past'.[107] Even in the 1750s, at the earliest stage of his public career, Burke had endeavoured to shield two British institutions from attack: post-Enclosures, private-property-centric, constitutional liberty and the Anglican Church.[108] In his thinking, the two were inextricably linked. 'A regime of property depended on the prior institution of civil obedience so that the acquisition of goods might be secure', and Anglicanism would underpin that obedience.[109] For Burke, the seizure of church lands in 1790s France (and perhaps soon also in Britain) was doubly terrifying; as well as being a violation of private property, it eroded the stature of the church and thus deprived the ruling elite of the legitimising glow that he felt religion conferred on private property.[110] When Burke said, six months before his death, that he hated Jacobinism 'as we hate the Gates of Hell',[111] he does seems to have meant this in a theological sense. 'Private property was very near to divinity in the mind of the English ruling class of the time'[112] and a world without private property would be hell on earth.

The destruction of private property was a result of irreligion, and in turn fomented that godlessness.[113] Moreover, the destruction of private property is a form of general deracination. Burke claimed, with a fair dose of hyperbole, that few 'barbarous conquerors have ever made so terrible a revolution in property' as the barbarians of the French Revolution.[114] He called the French Revolutionaries a 'gang of assassins', a term with some blatant Orientalist connotations.[115] More to the point, Burke compared the new leaders in France to 'a gang of Maroon slaves, suddenly broke loose from the house of bondage'.[116] Like ex-slaves, they supposedly displayed no ability to exercise liberty in a 'responsible' manner.[117] And slaves, like Jacobins, are ignorant of the dignity of private property. Burke said of one landed aristocrat killed by his tenants during the Revolution: 'I am persuaded that the sands of Africa and the wilds of America would not have shewn [sic] any thing so barbarous and perfectly savage'. He compared the Revolutionaries to the Jews of the deicide and '[w]hen they suffer as the Jews, they will have more pity from good men, than they are intitled [sic] to from any they have shewn to suffering dignity and innocence'. And he claimed to be ashamed to have 'the same form and nature with such wretches'.[118] With Burke racialising them, their politics placed them outside the boundaries of normative humanity. Proper citizenship collapses here into racial stereotypes.[119] Since the threat to the social order was simultaneously imagined in terms of property and racial outsiders, to reject private property was therefore to become a racialised outsider.

Burke continued on this trajectory when he came to issues of gender. In one of the most famous passages of the *Reflections*, he assailed the treatment of Marie Antoinette in the new France. He recalled meeting the queen almost two decades earlier, when she was still 'a delightful vision'. But he now had a melodramatic lament for her:

> little did I dream that I should have lived to see such disasters fallen upon her in a nation of gallant men, in a nation of men of honour and of cavaliers. I thought ten thousand swords must have leaped from their scabbards to avenge even a look that threatened her with insult. – But the age of chivalry is gone. – That of sophisters, oeconomists, and calculators, has succeeded; and the glory of Europe

is extinguished for ever. Never, never more, shall we behold that generous loyalty to rank and sex, that proud submission, that dignified obedience, that subordination of the heart, which kept alive, even in servitude itself, the spirit of an exalted freedom ... the nurse of manly sentiment and heroic enterprize is gone!'[120]

Burke sexualised his subject matter, portraying the revolutionary mob as literally rapacious villains, with the queen of France the innocent victim of their lusts.[121] Thomas Paine observed that Burke, in his abounding sympathies for the plight of the royal family alongside his simultaneous silence on the struggles of those lower down the social ladder, 'pities the plumage but forgets the dying bird'.[122] It is certainly hard to take his tone seriously here and indeed, as Don Herzog points out, Burke privately confided that the French royals were ridiculous.[123]

Yet, beneath his fanciful embellishments, Burke was building up his vision of the proper social order, and of the threats to it. This is perhaps the central (intersectional) theme of the *Reflections*; the gender order, the racial order, the religious order, the social order and the continued existence of private property – the survival of each depended on the survival of the others.[124]

Burke was one of the first writers to use the word 'civilisation' in the English language,[125] and he understood this term in simultaneously propertied, racialised and gendered registers. In Burke's broadside against the Revolution, gender, the sanctity of private property and normative racial ideals were all coterminous and the loss of one brings about the loss of the other two. The French had lost all three, and thus had exited civilisation itself. They had become 'a nation of gross, stupid, ferocious, and at the same time, poor and sordid barbarians, destitute of religion, honour, or manly pride, *possessing nothing at present*, and hoping for nothing hereafter ... Their humanity is savage and brutal.'[126] This is one of the most familiarly conservative strands of the *Reflections*; the conservative sense that private property is 'almost sacred' and is 'integral to human nature'. Once this is accepted, anything that threatens property is both sacrilegious and inherently unnatural.[127]

Burke's conception of the property order was simultaneously a conception of gender, race and civilisational normativity. He spoke of the danger that the Revolution posed for the 'rational and manly freedom' that had once predominated in France.[128] He believed that the best religion was that which is 'rational and manly', a form of 'manly worship', where 'manly' was more a synonym for 'good' than a reference to biological masculinity *per se*.[129] He claimed the foot-soldiers of the Revolution were 'a mixed mob' made up of men with a failed masculinity ('ferocious men') and 'women lost to shame' who cheer on these fallen men.[130] The Revolution was an unseating of all gender norms. Chivalry is the source of modern Europe's character; '[i]t is this which has distinguished it under all its forms of government, and distinguished it to its advantage, from the states of Asia'.[131] Thus, without the proper attitude towards gender, all Europeans would slip into an inferior, Asiatic existence. In the passage on Marie Antoinette, he ranges from the threat of economic wreckers (sophisters, 'oeconomists' and calculators), to the fragility of both the gender order and the broader social order, and his readers' threatened status as civilised Europeans. Happy it was then, that the British 'have not yet been completely embowelled of our national entrails; we still feel within us, and we cherish and cultivate, those inbred sentiments which are the faithful guardians, the active monitors of our duty, the true supporters of all liberal and manly morals'.[132] It is surely no coincidence then that the British would never seek to enact confiscations of private property.[133] Property, gender and race all remain pure in post-Enclosures Britain (even if such claims elide his anxieties that Britain is never as harmonious as he wanted his readers to believe).

The counter-revolution

The Revolution was Burke's central political concern after 1789,[134] and the intersectional conflation of property, masculinity and an eighteenth-century variant of racial stereotypes, as well as overwrought and overwritten fears of the Jacobin mobs, surfaced again and again in his subsequent writings. In his May 1791 'Letter to a Member of the National Assembly' he assailed the new rulers of France as 'adventurers, gamesters, gipsies, beggars, and robbers' who had whipped up the 'more active and stirring part of the lower orders' with promises of plunder and property seizures. Returning to his antisemitic accusations, Burke said that 'the whole gang of usurers; pedlars, and itinerant Jew-discounters at the corners of streets' now gorge themselves on the spoils of the Revolution. He was aghast that 'the very sons of such Jew-jobbers have been made bishops'; Jewish figures that, he said, are 'bred at the feet of that Gamaliel', one of the New Testament Pharisees. The Revolutionaries are 'low, sordid, ungenerous, and reptile souls ... they display their odious splendour, and shine out in the full lustre of their native villainy and baseness ... no man of sense or honour can be mistaken for one of them'. Members of the lower orders, 'half-domesticated', are now treated as the equal of those who had previously been at the top of the French social order. He suggested that the men of France may no longer 'deserve the name' of men and that a man's status as the head of his household had been eroded. This was the result of France's 'ignoble, unmanly, and perfidious rebellion'. 'To what a state of savage, stupid, servile insensibility must your people be reduced', he rhetorically asked of the French.[135]

As before, Burke placed this image of French plundering, deracination and gendered degeneration in contrast to the British. Ignoring the very real radicalism that had swirled through the 1640s – when Levellers, Ranters and Diggers all questioned private property and even advocated communism[136] – he claimed that the result of the Cromwellian revolution was that '[e]very man was yet safe [in England] in his house and in his property'. The Enclosures were secure. Yet at the same time, Burke recognised the dangers of infection from France. 'Jews' also exist in London. They are mostly 'very respectable persons of the Jewish nation, whom we will keep'. But there also exist, 'others of a very different description, housebreakers, and receivers of stolen goods, and forgers of paper currency, more than we can conveniently hang'. The mob was too multitudinous to be stamped out completely and safely. Burke also asserted that no ordered state in Europe will be safe as long as France remains a source of 'assassination, robbery, rebellion, fraud, faction, oppression, and impiety'.[137] Writing in 1792, he admitted that property itself in France had survived the Revolution, but still argued that faith in property had been shattered.[138] Burke's writings in the 1790s are marked by a continuous fear of the spread of Jacobinism into Britain. He later confessed that he wrote the

Reflections to speak out against the 'new, republican, frenchified, Whiggism' that was 'gaining ground in this Country'. And Burke said he wanted to promote 'Sentiments of Liberty which were not at war with order, virtue, Religion and Good Government'. He spoke of the pre-1789 Whigs as 'a Party, in its composition and in its principles, connected with the stolid, permanent long possessed property of the Country ... a party therefore essentially constructed upon a Ground plot of stability and independence'. Burke was clearly upset that this party of property had been changed by the Revolution.[139]

His opposition to the Revolution put him strongly at odds with his party, and in his 1791 'Appeal from the new to the old Whigs' he urged his former political friends to abandon their Jacobin sympathies. He denounced both the 'French usurpation' and the 'mad' Englishmen who supported it: 'what was done in France was a wild attempt to methodize anarchy; to perpetuate and fix disorder ... it was a foul, impious, monstrous thing, wholly out of the course of moral nature ... a tyranny far beyond any example that can be found in the civilized European world of our age'. Burke warned that the Jacobins looked upon Britain as the 'principal object of their machinations'. He urged the Whigs to recognise that primogeniture – the prescriptive patrilineal inheritance of property – helped preserve social order and harmony. Those who called for its destruction 'do this for political reasons that are very manifest'. As in the *Reflections*, Burke presented male ownership of landed property as the bedrock of the social order. A change in property-relations would usher in adverse changes across society:

> when you disturb this harmony; when you break up this beautiful order, this array of truth and nature, as well as of habit and prejudice; when you separate the common sort of men from their proper chieftains so as to form them into an adverse army, I no longer know that venerable object called the people in such a disbanded race of deserters and vagabonds.

In 1791, Burke also compiled his 'Thoughts on French affairs'. Here, he again levelled the charge that the Revolutionaries had dedicated themselves to destroying 'all traces of antient establishments'. Burke presented their goals as an all-embracing assault on private property: 'totally abolishing hereditary name and office, levelling all conditions of men (except where money *must* make a difference), breaking all connexion between territory and dignity, and abolishing every species of nobility, gentry, and church establishments'. And again he described these actions as an affront to 'the natural operation of things'. That the National Assembly was composed of men 'wholly unconnected with birth or property' was the source of much anxiety for Burke. As well as being the wrong class, he depicted the Jacobins in exoticised and racialised terms: 'monstrous as the Republick of Algiers', as strange as the 'Republick of the Mammalukes in Egypt'.[140] By the middle of the 1790s, Burke was still alleging a Jewish provenance for the Revolution, making comments in a private letter about 'the broad phylacteries'[141] and 'the imposing gravity of those magisterial rabbins [sic] and doctors in the cabala of political science'.[142]

The shadow of the Revolution can even be seen in a sketch he wrote for William Pitt (the Younger) on the seemingly innocuous topic of economic scarcity. In a disarmingly casual tone, Burke warned against the temptation to cut the throats of the rich and redistribute their property to the poor. Such an action would undo the reciprocal social relationship wherein the job-creating, propertied rich provide paid work to the propertyless poor. Burke also cautioned against visions of social equality, which he held were impossible to achieve, and against any government distribution of foodstuffs. State-run granaries, he claimed, would inevitably become targets for protests and 'popular frenzy' to seize the food and redistribute it. The danger of mobs, violent social transformation and property seizure continued to loom large in Burke's political imagination. He claimed that he could not think of the 'nefarious monsters' of the Revolution 'without a mixed sensation of disgust, of horror, and of detestation, not easy to be expressed'.[143] In his 'Letters on a regicide peace' (1796) he claimed Revolutionary France was not a state or a political force, but 'a general evil'. War between the old regimes of Europe and this evil entity 'is a war between the partisans of the ancient civil, moral, and political order of Europe against a sect of fanatical and ambitious atheists which means to change them all'. Elsewhere, he addressed the root of Jacobinism's threat as being Jacobins' 'contempt of Property'.[144]

In 'A letter to a noble lord', a publicly addressed epistle of 1796, Burke went even further in his views of the Revolution and tied together the themes of social order and the proper gender order. Taking an astronomical turn, he made one of his most overt yet also most bizarre statements on the fragility of the post-Enclosures order as well as the fragility of time, history and civilisation, and on understanding Britain and France together:

> Astronomers have supposed, that if a certain comet, whose path intersected the ecliptick, had met the earth in some (I forget what) sign, it would have whirled us along with it, in it's excentrick course, into God knows what regions of heat and cold. Had the portentous comet of the rights of man (which 'from it's horrid hair shakes pestilence, and war,' and 'with fear of change perplexes Monarchs'[145]), had that comet crossed upon us in that internal state of England, nothing human could have prevented our being irresistibly hurried out of the highway of heaven into all the vices, crimes, horrours and miseries of the French revolution.

The Earth could have easily moved along a different trajectory, time could have taken a different path, Britain could easily have slipped into the uncivilised barbarity of France or, as Burke describes a potentially post-private-property Britain, '[w]ild and savage insurrection quitted the woods, and prowled about our streets in the name of reform. Such was the distemper of the publick mind, that there was no madman, in his maddest ideas, and maddest projects, who might not count upon numbers to support his principles and execute his designs.' Burke calls this 'the death-dance of Democratick Revolution' and he says that his native Ireland was even more dangerous in this regard: 'In Ireland things ran in a still more eccentric course. Government was unnerved, confounded, and in a manner suspended.'[146] He then moves on to discuss his horror of those women who took a role in the Revolution, with his language shifting from the cosmological to the scatological:

> The revolution harpies of France, spring from night and hell, or from that chaotick anarchy, which generates equivocally 'all monstrous, all prodigious things,' cuckoo-like adulterously lay their eggs, and brood over, and hatch them in the nest of every neighbouring State. These obscene harpies, who deck themselves, in I know not what divine attributes, but who in reality are foul and ravenous birds of

prey (both mothers and daughters) flutter over our heads, and souse down upon our tables, and leave nothing unrent, unrifled, unravaged, or unpolluted with the slime of their filthy offal.

The quote here is, again, from *Paradise Lost*, another description of Hell.[147] Unnaturally monstrous mobs continued to haunt Burke's fears of social revolution.

Burke's America

Edmund Burke's condemnation of the French Revolution – emotive, overwrought, vociferous – shocked many of his contemporaries. He had long been found on the liberal, Whiggish end of English politics. Indeed, Charles-Jean-François Depont had originally written to Burke on the presumption that, *because of* his political record, he would be an amiable supporter of the French Revolution. The *Reflections* can thus appear as something of aberration, a late-career turn to conservatism after a lifetime as a liberal. In fact, there is a strong continuity across Burke's writings, as Daniel O'Neill recently pointed out.[148] The idealisation of private property and the claim that it was intimately linked with race and gender united a large fraction of his political writings.

Some two decades before Burke looked on with horror at events in France, he had shown a far greater level of sympathy for a different revolution. In the years leading up to 1776, Edmund Burke was a major voice in British politics for conciliation with the American colonies. Burke's statements on that crisis were based around a number of recurring tropes: the colonists were essentially British, where Britishness was understood in terms of attitudes towards politics and relationship to private property. And yet, there was also a fragility to this. The British-Americans could easily lose their normative respect for private property and slip into a deracinated and less manly mode of existence. In a 1774 Parliamentary speech on the topic of American taxation, Burke discussed how the colonists had constructed something akin to 'antient nations grown to perfection' in a land that once been 'a desolate wilderness'; that is, the colonists had, like good Lockeans, transplanted the 'antient'

British social order into this *terra nullius*. This new/old society displayed 'every characteristic mark of a free people in all her internal concerns. She had the image of the British constitution.' In other words, the Americans were essentially British and they had a British constitution with private-property ownership as its hard core. What Burke called the 'present cruelty to America' was that this British manly freedom was being abused.[149] He warned his Parliamentary colleagues to recognise this British sense of freedom in their dealings with the Americans.[150]

In a much-cited speech delivered in 1775, Burke advanced these ideas as the means of achieving conciliation with the colonies. The Americans, he said, were 'Two Millions of inhabitants of our own European blood' and Britain was their 'Mother Country'. They were a people defined by 'a love of Freedom':

> This fierce spirit of Liberty is stronger in the English Colonies probably than in any other people of the earth; and this from a great variety of powerful causes ... First, the people of the Colonies are descendants of Englishmen. England, Sir, is a nation, which still I hope respects, and formerly adored, her freedom. The Colonists emigrated from you, when this part of your character was most predominant; and they took this biass [sic] and direction the moment they parted from your hands. They are therefore not only devoted to Liberty, but to Liberty according to English ideas, and on English principles.

Such a people, a product of the culture of post-Enclosures England, would not tolerate any limits on their propertied freedom, an observation that led Burke to consider both the perilous consequences of Parliament imposing the wrong policies and the fragility of property ownership, whiteness and civilisation. American colonists, he stated, had moved so far into the continental interior as to be almost out of reach of British law. A coercive response would only push them further away. Where the Britons of North America had thus far respected the laws of private property and the need for formally recognised deeds of ownership ('We have invited the husbandman, to look to authority for his title. We have taught him piously to believe in the mysterious virtue of wax and parchment'), if they crossed to the far side of Appalachia they would be lost: 'Already they have topped the Apalachian [sic] mountains. From thence they behold before them an immense plain, one vast, rich, level meadow; a square of five hundred miles. Over this they would wander, without a possibility of restraint; they would change their manners with the habits of their life; would soon forget a government, by which they were disowned.' They would become, Burke said, '[h]ordes of English Tartars'.[151] Private property was the basis of a harmonious social order, but that order could easily slip away. Proper Englishmen would be reduced to violent, Oriental terrors.[152] Burke's idealised vision of the British Empire was based on an 'Ornamentalist' belief that all the differing groups and nations of the Empire were united by a shared political culture;[153] that culture was, for Burke, defined by its respect for private property.[154] Yet Burke clearly also sensed that that Ornamentalism was immensely brittle, and could easily shatter.

Shortly after the American Revolution, Burke wrote of the dangers of forced equality, a popular clamour for which had been encouraged by 'the Flames of this present cursed War in America'. Burke argued that inequality was actually a good thing, since it grew out of the best use of property: 'I am, for one, entirely satisfied, that the inequality, which grows out of the *nature of things* by time, custom, succession, accumulation, permutation, and improvement of property, is much nearer that true equality, which is the foundation of equity and just policy, than any thing which can be contrived by the Tricks and devices of human skill'.[155] That the American revolution, unlike the French, never threatened the property ownership upon which Burke believed an ordered society was built, surely goes a long way to explaining his sympathies in 1776 and his hostility in 1789. It is for no small reason that one scholar of Burke has labelled his writings and speeches on America 'a testing ground where he first tried out many of the conservative guns he would later train on the French or even sooner on English radicals'.[156]

'Ten degrees to the right of center'

Burke would come to be seen, in the nineteenth century, as a forebear of modern conservatism, an emblematic voice of the reaction that came after the Revolution.[157] Even before 1789, James

Boswell, prominent biographer and diarist, was convinced that Burke was a Tory at heart.[158] There is, however, a lively debate among scholars as to whether Burke was genuinely a conservative or should be classed as a liberal. The conservative writer Yuval Levin, who proudly wears his Burkean sympathies, has cut this Gordian knot by calling Burke's ideas 'conservative liberalism',[159] contending that all mainstream politics after the Enlightenment was 'liberalism' (in the Anglophone world, at least) and that Burke was on the right-hand side of this new mainstream. From the other end of the political spectrum, Immanuel Wallerstein has discussed how a shared fear of the lower orders after 1789 helped to soften the borders between liberalism and conservatism.[160] Following this lead, it is perhaps more worthwhile to discuss how Burke signposts the fuzziness of liberalism and conservatism in the nineteenth century. Moreover, both ideologies continued Burke's conflations of race, gender and private property, seeing the three as sanctified and often inviolable ideals.

What unites both 'conservatism' and 'liberalism' (if those two ideologies can even be said to have discrete and separate existences after 1789) is their shared veneration of private property, made sharper with the apprehension of the spectre of communism in the nineteenth century. However, for sure, conservatives favour 'old' property – the landed gentry, the patrician rural landlords – and liberals lean in to the 'new' – urban speculators and modernised real estate traders (the kinds of reckless risk takers that unnerved Burke). As discussed earlier, Locke's writings on private property represent a concerted attempt to defend both the individual's right to private property and the right of English colonists to privatise the New World. With a major debt to Locke, Rousseau's *Social contract*, the kind of text Burke feared as too radical and dangerous, is built on the (very Lockean) assumption that society exists to protect property and the move away from a state of nature is simultaneously a codification of the rules by which private property will be preserved. The social contract is a mass association that exists to 'defend and protect, with the whole of its joint strength, the person and property of each associate'. Such a society, for Rousseau as for Locke, is defined by a flat equality in which all citizens are politically equal, while economic equalities are ignored. Rousseau disdained genuinely egalitarian democracy, instead arguing for a polity in which 'the wisest should govern the multitude'.[161] And that avatar of high-Victorian liberalism, John Stuart Mill, provided a staunch defence of freedom of thought and association, but still saw fit to warn about mobs and the danger they posed to private property: 'An opinion that corn-dealers are starvers of the poor, or that private property is robbery, ought to be unmolested when simply circulated through the press, but may justly incur punishment when delivered orally to an excited mob assembled before the house of a corn-dealer, or when handed about among the same mob in the form of a placard'.[162] Freedom is all well and good, provided the wrong people never use it to hurt the property of the rich or to get into power.[163] As Mill told the Land Tenure Reform Association in London on 15 May 1871, he uncritically believed that '[i]t is a rule, to which history as yet furnishes few exceptions, that nations are governed by their landed proprietors'.[164] In *Utilitarianism* (1861), Mill struck a Burkean note when he described 'security of person and property' as 'the first needs of society'.[165] Jeremy Bentham, whom Mill had known as a child, believed, in another Burkean formulation, that '[a] single mistake in extending equality too far may overthrow the existing social order and dissolve the bonds of social order'.[166] It was views such as this that led Mark Neocleous to observe that 'security', 'liberty' and 'property' all became overlapping concepts in liberalism, with 'the liberty of private property' and 'the security of private property' being the central concerns of the liberal state.[167]

Both Mill and Rousseau, to differing degrees, understood their propertied freedom in racialised and gendered terms. Rousseau's *Social contract* is founded on the assumption that 'citizen' and 'property owner' are synonymous with being 'male'. In one particular historiographical turn, he explains the origins of political societies, while tacitly omitting women from the narrative: 'the family may be regarded as the first model of political society: the leader corresponds to the father, the people to the children'.[168] Rousseau believed that nations, like men, can be more or less mature, and that, as such, the more child-like nations were not yet ready for freedom.[169] Mill, an early feminist, avoided these kinds of patriarchal formulation. But as an administrator for the East India

Company he did see colonisation as a positive means of modernising the supposedly less mature nations of the world and of making them ready for a liberal social order.[170] In *On liberty*, he quite openly said, in discussing who had the ability to wield responsible freedom, that 'we may leave out of consideration those backward states of society in which the race itself may be considered in its nonage'.[171] For Mill as for many other thinkers, both liberal and conservative, the 'responsible freedom' required in a propertied social order, was a racialised freedom only available to certain (white) sub-sections of humanity.

If conservatism and liberalism operate according to a roughly hewn, shared set of ideals and practices, then one obvious conclusion is that there is a lode of illiberalism running through liberalism. Thomas Holt argues that 'in all putatively democratic societies' political power is 'mediated by institutional arrangements that [make] realization of majority rule very difficult'. And nineteenth-century liberalism invested tremendous energy in various means of political pacification and social control.[172] Liberalism follows the 'typical bourgeois pattern' of praising freedom when in opposition, but repressing it when in power.[173] J.G.A. Pocock talks of how Burke's writings 'became part of the liberal conservatism of late Georgian and early Victorian Britain'.[174]

This 'liberal conservatism' was already on display in the 1790s when, for all the talk of protecting the British constitution, some of the most fundamental liberal rights were being abrogated in Britain. As working-men's associations mushroomed in the 1790s, so also did a ruling class desire to crack down on them. *Habeas corpus* was suspended in May 1794 as Pitt's government went to war against the likes of the London Corresponding Society (which advocated for political representation for male non-property owners and was perceived as a threat to the privileges of property).[175] When the bogus case for treason against the leaders of that Society collapsed in December 1794, Burke wrote with exasperation that there could be 'no compromise with Jacobinism'.[176] In Burke's native Ireland, incorporated into the newly established United Kingdom after a failed French-inspired uprising, *habeas corpus* was suspended for twelve of the years from the passing of the Act of Union in 1800 to the founding of Daniel O'Connell's

Catholic Association in 1823. And the 1833 Coercion Bill provided that 'any county in Ireland could be placed under martial law, with a sun-down to sun-up curfew, violators to be transported to penal colonies in Australia'.[177] Luckily for Burke, he died before the 1798 'United Irishmen' rebellion in Ireland, an event that would have horrified him, as also would the 'sizeable support' for the rebellion 'amongst the radicals in the northern manufacturing districts' of England.[178]

The years after 1789 saw a coerced conformity in Britain; heterodox thinkers such as Mary Wollstonecraft were condemned as unnatural. Publications like the *Anti-Jacobin* and groups like the clumsily named Association for the Preservation of Liberty and Property Against Republicans and Levellers – at one point the largest political organisation in the country – helped to enforce this.[179]

We could certainly hear echoes of Burke in the 1818 speech by the future Tory Prime Minster George Canning, in which he referred affectionately to property as 'the conservative principle of society', offered as explanation for why he would never provoke the nation with complaints about 'incurable imperfections' or tantalise them with visions of 'imaginary or unattainable excellencies'.[180] It would take time, though, for Burke to find his permanent audience. William Pitt, Tory Prime Minister through the 1790s, was dismissive, finding 'nothing to agree with' in Burke's warnings (notwithstanding that Pitt later led the crackdown on radicals).[181] Thomas Jefferson, a staunch liberal, a slaveowner and American ambassador to the French from 1785 to 1789, took Burke's condemnation of the Jacobins to be evidence of the 'rottenness of his mind'.[182] After his death, Burke had 'few disciples – political or intellectual'. His Irish background, and the regular accusations of crypto-Catholicism that had dogged him in life, continued to cast an odour on him in death.[183] His public rehabilitation was not forthcoming until after the rise of Chartism in the 1830s, when his defence of tradition and property became obviously useful. Emily Jones' recent study of Burke's place within conservatism notes that 'cautious reformism' and 'distrust of democracy' were 'stock features of nineteenth-century political commentary, Liberal as well as Conservative'.[184] Moving into the nineteenth century, liberals and conservatives alike would come to share Burke's fears of the masses and to see in them a threat to a property order always understood in simultaneously racialised and gendered terms.

Slowly, out of the ashes of the French Revolution, there emerged a third political option, alongside conservatism and liberalism: communism. As the spectre of communism began to haunt more and more Europeans, Burke found his readers. Burke was an eighteenth-century liberal, but ended his career as a formulator of the ideas that defined this latter-day liberal conservatism and its fear of the communist mob, though one of his harshest communist critics simply dismissed him as nothing but a 'celebrated sophist and sycophant'.[185] That parsimonious critic and his famous collaborator are the focus of the next chapter.

Notes

1 Jean-Paul Sartre; George J. Becker, trans. *Anti-semite and Jew* (New York, 1948), 23–4.
2 E.P. Thompson. *The making of the English working class* (New York, 1966), throughout.
3 Yuval Levin. *The great debate: Edmund Burke, Thomas Paine, and the birth of right and left* (New York, 2014), 27.
4 The Society for Commemorating the Revolution not only published Price's speech as a pamphlet but also sent a copy to the French National Assembly with a letter building on his themes, noting especially 'the glorious example given in France to encourage other nations to assert the unalienable rights of Mankind, and thereby to introduce a general reformation in the government of Europe, and to make the world free and happy': Levin, *The great debate* (2014), 27–8.
5 Richard Price. *A discourse on the love of our country* (London, 1789).
6 Adam Zamoyski. *Phantom terror: political paranoia and the creation of the modern state* (New York, 2015), 10, 12, 13, 14. Paranoia about the Revolution reached such heights that the Bavarian government banned any book that mentioned it, 'and in so doing relegated Burke's *Reflections* to the forbidden list': *Phantom terror*, 28–9.
7 In truth, though, Burke was not much more than 'a figure of secondary importance' before the Revolution and his political status had been in decline for a decade prior to this; the death of his patron, the Marquess of Rockingham, had deprived him of an important

and much-needed supporter: Emily Jones. *Edmund Burke and the invention of modern conservatism, 1830–1914: an intellectual history* (Oxford, 2017), 2; Drew Maciag. *Edmund Burke in America: the contested career of the father of modern conservatism* (Ithaca, NY, 2013), 8–9. In 1777, about fifteen years before his *Reflections*, Burke had taken issue with Price, his politics and his *Observations on the nature of civil liberty*. In his 'Letter to the sheriffs of Bristol', Burke had written with trepidation that '[t]here are people, who have split and anatomized the doctrine of free Government, as if it were an abstract question concerning metaphysical liberty and necessity; and not a matter of moral prudence and natural feeling': Richard Bourke. *Empire and revolution: the political life of Edmund Burke* (Princeton, NJ, 2015), 682–3.

8   Richard Whatmore. 'Burke on political economy', in David Dwan, Christopher J. Insole, eds. *The Cambridge companion to Edmund Burke* (Cambridge, 2012), 80.

9   Letter from Edmund Burke to the Earl of Charlemont, 9 August 1789 in Alfred Cobban, Robert A. Smith, eds. *The correspondence of Edmund Burke*, Vol. VI: July 1789–December 1791 (Chicago, 1967), 10; Levin, *The great debate* (2014), 25.

10 Bourke, *Empire and revolution* (2015), 613; Iain Hampsher-Monk. 'Reflections on the Revolution in France', in Dwan and Insole, *Cambridge companion* (2012), 97; Levin, *The great debate* (2014), 24.

11 Zamoyski, *Phantom terror* (2015), 45. Daniel I. O'Neill calls this idea of Jacobinism-as-infectious disease 'one of Burke's favorite metaphors for the spread of the principles of liberty', an epidemic 'that would obliterate all of the social hierarchies definitional of civilized society in Europe – between nobles and commoners, men and women, rich and poor, parents and children': *Edmund Burke and the conservative logic of empire* (Berkeley, CA, 2016), 89.

12 Hampsher-Monk, 'Reflections', in Dwan and Insole, *Cambridge companion* (2012), 195.

13 As early as September 1789, Burke was writing of the 'miserable and precarious situation of all people of property' in France: letter from Edmund Burke to William Windham, 27 September 1789, in Cobban and Smith, *Correspondence*, Vol. VI (1967), 25–6.

14 Isaac Kramnick. *The rage of Edmund Burke: portrait of an ambivalent conservative* (New York, 1977), 4, 39; R.R. Fennessy. *Burke, Paine and the rights of man: a difference of political opinion* (The Hague, 1963), 185. 'If conservatism has a master text, that text is

Edmund Burke's *Reflections on the Revolution in France*, published on 1 November 1790 ... By turns garrulous and telegraphic, lachrymose and acidulous, haunted and haunting, the *Reflections* are brilliant. They're also frustrating, at least for readers inclined to reconstruct a theory, to articulate a text's implicit presuppositions and trace the inferences supposed to generate its conclusions ... We can think of the *Reflections* not as a master text or blueprint, but as a quirky crystallization of a disparate ensemble of practices and views, a window into the rich and bizarre tapestry of Britain': Don Herzog. *Poisoning the minds of the lower orders* (Princeton, NJ, 1998), 13.

15 See letter from Edmund Burke to Charles-Jean-François Depont (November 1789), in Edmund Burke; Daniel Ritchie, ed. *Further reflections on the Revolution in France* (Indianapolis, IN, 1992). This letter is Burke's first in-depth analysis of the French Revolution, and presages much of what he would later discuss in the *Reflections*. For Depont's letters see Cobban and Smith, *Correspondence*, Vol. VI (1967), 31–2 and 59–61.

16 Edmund Burke; Conor Cruise O'Brien, ed. *Reflections on the Revolution in France and on the proceedings in certain societies in London relative to that event* (London, 1986 [1790]), 2.

17 Writing to Philip Francis on 20 February 1790, Burke discussed Francis' criticism of the structure of the *Reflections*: 'The composition, you say, is loose, and I am quite sure of it: I never intended it should be otherwise. For, purporting to be, what in truth it originally was, a letter to a friend, I had no idea of digesting it in a systematic order': letter from Edmund Burke to Philip Francis, 20 February 1790 in *Further reflections* (1992), 22.

18 Burke, *Reflections* (1986 [1790]), 86–7.
19 Burke, *Reflections* (1986 [1790]), 91.
20 Burke, *Reflections* (1986 [1790]), 97.
21 Burke, *Reflections* (1986 [1790]), 94.
22 Burke, *Reflections* (1986 [1790]), 115.
23 Burke, *Reflections* (1986 [1790]), 101.
24 Burke, *Reflections* (1986 [1790]), 157. Pisgah is the name traditionally given to the mountain from which Moses first viewed the Promised Land. See Deuteronomy 3:27.
25 Letter from Edmund Burke to Philip Francis, February 20, 1790, in Burke; Ritchie, *Further reflections* (1992) 25. 'Indian delinquents' is most probably a reference to Warren Hastings and the East India Company, with whom Burke had a long-running and well-known

The poet of real property

    legal spat, though he does seem to be playing off the double meaning of Indian as a person from India and a Native American.
26. Burke, *Reflections* (1986 [1790]), 159. For 'savage', see Chapter 1, fn 85.
27. Burke, *Reflections* (1986 [1790]), 159.
28. Burke, *Reflections* (1986 [1790]), 99–100.
29. Burke, *Reflections* (1986 [1790]), 110.
30. Burke, *Reflections* (1986 [1790]), 115–17.
31. Letter from Edmund Burke to the Comte de Provence, 17 September 1791, in Cobban and Smith, *Correspondence*, Vol. VI (1967), 399–400.
32. Hampsher-Monk, 'Reflections', in Dwan and Insole, *Cambridge companion* (2012), 195. Levin similarly says 'Burke's audience in the *Reflections* was clearly British and not, as his epistolary mode would have it, a French gentleman'. Indeed, Burke was so fearful of a Jacobin uprising in Britain that a dying wish was for his body to be buried in an unmarked grave, since he believed not only that a massive social upheaval was inevitable, but that English Jacobins would want to desecrate his corpse: *The great debate* (2014), 31, 223. That Burke's primary target was British, not French, radicals, is reflected in the book's original title: *Reflections on certain proceedings of the [London] Revolution Society, of the 4th of November, 1789, concerning the affairs of France*: Maciag, *Edmund Burke in America* (2013), 16. See also Mike Goode. *Sentimental masculinity and the rise of history, 1790–1890* (Cambridge, 2009), 9; Albert Goodwin. *The friends of liberty: the English democratic movement in the age of the French Revolution* (Cambridge, MA, 1979), throughout.
33. James Chandler has made note of how often Burke speaks of 'we' Englishmen, in contrast to the targeted 'you' French: 'Poetical liberties: Burke's France and the "adequate representation" of the English', in François Furet, Mona Ozouf, eds. *The French Revolution and the creation of modern political culture*, Vol. 3: *The transformation of political culture, 1789–1848* (Oxford, 1989), 47. Moreover, Burke's claim to speak *de facto* for all Englishmen was a function of a political culture in which only property owners could legally serve as politicians and thus as the voices of the nation: Chandler, 'Poetical liberties' (1989), 46.
34. This binary opposition – violent France *versus* peaceful Britain – relied on historical amnesia: 'Burke wants to labor over the contrast between the ghastly events of 1789 and the inspiring events of 1688, between grotesque French gyrations and phlegmatic English plodding.

In England's Glorious Revolution, after all, no crazed mobs marched through the streets with bishops' heads on pikes ... But Burke is conspicuously silent over the gory events of 1649, when Cromwell and his Puritan minions put Charles I to death; later they would declare England a republic': Herzog, *Poisoning the minds* (1998), 15–16. Daniel O'Neill has aptly commented that Burke had a 'remarkable capacity for self-deception': *Conservative logic* (2016), 158.

35 Bourke, *Empire and revolution* (2015), 248.
36 Bourke, *Empire and revolution* (2015), 13.
37 Bourke, *Empire and revolution* (2015), 246–7. 'To secure possession, Burke believed, was the grand objective of all law. This was of course the achievement of civil society under sovereign authority, yet effective authority had to be underpinned by supporting popular opinion. Property, that is, was secured by political power on the basis of an opinion of its justice. Burke's most famous intervention into public debate, the *Reflections on the Revolution in France*, took its bearings from this fundamental commitment to the original right of property as based on the law of nature': *Empire and revolution*, 249.
38 Burke, *Reflections* (1986 [1790]), 119.
39 Burke, *Reflections* (1986 [1790]), 120. Usually held by a religious body, a mortmain is an inalienable piece of property, which the property holder is prohibited in perpetuity from selling.
40 Laura Brace. *The politics of property: labour, freedom and belonging* (Basingstoke, 2004), 139.
41 Burke, *Reflections* (1986 [1790]), 120. Also notice how Burke views religion, the family, social stability and private property as conjoined phenomena.
42 Richard Bourke calls this 'The Great Primeaval Contract' in Burkean thought: *Empire and revolution* (2015), 676.
43 Levin, *The great debate* (2014), 117.
44 Levin, *The great debate* (2014), 216. 'Burke's model of nature does not point to social equality. In a society sustained by inheritance, social eminence and great wealth will tend to stay in certain families and beyond the reach of others. Not that change and reform cannot happen, or that those who are able to rise in society are somehow unworthy of it, but equality itself should not be a primary goal of politics. Social peace, prosperity and stability are more important for everyone, and are often not well served by the pursuit of equality – especially because true social equality is ultimately an unachievable goal': *The great debate*, 82–3.

45 Christopher Pierson. *Just property, a history in the Latin West*, Vol. 1: *Wealth, virtue and the law* (Oxford, 2013), 49. On Burke's receptiveness to Cicero, see *Just property*, Vol. 2: *Enlightenment, revolution, and history* (Oxford, 2016), 116.
46 Burke, *Reflections* (1986 [1790]), 120.
47 Burke, *Reflections* (1986 [1790]), 112.
48 Burke, *Reflections* (1986 [1790]), 304.
49 Burke, *Reflections* (1986 [1790]), 110.
50 Bourke, *Empire and revolution* (2015), 250.
51 Letter to Depont, November 1789 in Burke; Ritchie, *Further reflections* (1992), 10–12.
52 Burke, *Reflections* (1986 [1790]), 90.
53 Letter from Edmund Burke to Earl Fitzwilliam, 12 November 1789 in Cobban and Smith, *Correspondence*, Vol. VI (1967), 37.
54 Burke, *Reflections* (1986 [1790]), 91.
55 Burke, *Reflections* (1986 [1790]), 122.
56 Letter from Edmund Burke to Adrien-Jean-François Duport, after 29 March 1790, in Cobban and Smith, *Correspondence*, Vol. VI (1967), 107.
57 Burke, *Reflections* (1986 [1790]), 141–2.
58 Burke, *Reflections* (1986 [1790]), 193–4.
59 Burke, *Reflections* (1986 [1790]), 207.
60 Burke, *Reflections* (1986 [1790]), 223.
61 Burke, *Reflections* (1986 [1790]), 326.
62 Burke, *Reflections* (1986 [1790]), 207.
63 Pierson, *Just property*, Vol. 2 (2016), 114.
64 Patrice Higonnet. *Goodness beyond virtue: Jacobins during the French Revolution* (Cambridge, MA, 1998), 21–2. Higonnet is one of a number of late-twentieth-century historians of the French Revolution who, in the post-1989 *Zeitgeist* of the end of history, disclaim any kind of ideological perspective, whilst being strikingly (if unconsciously) ideological themselves. His biases are present in the overly emotive language used here; did these acts of identity-definition serve those lower down the social hierarchy? Did they see this 'bonfire' as a sacrifice?
65 Georges Lefebvre; Elizabeth Moss Evanson, trans. *The French Revolution: from its origins to 1793* (London, 1962 [1957]), 126.
66 Eric Hazan; David Fernbach, trans. *A people's history of the French Revolution* (London, 2014), 75.
67 Lefebvre, *French Revolution* (1957), 154. The 'secularization of Church lands reduced clerics to salaried civil servants': *French Revolution*, 161.

68 Lynn Hunt. *Politics, culture and class in the French Revolution* (Berkeley, CA, 1984), 27, 75. On the broader issue of the material culture of the Revolution, see Leora Auslander. *Cultural revolutions: everyday life and politics in Britain, North America and France* (Oxford, 2008).
69 Hunt, *Politics, culture and class* (1984), 206.
70 Higonnet, *Goodness beyond virtue* (1998), 4.
71 O'Neill, *Conservative logic* (2016), 15.
72 Lefebvre, *French Revolution* (1957), 128–9.
73 'Burke dwelt at great length on the events of 5–6 October 1789 in the *Reflections* because they so perfectly captured the revolt against humanity that governed the Revolution. It was, he proposed, "the most horrid, atrocious, and affecting spectacle, that perhaps ever was exhibited to the pity and indignation of mankind." The descent of the *poissardes* [female fishmongers] upon Versailles, the assault on the queen's bedchamber, the forced address to the crowd from the royal balcony, the procession to Paris with the heads of decapitated guards on pikes, and the triumphal return of the captive royals to the Tuileries palace, together depicted a world turned upside down. Such events could not fail to shock "the moral taste of every well-born mind." To Philip Francis [a friend of Burke's], however, the meditation on the queen's suffering was "mere foppery," as indeed it has often appeared to subsequent readers': Bourke, *Empire and revolution* (2015), 706–7.
74 Antonio Gramsci. 'Passive revolution, Caesarism, fascism', in David Forgacs, ed. *The Antonio Gramsci reader: selected writings, 1916–1935* (London, 1988), 254.
75 Lefebvre, *French Revolution* (1957), 93.
76 Lefebvre, *French Revolution* (1957), 102.
77 Hazan, *People's history* (2014), 92.
78 Hazan, *People's history* (2014), 67.
79 Ellen Meiksins Wood. *The pristine culture of capitalism: a historical essay on old regimes and modern states*, 2nd edition (London, 2015), 77.
80 R.B. Rose. *Gracchus Babeuf: the first revolutionary communist* (Stanford, CA, 1978), 38.
81 Jean-Pierre Hirsch. 'Terror and property', in Keith Michael Baker, ed. *The French Revolution and the creation of modern political culture*, Vol. 4: *The Terror* (Oxford, 1994), 211. See also Lefebvre, *French Revolution* (1957), 146. Jacobin imitators across the English Channel were likewise not as anarchically radical as Burke supposed. Isaac

Kramnick's description is overstated, but has a solid core of truth to it: 'The radical dissenters of Burke's day were men and women of property. The English Jacobins, indeed, worshiped private property. They have had little respect for ancient baronial estates, but they were bourgeois to the core': *Rage of Edmund Burke* (1977), 15.

82 Hazan, *People's history* (2014), 106; Ronald Schechter. *Obstinate Hebrews: representations of Jews in France, 1715–1815* (Berkeley, CA, 2003), 155; Malcolm Crook, 'The rights of man and the right to vote: the franchise question during the French Revolution', in Gail M. Schwab, John R. Jeanneney, eds. *The French Revolution of 1789 and its impact* (Westport, CT, 1995), 191, 193, 195. Crook says there was a 'prevailing consensus' in the National Assembly that the franchise should be kept restricted through taxes (which is to say, by income and property), which ignores that leading figures, Robespierre not least among them, had strongly differing opinions. Full adult male suffrage was introduced under Robespierre's guidance in August, 1792, erasing the distinction between active and passive male citizens: Hazan, *People's history* (2014), 168.

83 Higonnet, *Goodness beyond virtue* (1998), 15–16; Hunt, *Politics, culture and class* (1984), 12–13.

84 Immanuel Wallerstein. *The modern world-system*, Vol. III: *The second era of great expansion of the capitalist world-economy*, 2nd edition (Berkeley CA, 2011), 111.

85 Hunt, *Politics, culture and class* (1984), 92.

86 From a very different ideological perspective to Burke's, Linebaugh and Rediker characterise the Revolution as 'a world-wide movement for liberty, equality and fraternity': Peter Linebaugh, Marcus Rediker. *The many-headed hydra: sailors, slaves, commoners, and the hidden history of the revolutionary Atlantic*, 2nd edition (Boston, MA, 2013), 254. And yet the effect of this is largely the same: a political conjuncture defined by opposing ideological strains becomes, instead, a clearly unambiguous and radical event.

87 Burke, *Reflections* (1986 [1790]), 211. For Minsky's conceptions of finance capitalism, see Hyman P. Minsky. *Stabilizing an unstable economy* (New Haven, CT, 1986).

88 Burke, *Reflections* (1986 [1790]), 308.

89 Bourke, *Empire and revolution* (2015), 612.

90 Raymond Williams. *The country and the city* (Oxford, 1973), 110, 112–13, 115.

91 'Like [Adam] Smith, Burke holds that a natural aristocracy of the landed class should be a moderating and directing influence in

governing commercial society. For the historical record, Burke, not Smith, seems to be the first British [sic] thinker to employ the word "capitalist", two years before his friend Arthur Young did in *Travels in France* (1792) ... the expression "landed capitalist" occurs in Burke's *Reflections on the French Revolution* (1790)': Neal Wood. *Tyranny in America: capitalism and national decay* (London, 2004), 33.

92 Burke, *Reflections* (1986 [1790]), 129. Emphases added.
93 Burke, *Reflections* (1986 [1790]), 132.
94 Burke, *Reflections* (1986 [1790]), 129.
95 Burke, *Reflections* (1986 [1790]), 129.
96 Burke, *Reflections* (1986 [1790]), 134.
97 Burke, *Reflections* (1986 [1790]), 261.
98 Burke, *Reflections* (1986 [1790]), 141.
99 Burke, *Reflections* (1986 [1790]), 91. There was an obvious double standard here: Burke was an *arriviste* lawyer who migrated from Ireland to London, precisely the social type he distrusted in France.
100 Burke, *Reflections* (1986 [1790]), 136.
101 Burke, *Reflections* (1986 [1790]), 138.
102 Burke, *Reflections* (1986 [1790]), 166.
103 Burke, *Reflections* (1986 [1790]), 179–80.
104 Burke, *Reflections* (1986 [1790]), 144.
105 Burke, *Reflections* (1986 [1790]), 204. For a further discussion of Burke's anti-Judaism, see David Nirenberg. *Anti-Judaism: the Western tradition* (New York, 2013), 376–83.
106 Antoine de Baecque describes 'a political cartoon from the autumn of 1789 called "The Patriotic Fat Remover," printed in Paris at the time of the nationalization of the clergy's wealth. In this engraving, an obese prelate is pressed into a "physiological machine" activated by a revolutionary soldier: pieces of gold fall into the "national treasury" as the ecclesiastic loses weight. In the background are two spindly emaciated priests, "their fat removed" in keeping with the title of the picture': Antoine de Baecque; Charlotte Mandell, trans. *The body politic: corporeal metaphor in revolutionary France, 1770–1800* (Stanford, CA, 1993), 1.
107 Hunt, *Politics, class and culture* (1984), 28.
108 Bourke, *Empire and revolution* (2015), 84. Though it is not clear whether the legitimising religion *had to be* Anglican Protestantism. Burke also made claims about the comparability of Christian Britain and Islamic India: he 'analogized Britain's ancient constitutions – with [their] protections of historically derived rights (including property rights), the rule of law, and a set of individual liberties – to Mughal

India. He depicted the British as the inheritors of a Muslim constitutional framework in India much like their own, which they were duty bound to protect.' In his native Ireland, he supported a limited Catholic emancipation from the Penal Laws, in the hope that it would promote a home-grown aristocracy more suited to rule over the island. And, as with his views of Islam and Hinduism, he saw Catholicism in Ireland as a potential source of social stability: O'Neill, *Conservative logic* (2016), 103, 143, 149.

109 Bourke, *Empire and revolution* (2015), 106–7.
110 Bourke, *Empire and revolution* (2015), 250. 'By uprooting the foundations of their existing regime and by confiscating the property of the church, the French had undone both the balance of their politics and the freedom of their people, Burke argued, and they were headed for disaster': Levin, *The great debate* (2014), 28.
111 Quoted in Kramnick, *Rage of Edmund Burke* (1977), 143.
112 Peter Linebaugh. *The Magna Carta manifesto: liberties and commons for all* (Berkeley, CA, 2008), 112.
113 Burke said that the 'new people' were defined by 'an insolent irreligion in opinions and practices': Burke, *Reflections* (1986 [1790]), 125.
114 Burke, *Reflections* (1986 [1790]), 216–17.
115 Burke, *Reflections* (1986 [1790]), 160. Zamoyski has identified a fear of the Orient, common at the time, in which the Revolutionaries were 'modern Caliphs', said to be motivated by 'this new species of Mahometanism ... fired by a message which some referred to as their "Khoran"': *Phantom terror* (2015), 35–6. See also Farhad Daftary. 'The "Order of the Assassins": J. von Hammer and the orientalist misrepresentations of the Nizari Ismailis', *Iranian Studies*, Vol. 39, No. 1 (2006), 71–81.
116 Burke, *Reflections* (1986 [1790]), 123. Maroon refers to ex-slaves in the plantation colonies of the Caribbean who had escaped slavery by moving to remote and inaccessible parts of the interior of Jamaica or Barbados. 'In Spanish the self-emancipated were called *cimarrones*, a word deriving from the Taíno language that became *marron* in French and *maroon* in English': Ned Sublette, Constance Sublette. *The American slave coast: a history of the slave-breeding industry* (Chicago, 2016), 76fn. For discussions of the fears of maroons and deracination, see Thomas C. Holt. *The problem of freedom: race, labor, and politics in Jamaica and Britain, 1832–1938* (Baltimore, MD, 1992), 301; Catherine Hall. *Civilising subjects: metropole and colony in the English imagination, 1830–1867* (Chicago, 2002), 61.

117 'One of Burke's greatest fears was the unruly democratic consciousness of the uncivilized, acutely emblematized by the image of former French slaves as diplomats in the British slave colonies of the West Indies': O'Neill, *Conservative logic* (2016), 90.
118 Letter from Edmund Burke to the Marquis de Bouillé, 13 July 1791 in Cobban and Smith, *Correspondence*, Vol. VI (1967), 291.
119 Paul Gilroy has shown how even Burke's aesthetics, privileging whiteness as a form of beauty and darkness as a source of sublime terror, had an obvious racialised essence: *The Black Atlantic: modernity and double consciousness* (Cambridge, MA, 1993), 9.
120 Burke, *Reflections* (1986 [1790]), 169.
121 Goode, *Sentimental masculinity* (2009), 40.
122 Levin, *The great debate* (2014), 69.
123 Herzog, *Poisoning the minds* (1998), 27. Albeit in a private letter to Philip Francis in early 1790, Burke repeated his romantic views of the queen and his hostile views of those disrespecting her: 'why is it absurd in me to think, that the chivalrous spirit which dictated a veneration for women of condition and of beauty, without any consideration whatever of enjoying them, was the great source of those manners which have been the pride and ornament of Europe for so many ages? And am I not to lament that I have lived to see those manners extinguished in so shocking a manner, by means of speculations of finance, and the false science of a sordid and degenerate philosophy?' Letter from Edmund Burke to Philip Francis (February 20, 1790) in Burke; Ritchie, *Further reflections* (1992), 24.
124 Kristen R. Ghodsee has noted that noticeable increases in female economic independence are often accompanied by 'a loosening of social mores around sexuality': *Why women have better sex under socialism, and other arguments for economic independence* (New York, 2018), 114. Conservatives generally view both female independence and the relaxing of sexual norms with a visceral horror. The idea that publicly active and independent women were a source of horror dovetails with the analysis of Joan Landes: 'The public and the private sphere: a feminist reconsideration' in Joan D. Landes, ed. *Feminism, the public and the private* (Oxford, 1998), 143. In keeping with the notion that 'ideology' was born in the French Revolution, Daniel O'Neill has seen Burke's horror of female political activism and his clashes with Mary Wollstonecraft as giving rise 'to what we now understand as conservatism and feminism': *The Burke–Wollstonecraft debate: savagery, civilization, and democracy* (University Park, PA, 2007), 3.

125 Maciag, *Edmund Burke in America* (2013), xii.
126 Burke, *Reflections* (1986 [1790]), 174. Emphases added.
127 Brace, *Politics of property* (2004), 138.
128 Burke, *Reflections* (1986 [1790]), 121.
129 Burke, *Reflections* (1986 [1790]), 95.
130 Burke, *Reflections* (1986 [1790]), 161.
131 Burke, *Reflections* (1986 [1790]), 170.
132 Burke, *Reflections* (1986 [1790]), 182.
133 Burke, *Reflections* (1986 [1790]), 204.
134 'Burke's animosity against the French Revolution stemmed from two sources: first its violation of the laws of nature in the form of an assault on the rights to property; and second its hostility to the institutions of religion insofar as these inculcated fundamental duties': Bourke, *Empire and revolution* (2015), 14. However, the two concerns have fuzzy borders, since Burke was particularly incensed by the seizures of ecclesiastical land and, more importantly, he saw obedience to religious authority as being key for the social reproduction of private property.
135 'A letter to a Member of the National Assembly' in Burke; Ritchie, *Further reflections* (1992), 35, 39, 45, 58.
136 Andrew Bradstock. *Radical religion in Cromwell's England: a concise history from the English Civil War to the end of the Commonwealth* (London, 2011); Christopher Hill. *The world turned upside down: radical ideas during the English Revolution* (London, 1975); David W. Petegorsky. *Left-wing democracy in the English Civil War: a study of the social philosophy of Gerrard Winstanley* (New York, 1972); John Rees. *The Leveller revolution: radical political organisation in England, 1640–1650* (London, 2016); John Walter. *Understanding popular violence in the English Revolution: the Colchester plunderers* (Cambridge, 1999).
137 'A letter to a Member of the National Assembly', 39, 40, 57.
138 Bourke, *Empire and revolution* (2015), 24. Richard Bourke did not directly quote Edmund Burke, though this passage does give a precise summation of Burke's thinking.
139 Letter from Edmund Burke to William Weddell, 31 January 1792, in P.J. Marshall, John A. Woods, eds. *The correspondence of Edmund Burke*, Vol. VII: *January 1792–August 1794* (Chicago, 1968), 52. Several of Burke's letters from 1792 are concerned with the danger of revolutionary contagion from France.
140 'Thoughts on French affairs' (December 1791) in Burke; Ritchie, *Further reflections* (1992), 236.

141 Phylacteries, or *Tefillin*, are sets of small black leather boxes containing passages from the Torah, which Jewish men traditionally wear during their morning prayers.
142 Letter from Edmund Burke to William Elliot, 27 May, 1795 in Burke; Ritchie, *Further reflections* (1992), 263.
143 'Thoughts and details on scarcity. Originally presented to the Right Hon. William Pitt in the month of November' (1795), in Edmund Burke. *The works: twelve volumes in six* (Hildesheim, 1975 [1887]), Vol. V, 134, 153, 167–8. It is also in this piece that Burke talks of 'the laws of commerce, which are the laws of Nature, and consequently the laws of God'. Burke seems to mean this both in the sense that commercial activity is dependent on harvests and other natural [i.e. God-given] events, and also that his vision of the socio-economic order is supposedly ordained by God.
144 Letter from Edmund Burke to Florimond-Claudee, Comte de Mercy-Argenteau, *c.* 6 August 1793 in Marshall and Woods, *Correspondence*, Vol. VII (1968), 389. Elsewhere, he claimed that '[n]ext to religion, *property* is the great point of Jacobin attack': letter from Edmund Burke to Sir Hercules Langrishe, 26 May 1795, in R.B. McDowell, ed. *The correspondence of Edmund Burke*, Vol. VIII: *September 1794–April 1796* (Chicago, 1969), 256.
145 The quotes here are from *Paradise Lost*.
146 Burke had long feared that Ireland could easily slip into chaos. As early as 1762, he spoke of the weakness of the 'landed interest' in Ireland and said 'if this is broke and crumbled to pieces, you are gone without redemption': letter from Edmund Burke to Charles O'Hara, 30 December 1762, in Thomas W. Copeland, ed. *The correspondence of Edmund Burke*, Vol. 1: *April 1744–June 1768* (Chicago, 1958), 162. A decade later, he warned that a proposed tax on absentee landowners in Ireland (of which he was one) would cause deracination on both sides of the Irish Sea: 'We shall sink into surly, brutish Johns, and *you* will degenerate into wild Irish'. He went on to talk of the proposed tax as 'something monstrous and unnatural' [emphases in original]: letter from Edmund Burke to Charles Bingham, 30 October 1773, in Lucy S. Sutherland, ed. *The correspondence of Edmund Burke*, Vol. 2: *June 1768–June 1774* (Chicago, 1960), 474–5. That he himself, as an absentee Irish landowner, would have seen a tax increase under this change, surely also played a role in his opposition. On the other hand, Burke feared that the Protestant ascendancy in Ireland (of which he was a product) existed at too much of a remove from the Catholic majority to provide effective, propertied leadership.

He favoured lifting the Penal Laws as a means of boosting a Catholic aristocracy: O'Neill, *Conservative logic* (2016), 17. See also Theodore W. Allen. *The invention of the white race*, Vol. 1: *Racial oppression and social control*, 2nd edition (London, 2012), 92–4, which discusses the practical attempts to enfranchise Catholic property owners and make them a keystone of the system of social control.

147 'Letter to a noble lord' (February, 1796) in Burke; Ritchie, *Further reflections* (1992) 279–326. The 'noble lord' was the 4th Earl Fitzwilliam, a close ally of Burke's.

148 O'Neill, *Conservative logic* (2016), 45–6 and throughout. But where O'Neill sees continuity in Burke's attitudes towards British imperialism, I see it in terms of private property. In this vein, Isaac Kramnick has argued: 'His conservatism was not simply a reaction to the Revolution in France. It was a life-long response to what he perceived as dreaded tendencies of his age. *The Reflections on the Revolution in France* elaborates and develops themes and concerns he had articulated throughout his career': *Rage of Edmund Burke* (1977), 12.

149 'Speech of Edmund Burke, Esq. on American taxation. April 19, 1774' (3rd edition, 1775), in Edmund Burke; David Womersley, ed. *A philosophical enquiry into the origin of our ideas of the sublime and beautiful, and other pre-revolutionary writings*, 2nd edition (London, 2004), 300, 306. Ironically, for all his conservative and propertied emphasis on law and order, the publication of Burke's Parliamentary speeches broke the law: 'Through the eighteenth century, it was illegal to publish Parliamentary debates': Herzog, *Poisoning the minds* (1998), 71.

150 In his private letters he addressed the plan to coerce the colonies back into submission: 'I think that a more complete Scheme of senseless Tyranny never was devised by the pride and folly of man'. And on 'that most famous Bill for famishing the four Provinces of New England' he said that '[m]y soul revolts at it. No cruelty, no Tyranny ever heard of in History or invented in Fable has at all equalled it': letter from Edmund Burke to John Noble, 21 February 1775 and letter from Edmund Burke to John Noble, 9 March 1775, in George H. Guttridge, ed. *The correspondence of Edmund Burke*, Vol. III: *July 1774–June 1778* (Chicago, 1961), 118 and 131–2.

151 Burke was perhaps echoing contemporary fears about the dangers of Black escape into the American interior or the uplands of Jamaica, and the deracination this would supposedly entail. See Gerald Horne. *The counter-revolution of 1776: slave resistance and the origins of the United States of America* (New York, 2014), 78–9, 99, 101.

152 Indeed, in the same speech Burke discussed the opposite move; English property laws had introduced civility to previously wild peoples in Ireland, Wales and the north of England. All the 'rigorous laws' that aimed at subduing 'the fierce spirit of the Welsh' had failed. Harmony could only emerge when military control gave way to civil rule, the unorganised border marches were turned into rational counties and property ownership was put on a correct legal footing: 'The speech of Edmund Burke, Esq., on moving his resolutions for conciliation with the colonies, March 22, 1775' (third edition, 1775) in Burke; Womersley, *Sublime and the beautiful* (2004), 343, 340, 350–3, 359, 371.

153 O'Neill, *Conservative logic* (2016), 67. See also David Cannadine. *Ornamentalism: how the British saw their empire* (Oxford, 2001), which O'Neill uses (to generally strong effect). Though my argument is that Burke's Ornamentalism was never as neat as O'Neill suggests.

154 Indeed, it was the respect for private property that made the British Americans so suitable and ready for freedom. There is also an obvious contradiction here: the colonists deeply respect private property, and yet that respect is potentially ephemeral and could disappear at any moment.

155 Letter from Edmund Burke to John Bourke, November 1777 in Guttridge, *Correspondence*, Vol. III (1961), 403. There is a subtle difference here between Locke, who believed private property was artificial (i.e. unnatural) and Burke, who assumed it was 'natural', though never really examined the form and content of that assumption.

156 Kramnick, *Rage of Edmund Burke* (1977), 23.

157 Corey Robin. *The reactionary mind: conservatism from Edmund Burke* (Oxford, 2011), 41. Slavoj Žižek has said that '[t]he identifying mark of all kinds of conservative is a predictably flat rejection' of the French Revolution, 'a catastrophe from its very beginning': 'Foreword: The dark matter of violence, or, putting terror in perspective', in Sophie Wahnich; David Fernbach, trans. *In defence of the Terror: liberty or death in the French Revolution* (London, 2012), xii.

158 Herzog, *Poisoning the minds* (1998), 17.

159 Levin, *The great debate* (2014), 237.

160 Immanuel Wallerstein. *The modern world-system*, Vol. IV: *Centrist liberalism triumphant, 1789–1914* (Berkeley, CA, 2011), throughout.

161 Jean-Jacques Rousseau; Christopher Betts, trans. *The social contract* (Oxford, 1994 [1762]) 54–5, 102–3. However, Rousseau did not believe in an absolute right to private property. As a staunch republican, he believed that the state retains the right to seize property, if it is in the general interest to do so: *Social contract*, 62.

162 J.S. Mill; Elizabeth Rapaport, ed. *On liberty* (Indianapolis, IN, [1859]), 53.
163 'An important though muted purpose behind his great treatise, *On Liberty*, was to justify protection of the intellectual elite from the presumably illiberal masses. Defining their conflict as one of enlightenment *versus* ignorance rather than wealth *versus* poverty, he argued that the well-being of the whole society, rather than the special interests of the elite, was at stake': Holt, *Problem of freedom* (1992), 6. Though as the quote above about mobs outside the homes of corn merchants shows, Mill overtly presented this as an issue of wealth, poverty and property.
164 Quoted in Brett Christophers. *The new enclosure: the appropriation of public land in neoliberal Britain* (London, 2018), 74. Mill could thus perhaps be placed in the 'common aristocratic assumptions about the importance of landed property as a social and political institution of nineteenth-century British society': Desmond Fitz-Gibbon. *Marketable values: inventing the property market in modern Britain* (Chicago, 2018), 1.
165 Mark Neocleous. *A critical theory of police power*, 2nd edition (London, 2021), 113.
166 Satnam Virdee. *Racism, class and the racialized outsider* (London, 2014), 9.
167 Neocleous, *Critical theory of police power* (2021), 114.
168 Rousseau, *Social contract* (1994 [1762]), 46.
169 Rousseau, *Social contract* (1994 [1762]), 80–81, 111–16.
170 Hall, *Civilising subjects* (2002), 30–1.
171 Mill; Rapaport, *On liberty* (1859), 10.
172 Holt, *Problem of freedom* (1992), 35, 53, 215.
173 Marshall Berman. *All that is solid melts into air* (New York, 1988), 113. In Perry Anderson's view, 'liberalism is a metal that rarely comes unalloyed': *The Indian ideology* (London, 2013), 133.
174 J.G.A. Pocock, 'Edmund Burke and the redefinition of enthusiasm: the context as counter-revolution' in Furet and Ozouf, *French Revolution* (1989), 19. Burke perhaps fits Phil Ochs' famous definition of a liberal: 'ten degrees to the left of center in good times, ten degrees to the right of center if it affects them personally'.
175 Zamoyski, *Phantom terror* (2015), 58. 'In 1794 twelve radicals, including John Horne Tooke, John Thelwall, and Thomas Hardy, a founding member and secretary of the London Corresponding Society, were arrested for high treason. In 1795 the Treasonable and Seditious Practices and Unlawful Assemblies Acts were passed,

criminalizing certain public meetings and political discussions. In 1799 the LCS and other associations deemed dangerously radical were proscribed, and *habeas corpus* was suspended. These actions effectively put an end to the "Revolution controversy" and made Burke its posthumous *de facto* winner': O'Neill, *Burke–Wollstonecraft debate* (2007), 5.
176 Quoted in Bourke, *Empire and revolution* (2015), 899.
177 Allen, *Invention of the white race* (2012), 99, 102.
178 Virdee, *Racism* (2014), 14.
179 Zamoyski, *Phantom terror* (2015), 46, 66.
180 Quoted in Herzog, *Poisoning the minds* (1998), 54.
181 Zamoyski, *Phantom terror* (2015), 47.
182 Kramnick, *Rage of Edmund Burke* (1977), xi.
183 Jones, *Edmund Burke* (2017), 11, 34–5.
184 Jones, *Edmund Burke* (2017), 7. By the 1970s, he was being praised by cold warriors as a defender of Western values from Jacobins/Communists: Kramnick, *Rage of Edmund Burke* (1977), xi. 'In a 2005 *New Yorker* interview, a neoconservative Pentagon official defended the Bush administration's invasion of Iraq by invoking the name of the eighteenth-century British [*sic*] politician Edmund Burke ... To certain conservative intellectuals, the use of Burke's philosophy to justify the toppling of Saddam Hussein made sense: not because the situation called for it, or the "facts on the ground" justified it, but because the ritualistic mention of Burke, the "father of conservatism," had by 2005 established itself as a standard rhetorical ploy': Maciag, *Edmund Burke in America* (2013), 1.
185 Karl Marx; ed. Frederick Engels, ed., trans. Samuel Moore, Edward Aveling. *Capital: a critique of political economy*, Vol. I: *The process of production of capital* (London, 1954), 306.

3

The Moor's laboratory

These Irish are really shocking, abominable people – not like any other civilized nation.

Queen Victoria[1]

Give me two hundred thousand Irishmen and I could overthrow the entire British monarchy

In May 1856, an obscure international industrialist and his common-law Irish wife arrived in Ireland for a tour of the country. The pair travelled from east to west, from Dublin to Galway, followed the Shannon southward through Limerick and went on to Kerry (the traditional tourist spots),[2] before looping back up to Dublin. Altogether, they covered some 500 miles. Writing to an old friend in London, the wealthy tourist described the bleak landscape he passed through. Post-Famine Ireland was an island of ruins, some dating back to the early Middle Ages, some more recent: 'The land is an utter desert which nobody wants'. Galway was an especially egregious example; 'covered with ruined peasant houses, most of which have only been deserted since 1846'. There was 'a total absence of any industry at all' across the island and a mixture of priests, lawyers and assorted other 'parasitic growths' lived off the 'distress of the peasants'. The 'Celtic character of the population [has] gone to the dogs'. The level of policing was intrusive and shocking in 'England's first colony' and this particular tourist had 'never seen so many gendarmes in any country ... armed with carbines, bayonets and handcuffs'. In fact, 'one can already notice here that the so-called liberty of English citizens is based on the oppression of the colonies'. What little economic activity there was in Ireland was observable only in the richer pasture lands of Munster and east Leinster, 'gradually coming into the hands of big farmers'.

The farming peasants of Ireland had been systematically dispossessed, in a centuries-long process that had started in the early modern period. Paralleling and sometimes informing analogous developments in North America, native dispossession meant that lands were freed up for privatisation and the growing of capitalist cash crops and, by the later nineteenth century, capitalist livestock. Additionally, the locals, notwithstanding 'their Irish fanaticism', were being made to feel increasingly unwelcome: 'By consistent oppression they have been artificially converted into an utterly impoverished nation and now, as everyone knows, fulfil the function of supplying England, America, Australia, etc., with prostitutes, casual labourers, pimps, pickpockets, swindlers, beggars and other rabble'.[3] Dispossession fed into migration and proletarianisation.

This tourist observer was Friedrich Engels; his common-law wife and travelling companion was Mary Burns (older sister of Lizzie Burns, who would later be Engels' second wife); and the correspondent in London was, of course, Karl Marx. Indeed, Engels ended his letter not only by discussing his own desire to write a history of Ireland but adding an admonitory request that if his old comrade would not visit and write about Ireland, Engels would have to do it himself.[4]

Ireland had a well-established status as a laboratory for private property, for enforcing enclosures and for experimenting with methods of dispossession that would also be used on the other side of the Atlantic. Various plantation efforts were implemented from the 1560s onwards, some unsuccessfully, others more long-lasting such as the Ulster Plantation of the early 1600s and the notoriously violent Cromwellian plantations of the 1650s. *A view of the present state of Ireland* (1596) by Edmund Spenser, poet at the Elizabethan court, in which the Gaelic Irish were presented as savages in need of civilising and privatising, is a good example of the ideology deployed. Claims that the Irish were nomads, pagans or even cannibals were common currency. They were already being classified as not fully European. As with the Native Americans, the accusations levelled against the Irish legitimised their dispossession and the privatisation of Irish land.⁵ The ideology underpinning the plantation of Ireland was of a piece with the Atlantic Lockeanism of New World settlement and the Enclosures from the sixteenth century onwards.⁶ Immanuel Wallerstein situates the expansion of English colonialism into Ireland from the later sixteenth century in the larger context of post-Enclosures England and the perceived need for an external safety valve for a surplus population, all familiar tropes from Locke's context. This colonisation of Ireland acquired a 'new seriousness' early in the following century, concomitant with a general strengthening of the British state after James I/VI personally consolidated a single rule over England and Scotland. Irish forests were singled out for their timber and Ireland was turned into a supplier of wool for English markets.⁷ The island rapidly changed from being a 'lightly settled, overwhelmingly pastoral, heavily-wooded country'⁸ into having 'modern' privatised land holdings.

The Penal Laws implemented concurrently from the 1600s onwards formalised this dispossession, explicitly denying full citizenship to the Gaelic Irish, implicitly denying their masculine sovereignty. Even if these laws remained 'imperfectly implemented', their end result was the exclusion of Catholics from land ownership and formal political power.⁹ In the long term, this Lockean remaking of Ireland hardly had the effect of 'civilising' the country. Edmund Burke, for example, while a defender of the property regime produced by the Enclosures in England, had a long-standing concern that the Cromwellian plantations in Ireland, whose victims included his own Catholic ancestors, had deprived the country of a 'natural' ruling elite.¹⁰ In the Burkean schema, therefore, Ireland was an implicitly unnatural place, where Catholic peasants – dispossessed and disaffected – remained at odds with their Protestant landlords. A drastic increase in population – from almost 5 million in 1780 to just under 7 million in 1821, then over 8 million in 1841¹¹ – meant that a finite supply of land was being shared among an ever-increasing pool with the Famine of the later 1840s as the direct result. Alongside the mass death and high levels of emigration, 70,000 evictions took place during the Famine, feeding into a general feeling of economic insecurity that would not be soon forgotten.¹² While evictions were far more rare than later nationalist accounts would suggest, about 1 million eviction notices were issued in Ireland between 1850 and 1886. In a country that had 500,000 tenants, this meant that, on average, each tenant received two notices to quit in these years. As Alexander Richey, a professor of law at Trinity College Dublin, explained in 1880, 'every notice to quit brought home to the tenant the power of the landlord to evict him; every use by a landlord of his legal power for the purpose of raising the rent ... was a conclusive proof that this power might be harshly and inequitably used'. And indeed, as the social historian Fergus Campbell points out, even if landlords were not the rack-renting tyrants of nationalist imagination, they still wielded a great deal of social control over their tenants.[13]

Engels' short epistolary travelogue was describing the most recent version of a Lockean process of dispossession that had been rinsed and repeated since at least the Cromwellian plantations of the 1650s, if not earlier. And in Ireland, as in the New World, the outcome was somewhat similar; the post-Famine country that Engels and Mary Burns visited was defined by profound inequalities, in private land ownership as much as any other arena. Agrarian violence was common, but where their Victorian contemporaries saw only a dangerous Celtic mob targeting privately owned estates, Engels, as well as Marx, would haltingly come to develop a very different view.

Engels had long had a fascination with the Irish (not least with his two Irish wives).[14] Echoing his observations about Irish migrant labour in his 1856 letter to Marx, Engels' famous 1844 work on *The condition of the working class in England* features a detailed *excursus* on the indigent population in Manchester's 'Little Ireland' slum district. Placing Ireland's incorporation into the British industrial system in a broader historical frame, Engels talked of how Limerick and Kerry, counties he would later travel through, had been forcibly remade in a modern and privatised, capitalist image: 'hitherto a wilderness wholly without passable roads, and serving, by reason of its inaccessibility, as the refuge of all criminals and the chief protection of the Celtic Irish nationality in the South of Ireland. It has now been cut through by public roads, and civilization has thus gained admission even to this savage region.'[15] The transition to capitalism, the ongoing inculcation of individualised forms of private property ownership, was thus a process of civilising a savage mob.[16] As Engels' descriptions progressed, this racialised pitch intensified.

With the exponential growth of the early Victorian economy, the Irish, having 'nothing to lose at home', flocked across the Channel seeking 'steady work and good pay for strong arms'. They arrived 'like cattle' and 'insinuate themselves everywhere'. In quasi-ethnographic terms, Engels claimed that '[w]henever a district is distinguished for especial filth and especial ruinousness, a man may safely count upon meeting chiefly those Celtic faces which one recognises as different from the Saxon physiognomy' and he even wrote in surprise that 'I have occasionally heard the Irish-Celtic language spoken in the most thickly populated parts of Manchester'.[17] With talk of 'filth and drunkenness' and a 'lack of cleanliness ... which is the Irishman's second nature', Engels revealed his own biases along the way. 'The Irishman', he wrote, in the singular, 'loves his pig as the Arab his horse, with the difference that he sells it when it is fat enough to kill.'[18] As Saree Makdisi has recently shown, in early Victorian England 'Arab' was an often malleable and generally negative label. Connoting racial as well as lower-class barbarism, it suggested a civilisational inferiority.[19] It is clear where Engels was placing the Irish mob within a broader class/race hierarchy. The Irish were a people with 'a southern facile character ... little above the savage' and '[f]or work which requires long training or regular, pertinacious application, the dissolute, unsteady, drunken Irishman is on too low a plane'. They were too different, and too backward, to ever be properly assimilated into British life: 'even if the Irish, who have forced their way into other occupations, should become more civilized, enough of the old habits would cling to them to have a strong degrading influence upon their English companions in toil, especially in view of the general effect of being surrounded by the Irish'.[20] As with so many other political actors before and since, Engels was denouncing impoverished migrants as a menacing mob and an economic threat; indeed, he was repeating the kinds of accusations that had been used to justify the seizure and privatisation of Irish lands. Yet, there was more going on here than mere racialised slurs.

Engels' racialised discussion of the Irish was a discussion of the problems of capitalism, not least the problem of how private property changes our very way of thinking about the world. He claimed that 'with the possible exception of the Irish, the degree of intelligence of the various workers is in direct proportion to their relation to manufacture ... the factory-hands are most enlightened as to their own interests, the miners somewhat less so, the agricultural labourers scarcely at all'.[21] Irish workers might work like factory hands, but they still had a pre-private-property, agricultural, class-consciousness. Their agrarian origins made them a contradictory people and Engels' views of the Irish bear comparison to his ambiguous depictions of premodern (which is, to say, pre-private-property) agrarian England. In the early pages of *The condition of the working class in England*, Engels cast a *somewhat* harmonious gaze on the agrarian lives of non-privatised and precapitalist England. Before the arrival of factories, craft labour was built on patriarchal relations. Men worked from home, a quite different environment to the surveillance of the future capitalist workplace, and they had their wives and children as convenient helpers.[22] Living conditions were superior to those of their urban proletarian successors:

> They did not need to overwork; they did no more than they chose to do, and yet earned what they needed. They had leisure for healthful work in garden or field, work which, in itself, was recreation for them, and they could take part besides in the recreation and games of their neighbours, and all these games – bowling, cricket, football, etc., contributed to their physical health and vigour. They were, for the most part, strong, well-built people, in whose physique little or no difference from that of their peasant neighbours was discoverable. Their children grew up in the fresh country air, and, if they could help their parents at work, it was only occasionally; while of eight or twelve hours' work for them there was no question.

And yet, undermining his romantic vision of pastoral England, Engels also spoke of the rural craft labourers of precapitalist England as a people who 'vegetated throughout a passably comfortable existence':

> intellectually they were dead; lived only for their petty private interest, for their looms and gardens, and knew nothing of the mighty movement which, beyond their horizon, was sweeping through

mankind. They were comfortable in their silent vegetation [*in ihrem stillen Pflanzenleben*], and but for the industrial revolution they would never have emerged from this existence, which, cosily romantic as it was, was nevertheless not worthy of human beings. In truth, they were not human beings; they were merely toiling machines in the service of the few aristocrats who had guided history down to that time.[23]

The romantic notion that non-privatised rural dwellers lead an idyllic existence was not uncommon in Victorian Britain.[24] And for Engels, certainly, the social world of precapitalist times was a mixture of a romantic and subtly gendered manly freedom and an uncivilised backwardness. For sure, the rapidity and dynamism of the new industrial time stood in marked contrast to what Engels and Marx would later call 'the idiocy of rural life'.[25] But conversely, the wholesome masculinity of that earlier time also stood in contrast to the oppressiveness of factory labour, and the miseries of unemployed men forced to do women's work ('[i]n many cases the family is not wholly dissolved by the employment of the wife, but turned upside down. The wife supports the family, the husband sits at home, tends the children, sweeps the room and cooks').[26] Capitalism was 'an insane state of things', a new social world that 'emasculates the man and takes from the woman all womanliness'.[27] The 'righteous and peaceful life in all Godliness and respectability'[28] of precapitalist England had been replaced by the sexual exploitation of female workers and a 'factory servitude' that, Engels claimed, 'confers the *jus primae noctis* upon the master'.[29] The transition from pastoral feudalism to privatised industrial capitalism was accompanied by adverse shifts in gender roles.

Engels saw the Irish immigrants moving in large numbers into Manchester as a living example of this older social world of precapitalism, before private property. Where English workers had been irreparably changed by the industrial experience, Irish workers inhabited a contradictory existence: they lived and even worked within capitalism, but maintained anachronistic social practices, ontologies and epistemologies. Unlike English workers, the Irish remained unconscious of the power of socialised factory labour, but yet, for all their seemingly innate faults, the Irish also continued to exist outside the coercive social discipline of capitalist modernity, and this held out some revolutionary possibilities. At a later point in the book, Engels discusses the latent discontent of industrial England and says 'to this the Irish immigration further contributes by reason of the passionate, mercurial Irish temperament, which it imports into England and into the English working class ... the mixing of the more facile, excitable, fiery Irish temperament with the stable, reasoning, persevering English must, in the long run, be productive only of good for both'.[30] Precapitalist and manly Irish communalism would mix productively with the dynamic power of the modern divisions of labour that English workers had learned under capitalism.

Writing for *Der Schweizerische Republikaner* [*The Swiss Republican*] in June 1843 (roughly the same time that he wrote *Condition of the working class in England*), Engels jealously eyed up Irish male agrarian muscularity as well as the famous nationalist 'monster meetings' of Daniel O'Connell (with an almost erotic tinge):

> The wily old fellow [*der alte Schlaukopf*] gets around from town to town always surrounded by two hundred thousand men, a bodyguard such as no king can boast of ... Two thousand men, and what kind of men! Men who have nothing to lose, two-thirds of them not having a shirt to their backs, they are real proletarians and *sansculottes* [sic], and moreover Irishmen – wild, headstrong [*unbändige*], fanatical Gaels. If one has not seen the Irish, one does not know them. Give me two hundred thousand Irishmen and I could overthrow the entire British monarchy.[31]

Running through both the youthful bombast of this journalistic piece and the more serious analyses of *The condition of the working class in England* are a number of tropes that would recur throughout Engels and Marx's writings: the 'time' of precapitalism, before private property, was defined by both stagnancy and masculinity, vegetation and freedom. Non-privatised, precapitalist races not only continued to exist synchronically with capitalism, but they also continued to manifest signs of both racial stagnancy and decadence *and* romantic freedoms from that earlier time. For all this, the Irish continued to be one of the examples he most regularly employed and Engels moved from seeing them as a dangerous mob in need of condemnation to a liberatory mob that should be politically embraced. Where Locke looked at America and primarily saw 'empty' lands filled with savages and waiting to be privatised, and where Burke looked with extreme terror at France and the Jacobins' ostensible threats to private property, Marx and Engels drew far more positive conclusions from the supposedly unprivatised spaces and peoples of Ireland.[32] 'Ireland' was a laboratory for understanding the emergence of private property and, for Engels and Marx, the Irish were a potentially revolutionary force; not only were they as yet unschooled in private property, they were also, in a sense, an un-privatised people. Marx and Engels' thinking on Ireland was of a piece with how they thought about some of the broader themes in their work: race, masculinity and the 'times' of capitalist development. Compared to Engels, Marx was less inclined to the use of such racial stereotypes. But moving across what Mike Davis has called a 'panoramic view of the *oeuvre*',[33] it is clear that from the humanist early Marx to the seeming coldness of the mature Marx there was a continuity in how he employed the Irish mob in his discussions of private property and capitalism.

We must travel for a moment to Ireland

In the first volume of *Capital*, in the context of a discussion of 'The general laws of capitalist accumulation', Marx engaged in a focused examination of Ireland, the only non-English region analysed at systematic length in his monumental work; 'we must travel for a moment to Ireland' he informs the reader.[34] Throughout his discussion, Marx distinguishes between England, 'an industrial country', and Ireland, 'an agricultural country', a distinction that is not just socio-economic but also temporal. England resides within the space–time of fully privatised and modern industrial capitalism; Ireland has not yet made the full transition from the *time* of feudalism. In Ireland, social relations still bear the trace of the precapitalist and Marx laments the eradication of harmonious and traditional, precapitalist social forms, in existence in Ireland 'from time immemorial':

> The first act of the agricultural revolution was to sweep away the huts situated on the field of labour. This was done on the largest scale, and

as if in obedience to a command from on high. Thus many labourers were compelled to seek shelter in villages and towns. There they were thrown like refuse into garrets, holes, cellars and corners, in the worst back slums. Thousands of Irish families, who according to the testimony of the English, eaten up as they are with national prejudice, are notable for their rare attachment to the domestic hearth, for the gaiety and the purity of their home life, found themselves suddenly transported into hotbeds of vice.[35]

Where others lamented the continued existence of Irish opponents of private property, Marx instead saw the transition to capitalism and private property as a transition away from Irish gaiety and purity, into a world of English vice. Even the environment of Ireland seemed more conducive to a 'natural' life. In his unfinished *History of Ireland*, Engels claimed that '[t]he weather, like the inhabitants, has a more acute character, it moves in sharper, more sudden contrasts; the sky is like an Irish woman's face: here also rain and sunshine succeed each other suddenly and unexpectedly and there is none of the grey English boredom'.[36] In *Capital*, Marx approvingly noted the 'Irish warmth'[37] with which early trade unionists in Ireland organised their meetings, a warmth that was presumably born out of the country's lingering precapitalist traits; the precapitalist and unprivatised base of Ireland determined the superstructural warmth of the country's inhabitants. Whatever dynamism capitalism and private property were bringing to Ireland, these changes also meant that the bucolic warmth of the Irish would be lost forever and Marx's thoughts on the nature of Irish society were a development of his thoughts on precapitalist societies more broadly.

As early as the early 1840s, Marx was talking of 'the abstraction of private life', by which he meant the remaking of our sense of selfhood from a feudal self to the privatised sense of self under capitalism, the latter of which 'belongs only to modern times'. He talked of the Middle Ages as 'the animal history of mankind', the time when people lived a primitive but non-alienated life.[38] In the roughly contemporaneous 1844 manuscripts, he spoke of the goal of capitalism as being 'the unhappiness of society'. Capitalism degrades each worker to 'a beast reduced to the strictest bodily needs'. It is a system that 'perfects the worker and degrades the man'³⁹ and '[p]roduction does not simply produce man as a *commodity*, the *human commodity*, man in the role of *commodity*; it produces him in keeping with this role as a *mentally* and physically *dehumanised* being'.⁴⁰ The true meaning of the Irish, for Marx, was that they continued to exist outside this unhappy capitalist dehumanisation; they were not a mob in any conventional, negative sense but instead were a still warm and more fully human people, examples of a feudal earthiness from before the imposition of capitalist private property.⁴¹ Marx contended that '[p]rivate property has made us so stupid and one-sided',⁴² a condition that clearly did not affect the Irish, who were as yet unaffected by the 'generalized form of domination, novel to modernity ... the impersonal domination suffered by members of commercial society'.⁴³ The Irish embodied the 'human, *intimate*' [*eine gemütliche Seite*, literally 'a cosy side'] ontology of feudalism; they were what Marx elsewhere called 'real, corporeal *man*, man with his feet firmly on the solid ground, man exhaling and inhaling all the forces of nature'.⁴⁴ The gendered connotations are less blatant in the original German. Nonetheless, Stuart Hall was correct to point out that in the vocabulary of the 1844 manuscripts, '[i]t is *Man*, not merely because that was the available generic term, but also because it reflected the sexual division of labour at the time. It was taken for granted that those who were remaking the world were gendered ... It is Man the producer, Man as the active practitioner – human practice rather than the economy – that stands as the determining center.'⁴⁵ The slippage between universal mankind and *men* more narrowly defined is a well-known phenomenon in feminist thought: 'historically, the human has been most commonly marked as male'.⁴⁶ And Marx and Engels did seem to be participating in that slippage here, seeing feudal people like the Irish as more fully human, more natural and thus more masculine.⁴⁷ Marx and Engels were moving away from the notion that the Irish were an inferior mob, but retained the idea that the most normal kind of politics was a male politics.

These views of the Irish as a pre-industrial people whose naturalistic human warmth was being destroyed by English economics and private property resurfaced in a number of interesting ways throughout Marx's work.⁴⁸ In an 1853 article on 'Irish tenant right' for the *New York Daily Tribune*, Marx critiqued the landlord system in Ireland and its negative effects on the country. He laid the blame on the elite across St George's Channel:

> England has subverted the conditions of Irish society. At first it confiscated the land, then it suppressed the industry by 'Parliamentary enactments', and lastly it broke the active energy by armed force. And thus England created those abominable 'conditions of society' which enable a small *caste* of rapacious lordlings to dictate to the Irish people the terms on which they shall be allowed to hold the land and to live on it.[49]

Private property was the source of an 'abominable' social order and was making the Irish a literally degraded people. In the notes for an undelivered speech to the General Council of the International Working Man's Association in November 1867, Marx talked of how, concurrent with the post-Famine Irish agricultural revolution, 'the number of the deaf-mutes, the blind, the decrepit, the lunatic, and idiotic increased relatively to the numbers of the population'. He argued that the supposed progress of the agricultural revolution in Ireland 'did not bring improvement but rather the destruction of life'; 'the physical sickness [of the Irish people] and soil exhaustion of Ireland' were both seemingly of a piece with each other.[50] And livestock numbers eerily matched the drop in human population: '1,032,694 Irishmen have been displaced by about one million cattle, pigs, and sheep'.[51]

His vision of Ireland was broader, though, than just a singular narrative of poverty and violent economic restructuring, because for Marx, as for Engels, Ireland still displayed traits of feudalism but was now being violently dragged into propertied capitalist modernity and this traumatic transformation held out a revolutionary possibility. In contrast to the 'solid, but slow' conservatism of 'the Anglo-Saxon Worker', Irish immigrant labourers had a 'revolutionary fire'.[52] Not fully schooled in the rules of private property, they carried their essentially non-capitalist consciousness to the very heart of capitalist Britain. This was a contradiction that needed to be exploited. Indeed, Engels and Marx were of one mind in their view that Fenianism, a product of this contradiction, could be a revolutionary force on both sides of the Irish Sea:

What the English do not yet know is that since 1846 the economic content and therefore also the political aim of English domination in Ireland have entered into an entirely new phase, and that precisely because of this, Fenianism is characterised by a socialistic tendency (in a negative sense, directed against the appropriation of the soil) and by being a lower orders movement.[53]

Which is to say that, by Marx and Engels' lights, Irish nationalists were unconscious socialists. Giving voice to the resentments of dispossessed Irish feudal peasants, they stood in unwitting opposition to the transformation of rural Ireland into a privatised capitalist economy. Not that any of this detracted from Engels' perception (at the time of the 1867 trial of the 'Manchester Martyrs') that the leaders of Fenianism were 'mostly asses'.[54] Just as Engels had written in *Der Schweizerische Republikaner* in 1843, Marx continued to feel that the Irish could be the ones to bring down the British state. He saw Ireland as the 'weakest point' in the British Empire,[55] and looked forward to a social revolution that would be 'Ireland's revenge' upon England.[56]

There is much about Marx and Engels' writings on Ireland that is selective in its approach. Their view of the Irish-as-peasants ignores the major industrialisation already under way in Ulster; Belfast was the fifth largest industrial city in the world in the mid-nineteenth century.[57] Religious divisions were almost totally absent from Marx and Engels' discussions of Ireland.[58] This is curious, since a number of Irish historians have pointed out the key role that the Catholic Church has played in the country's capitalist development, in legitimating property rights and in the promotion of a disciplined sexual culture that would fit with the new use of primogeniture after the Famine.[59] Yet such seemingly non-materialist considerations were clearly not considered relevant by Marx and Engels. The outsized role of the Church in post-Famine Ireland is almost completely ignored in their writings. Moreover, the Irish were never as uniformly anti-capitalist, nor the English proletariat so disciplined and regulated by private property and capitalism, as Marx and Engels had it.

David Roediger has noted the common American view in the 1850s that the Irish 'symboliz[ed] preindustrial license'.[60] Much of the contemporary British discussion of the rural Irish was similarly couched in a 'myth of the West', which suggested that the 'real' Irish mob, in all of their 'old barbarities', could still be found in the pre-industrial west of Ireland, with its tenant farmers and landless labourers.[61] Irish wildness also had a rough political analogue; violent agrarian outrages by secret societies were a common occurrence across nineteenth-century Ireland, often taking a ritualistic form but in the main targeting livestock rather than persons or property.[62] 'Usually, the [secret] societies did not dispute [a] landlord's ownership of the soil, but they acted on the conviction that all members of the community should have access to sufficient land or food to ensure survival.' The more affluent leaders of secret societies generally withdrew their support if the actions targeted private property.[63] Whatever respect was shown for private property, the widespread agitation was *the* major reason why Ireland was so heavily policed at mid-century, which Engels easily recognised during his 1856 visit.[64] The western province of Connacht, rural and with an economy dominated by small tenant farmers, was 'the most politically active province in Ireland between 1879 and 1918',[65] the site of intense agrarian agitations in 1878–82 and again in 1898. The urban anxieties about the rural 'wild men on the land', identified in the early 1960s by the west of Ireland socialist, Peadar O'Donnell, had a long pedigree.[66]

Yet talk of the rebellious and pre-industrial Irish hid a more complicated reality. The Irish economy was growing rapidly from the mid-eighteenth century onwards. Transport infrastructure was being developed by local government from the mid-1700s, the country was being incorporated more and more into global markets and an economy that privileged 'communal rights and responsibilities' was already giving way 'to one of individualized risk' even before the Famine.[67] 'Between 1750 and 1810 the value of annual exports increased from less than £2 million to over £6 million, and the value of yearly imports rose at a comparable rate.' Paper money was in high circulation,[68] as were fashionable imported clothing and luxury goods like tea, spirits and tobacco.[69] Even if the benefits of this commercialisation were distributed unequally, Ireland was already a recognisably capitalist and propertied space well before the 1850s.[70] Not least in the areas of rent and land, 'harsh and competitive conditions'[71] had already come to prevail in Ireland.

Nor were the Irish peasants as ripe for anti-capitalist radicalism as Marx and Engels believed; they were not a negative, vile mob but that does not necessarily mean that they were automatically a positively liberatory, anti-capitalist mob either. Kerby Miller has noted that 'many travellers in pre-Famine Ireland complained that peasant deference too often descended to depths of shameless dissimulation and obsequious flattery'. Other visitors were shocked by the social obedience that supposedly prevailed. Miller quotes an 1853 observation from a tenant farmer in west Munster: 'Any man must obey his landlord, when he has got a good landlord'. This obsequiousness seems to have been linked to a desire on the part of small tenant farmers to purposely exaggerate their poverty so as to avoid rent increases.[72] And prior to the militant agitation of the Land War of 1878–82, agrarian demonstrations tended to be 'deferential and conciliatory', part of 'the longstanding discourse of conciliation from which moderate reformers of the land and political structures operated'.[73] Their 'feudalism' was just as likely to make the Irish 'more fatalistic than optimistic, more prone to accept conditions passively than to take initiatives for change, and more sensitive to the weight of tradition than to innovative possibilities for the future'.[74] Stagnancy and radicalism are, by definition, mutually contradictory; there are complexities and tensions here that Marx and Engels did not fully explore. Conversely, Miller argues that it was 'the "progress" of the late eighteenth and early nineteenth centuries [capitalism and changes in the property order] that transformed landlord–tenant relations in ways that destroyed traditional mechanisms of social control'. In other words, with the deepening of private property's roots, the rural Irish became less obsequious and more radical, rather than carrying over a radicalism derived from their earlier 'feudal' economics.[75]

Likewise, the image of the heavy-drinking and undisciplined Irish was something of a myth. Alcohol consumption in nineteenth-century Ireland was slightly below the English average and, by the broader standards of the British Isles, the level of Irish alcohol consumption was quite unexceptional.[76] The Irish were never quite the fiery, revolutionary people that Marx and Engels wanted them to be. Marx accepted the idea that Ireland was a feudal, agrarian space, less developed along a set path of economic/historical development. But he ignored the fact that Ireland's economy had, by some measures, been better in the eighteenth century than in the nineteenth, that uneven Irish economic underdevelopment had itself been *developed* since the Act of Union of 1800. Engels later talked about the antithesis of urban and rural spaces as being as central to capitalism as the antithesis of workers and capitalists;[77] that Ireland was itself produced as a rural space and as a supplier of cheap agrarian goods by British urban capitalism goes unexamined in Marx's analyses in favour of an unquestioned assumption that Ireland had always been rural, always trapped in a primordial, precapitalist time. The Irish 'misery' and precapitalist ontology Marx and Engels identified were, in large extent, post-Famine phenomena.

Marx was not a historian, however; rather, he used empirical historical evidence to bolster his underlying theories about capitalist discipline and the capitalist social order.[78] Unsurprisingly, he gave less attention to these messy historical realities, instead favouring investigations of the *tendencies* of capitalist development. His interest in the Irish was not an interest in uneven and inconsonant Irish realities, but rather an interest in developing a theory of how feudalism becomes capitalism, of how property becomes privatised and of which workers might move beyond capitalist property-relations.[79] Locke had looked at America and had seen a primordial space akin to the world in its earliest history, a space that could now be privatised once the 'savage' inhabitants were cleared out. Marx looked at Ireland and saw an island that still existed within feudal time and thus he believed he was witnessing a conveniently contemporaneous transition to a modern capitalist property order. And rather than seeing the inhabitants as a savage mob, he valorised them as wonderfully non-capitalist.

It would be easy to state simply that Marx and Engels were 'wrong' in their discussions of Ireland. It is more accurate, though, to say that Marx overemphasised capitalism's power, including its power to remake the proletariat and to convert all the globe into private property. And of a piece with how he imagined the despotic power of capitalism in England was the idea that the Irish had escaped this propertied despotism and remained a lovable mob, freer and perhaps even more manly. English capitalist dystopia was imagined with and through Irish feudal utopia. But as with so many other dialectically opposed notions in Marx, the thesis and antithesis broke down into a contradiction; the Irish were no longer fully feudal but had not yet become altogether capitalist. The feudal Irish became not just the opposite of the capitalist English. They were also flooding as a mob into England. The Irish had become a living supersession of feudal thesis and capitalist antithesis, an inherent contradiction of capitalist development that needed to be exploited. Yet even then, Marx's views of the Irish were not all that radical or innovative.

It has long been recognised that Marx accepted the ideas of Adam Smith, David Ricardo et al. and tried to rework them in an anti-capitalist direction, but that in doing this he remained trapped in classical economy's epistemological categories. Something similar is true with race; he accepted racial stereotypes about the anti-property mob, tried to rework them, but remained trapped by them. Cedric Robinson, in his critique of Marxism, noted that 'at base, that is at its epistemological substratum, Marxism is a Western construction – a conceptualization of human affairs and historical development that is emergent from the historical experiences of European peoples mediated, in turn, through their civilization, their social orders, and their cultures'.[80] More specifically, the environmental historian Andreas Malm has recently noted how invested Marx was in the Victorian British discourse of 'steam demonology' as a critique of industrial capitalist working conditions.[81] Marx, something of a product of Victorian Britain himself, accepted the racialised notions about the Irish while simultaneously working to repurpose them in an anti-capitalist direction; in his writings, the negative racial and economic stereotypes of the Irish mob were converted into positives. The 'bio-social theories'[82] of gender, race and class, which were all simultaneously used to understand civilisational differences in Victorian Britain, were all drawn on by Marx in ways that were similar, and yet markedly different, to the thinking of his contemporaries; similar and yet very different to how Locke and Burke used imaginary depictions of America or France to construct their theories of private property.

Irish indeterminacy, the sense that this nation defied categorisation, was certainly a familiar Victorian concern:

They were national subjects incorporated into the nation-state through parliamentary and economic structures, but they remained a colonized and alien population, denied fundamental rights of citizenship and subjecthood, and constructed as culturally, religiously, and racially other. This position rendered the Irish within the newly created United Kingdom vexatious in relation to questions of national belonging.

The Irish were an 'ambivalent' people who 'defied' any easy 'visual coding'.[83] Irish migrant workers were perceived as diseased interlopers, spreading their pathogens in the English social body. 'Indeed the very notion of a coherent British body politic relied on such fears of alien invasion.'[84] Ireland was seen as a country that stubbornly refused to enter modernity and the Irish were a mob unsuited for the rigours of private property and an industrialised society.[85] The notion that there was something *different* about the Irish, and that this difference was somehow connected to Irish people's anomalous relationship with private property, was a commonplace of Victorian Britain.[86] For Victorian elites, the instability of post-Famine Irish society was the result of a society where there were too many indigent tenant farmers and not enough responsible owners of private property. Marx and Engels operated within such popular ideas, while also retooling them into the idea that the Irish were trapped between feudalism and capitalism and would help enact the transition to socialism.[87]

Similarly, Engels' short 1856 travelogue is perhaps best understood in the broader context of Victorian-era travel literature in which mainly male visitors interpreted the exotic experiences of Ireland for readers on the other side of St George's Channel. Political speculations about the subversive and unpropertied Irish were a regular feature in such travelogues; likewise the proto-anthropological language and a focus on the economic miseries of an Ireland seen as implicitly precapitalist. Tourists regularly described the island as 'shockingly strange' and 'an uncultivated and raging landscape'.[88] To travel to Ireland was, allegedly, a way to experience a primitive Gaelic space that had somehow survived from another time before private property, where even the local residents were perceived in the tourist's gaze as being part of the curious natural *mise-en-scène*.[89] There was also a supposed therapeutic quality to experiencing Ireland directly: 'Coming from an increasingly urban, industrial society, some tourists wanted to imagine the Irish peasantry as untouched and unspoiled by materialism, leading simple lives untrammeled by modern complexities, pressures and discontents'. And yet, at the same time, '[t]he sense that something was wrong with Ireland permeated many of the travel narratives, especially in the last two decades before the Famine'.[90] Even when the Irish were seemingly being praised, they remained a racially inferior mob. Engels ploughed all these furrows in his travelogue and in his writings on Ireland in general, albeit in an anti-capitalist, anti-private property direction.[91]

Marx and Engels rehearsed and borrowed from a number of conventional racial stereotypes about the wild and primitive Irish mob, but also used these racialist ideas in a malleable and strategic manner. That racial divisions are inherent to the workings of capitalism is a point well received.[92] What is less discussed is how central race was to how Marx and Engels *conceived* of capitalism; 'race' was actually of major importance for their understanding of private property and the origins of capitalism.

Those societies in which the capitalist mode of production does not prevail

Marx began the first volume of *Capital* by claiming that this would be a study of 'those societies in which the capitalist mode of production prevails'.[93] There is a certain dissimulation at work here; his *magnum opus* in fact devotes a notably large amount of attention to non-capitalist societies, the role they play for capitalism and the process through which these peoples, conventionally seen as racialised mobs, move towards capitalism and towards private property. Marx's project was to study the geographical spread of capitalism (what we might today call globalisation) and the historical development of capitalism (the transition from feudal conceptions of private property to capitalist ones). Confirming Alexander Saxon's observation that it is 'fundamentally a theory of history',[94] *race* played a major role in how Marx understood both of these interrelated phenomena of capitalist historical time and geographic space.[95]

Marx's views of the Irish regularly intersected with his views of other racial or ethnic groups that he believed were in the process of moving from feudalism to capitalism. He regularly compared the end of feudalism in Ireland, for example, to its Gaelic cousin in 'the promised land of modern romance, the Highlands of Scotland', where once 'independent peasants' were systematically dispossessed so that '[t]he remnant of the aborigines' were removed from their lands and 'flung on the sea-shore'. The difference between the two was only one of scale: 'in Ireland landlords have gone to the length of sweeping away several villages at once; in Scotland areas as large as German principalities are dealt with'.[96] Further afield, in a note to the first English edition of *The communist manifesto*, Engels talked of 'common ownership of land' as being 'the primitive form of society everywhere from India to Ireland'.[97] 'Primitive accumulation' [*ursprüngliche Akkumulation*] in Ireland, as in Scotland and India, had destroyed communal property-relations supposedly in existence, in all three countries, since 'time immemorial'.[98] In all three cases, an ancient, communal form of property ownership had been rapidly erased by the dynamism of industrial capitalism.

That global industrial capitalism had shown itself capable of destroying ancient systems of property reinforced Marx and Engels' arguments about the power of capitalism to remake the world after its own image, the power 'with which it batters down all Chinese walls'.[99] There is a discursive strategy at work here. Marx and Engels accepted that primitive and 'Asiatic Societies' are defined by their 'unchangeableness'.[100] But this unchanging nature is also in striking contrast with the dynamism of capitalism, the one social form that ultimately proved capable of destroying these seemingly rigid ancient societies. The stereotype of ancient unchangeableness is a counterfoil that sharpens Marx and Engels' vision of rapid and revolutionary change under industrial capitalism. Marx was engaging in a broader argument about the geographical spread and historical development of capitalism and about how different races and ethnicities were assimilated into this global propertied system in differing ways. The diversity of the world (understood in terms of capitalist development) is the essence of this argument. As Teodor Shanin argues, the 'societal map' in late Marx 'assumed the global co-existence of potentially progressive social formations and of essentially static "ahistorical" ones',[101] a diachronic way of seeing both the world and divergent global attitudes towards private property (and a way of seeing in which Locke also engaged). Marx understood the world in terms of where certain places and people, certain 'races', fit into the hierarchies of a global capitalist system, a system that assimilates all the races of the world – 'the entanglement of all peoples in the net of the world-market'.[102] Race, therefore, is not a sidebar to Marx's analysis, it is actually a category at the heart of his understanding of private property and of capitalism as a world-system. How Marx understood 'races' like the Irish, the Scottish or the Indians was fully bound up with how he understood primitive accumulation and the rise of private property.

Locke believed that private property arose for essentially good, if very gendered, reasons; legally recognised private holdings allowed each father to raise his family in secure conditions. Private property secured the patriarchal family, which in turn secured the continuity of private property into the next generation. Conversely, for Marx, the story of private property 'is written in the annals of mankind in letters of blood and fire'.[103] Essentially, Marx inverted the standard Lockean narrative of private property's rational and clean emergence, instead exposing the inherent violence of domestic and colonial expropriation. When he looked at the Irish, he believed he was looking at latter-day victims of this propertied violence.

Marx's writings on Ireland employed a set of familiar racial stereotypes about the Irish – that they were backward and primitive like other 'savage' races, but also warm, loveable and poetic – that resonated throughout his Victorian world.[104] Engels' earliest forays into Irish studies were even more pronounced in this regard. And yet, such stereotypical imaginings co-existed with something quite different: a sense of respect, a belief that the Irish could be an active and revolutionary force within global history. The Irish stood to lose something of great value in their transition from feudalism into a world of private property and capitalism. They were not like passive and primitive Indians or Chinese, who could only benefit from being dragged into Western capitalist orbits. The Irish had an impressive sense of freedom and perhaps even a muscular masculinity. They could readily take part in history rather than being acted upon by it. The non-privatised Celts were, Marx said, 'gallant young men'.[105] And in Marx and Engels' writings on Ireland there was a romance and a respect that remained absent from analyses of Jews, Indians or other non-'white' races.[106] Likewise there is none of the clear disdain that Marx exprressed for individualistic and selfish French farmers, scorned as atomised and selfish 'potatoes in a sack', or Engels' more guarded critique of peasants in the Wuppertal in Germany.[107]

Teodor Shanin has noted that Marx's dismissive views of communal property in India or China was in marked contrast to his greater sympathies for Russian communalism: 'while the picture of India or China was to Marx's generation of Europeans remote, abstract and often misconceived, Russia was closer not only geographically but in the basic sense of human contact, possible knowledge of language and of availability of evidence and analysis, self-generated by the natives'.[108] This is overstated; Marx was far less favourable about Russia than Shanin allows.[109] There was less ambiguity in Marx's views of the Irish, who were more culturally familiar (or racially familiar?) to Marx as well as to Engels. Hibernian romance – and perhaps also a sense that the Irish were white Europeans and thus active agents in their own history – led Marx and Engels away from harsh condemnations of Irish mobs.[110]

They become corruptible as soon as they stop being peasants and turn bourgeois

In seeking to transform his readers and to urge them to political action, Marx was faced with a basic intellectual problem: 'In his effort to so transform us, he must work with the materials at hand, the economic, philosophical, and religious forms of thought that weigh like a nightmare upon his brain',[111] as William Roberts has said. The reference, of course, is to the notion of historical determinism as described in *The Eighteenth Brumaire of Louis Bonaparte*: 'Men make their own history, but they do not make just as they please ... The tradition of all of the dead generations weighs like a nightmare on the brain of the living.'[112] Not only is historical determinism one of the foundational concepts of Marx's writings, but the validity of this idea is shown by the fact that Marx himself was trapped in his own past and present: in nineteenth-century Europe's prevailing ideas about race and gender, both of which were always assumed to be created and recreated through private property. Marx and Engels operated within a discourse about racialised mobs and the threat they posed to private property, even if they welcomed rather than feared such mobs. Maria Mies has similarly written of how conventional and of their time Marx and Engels could be on questions of gender;[113] both thinkers operated within a set of ideas about Irish masculinity and muscular primitivism that contemporary British or American audiences would not have found unconventional. Even so, Marx and Engels also showed themselves capable of repurposing these racial and gendered ideas for anticapitalist purposes. Their views of the Irish mixed stereotypes of precapitalist and pre-private-property primitivism with a respectful sense of nostalgia, masculinity and even romance.[114] Marx and Engels' discursive use of the Irish echoes what Kristin Ross has called 'the possibility of anachronism ... allowing encounters in one's own moment with actually embodied aspects of the past, stranded or land-locked, as it were, but still sporadically perceptible. Evoking communitarian or tribal societies of the past may provide clues to the free forms of a whole new economic life.'[115] Marx's vision of Britain before primitive accumulation, for instance, borrowed from broader currents of contemporary British radicalism with its desire for 'restitution and reform of the British constitution, deploying an updated version of "the Norman yoke" to explain the present misery of the laborer'. This has led William Roberts to claim, in his recent innovative reading, that 'Marx seems to have saddled himself with a nostalgia for a bygone era of independent petty production that is hardly compatible with his own obvious preference for large-scale cooperative production'. Roberts even speaks of a 'Romantic radicalism' at work in Marx's descriptions of precapitalism.[116] The Irish were a people from the precapitalist past whose supposed communalism simultaneously signposted the socialist future after the abolition of private property.[117]

For Marx and Engels, unlike Locke, Burke and bourgeois theorists of private property in general, 'the mob' were less a frightening spectre, more a welcome presence whose humanity was fully recognised (albeit sometimes romanticised). Like many before and since, Marx's understanding of private property existed in an intimate relationship with his views on race and gender.[118] But where Locke and Burke saw private-property ownership as a marker of masculine sovereignty and white racial identity,[119] Marx saw private property, and capitalism in general, as destructive of masculinity (what he and Engels elsewhere lamented as 'the vanished status of the workman of the Middle Ages').[120] Whatever anyone says about 'the universal logic of capitalism',[121] 'race' and 'gender' are not universal concepts; they change over time. The ways in which Marx and Engels deployed 'race' and 'gender' as categories of capitalist analysis surely demonstrates the malleability and dynamism of these concepts, as well as the onerous difficulties of discussing private property outside these two categories.

All the recurring tropes of Marx and Engels' treatment of the Irish surfaced in the latter's *Origins of the family, private property and the state*, 'a highly speculative work based on Marx's handwritten and difficult-to-decipher notes on compendious volumes [by the anthropologist Lewis Morgan] that Engels himself had not read at the time of writing'.[122] This book is a grand stadial history of the races of the world, gender relations and capitalist development.[123] As with earlier works in the Marx–Engels canon, Engels takes extant conceptions of race and history and repurposes them here, to craft a more materialist history. The work repeated the idea of development as decline; the civilising process also means the 'downfall from the simple moral grandeur' of earlier social orders,[124] though his earlier emphasis on manly liberty was now toned down, with Engels here asserting that women had more freedom in the earlier stages of human development.[125] Like Locke, however, he sees the family as existing prior to the rise of society, perhaps even predating history itself, with private property reproducing itself through (and for) the family. In a chapter devoted to the Irish, Engels claimed that there was a Celtic communalism that 'is alive in the popular instinct to this day' in Ireland and stated that during his trip to Ireland he had been able to experience the remnants of this ancient Celtic '*gens*'.[126] There is a clearly essentialist sense of race here, with 'nineteenth-century ideas about race and reproduction' surfacing throughout the work.[127]

Such depictions of the Irish were themselves *passé* by the end of the nineteenth century. And while Engels never stopped seeing the Irish in racialised terms, his later writings were far less hopeful for the island's revolutionary future. Visiting Ireland again in September 1869, with Lizzie Burns and Marx's daughter Eleanor, he saw some important changes.[128] While some parts of the country still remained 'downright depopulated', Dublin was now 'unrecognisable'. Likewise, trade was at a high level in Cork and the city and its port had acquired a newly cosmopolitan air: 'I heard a lot of Italian, also Serbian, French and Danish or Norwegian spoken'. All of this pointed to a regrettable conclusion: 'The worst about the Irish is that they become corruptible as soon as they stop being peasants and turn bourgeois. True, that is the case with most peasant nations. But in Ireland it is particularly bad.'[129]

Ireland certainly underwent transformative economic changes in the later nineteenth century, as various British-backed schemes broke up many of the large landed estates and converted tenants into owner-occupiers, thus effectively defanging the Irish agrarian radical mob by the time of the War of Independence (1919–1921).[130] It was not until the start of the twentieth century that the Lockean project of civilising and privatising Ireland finally succeeded, in which process Irish nationalism played a helpful role.[131] All of this happened against the backdrop of a broader strengthening of global capitalism from the 1890s onwards (which did affect Engels' hopes for an imminent socialist revolution).[132] It would appear that Ireland had made the final leap from feudalism to capitalism.[133] And in parallel to economic changes there was an important change in racial representations. The kind of overtly racialised depictions of the Irish mob in which Engels engaged (present in subtler ways in Marx), disappeared. Social Darwinism and the scramble for Africa solidified phenotype as *the* key signifier of 'race'. The Irish became more fully assimilated into whiteness, something that formal sovereignty in 1922 would help reinforce. The Irish mob had embraced private property and turned conformist and capitalist.

Indeed, in what was probably his last public comment on Irish affairs, Engels used an 1888 interview with the *New Yorker Volkszeitung* [*New Yorker People's Newspaper*] to confess that the country was moving from 'semi-feudal conditions to capitalist conditions' and a 'purely socialist movement cannot be expected in Ireland for a considerable time. People there want first of all to become peasants owning a plot of land, and after they have achieved that mortgages will appear on the scene and they will be ruined once more.'[134] Bringing his career as a before-the-fact Irish Studies scholar to an end, Friedrich Engels looked into the bleak capitalist future with an intriguing prophecy; before any socialist revolution can take root in Ireland, the country will first have to be ruined by a mortgage-based crisis of financial capitalism.

Marx and Engels took existing ideas about private property and white male racial normativity and inverted them into a communist spectre that has continued to haunt the propertied imagination. They took a somewhat vague set of ideas about a communal future and developed them into a coherent vision of a world that no longer needs private property. Liberals and conservatives obviously did not support such visions; they would try to ignore or forget them and yet regularly needed the cypher of socialism; claiming that socialism would be chaotic and violent was a commodious means of reifying a normativity that was always understood as propertied, white, male and capitalist. 'Marxism', 'socialism' and 'communism', as accusations pregnant with meaning, would become common currency in the history of private property, often employed by the same people who were influenced by Locke or Burke.

Taken collectively, Marx and Engels, Burke and Locke provide a very broad introduction to the three dominant strands of politics within Anglophone Atlantic capitalism, their understanding of private property and their conceptions of the 'mob' that threatened it: socialism and communism, which were suspicious if not outright hostile to private property; conservatism, which stressed unchangeability and a prescriptive emphasis on tradition and order; and liberalism, advocating a horizontal equality in which all citizens were said to have *equal rights* to own property, even if all the economic and social barriers to that property ownership were elided and who actually counted as a citizen was often defined in restrictively narrow terms. The latter two ideologies are predicated on a fear of the mob, the former embraces the mob. These three bodies of thought clearly diverged in important ways. Yet Locke and Marx both imagined the world in diachronic terms, where the 'primitive' and the 'advanced' existed simultaneously in different places; England was advanced for both, and both saw Ireland as primitive and even primordial; Locke saw the Americas as a prelapsarian survival. Partitioning the world in these terms – in which certain places and races were depicted as less advanced along a set path of historical development – meant that race was inherent in how they imagined the world, actively so for Locke and Engels, more passively and ambiguously for Marx. Both Locke and Marx believed they could identify the specific 'moment' when private property came into the world – whether in the progression away from the state of nature or in primitive accumulation and the move from feudalism to capitalism. Both similarly defined private property as artificial, but obviously they part ways as to whether it is a good thing. One of the frustratingly underdeveloped elements in Burke's conception of private property is whether or not he believed it was 'natural' or whether, like Locke, he saw it as artificial but socially positive; he regularly described opponents of private property as being somehow or another 'unnatural', but also seemed to think one could slip out of civilisation, out of private property, and presumably back into a Lockean State of Nature. Yet Burke shared Locke's sense that private property ownership was a marker of masculinity, albeit going into the parallel conception that the erasure of private property would erase men's normative gender roles. And Burke shared the fears that animated Locke and his contemporaries a century earlier, that Britain could be easily devoured by mobs of masterless men. Marx, unsurprisingly, took a directly opposite view of the lower classes, believing their agitations could create a better world, though he never broke from gendered understandings of private property. Engels ended his life by writing perceptively on the origins of private property within the family, even as he continued to accept that heteronormative family as so certainly natural as to exist outside of any and all historical change. All of these thinkers were attempting to figure out what it meant to live within the world created by the Atlantic Enclosures, starting in Britain and then circulating out from there; an enclosure culture in which private property, race and gender were always apprehended together. Locke and Burke's ways of thinking and imagining a privatised world became the dominant ones in capitalist modernity; Marx's always remained a spectre that haunted the mainstream, a codifying of anti-private property attitudes that have always existed alongside the attitudes of pro-private property partisans. The rest of this book will examine less philosophically minded, more practical wayfarers and how all these myriad liberal, conservative and socialist ideas went into practice in the history of private property.

For Marx, Ireland was a test case for the entire global history of private property and capitalism. A third of the way through the first volume of *Capital*, he professed that American capitalist development could be swapped with this Irish and British narrative because *mutato nomine de te fabula narratur* [with the name changed, the story is told of you]. The role that Irish immigrants played for Britain, Marx intimated, was the role played by the slaves of Kentucky and Virginia for American industry.[135] The next chapter follows this Marxian thread to Virginia, and a writer there who utilised some rhetoric remarkably similar to Marx's (and also expounded a variety of Burkean and Lockean designs), to reach some radically different conclusions from the Moor.

Notes

1 Quoted in Kevin Anderson. *Marx at the margins: on nationalism, ethnicity, and non-Western societies* (Chicago, 2010), 126.
2 Glenn Hooper. *Travel writing and Ireland, 1760–1860: culture, history, politics* (London, 2005), 82.
3 For a Marxian-influenced interpretation of the role of emigration in nineteenth century Ireland's political economy, see Jim Mac Laughlin. *Emigration and the peripheralization of Ireland in the global economy.* Review (Fernand Braudel Center) Vol. 17, No. 2 (1994), 243–73.
4 Letter from Engels to Marx (23 May 1856). Reprinted in full in Karl Marx, Frederick Engels; I.L. Golman, V.E. Kunina, eds. *Ireland and the Irish question* (Moscow, 1971), 83–5. Kevin Anderson says that Marx himself was preparing 'a lengthy study of Ireland' in the autumn of 1869: *Marx at the margins* (2010), 134. Engels' sadly unfinished Irish history was abandoned in favour of more immediate political work after the Franco-Prussian War: *cf.* 'letter from Engels to Sigismund Borkheim (March 1872)' in Golman and Kunina, *Ireland*

and the Irish question (1971), 299. Engels intended his planned history of Ireland as a 'pendant' to *Condition of the working class in England*: see Yvonne Kapp. *Eleanor Marx*, Vol. 1: *Family life (1855–1883)* (New York, 1972), 117.

5 Nicholas P. Canny. 'The ideology of English colonization: from Ireland to America', *William and Mary Quarterly*, Vol. 30, No. 4 (1973), 575–98.

6 Joe Cleary. *Outrageous fortune: capital and culture in modern Ireland* (Dublin, 2006), 25.

7 Immanuel Wallerstein. *The modern world-system*, Vol. I: *Capitalist agriculture and the European world economy in the sixteenth century*, 2nd edition (Berkeley, CA, 2011), 228, 261, 281.

8 Cleary, *Outrageous fortune* (2006), 26.

9 Conor Morrissey. *Protestant nationalists in Ireland, 1900–1923* (Cambridge, 2019), 5–6.

10 Richard Bourke. *Empire and revolution: the political life of Edmund Burke* (Princeton, NJ, 2015), 38, 161.

11 Cormac Ó Grada. 'The population of Ireland, 1700–1900: a survey', *Annales de Démographie Historique* (1979), 283.

12 Fergus Campbell. *Land and revolution: nationalist politics in the west of Ireland, 1891–1921* (Oxford, 2005), 13.

13 Fergus Campbell. *The Irish establishment, 1879–1914* (Oxford, 2009), 16, 43–4.

14 Aidan Beatty. 'The two Irish wives of Friedrich Engels: recovering the narratives of Mary and Lizzie Burns', *Socialist History*, 60 (2021), 5–22. Both Mary and Lizzie Burns appear to have been uneducated and, at most, only nominally literate. Little direct evidence of them survives: Tristram Hunt. *Marx's general: the revolutionary life of Friedrich Engels* (New York, 2009) 94–6. The Irish playwright Frank McGuinness, however, did reconstruct them in *Mary and Lizzie* (1989), a surreal work that explores themes of gender identity, nationalism and Irish Catholicism. At the end of the play, 'Lizzie' accurately forecasts that 'you will be remembered, because you loved the earth ... I will be remembered by a line in your life. Frederick Engels lived with two Irish women, Mary and Lizzie Burns. Little does that tell. Little do they know.' Nonetheless, 'Lizzie' also recounts her and her sister's important role in Engels' life and career: 'Years ago in this country they say two women met a man and they went walking through Manchester. The women gave the man safe passage through the dangerous poor ... They showed him the poor and they showed him their father and they showed their race and themselves to

him.' In another scene, 'Jenny von Westphalen', Marx's wife, questions the Burns sisters' sexual propriety before reading some of the more overtly anti-Irish passages from *Condition of the working class* to the sisters: 'Shall I tell you what he's said ... He's named your race ... Do you think he loves you?' Frank McGuinness. *Plays Two* (London, 2002), 53, 64, 74.

15 Friedrich Engels; David McLellan, ed. *The condition of the working class in England* (Oxford, 1993 [1844]), 27.
16 For the notion that the bogs and rural landscapes of eighteenth- and nineteenth-century Ireland had a wildness that matched that of the Irish people themselves, see Hooper, *Travel writing* (2005) 27; Declan Kavanagh. *Effeminate years: literature politics and aesthetics in mid-eighteenth-century Britain* (Lewisburg, PA, 2017), 99–134.
17 Engels, *Condition of the working class* (1993 [1844]), 101–2.
18 Engels, *Condition of the working class* (1993 [1844]), 103.
19 Saree Makdisi. *Making England Western: occidentalism, race and imperial culture* (Chicago, 2014), 77–8 and throughout.
20 Engels, *Condition of the working class* (1993 [1844]), 103–4.
21 Engels, *Condition of the working class* (1993 [1844]) 32. Anderson takes a positive view of Engels' *Condition of the working class*, talking of it as 'a subtle analysis of the relationship [of] class to ethnicity, singling out Irish immigrant labor from a number of vantage points' and goes on to say that '[d]espite the condescending language about "race" and "civilization," Engels's pro-Irish sympathies are clear enough': *Marx at the margins* (2010), 116–17. What this amounts to, though, is a denial of the important role of racialised stereotypes in Engels' analysis of Irish immigrant labourers in Victorian England.
22 This echoes Marx's ambiguous (and not always critical) views of 'the rural patriarchal system of production': Karl Marx; Maurice Dobb, ed. *A contribution to the critique of political economy* (New York: 1970 [1859]), 33. This work was produced between August and September 1857.
23 Engels, *Condition of the working class* (1993 [1844]), 15–17.
24 Elizabeth K. Helsinger. *Rural scenes and national representation: Britain, 1815–1850* (Princeton, NJ, 1997), 8–9; William H.A. Williams. *Tourism, landscape and the Irish character: British travel writers in pre-Famine Ireland* (Madison, WI, 2008), 142.
25 Karl Marx, Friedrich Engels; A.J.P. Taylor, ed. *The communist manifesto* (London, 1985 [1848]), 84. In the original German, this term carries a connotation of child-like simplicity as well as lower intelligence.

26 Engels, *Condition of the working class* (1993 [1844]), 154.
27 Engels, *Condition of the working class* (1993 [1844]), 155.
28 Engels, *Condition of the working class* (1993 [1844]), 16.
29 Engels, *Condition of the working class* (1993 [1844]), 158.
30 Engels, *Condition of the working class* (1993 [1844]), 134.
31 'Letters from London' (1843), in Golman and Kunina, *Ireland and the Irish question* (1971), 33–6. Originally published in *Der Schweizerische Republikaner* 39 (27 June 1843).
32 As already discussed, 'Ireland' also mattered for Locke, who saw in it a source of privatisable real estate, and for Burke, who feared the easy reception there of Jacobinism. Indeed, 'Ireland' has often served as a space for the imaginative free play of capitalist modernity. Along with many of our conceptions of private property, it was here that 'terrorism' was invented, as well as colonial policing and modern conceptions of human dignity: Samuel Moyn. 'The secret history of constitutional dignity', *Yale Human Rights and Development Journal*, Vol. 17, No. 1 (2014), 39–73; Amy Martin. *Alter-nations: nationalisms, terror, and the state in nineteenth-century Britain and Ireland* (Columbus, OH, 2012); Alex Vitale. *The end of policing* (London, 2017), 34–5.
33 Mike Davis. *Old gods, new enigmas: Marx's lost theory* (London, 2018), xiv.
34 Karl Marx; Frederick Engels, ed.; Samuel Moore, Edward Aveling, trans. *Capital: a critique of political economy*, Vol. I: *The process of production of capital* (London, 1954 [1887]), 652. On the importance of Ireland in Marx's thought, see the brief mentions in Ernest Mandel. *Late capitalism* (London, 1978), 86; Norman Levine. *The tragic deception: Marx contra Engels* (Oxford, 1975), 66.
35 Marx, *Capital*, Vol. I (1954 [1887]), 661.
36 Engels, 'History of Ireland', in Golman and Kunina, *Ireland and the Irish question* (1971) 184. See also Eamonn Slater. 'Engels on Ireland's dialectics of nature', *Capitalism, Socialism, Nature*, Vol. 29, No. 4 (2018), 31–50.
37 Marx, *Capital*, Vol. I (1954 [1887]), 241.
38 Karl Marx; Joseph O'Malley, ed.; Annette Jolin, Joseph O'Malley, trans. *Critique of Hegel's 'Philosophy of Right'* (Cambridge, 1970), 32, 82.
39 Marx is here quoting Antoine-Eugène Buret's *La misère des classes laborieuses en France et en Angeleterre* (1841).
40 Karl Marx. 'Economic and philosophic manuscripts of 1844', in *Collected works*, Vol. 3: 1843–1844 (London, 1975), 239, 242, 245,

284; emphases in original. The effects of the transition to capitalism as summed by Marx, was reiterated by Ernest Mandel as the 'corrosive influence of commerce': *Late capitalism* (1978), 44.

41 Marx's stadial conception of history had an inherent circularity that allowed 'primitive peoples' to be valorised for the reason that their precapitalist ideals would return in the socialist future. As Nick Yablon has discussed, stadial views of history often recognised that rather than offering a narrative of never-ending progression, societies were actually progressing toward their own demise: *Untimely ruins: an archaeology of American urban modernity* (Chicago, 2009), 28–30. For Marx, capitalist society was progressing to its own regression, 'back' to earthiness but forward to socialism.

42 Marx, 'Economic and philosophical manuscripts' (1975 [1844]), 300.

43 William Clare Roberts. *Marx's inferno: the political theory of capital* (Princeton, NJ, 2017), 85.

44 Marx, 'Economic and philosophic manuscripts' (1975 [1844]), 266, 336. Emphases in original. This fits with Dipesh Chakrabarty's observation that 'Marx's critique of "capital" builds into the category two aspects of nineteenth-century European thought', namely, 'the abstract human of the Enlightenment and the idea of history': *Provincializing Europe: postcolonial thought and historical difference*, 2nd edition (Princeton, NJ, 2007), 47. See also Jason Moore. *Capitalism in the web of life: ecology and the accumulation of capital* (London, 2015), which uses a rereading of Marx to argue that 'Nature' is always internal to capitalism. What Marx is saying here about the Irish contradicts Moore's reading.

45 Stuart Hall; Jennifer Daryl Slack, Lawrence Grossberg, eds. *Cultural studies 1983: a theoretical history* (Durham, NC, 2016), 39. In a study of nineteenth-century labour movements, Joan Scott identifies 'a construction of class that equated productivity and masculinity' and talks of how '[t]he masculine construction of class assumed a (gendered) family division of labor': *Gender and the politics of history*, revised edition (New York, 1999), 64–5. Mike Davis recently stated that both patriarchy and white supremacy plagued the early labour movement: 'The "modern Hercules" viewed the single working woman, not as a sister and comrade, but as a strike-breaker and enemy of the family': *Old gods* (2018), 51.

46 Joanna Bourke. *What it means to be human: reflections from 1791 to the present* (Berkeley, CA, 2011), 5. Wendy Brown has sketched out a genealogy of *homo oeconomicus* as the gendered male subject of capitalism, and 'his' work in different historical instantiations of

capitalism: *Undoing the demos: neoliberalism's stealth revolution* (New York, 2015), 99–107. And Hannah Arendt has critiqued the tendency of nineteenth-century socialists to be 'so neglectful of the political consequences of their own inherited concepts': *The origins of totalitarianism*, 2nd edition (New York, 1968), 41.

47 For a discussion of the gendered blind spots of Marxism, see Silvia Federici. *Caliban and the witch: women, the body and primitive accumulation* (New York, 2014). Federici makes the point that Marx could not have seen the transition from feudalism to capitalism as a form of liberation 'had he looked at its history from the viewpoint of women'. I do not agree that Marx saw the transition to capitalism as an untroubled liberation, but Fedrici's point that Marx ignores women has obvious weight to it.

48 Such views bear comparison to Hegel's view of Black slaves: 'the Negro ... exhibits the natural man in his completely wild and untamed state': G.W.F. Hegel, *The philosophy of history* (New York, 1991 [1837]), 111. Such attitudes, Tommy Curry observes, were not 'the rambling of a ... racist posing as a philosopher' but 'reflected the most authoritative ethnological thinking of the nineteenth century': *The man-not: race, class, genre and the dilemmas of Black manhood* (Philadelphia, PA, 2017), 43. Susan Buck-Morss has said that 'Hegel was perhaps always a cultural racist if not a biological one': *Hegel, Haiti and universal history* (Pittsburgh, PA, 2009), 74. As I will discuss below, I am not interested in 'outing' Marx as a racist in this manner, but it is certain that race played a prominent role in his writings.

49 'The Indian question – Irish tenant right', *New York Daily Tribune* (11 July 1853), in Golman and Kunina, *Ireland and the Irish question* (1971), 59–65. Emphases in original.

50 Kohei Saito. *Karl Marx's ecosocialism: Capital, nature, and the unfinished Critique of political economy* (New York, 2017), 207–8.

51 'Notes for an undelivered speech on Ireland' (n.d.), in Golman and Kunina, *Ireland and the Irish question* (1971), 121. The notes for this entry state that the speech was prepared for a discussion of the Irish question at the General Council of the International Working Man's Association on 26 November 1867. Marx returned to the theme of Irish physical degeneration under British rule in his 'Outline of a report on the Irish question to the Communist Educational Association of German Workers in London' (16 December 1867), in Golman and Kunina, *Ireland and the Irish question*, 137, where he talks of the 'physical deterioration [*Verschlachterhöhung*] of the population' in

post-1847 Ireland, 'not only a relative, but an absolute increase in the number of deaf-mutes, blind, insane, idiotic, and decrepit inhabitants'.

52 Karl Marx, 'Confidential communication' [of the First International] (*c*. March 1870). Initially published in *Die Neue Zeit*, Vol. 2, No. 15 (1902); in Golman and Kunina, *Ireland and the Irish question* (1971), 160–63.

53 Letter from Karl Marx to Friedrich Engels (30 November 1867), in Golman and Kunina, *Ireland and the Irish question* (1971), 147. In reality, early Fenians were suspicious of land reform, believing, as bourgeois nationalists often do, that social issues should be secondary to the national question: Anne Kane, *Constructing Irish national identity: discourse and ritual during the land war, 1879–1882* (New York, 2011), 47.

54 Letter from Friedrich Engels to Karl Marx (29 November 1867), in Golman and Kunina, *Ireland and the Irish question* (1971), 145.

55 Letter from Karl Marx to Paul and Laura Lafargue (5 March 1870), in Golman and Kunina, *Ireland and the Irish question* (1971), 290.

56 Karl Marx. 'Ireland's revenge', *Neue Oder-Zeitung* (16 March 1855), in Golman and Kunina, *Ireland and the Irish question* (1971), 74–6.

57 Cleary, *Outrageous fortune* (2006), 66. 'In a variety of ways, great and small, Ulster's social structure and habits varied from those in the rest of the country': Michael Laffan, *The partition of Ireland, 1911–1925* (Dundalk, 1983), 3. Among these, Laffan lists the Ulster Custom, which made agriculture in Ulster different from the rest of the country. Also, '[i]n the nineteenth century sexual behaviour was more easygoing and illegitimacy more common there than elsewhere in Ireland. In its physical appearance Ulster seemed more "British" and even in the eighteenth century visitors contrasted the orderliness and neatness of its farms with those of the south … The industrialization of Belfast in the course of the nineteenth century drew Ulster further apart from the Catholic south … In economic terms Belfast was an anomaly, a British industrial outpost in agrarian Ireland.'

58 Stuart Hall has rightly noted that 'religion is the great lost subject in Marxist scholarship': *Cultural studies* (2016), 49. Mike Davis' analysis situates this in a historical problematic; 'all signs in Marx's day pointed to the continued erosion of belief and the secularization of industrial society. After the early writings, religion was quite understandably not a topic on his agenda': *Old gods* (2018), xv.

59 Raymond Crotty. *Ireland in crisis: a study in capitalist colonial undevelopment* (Dingle, 1986), 55; Tom Inglis. *Moral monopoly: the rise*

and fall of the Catholic church in modern Ireland, 2nd edition (Dublin, 1998), 8–9, 75; Kane, *Constructing Irish national identity* (2011), 43–4; J.H. Whyte. *Church and state in modern Ireland, 1923–1970* (Dublin, 1971), 32–3, 36; Aidan Beatty. 'Where does the state end and the church begin? The strange career of Richard S. Devane', *Studi Irlandesi: A Journal of Irish Studies* 9 (2019). For a comparable discussion of the role the church played in assimilating Irish immigrants to American racial capitalism, see Peter O'Neill. *Famine Irish and the American racial state* (New York, 2017).

60 David Roediger, *The wages of whiteness: race and the making of the American working class* (London, 1991), 107.
61 Williams, *Tourism* (2008), 164. Williams is here quoting Joep Leerssen. *Mere Irish and Fíor-Ghael: studies in the idea of Irish nationality, its development and literary expression prior to the nineteenth century* (Notre Dame, IN, 1997), 66.
62 Tom Garvin. *The evolution of Irish nationalist politics* (Dublin, 2005), 60–76; James S. Donnelly, Jr. *Captain Rock: the Irish agrarian rebellion of 1821–1824* (Madison, WI, 2009).
63 Kerby Miller. *Emigrants and exiles: Ireland and the Irish exodus to North America* (Oxford, 1985), 62, 64.
64 Jonathan Sperber calls Victorian Ireland the closest thing in contemporary Europe to a police state, with fourteen times as many armed policemen per capita as absolutist Prussia: *The European revolutions, 1848–1851* (Cambridge, 1984), 242; R.M. Douglas. *Architects of the revolution: Ailtirí na hAiséirghe and the fascist 'new order' in Ireland* (Manchester, 2009), 12. Needless to say, an armed constabulary was not deemed necessary for the rest of the United Kingdom.
65 Campbell, *Land and revolution* (2005), 3 and throughout.
66 Peadar O'Donnell. *There will be another day* (Dublin, 1963), 19.
67 Breandán Mac Suibhne. *The end of outrage: post-Famine adjustment in rural Ireland* (Oxford, 2017), 6–8, 85.
68 Marx wrongly claimed that '[b]efore the famine, the great mass of agricultural wages were paid in kind, only the smallest part in money; to-day [1860s], payment in money is the rule': *Capital*, Vol. I (1954 [1887]), 661.
69 Miller, *Emigrants and exiles* (1985), 29, 31.
70 Indeed, absent this capitalist development, under the watchful eye of an 'activist state', it is questionable whether Engels could have carried out his two trips to Ireland. Mac Suibhne, *Outrage* (2017), 46.
71 Laura Brace. *The politics of property: labour, freedom and belonging* (Basingstoke, 2004), 212.

72 Miller, *Emigrants and exiles* (1985), 43, 50, 100. This practice of pretending poverty to gain sympathy from others was referred to in Ireland (and still is) as 'putting on the poor mouth' (*ag cur an béal bocht*). The very fact that a term exists to describe it points to its wide prevalence and recurring use!
73 Kane, *Constructing Irish national identity* (2011), 67, 88.
74 Miller, *Emigrants and exiles* (1985), 107. Miller also notes how this passivity might even have surfaced in the Irish language, which favours a passive voice and avoids direct statements: *Emigrants and exiles*, 119–20.
75 Miller, *Emigrants and exiles*, 44. Miller specifically critiques Marx's views of Ireland in this regard, *cf. Emigrants and exiles*, 60.
76 J.J. Lee. *The modernisation of Irish society, 1848–1918* (Oxford, 1973), 14. Similarly, '[t]hough drinking was a central part of social life for males in Ireland, per capita alcohol consumption there in the early twentieth century trailed that of the United States': Roediger, *Wages of whiteness* (1991), 152.
77 Frederick Engels; C.P. Dutt, ed. *The housing question* (Moscow/Leningrad, 1935 [1872]), 54, 95.
78 Buck-Morss has similarly discussed how Hegel embellished, distorted and exaggerated the reality of African life 'to serve his philosophical purpose of making a certain developmental scheme seem logical': *Hegel* (2009), 117. For comparable analyses of Marx and Hegel's historiographies, see Lucio Colletti; Lawrence Garner, trans. *Marxism and Hegel* (London, 1973), 112, 130–1.
79 A comparison with Marx and Engels' fragmentary writings on Scotland is useful here; much of the empirical historical evidence they utilised was wrong, but the theories of capitalist development seem to be what interested them more. See Neil Davidson. 'Marx and Engels on the Scottish Highlands', *Science & Society*, Vol. 65, No. 3 (2011), 286–326.
80 Cedric J. Robinson, *Black Marxism: the making of the Black radical tradition*, 2nd edition (Chapel Hill, NC, 2000), 2. In a comparable vein, Susan Buck-Morss has noted that '[t]here is an element of racism in official Marxism, if only because of the notion of history as teleological progression': *Hegel* (2009), 57.
81 Andreas Malm. *Fossil capital: the rise of steam power and the roots of global warming* (London, 2016), 311.
82 Vron Ware. *Beyond the pale: white women, racism and history* (London, 2015), 37, 65.
83 Martin, *Alter-nations* (2012) 3, 5, 7. See also Sikata Bannerjee, *Muscular nationalism: gender, violence, and empire in India and*

Ireland, 1914–2004 (New York, 2012); Joseph Valente. *The myth of manliness in Irish national culture* (Champaign, IL, 2011); Sharrona Pearl. *About faces: physiognomy in nineteenth-century Britain* (Cambridge, MA, 2010), 110, 127–8.
84 Alison Winter. *Mesmerized: powers of mind in Victorian Britain* (Chicago, 1998), 20, 61–2. For what the contemporary Irish thought about their supposed indeterminacy, see Aidan Beatty. *Masculinity and power in Irish nationalism, 1884–1938* (London, 2016), Ch. 5; Brian Ó Conchubhair. *Fin de siècle na Gaeilge: Darwin, an athbheochan agus smaointearacht na hEorpa* [*Irish-language fin de siècle: Darwin, the Gaelic revival and European intellectual thought*] (Indreabhán, 2009), Ch. 3.
85 Hooper, *Travel writing* (2005) 185; Caomhín de Barra. *The coming of the Celts, AD 1860: Celtic nationalism in Ireland and Wales* (Notre Dame, IN, 2018), 27.
86 Aidan Beatty. 'An Irish revolution without a revolution', *Journal of World-Systems Research*, Vol. 22, No. 1 (2016), 54–96; Campbell, *Land and revolution* (2005); Kane, *Constructing Irish national identity* (2011); W.E. Vaughan. *Landlords and tenants in mid-Victorian Ireland* (Oxford, 1994).
87 Engels – always the more overtly racialist of the two – was directly influenced by Thomas Carlyle's mainly negative views of the Irish: Pearl, *About faces* (2010), 111–12; Amy Martin, 'Blood transfusions: constructions of Irish racial difference, the English working class, and revolutionary possibility in the work of Carlyle and Engels', *Victorian Literature and Culture*, Vol. 32, No. 1 (2004), 83–102.
88 Hooper, *Travel writing* (2005), 5, 7–10, 21, 22, 102, 113.
89 Williams, *Tourism* (2008), 37, 52. This is worth comparing to the perception that tours to the Highlands were a form of 'Northern time travel': 'The pleasure of the experience was to a great degree temporal. Highland tours offered a time machine for the adherents of stadial history ... The space of the Highlands seemed to participate in two stages of history at the same time': Fredrik Albritton Jonsson, *Enlightenment's frontier: the Scottish Highlands and the origins of environmentalism* (New Haven, CT, 2013), 50.
90 Williams, *Tourism* (2008), 60, 196.
91 Judith Walkowitz has placed Engels' urban writings in the context of the 'throng of missionaries and explorers, men who tried to read the "illegible" city', such as Dickens and Henry Mayhew. Engels' rural forays were also part of a broader Victorian tradition: *City of dreadful delight: narratives of sexual danger in late-Victorian London*

(Chicago, 1992), 18. And indeed, Walkowitz goes on to point out – by way of Peter Stalybrass, Allon White. *Politics and poetics of transgression* (Ithaca, NY, 1986), 132 – that Engels still retained 'an essentialist category of the sub-human nomad: the Irish': *City of dreadful delight*, 19.

92 Michael Lebowitz. 'The politics of assumption, the assumption of politics', *Historical Materialism*, Vol. 14, No. 2 (2006); Robinson, *Black Marxism* (2000). See also Keeanga-Yamahtta Taylor's discussion of 'The political economy of racism', an analysis that directly draws on Marx's writings on Irish workers: *From #BlackLivesMatter to Black liberation* (Chicago, 2016), 205–9.

93 Marx, *Capital*, Vol. I (1954 [1887]), 43.

94 Alexander Saxton. *The rise and fall of the white republic: class politics and mass culture in nineteenth-century America* (London, 1990), 14.

95 Anderson, *Marx at the margins* (2010), 3.

96 Marx, *Capital*, Vol. I (1954 [1887]), 681–3. See also Davidson, 'Marx and Engels on the Scottish Highlands'. Marx was a 'great admirer' of Sir Walter Scott and may have taken some of his perceptions of feudalism from him: Roberts, *Marx's inferno* (2017), 198, fn 39. Engels praised Scott's novels for the ways they brought the 'Scottish highland clan [*diesen hochschottischen Clan*] vividly before our eyes': *The origin of the family, private property and the state* (Chicago, 1909 [1884]), 162. On the broader history of land ownership in Scotland, see T.M. Devine. *The Scottish clearances: a history of the dispossessed, 1600–1900* (London, 2018).

97 Marx, Engels; Taylor, *Communist manifesto* (1985 [1848]), 79, fn 2.

98 The small pieces of land held by farm labourers 'from time immemorial' in Ireland were being 'systematically confiscated'. In Scotland, land that had belonged collectively to the clan 'from time immemorial' was appropriated by the Duchess of Sutherland. And in the sub-continent, Marx talks of the state taking a payment 'from time immemorial' from 'small and extremely ancient Indian communities … based on possession in common of the land, on the blending of agriculture and handicrafts, and on an unalterable division of labour'. Indeed, Indian politics in general was unchanged 'from immemorial times': Marx, *Capital*, Vol. I (1954 [1887]), 661, 682, 337. Sperber says that 'primal accumulation' or 'original accumulation' would be better translations of the original *ursprüngliche Akkumulation* than the standard term 'primitive accumulation': *Karl Marx: a nineteenth century life* (New York: 2014), 435. Conversely, Roberts' view is that 'primitive accumulation' is a perfectly acceptable translation of Marx's *ursprünglich*:

Marx's inferno (2017), 188, fn 2. The problem, of course, is that 'primitive' has a racial register uncomfortable to twenty-first-century readers, though Marx was comfortable with it.
99 Marx, Engels; Taylor, *Communist manifesto* (1985 [1848]), 84.
100 Marx, *Capital*, Vol. I (1954 [1887]), 338–9.
101 Teodor Shanin. 'Gods and craftsmen' in *Late Marx and the Russian road: Marx and the peripheries of capitalism* (New York, 1983), 5.
102 Marx, *Capital*, Vol. I (1954 [1887]), 714.
103 Marx, *Capital*, Vol. I (1954 [1887]), 669.
104 L. Perry Curtis. *Apes and angels: the Irishman in Victorian culture*, 2nd edition (Washington, DC, 1997); Michael de Nie. *The eternal Paddy: Irish identity and the British press, 1798–1882* (Madison, WI, 2004); Sinéad Garrigan Mattar. *Primitivism, science and the Irish revival* (Oxford, 2004); Noel Ignatiev. *How the Irish became white* (New York, 2008); Bruce Nelson. *Irish nationalists and the making of the Irish race* (Princeton, NJ, 2013). My argument directly contradicts the claim of Perry Anderson that Marx and Engels 'remained largely outside the local cultural and political framework' in England: *Considerations on Western Marxism* (London, 1984), 4. That they were so heavily invested in Irish questions suggests that the analysis should shift when we consider not 'England' but the United Kingdom. As one recent reader of Marx's *Capital* has noted, the work 'proceeds both within and against the categories of the day': Ivan Ascher. *Portfolio society: on the capitalist mode of prediction* (New York, 2016), 27. Presumably those 'categories' were primarily those of the United Kingdom within which Engels and Marx lived for so long. It is untenable to think that their time there did not affect them! For an analysis that does place Marx in his specifically British context, see Christopher Hill. 'Karl Marx and Britain' (1983), in *The collected essays of Christopher Hill* (Amherst, MA, 1986), 236–44.
105 Quoted in Anderson, *Marx at the margins* (2010), 140.
106 Though Marx did believe that the Indians – allegedly gifted in mathematics – would soon enter capitalist modernity: 'The future results of British rule in India', *New York Daily Tribune* (8 August 1853). Marx's notion of 'race' was not always an essentialised one.
107 *Eighteenth Brumaire of Louis Napoleon* (New York, 1963 [1852]), 109. In his earliest surviving letter to Marx, Engels writes in similar terms about the changing nature of the peasants of the Wuppertal: they were becoming more civilised but also express their politics through an individualist violence. He wrote of his hope that they would instead embrace Communist collective action and thus become

'human beings': letter from Friedrich Engels to Karl Marx (October 1844), available at www.marxists.org/archive/marx/works/1844/letters/44_10_01.htm, accessed 30 June 2022.
108 Shanin, 'Gods and craftsmen' (1983), 19.
109 Bruno Naarden's contention that Marx 'was afflicted with a very outspoken form of Russophobia' is polemically charged but carries a strong dose of truth: 'Marx and Russia', *History of European Ideas*, Vol. 12, No. 6 (1990), 783. Neither Marx nor Engels were completely innocent of racialised stereotypes when it came to Russian peasants, albeit to differing degrees; Marx was never as uncritically accepting of race as Engels.
110 Paul Gilroy, with an accusatory air, has said that 'Marx and Engels' assertion that the workers have no fatherland sits uncomfortably beside their practice as German nationalists'. This is something of an overstatement – they were hardly German nationalists in any conventional sense, and certainly not in any *völkisch* sense. But Gilroy is certainly correct to point to their perception that non-European nations are 'ruins of people': *'There ain't no black in the Union Jack': the cultural politics of race and nation* (Chicago, 1991), 69.
111 William Clare Roberts. 'Marx in Hell: the critique of political economy as *katabasis*', *Critical Sociology* Vol. 31, Nos 1, 2 (2005), 54.
112 *Eighteenth Brumaire* (1963 [1852]), 15. In the original German, Marx talks of tradition weighing *wie ein Alp* [like an Alpine mountain] on the brains of the living. The translation, by C.P. Dutt, is possibly a channeling of James Joyce/Stephen Dedalus, who famously had it that '[h]istory ... is a nightmare from which I am trying to awake': *Ulysses* (New York, 1986 [1922]), 28.
113 Maria Mies. *Patriarchy and accumulation on a world scale: women in the global division of labour*, 2nd edition (London, 1998), 33, 49.
114 Against the view that Marx was a cold materialist, David Harvey has discussed how 'Marx was undoubtedly influenced by early-nineteenth-century Romanticism. His early writings are infused with Romantic sentiments and meanings. And while this sensibility is subdued in his later writings, it is not hard to detect its presence': *A companion to Marx's Capital* (London, 2010), 115. Shlomo Avineri has made a similar argument that 'Marx's description of medieval Europe echoes some of the romantic notions prevalent at that period in Germany: Marx feels that the Middle Ages produced an integrated way of life': *The social and political thought of Karl Marx* (Cambridge, 1968), 20.
115 Kristin Ross. *Communal luxury: the political imaginary of the Paris Commune* (London, 2015), 74–5. This seems to be the same point

Marx was making in a discussion of the 'eternal charm' of 'the childhood of humanity' in the *Grundrisse*: Karl Marx; Martin Nicolaus, trans. *Grundrisse: foundations of the critique of political economy*, (London, 1973), 111. See also Hall, *Cultural studies* (2016), 49–50: 'Why is it that the critique of capitalism has always drawn on the supposed remembrances of precapitalist cultural forms as well as on the explicit dreams of postcapitalist forms? We all know the power and the appeal of such residual ideas as we are about to rush off to the countryside, a countryside that doesn't exist, a mythical countryside.' The use of such tropes counters the bold claim of Owen Hatherley – via Patrick Wright's *On living in an old country* (London, 1985), 155–6 – that socialism is 'inherently future-oriented', because socialism does not 'present itself as fully achieved or accomplished in the present as we know it, it cannot work up an easy public presence for its sense of history': *The ministry of nostalgia* (London, 2016), 10. Socialism might not exist in the present, but some of its practitioners clearly think it existed in the past, and will again in the future. There is an important Janus-faced style of thinking at work here that Hatherley overlooks.

116 Roberts, *Marx's inferno* (2017), 200, 201, 208. Both Teodor Shanin and Kevin Anderson have argued that Marx's views of human history moved from a unilinear model to a later and more multifaceted conception, a notion of historical time that Shanin succinctly labels 'back from the past/future to the present': Shanin, 'Gods and craftsmen' (1983), 15; Anderson, *Marx at the margins* (2010), 2. This circular stadial history, though, was already present in the 1844 manuscripts, as observed earlier.

117 On the subject of time and the socialist future, it might even be worth bringing Marx's views of the Irish and of the Jews into closer conversation with each other. If the Jews are thought of in terms of supersession (the bearers of the capitalist spirit who will cease to exist in the transition to socialism), as Marx described Jews in *On the Jewish question* (1843), are the Irish a messianic people, the heralds of the socialist millennium? Marxism has certainly not always been innocent of such messianism. Zinoviev once admitted, while chair of the Communist International, that the working class had a kind of messianic role: Davis, *Old gods* (2018), 18.

118 Marx certainly recognised that attitudes towards private property could intersect with other emotive concepts. In one of *Capital*'s most memorable pieces of prose-styling, he talks of how 'all fractions of the ruling-classes' in England, 'landlords and capitalists, stock-exchange

wolves and shopkeepers, Protectionists and Free-traders, government and opposition, priests and freethinkers, young whores and old nuns', were united by 'the common cry for the salvation of Property, Religion, the Family and Society': Marx, *Capital*, Vol. I (1954 [1887]), 270–1. Similarly, in the *18th Brumaire*, he talks of how 'property, family, religion, order' are the 'watchwords of the old society' that the bourgeoisie seeks to defend: (1963 [1852]), 25.

119 As Mrinalini Sinha has noted, '"manhood" in colonial societies was based on a particular relationship to property': *Colonial masculinity: the 'manly Englishman' and the 'effeminate Bengali' in the late nineteenth century* (Manchester, 1995), 5.

120 Marx, Engels; Taylor, *Communist manifesto* (1985 [1848]), 89.

121 Vivek Chibber. *Postcolonial theory and the spectre of capital* (London, 2013), 291 and throughout.

122 Alys Eve Weinbaum. *Wayward reproductions: genealogies of race and nation in transatlantic modern thought* (Durham, NC, 2004) 108. Though Engels made a point of saying that the discussion of the Celts was his, not borrowed from Morgan: *Origin of the family* (1909 [1884]), 11.

123 James Connolly, the premier figure in Irish Marxist thought, operated in the shadow of *Origin of the family*; his 1910 work, *Labour in Irish history* claims that a communal social order was regnant in premodern Ireland. This was borrowed from 'Morgan's monumental work on Ancient Society'. Morgan's methodology 'will yet unlock the doors which guard the secrets of our native Celtic civilisation': *Collected works*, Vol. 1 (Dublin, 1987), 24. Similarly, Karl Kautsky claimed in 1908 that contemporary Ireland exhibited the same mode of production as ancient Rome: *Foundations of Christianity*, trans. Henry F. Mins (New York, 1953 [1908]). And Emma Goldman saw something of political importance in the supposedly anarchist strains of Irish peasant culture: *Living my life*, Vol. II (New York, 1970 [1931]), 572–3. There is a subterranean history of this discursive use of 'the Irish' in left intellectual culture after Marx.

124 Engels, *Origin of the family* (1909 [1884]), 119.

125 Engels, *Origin of the family* (1909 [1884]), 60, 79.

126 Engels, *Origin of the family* (1909 [1884]), 158, 161–2fn.

127 Weinbaum, *Wayward reproductions* (2004), 115–17.

128 For background on this trip, see Kapp, *Eleanor Marx*, Vol. I (1972), 116–17. Queenstown in Cork had greatly expanded because of trade generated by the American Civil War.

129 Letter from Friedrich Engels to Karl Marx (27 September 1869), in Golman and Kunina, *Ireland and the Irish question* (1971), 273–4.
130 Beatty, 'An Irish revolution without a revolution' (2016); Campbell, *Land and revolution* (2005), 13, 48–9, 257–9, 290. A comparative imperial view of Ireland's 'New Political Economy, Old Political Order' is given in Thomas C. Holt. *The problem of freedom: race, labor, and politics in Jamaica and Britain* (Baltimore, MD, 1992), 318–36. For a contrasting view, which argues that agrarian radicalism continued to have major purchase into the twentieth century, see Conor Kostick. *Revolution in Ireland: popular militancy, 1917–1923*, 2nd edition (Cork, 2009).
131 Beatty, *Masculinity and power* (2016), Ch. 6. For land-ownership policies in post-1922 Ireland, see Terence Dooley. *The land for the people: the land question in independent Ireland* (Dublin, 2004).
132 Yvonne Kapp, *Eleanor Marx*, Vol. 2: *The crowded years, 1884–1898* (New York, 1976), 48.
133 The title of the 1904 Land War history by Michael Davitt, the foremost agrarian agitator of post-Famine Ireland, reveals how Marx's views were part of a broader discourse: *The fall of feudalism in Ireland, or the story of the Land League revolution* (London, 1904).
134 *New Yorker Volkszeitung* (20 September 1888), in Golman and Kunina, *Ireland and the Irish question* (1971), 343. A certain confirmation of Engels' bleak prediction might be found in, of all places, a confidential British Foreign Office intelligence report from July 1970: 'Although overdue for social reform, Ireland is markedly stony ground for Communism. In the first place, extremists and malcontents have an anti-Communist safety valve in traditional Republicanism … The Republic is the antithesis of the classical Communist society: it is rural, bourgeois and clerical. The Church certainly has great influence on opinion and most Irish, educated by the Church, regard even pink Socialism as atheistic dynamite. The Russians and their fellows are the legions of hell': National Archives of the United Kingdom, FCO33/124. Quoted in Brian Hanley, Scott Millar. *The lost revolution: the story of the Official IRA and the Worker's Party* (Dublin, 2009), 236.
135 Marx, *Capital*, Vol. I (1954 [1887]), 254.

Part II

Practices

4

The failure of free society

Negro property is certainly the most troublesome in the world.
John Berkley Grimball[1]

All concur that free society is a failure

George Fitzhugh was a Virginian journalist, lawyer, political commentator and amateur sociologist. He was also no friend of America's burgeoning industrial capitalism. In an 1854 study, Fitzhugh took on 'The failure[s] of free society' as he sought to construct an alternative *Sociology for the south*.[2] At about the same time that Karl Marx was uncovering the laws of capitalism in the British Museum, Fitzhugh was at work in Richmond, Virginia, making some intriguingly similar comments about the nature of American industrial capitalism. As with Marx, Fitzhugh developed a critique of the underlying assumptions of political economy. And indeed, Fitzhugh's critique, both in *Sociology of the south* and in his later work, *Cannibals all!* (1857), seems to echo much of the subsequent Marxist and radical analyses of capitalism and of private property.[3]

In *Cannibals all!*, he spoke of capitalism as a form of gambling and something that degraded the dignity of labour.[4] He referenced Adam Smith, and dismissed him as a partisan propagandist and a superstructural product of capitalist Britain.[5] Both of Fitzhugh's books seem to prefigure drain theory, postcolonial theory, dependency theory and world-systems analysis in his descriptions of the uneven development of global capitalism. So-called free trade masks the inequality that exists at a global scale: 'Free trade, when the American gives a bottle of whiskey to the Indian for valuable furs, or the Englishman exchanges with the African blue beads for diamonds, gold and slaves, is a fair specimen of all free trade when unequals meet ... Thus is Ireland robbed of her very life's blood, and thus do our Northern States rob the Southern'.[6] Touching on the issue of monoculture at the global capitalist periphery, Fitzhugh said that '[w]e are very sure that the wit of man can devise no means so effectual to impoverish a country as exclusive agriculture'.[7] With words familiar to postcolonial theorists, Fitzhugh says that '[p]olitical independence is not worth a fig without commercial independence'.[8] Fitzhugh's conception of the American south's dependent place in the world order comes strikingly close to postcolonial theory: 'Free trade doctrines, not slavery, have made the South agricultural and dependent, given her a sparse and ignorant population, ruined her cities, and expelled her people.'[9]

Fitzhugh demonstrated a certain critical awareness of Ricardian theories of comparative advantage,[10] and saw how wealth had a tendency to become globally centralised.[11] This centralised wealth leads, in turn, he argued, to a centralised and homogenised culture.[12] He also suggested that free trade leads to ecological destruction and soil depletion.[13] Fitzhugh developed a critique of capitalist ideology, in which selfishness masquerades as morality.[14] He even had a conception of the internalisation of this hegemonic ideology in capitalist society. Political economy serves to inculcate a privatised 'separate, individual action' and is 'calculated to prevent that association of labor without which nothing great can be achieved; for man isolated and individualized is the most helpless of animals'. And Fitzhugh saw this atomisation as being almost a repudiation of the most basic instincts of humanity.[15] As with his communist contemporary in the British Museum, Fitzhugh had little time for the false liberty of capitalist freedom: 'A liberty, we should infer from the descriptions we can get of it, very much like that of domestic animals that have gone wild'.[16] He elsewhere said that labourers in industrial society 'have not a single right or a single liberty, unless it be the right or liberty to die',[17] presaging the Marxist saw that the only freedom under capitalism is the 'freedom to starve'.[18] And in *Cannibals all!* he pointed out the large gap between the theory and

The failure of free society 161

praxis of British liberalism (as it existed prior to the Reform Act of 1867), claiming to promote freedom but simultaneously denying it to the proletarian mob:

> It is a favorite political maxim of Englishmen, that taxation and representation should go hand in hand; and that none shall be taxed without their own consent. Yet in Great Britain, the working men, who pay every cent of tax, are not represented at all, have no vote in elections, and are taxed without and against their own consent; whilst the capitalist class ... pay no taxes [and] are the mere conduits, that pass them from the laborers to the government.

With an almost Marxist accent, Fitzhugh denounced '[t]his vampire capitalist class', a parasitical blight on human nature.[19]

Capitalism, according to Fitzhugh, promises wealth but in actual fact promotes misery and social strife. Unemployment is an essential feature of this society, since the supply of labour always outstrips demand for labourers.[20] Capitalism is an anti-social war of the rich elite against the poor mob, and '[w]hat can such a war result in but the oppression and ultimate extermination of the weak?'[21]

With a hint of Thatcher (or maybe even Karl Polanyi), Fitzhugh observed how society itself ceases to exist under the onslaught of industrial capitalism (though for Polanyi that destruction of the social contract was not the positive result that it was for Thatcher).[22] The 'society' of industrial capitalism offers up a miserable existence:

> The free laborer rarely has a house and home of his own; he is insecure of employment; sickness may overtake him at any time and deprive him of the means of support; old age is certain to overtake him, if he lives, and generally finds him without the means of subsistence; his family is probably increasing in numbers, and is helpless and burdensome to him. In all this there is little to incite to virtue, much to tempt to crime, nothing to afford happiness, but quite enough to inflict misery. Man must be more than human, to acquire a pure and a high morality under such circumstances.

Both workers and capitalists in this 'society', he says, are 'blunted and debased by the continual war of competition'.[23] The misery of industrial capitalism seems inescapable: '[w]e do not know whether free laborers ever sleep. They are fools to do so; for, whilst they sleep, the wily and watchful capitalist is devising means to ensnare and exploitate [sic] them.'[24]

Fitzhugh, like Marx, adopted a labour theory of value and praised workers rather than denouncing them as a mob.[25] The working class is 'the class that alone produces all wealth, private and public' and, in a deft turn of phrase, 'speeds the car of human progress only to be crushed under its wheels'.[26] And because of this conception of value, 'where a country has gained a millionaire, it has by the same process gained a thousand pauper laborers'.[27] His polemical claim was that '[t]he normal state of free society is a state of famine'.[28] Fitzhugh said that on top of the exploitation, misery and overworking of capitalist 'free' society, 'far the worst feature of modern civilization' is the manner in which industrial capitalism cheats workers and channels their earnings into the funding of 'the vulgar pomp and pageantry of the ignorant millionaires'. He called this 'the tinsel glare and glitter of free society'.[29]

Capitalism is also to be feared for its adverse effects on the gender order. Defining women as inherently delicate, Fitzhugh claimed that '[w]oman fares worst when thrown into this warfare of competition',[30] recalling Engels' views in *Conditions of the working class in England* that capitalism is 'an insane state of things' that 'emasculates the man and takes from the woman all womanliness'.[31]

Also, resembling Marx's discussion of indigent Irish workers 'thrown like refuse into garrets, holes, cellars and corners, in the worst back slums',[32] Fitzhugh traced how the gendered, destructive forces of capitalism follow male and female workers at home as well as at the factory. The industrial proletariat 'work fourteen hours a day, cooped up in close rooms, with foul air, foul water, and insufficient and filthy food, and often sleep at night crowded in cellars or in garrets, without regard to sex'.[33] Even calling to mind the more humanistic focus of Marx's early writings, Fitzhugh suggested that owning capitalist property makes one love fellow humans less.[34]

There are a number of other similarities between Marx and Fitzhugh. Like Marx, Fitzhugh saw capitalism emerging out of the interstices of feudalism and he also had much to say about the contradictions of capitalism.[35] The development of a sophisticated division of labour under modern industrial capitalism had been in equal parts a blessing and a curse.[36] Fitzhugh held to an almost

Marxian determinism when it came to understanding the workings of capitalism. Free society has an inherently exploitative nature that is impossible to escape.[37] He came close to advancing a theory of commodity fetishism and reification, identifying the role of advertising in generating demand for capitalist commodities.[38] The miseries engendered under industrial capitalism make it an essentially evil system: 'None but Lucifer would have made such a world.'[39] Industrial capitalism is not divine, it is diabolical.

But where Marx could be (in)famously vague about what the post-capitalist future would look and feel like, Fitzhugh had a definite (and very propertied) alternative at hand.

The slave imaginary

Edmund Burke imagined British harmony with and through a parallel imagination of French chaos. Marx viewed Ireland's feudal, pre-private-property conditions from the vantage of point of hyper-capitalist Britain, and in so doing sharpened his sense of capitalist dynamism. Fitzhugh also saw the world, and saw private property, through conveniently opposing binaries. In contrast to the satanic mills of the industrialised north, Fitzhugh constructed a vision of a Godly southern society: 'God made no such world!' as industrial capitalism. Rather, 'He instituted slavery from the first, as he instituted marriage and parental authority'.[40] And just as a benevolent father rules over a contented family, so a slave is contented within a social world that mirrors that family; the privately owned slave as the obedient child, the white master the father.

> He [the slave] has a master to watch over and take care of him. If he be sick, that master will provide for him. If his family be sick, his master and mistress sympathise with his affliction, and procure medical aid for the sick. And when he comes to die, he feels that his family will be provided for. He does all the labor of life; his master bears all its corroding cares and anxieties. Here, again, we see harmonious relations, consistent with the wisdom and mercy of God. We see an equal and even-handed justice meted out to all alike, and we see life itself no longer a terrestrial purgatory; but a season of joy and sorrow to the rich and the poor.[41]

The American south, according to Fitzhugh, was a harmonious slavocracy, built on the foundation of humans-as-property. The industrialised and capitalist north paled in comparison to this idyll.[42] Fitzhugh depicted slavery as being, in every way, a more beneficent social order. Slavery is more efficient than 'free' wage labour. Slavery is kinder.[43] For Fitzhugh, slaves benefit from slavery. In fact, he attested, slaves 'own' their masters, in the sense that masters owe care and security to their slaves in a kind of feudal relation superior to the mob society of the American north.[44] Slavery is an organic social order, 'natural and universal' and in line with 'the ways of God'.[45] Race, similarly, is a natural hierarchy for Fitzhugh.[46] In this he went far beyond Locke or Marx, who always recognised the artificiality of private property, or Burke, who remained agnostic on this point.

Fitzhugh wanted Americans to uncritically accept slavery, presenting it as both natural and the system ordained by God.[47] The owning of slaves as private property was a perfect social order that could not be improved upon, whereas northern free society was 'a violation of the laws of Nature and the revealed will of God'.[48] And the supposed freedom that set off the north from the south was, in fact, 'an empty and delusive mockery' because, under capitalism, overburdened workers are never free from their social worries. Conversely, Fitzhugh wanted his readers to believe that Black slaves in the south were actually more free than white wage labourers in the north, since they allegedly had so many of their material needs taken care of by their owners. (He bizarrely claimed that the only one *not free* in the south was the slave owner, since he was never freed from the responsibilities of his plantation).[49] Fitzhugh favourably compared this imaginary ideal of slavery with the plight of propertyless men in the north, claiming that the latter are 'in a worse condition than slaves' in the south.[50] In contrast to the misery of northern workers, Fitzhugh asserted that '[t]he negro slaves of the South are the happiest and, in some sense, the freest people in the world'. Superannuated slaves and the children of slaves both enjoy a comfortable existence,[51] slave women do not have to work hard and, 'protected from the despotism of their husbands by their masters', do not have to fear domestic violence. Adult male slaves enjoy a relatively short, nine-hour, work day, with ostensibly sufficient time left over for recreation and rest.[52] No such relaxation exists in the north.

Fitzhugh described slavery as an effective system of mass education and moral inculcation, separating out the ignorant masses from each other and instead bringing them into a 'daily intercourse with the well-informed'. Panopticon-like, slaves were subject 'to the constant control and supervision of their superiors'. Slavery was simultaneously pedagogic and 'the best and most efficient police system'.[53] It was, in fact, these functions that made slaves so happy.[54] Showing how radically dissimilar he felt both societies were, Fitzhugh contrasted 'the proud humility of the Southerner' with 'the exacting and supercilious arrogance of the Northerner'.[55] Fitzhugh concluded *Sociology of the south* by stating that while free society 'is afflicted with disease', slave society is 'healthy'.[56]

Summing up the differences between free and slave societies, Fitzhugh said that northern industrialism represented 'a system of antagonism and war' whereas the slaveocracy was a world 'of peace and fraternity'.[57] Against the insecurity of free labour and the terrifying mobs of the north, there existed the social harmony of slavery.[58] Slavery brought together 'the interests of rich and poor, master and slave, and begets domestic affection on the one side, and loyalty and respect on the other'.[59] It was, he argued, a society devoid of class antagonisms.[60] Fitzhugh imagined slavery – a regime in which a select few are able to possess people as private property – as an altogether more moral, more harmonious and more stable regime than one in which all property is alienable but a taboo is placed on the ownership of men: 'free' men denied the security of slavery are condemned to a miserable and atomised existence.

Thus Fitzhugh had a ready-made social model at hand to both replace 'free' industrial capitalism and answer the anti-capitalist criticisms of radicals, socialists and communists. Indeed, he argued that 'socialism is the new fashionable name of slavery'.[61] Slavery provided the harmonious social order that socialists say they desire. Slavery did away with free competition, afforded 'protection and support at all times to the laboring class', and instituted 'a qualified community of property'.[62] Slavery avoided the problem of urban mobs.

A pastoral of racial harmony

Fitzhugh's work always lingered between being a serious analysis of American society and merely a crass propaganda; the one full-length study of his life and work pushes firmly for the latter view.[63] Fitting with his status as a propagandist, Fitzhugh switches, when it suits him, from sympathy with the plight of northern workers to disdaining them as a vile and dangerous mob. In a programmatic essay in 1857, Fitzhugh announced his intention of developing a movement for 'Southern thought', though he clearly saw this as, essentially, pro-slavery agitprop to justify and defend slavery as 'natural, normal and necessitous'.[64] He spoke of *Sociology for the south* as being part of an ideological attack against the north,[65] and it is worth observing that he only visited the north for the first time in 1855, *after* writing his first rhetorical assault on the entire region and its political economy.[66]

Fitzhugh's depictions of the evils of capitalism do have obvious points of comparison with those of Marx; he even lamented how much suspicion and ignorance there was between socialists and slave owners.[67] Fitzhugh's dalliances with radicalism caused southern reviewers to 'squirm',[68] despite his assurances that this was a marriage of convenience, and his 'socialism' has all the appearance of a strategically adopted stance, one that allowed him to shock his readers and satirise the north. Fitzhugh argued that the absence of the 'defects' of the free north in the slave-owning south meant that his compatriots are not 'troubled' by 'strikes, trade unions, phalasteries, communistic establishments, Mormonism, and the thousand other isms that deface and deform free society';[69] not troubled by all the mobs of the north. Fitzhugh clearly was not advocating socialism in any kind of good faith. Rather, he advocated slavery as a means of abrogating socialism and thus protecting property ownership.[70] Indeed at the very outset of *Sociology of the south*, Fitzhugh dedicated the work 'To the people of the south', saying that few people are aware 'of the blessings they enjoy, or of the evils from which they are exempt'. By 'evils' he meant the social ills of northern free society: 'the revolutionary tumults, uproar, mendacity and crime of free society … Its crimes, its revolutions, its sufferings and its beggary.'[71] Grace Elizabeth Hale has discussed how southern whites, from the era of Jim Crow onwards, constructed an imaginary vision of their recent past, which served to celebrate 'a plantation pastoral of racial harmony and a noble war of principle and valor, while making Reconstruction the fall that made segregation the only possible future'. What Fitzhugh's work shows is how much this constructed romance of the south was already in full bloom before Appomattox, as propagandists like Fitzhugh drafted what du Bois called 'the fairy tale of a beautiful Southern slave civilization'.[72] And they constructed that image in direct opposition to images of northern mobs.

Arguments made in bad faith are a common currency in ultraconservatism; across his two books, Fitzhugh slowly revealed that his ostensibly socialist posturing and condemnation of capitalism was a strategic ruse, a means of attacking the excesses of one particular form of capitalism so as to not only defend slavery but also boost it as an alternative to wage labour and free-market capitalism. In *Cannibals all!* – relatively, the more serious work, notwithstanding its aggressive title – Fitzhugh was openly anti-socialist, delineating his fears that radical social change necessarily also meant the annihilation of society's 'most essential institutions – religion, family ties, property, and the restraints of justice'.[73] He was openly alarmed at the rise of socialism in the north.[74] In his less sarcastic moments he revealed himself as a deeply and rigidly conservative thinker, dedicated to tradition and resistant to any political innovations.[75] His fears of capitalism always had a conservative tinge to them. Like many reactionary thinkers before and since, Burke not least among them, Fitzhugh was alarmed by the ways that capitalism could undermine social stability and existing social practices and hierarchies.[76]

For Fitzhugh, slavery was the fulfilment of the Aristotelian ideal that man is a social animal.[77] His slave imaginary – with its Burkean emphasis on property, order, harmony, stability – was of a piece with a larger social vision. Society is like a family;[78] slaves are lower down this hierarchy, like children, and masters have duties to these children, like parental authorities. Slaves could not be free because they were incapable, in Fitzhugh's imagination, of the requisite maturity and self-control.[79] Black people are not free because, for Fitzhugh, they cannot be free. Both God and nature have intended Africans to be slaves, which is to say: to be private property.[80]

Race was clearly central to his social vision, yet he also went beyond this. To properly govern a society it was necessary to control it first.[81] Slavery is thus not an aberration or only applicable to specific ethnic or racial groups. Rather, it is a system of beneficial control that echoes the systems of control that Fitzhugh believed should exist in varying scales across all human society. Against the idea that modern societies are freer, Fitzhugh observed that complex societies require complex systems of control.[82] Slave owners' control over their slaves performs the same social function as fathers' control of their wives and children.[83] This was a common claim about Atlantic slavery; '[i]n the southern colonies, the slaveholders stressed their paternalist responsibilities and portrayed the plantation as a large family within whose protective embrace child-like negroes received shelter and sustenance'.[84] The flipside of such arguments was the implicit claim that African Americans were essentially children who do not want freedom. As an 1835 editorial in the apologist *Southern Rose* magazine stated, 'it is not true that African slaves pine for "free breath"; they are the most careless, light-hearted creatures in the world'; slaves 'enjoy the service they render'.[85]

Imagining the south as not just a consensual racial hierarchy, but a happy family too, served to normalise 'the peculiar institution', allowing slavery to be associated with the biological normativity of the heterosexual family (a normalising move that Burke also made). Fitzhugh's fantasy of slavery was a fantasy of white male authority; primarily the owner's authority over slaves but also the father's rule over his wife and children. Thus, his imaginary depictions of the south extended to gender relations, which he depicted as being equally harmonious and friction-free. The obedient wives of the south were contrasted with the frequency of 'wife-murder' in the north, where a 'low, sordid, worldly view of the marriage tie' reigns; the capitalist north had capitalist marriage, in which women were bought and sold. Incongruously, and belying his ostensibly leftist sympathies, Fitzhugh named socialists as a major source of this capitalist problem.[86] He condemned radical abolitionists for, in his mind, attacking both marriage and all forms of private property ownership alongside their attacks on slavery.[87] In a rough-hewn base–superstructure model, the chaos of free society is reflected in the chaotic thinking of 'free' men: 'Where there is no slavery, the minds of men are unsettled on all subjects, and there is, emphatically, faith and conviction about nothing.' This is the reason, Fitzhugh said, that most abolitionists are 'infidels', atheists. The danger with social reformers, he believed, was that 'they propose wholly to disregard the natural relations of mankind, and profanely to build up states, like Fourierite Phalansteries, or Mormon and Oneida villages, where religion shall be banished, and in which property, wife and children shall be held somewhat in common'.[88] The problem with the north is that it was dominated by abolitionist mobs who revel in chaos.

For Fitzhugh, the abolition of slavery would lead inexorably to abolition of 'the relations of husband and wife, parent and child, [and] the institution of private property of all kinds'. In his political imagination, the racial hierarchy was so bound up with the gender hierarchy, the class hierarchy and the property order that the world, Fitzhugh says, 'will have to choose between Free Love and Slavery'.[89] Making more explicit what Burke only implied, Fitzhugh said that all were natural hierarchies and demolishing one would demolish the rest.

Slavery, violence and private property

It should go without saying that Fitzhugh, as a 'propagandist of the old South', presented a highly skewed vision of slave realities. Rather than any pseudo-familial bonds, slaves were, for their owners, 'just like any other piece of property that produces offspring, crops, or other goods'.[90] Given their high cost, planters had a vested interest in extracting as much as labour as possible from slaves, to quickly recoup their investment.[91] A harmonious slaveocracy, in which slaves would be peaceably content with their status as property, is an oxymoron. As W.E.B. du Bois said of slavery, from the vantage point of 1909:

it was scarce possible to overrate the price of repression. True, in these latter days men and women of the South, and honest ones, too, have striven feverishly to paint Negro slavery in bright alluring colors. They have told of childlike devotion, faithful service and light-hearted irresponsibility, in the fine old aristocracy of the plantation. Much they have said is true. But when all is said and granted, the awful fact remains congealed in law and indisputable record that American slavery was the foulest and filthiest blot on nineteenth-century civilization.[92]

Violence was essential to slavery's private ownership of human beings; as many as 10 per cent of potential slaves died in the process of capture in Africa, and another quarter in marches to the coast. Of the estimated 12.5 million transported via the 'Middle Passage', 2 million died at sea, from sickness, violence and malnutrition.[93] And this violence continued to define chattel slavery at the other end of the Middle Passage. For all of Fitzhugh's fanciful depictions, slave owners were keenly aware that 'the slavery regime could survive only with the most repressive and bestial force imaginable'. Legislation existed in most southern states to allow slave owners to punish their chattel 'with impunity'. Such laws also gave exacting detail about the instruments that could be used to torture slaves.[94] Short of killing slaves, which was technically illegal but not consistently punished, slave owners 'enjoyed tremendous autonomy to extract obedience from the men, women, and children' they owned as private property.[95]

It is not surprising then that 'the whip was the most common instrument of punishment – indeed, it was the emblem of the master's authority'. In the 1834 case *State v. Will* in North Carolina, the presiding judge summarised what he saw as the ideal power dynamics of slavery: 'Unconditional submission is the general duty of the slave; unlimited power is, in general, the legal right of the master.' One South Carolina judge confessed in 1847 that many slaveholders 'deserved no other name than fiends' because of the ways they delighted in the torture of their private property.[96] Fitzhugh alluded to such violence when he said that 'not a single negro was ever reclaimed from his savage state till he was caught, tied, tamed, and domesticated like the wild ox or the wild horse'.[97] A wild horse, of course, is 'broken' as part of domestication. Such bestialisation was inherent to this system of private property; slaves were sold at 'marts', the buyers inspecting them as they would a horse.[98] The US Department of Agriculture, founded by Lincoln in 1860, devised a rating system for meat that is still in use today, which employed the classifications used by slave-traders, rating humans (or beef) as, for example, 'prime', 'lean' or 'choice'.[99] The desire to have such full authority over property also extended to naming practices: 'Owners frequently renamed their slaves, forbidding the use of African names or [B]lack family names'.[100]

Slaves generally lived in, at best, poor-quality, 'cramped one-room buildings'. The use of lofts, barns and storage rooms as housing was not uncommon.[101] In such situations, stable family life would have been impossible; in any case slave families were regularly broken up. 'A planter might decide to sell a mother or her children to pay off a debt or to get rid of an unruly slave.' As with any other form of private property, slaves 'were devised in wills, wagered at horse races, and awarded in lawsuits. Bonded families were disbanded when the heirs of an estate decided not to continue the patriarch's business.'[102] A 1809 court ruling in South Carolina decreed that female slaves had no legal claims on their children, because 'the young of slaves ... stand on the same footing as other animals'.[103] This threat to sell off family members was regularly used to coerce and control slaves.[104]

A special terminology was invented to not only describe the emotions of slaves, but also erase the visibility of Black grief or trauma. 'When confronted with enslaved women's emotional responses to losing or being separated from their children, white southerners construed their grief as "the sulks," or even a form of madness – "vices," flaws, or pathological conditions – that made such women less valuable and less desirable in the slave market.'[105] On average, slave children had lower birth weights than white children and, as of 1850, the infant mortality rate among slaves was twice that of whites, with fewer than two out of three Black children surviving to age 10.[106] Female slaves were commonly used as wet-nurses, with the result that '[e]nslaved mothers were generally deprived of adequate food and nutrients to support and sustain their own health, much less that of two or three babies'.[107]

Fitzhugh's claims of domestic bliss obscured not just this abuse of children, but also the sexual violence endemic to the south, a place of 'social and sexual disorder ... of coerced production and reproduction, racial and sexual exploitation, and physical and psychological violence'.[108] The routine rape of slave women was an inherent part of slavery; after the banning of the importing of slaves in 1808, this was one of the primary methods through which new slave property could be generated.[109] The use of Black women in brothels, an outgrowth of the sexual abuse of female slaves, was a common practice; New Orleans, 'the largest slave market in the south', had 'plenty of brothels'. Often operated by white women, such 'disgusting affair[s]', as the *Daily Picayune* termed them in 1847, hardly accorded with Fitzhugh's morally upstanding slave-pastoral.[110] Likewise, the active involvement of white women in the slave trade and their commonplace presence as bidders at auction blocks confound Fitzhugh's patriarchal platitudes.[111]

The idea of a harmonious south devoid of class-based strife also ignored the class divisions unequivocally existent within white southern society. 'Poor whites', those who owned neither land nor slaves, comprised at least a third, possibly as many as a half, of Dixie's population in the immediate antebellum decades. This poor white mob 'had long posed a threat to the maintenance of the peculiar institution' and on the eve of secession were overtly resentful of domineering slaveholders. Both land prices and the Specie Circular Act of 1836, which mandated that all governmental land purchases be transacted with silver or gold, made it virtually impossible for this class to enter the ranks of the propertied. Likewise, the high prices of slaves – depending on how we calculate the cost of a slave (whether the purchase price itself, or the collateral needed to receive credit to make the purchase), the price of a slave adjusted for inflation to 2017 dollars was between $20,000 and $130,000 – also shut off this avenue of southern social mobility; only about one-third of southern whites owned slaves. Unemployment and underemployment among the other two-thirds were endemic, as was the attendant poverty engendered. Poor whites eked out an existence through hunting and fishing or by plundering plantations (for which they occasionally recruited slaves). Andrew Johnson, a product of a poor white background in the south, remembered being regularly beaten as a child by local, wealthy, slave owners. He would later return the compliment by saying that before 1860 the southern states were ruled over by 'an illegitimate, swaggering, bastard, scrub aristocracy, who assumed to know a great deal, but who, when the flimsy veil of pretension was torn off from it, was shown to possess neither talents, information, nor a foundation on which you can rear a superstructure that would be useful'.[112] A steady emigration occurred in the years before the Civil War, as poor whites moved west, often choosing to settle in states where slavery was illegal. 'However, moving an entire family was often unrealistic for the poorest whites.'[113] As a recent study of these socially dangerous 'masterless men' observed, to admit that 'the South had a very sizable percentage of its own poor – consistently plagued by unemployment, underemployment, and nonlivable wages' would have been tantamount to an abandonment of 'the rosy ideal of the humanitarian, caretaking paternalist' south;[114] the kind of social imaginary boosted by Fitzhugh.

The watchword of Frenchmen when they turn out to murder each other

Throughout his discussion of slavery and abolitionism, Fitzhugh continually conflates the dangers of abolition with a number of other 'dangers'. He spoke of how free society was bedevilled by agitators and by 'the unnatural remedies of woman's rights, limited marriages, voluntary divorces, and free love, as proposed by the abolitionists'.[115] Fitzhugh stated that all who follow current affairs in America will have noticed that:

> every abolitionist is either an agrarian [i.e. a supporter of land redistribution], a socialist, an infidel, an anti-renter, or in some way is trying to upset other institutions of society, as well as slavery at the South. The same reasoning that makes him an abolitionist soon carries him further, for he finds slavery in some form so interwoven with the whole frame-work of society, that he invariably ends by proposing to destroy the whole edifice and building another on entirely new principles.[116]

Like Burke and Locke before him, Fitzhugh was disturbed by visions of masterless men and Jacobin-like agitators. Indeed, Fitzhugh's descriptions followed a Burkean template. In his imagination, abolition threatened all property-relations, not just those of slaveholders.[117] That abolition of this one specific form of property (slaves) was really just a veiled attempt to abolish all private property was already being claimed in the later eighteenth century.[118] And since, in the conservative imagination, stability requires property and property requires stability, the abolition of slavery (itself a form of private ownership) would thus lead, in Fitzhugh's imagination, to the abolition of all private property as well as the destruction of stable gender roles (recalling Burke's fear of the Revolutionary harpies).[119] As Scott Henkel exclaimed in his analysis of *Cannibals all!* 'Fitzhugh's book ... reads like a threat to anyone who would challenge the relations between masters and slaves: without such a hierarchy, our communities would degenerate to the point where people would eat one another'.[120] The only two choices, according to Fitzhugh, are slavery or the abolitionist mob.

Fitzhugh claimed that marriage itself had broken down in the northern free states; there is an 'intimate connexion and dependence, of slavery, marriage and religion'. If slavery goes, so too will religion. In his frank formulation, he observed that '[m]arriage is too much like slavery not to be involved in its fate'. Abolitionists and socialists seek the same thing, 'to usher in the new golden age, of free love and free lands, of free women and free negroes, of free children and free men'.[121] The success of abolitionism would mean the subversion of 'all religion, all government, all order'.[122] He claimed that marriage was treated, north of the Ohio River, like a form of casual horse-trading. He felt that marriages were under attack in the north, alongside the attack on slavery, and claimed that marriages in northern states are 'contracted with as little formality as jumping over a broom'. The 'conservative South' was the indispensable bulwark, shielding both the racial and the gender order.[123] Fitzhugh was similarly aghast at the horrors of early feminism in the free states.[124] Women who demand their rights are, he said, 'coarse and masculine' and rightfully despised by men.[125] And, as always, where Fitzhugh saw the north degrading, the south provided the more healthful alternative: 'Woman *there* [the north] is in a false position. Be she white, or be she black, she is treated with kindness and humanity in the slave-holding South'.[126]

That the rise of radical abolitionism in the north had incited an aggressive southern defence of slavery is a well-known point among American historians, a phenomenon that was intensified by the Haitian revolution of the 1790s, the failed rebellions of Denmark Vesey in 1822 and of Nat Turner a decade later, and the abolition of slavery in the British Empire in 1832.[127] (As a native of Richmond, Virginia, Fitzhugh lived only seventy miles from Southampton County, where the Nat Turner slave rebellion took place between 21 and 23 August 1831, after which Turner was on the run for nine-and-a-half weeks. It is highly likely that this awareness of slave revolts formed some of the background for attitudes imbibed by Fitzhugh.)[128] Fitzhugh flipped mainstream abolitionist ideas about property-owning independence being the hallmark of free northern society by instead presenting slavery as the ideal means of preserving property and preserving the social order. The zealous obstinacy of his arguments is almost certainly a direct reaction to the growing strength of abolitionism in the 1850s.

Fitzhugh's sole biographer has foregrounded the huge contradictions that resulted; he was a defender of private property but also couched his defence of slavery in an attack on the evils of the unfettered use of private property.[129] Like many conservatives he was anxious about the fissiparous effects of capitalism and the instability of a world in which everything can be sold and all values can be called into question, yet remained obstinately unwilling to fully oppose that capitalism and was even more animated by the 'evils' of socialism. Fitzhugh believed that correct kinds of property ownership were necessary for social harmony and that the encroachment of northern-style capitalism was threatening this in the south.

As he developed his argument, he became more Burkean than Marxian: 'Philosophy will blow up any government that is founded on it. Religion, on the other hand, will sustain the governments that rest upon it.'[130] Greater democracy had created the need for conservative counter-forces: 'Universal suffrage [by which he means universal male suffrage] has given to the progressive element in society, the poor, the young, and the enterprising, so much power, that this conservative balance would not be amiss'.[131] And like

Burke, Fitzhugh's ideal society had a natural ruling class, defined by their property (whether in land or slaves, ideally both) and by their ability to wield power in socially positive ways.[132] And in perhaps his most full-throated defence of inequality, Fitzhugh said that '[m]en are not "born entitled to equal rights!" It would be far nearer the truth to say, "that some were born with saddles on their backs, and others booted and spurred to ride them" – and the riding does them good.' This echoed the anti-mob views of the South Carolina senator James Hammond, who used his infamous 'mud-sill' speech in 1858 to contend that, in all social systems, 'there must be a class to do the mean duties, to perform the drudgeries of life'.[133] John Randolph (1773–1833), a scion of one of Virginia's prestigious first families, is said to have proudly declared 'I am an aristocrat. I love liberty; I hate equality.'[134] In a like vein, in 1848 John C. Calhoun had attacked the Jeffersonian dictum that 'all men are born free and equal', calling it 'the most false and dangerous of all political error[s]'. Such statements became increasingly common in the south in the 1850s.[135] Even female planters such as Keziah Brevard, who did not have the right to vote herself, prayed that 'some thing be done to check this mobocracy ... Democracy has brought the South I *fear* into a *sad, sad* state'.[136] Such attempts to legitimate inequality were, of course, attempts to legitimate inequality in property ownership and to condemn the poor as a vile mob.

Fitzhugh prided himself on his supposed aristocratic lineage, claiming descent from the settler and lawyer William Fitzhugh (1651–1701), who had supported Governor Berkeley during Bacon's Rebellion of 1676–7. He favoured reintroducing primogeniture and entail, so as to ensure social stability in the south. 'An aristocracy founded upon estates regularly transmitted for generations within a family' would be the backbone of Fitzhugh's ideal and harmonious social order, echoing Burke's concept of prescription.[137] In his rigidly hierarchical dream-world, Fitzhugh saw it as a positive good that only a select few would own property, but also that many can and should be sold *as* property.[138]

In opposition to the free use of property under liberal capitalism, Fitzhugh described his ideal society as one in which property is held within families, cannot be alienated and cannot be deployed freely as its owner wishes. Channeling Burkean prescription, he said that '[p]roperty is too old and well-tried an institution, too much interwoven with the feelings, interests and affections of man, to be shaken by the speculations of philosophers'. As an arch conservative, he believed that land should only be distributed via primogeniture, never through any novel new ideas like the Free Soil Movement or the Homestead Act, both of which sought to parcel out land to aspirant white Americans.[139]

Lockean slavery

George Fitzhugh's literary career was brief; he was well into his forties before he published. Active for just over a decade, he wrote two books and a small amount of journalism (with much of the journalism acting as early drafts for the monographs).[140] After slavery, he lost his motivation to write, as well as a readership directly receptive to pro-slavery missives.[141] He died in poverty and obscurity in Texas in 1881, having been taken in by his daughter.[142]

And yet his work provides an emblematic example of pro-slavery thinking in the immediate antebellum years as well as a case study in ultra-conservatism. Couched in binary oppositions, Fitzhugh's contrasting of the perceived evils of the north with the unassuming bucolic simplicity of the south was standard pro-slavery fare, echoing the notions put forward by the likes of John C. Calhoun, senator, vice-president and anti-abolition tub-thumper. On the other hand, Fitzhugh himself was unusual among pro-slavery writers in his willingness to engage with abolitionist thought; 'he corresponded with antislavery periodicals', even travelled to New Haven in Connecticut to debate with the abolitionist and early feminist Wendell Phillips, and kept up to date with the journalism of both Horace Greeley and William Lloyd Garrison.[143] He was quoted by Lincoln – whose idea of a 'House Divided' may have come via Fitzhugh – and was read widely in the north.[144] During an eight-month lecture tour of North America Charles Mackay of the *Illustrated London News* described him as the 'ablest and most conscientious' of the pro-slavery thinkers. Mackay's *Life and liberty in America* (1859) subsequently devoted almost a whole chapter to a discussion of him.[145] And while *Sociology for the south* was reviewed by no northern journals and only a few foreign ones, it received a 'friendly response' in the south, something that encouraged Fitzhugh.[146] After reading *Cannibals all!*, James D.B. De Bow wrote in his eponymous *De Bow's Review*, a leading pro-slavery publication and 'the principal journal of the commercial South',[147] that Fitzhugh was 'one of the boldest and most daring thinkers of the age. He grapples with things as they are in reality.'[148]

In truth, though, Fitzhugh's claims about the south escaping the evils of capitalism were, at best, well-crafted propaganda, and at worst an American Victorian trolling *avant la lettre*. His binary opposition of chaotic capitalist north *versus* harmonious slave-owning south served to obscure an important fact: slavery was not an aberration in the history of capitalism and private property, but an essentially capitalist project and operated according to the rules of private property already discussed in this book; Fitzhugh deployed Burkean conceptions of prescription and primogeniture in his analysis of how to create a stable social order and presented connections between stable families and stability in property that would probably have satisfied Burke.[149]

Slavery 'combined the horrors of an archaic labor system with the rapacious efficiencies of capitalism'.[150] And many of the defining traits of a capitalist economic order – ever-increasing productivity, technological advancement, rational accounting, large-scale interstate trade (in both slaves and cotton), constant geographic expansion due to constant resource depletion – were all a part of slavery.[151] The development of slavery in the United States, not least the transport and sale by mortgage of slaves, was closely connected to the development of shipbuilding, insurance and banking.[152] The industrial textile mills of places like Manchester – which Marx and Engels saw as *the* most capitalist places on Earth – could not have existed without the raw cotton mass-grown by slaves in the Deep South.[153] Systems of labour management on plantations resembled Taylorist time-and-motion studies, decades before Frederick Taylor ostensibly coined this technique.[154] Slavery parallelled the livestock breeding industry and '[a]uction catalogues, similar to contemporary ones, listed the merchandise (in this case, human property) with detailed descriptions of physical attributes, skills, and sometimes, notes about personalities'.[155] Slavery also involved what

Daina Ramey Berry calls 'postmortem commodification', the selling of slaves' corpses, the emerging anatomists of medical schools across the United States, south and north, being the main buyers.[156] The cruelties of slavery existed *because of* its capitalist nature.

The wealth generated by slavery was classically capitalist, with slaves representing 'the nation's largest concentration of private property'.[157] More than the industrialised north, it was the south that fitted better with Marx's vision of capitalism's tendency towards extremes of wealth concentration at one end of society, and inexorable proletarianisation and immiseration at the other.[158] Eric Williams' classic study *Capitalism and slavery* notes that already in the eighteenth century, 100 per cent returns on profits were 'not uncommon' in the Liverpool-based slave trade, sometimes reaching as high as 300 per cent, and 'the average annual profit was over thirty per cent'.[159] Of the small numbers of Americans whose wealth surpassed $100,000 in 1860, two-thirds lived in the south; 'New York at that time had fewer millionaires per capita than Mississippi' and more money was being invested in slaves as a form of private property than in industry and railroads.[160] Slaves amounted to approximately $3 to $4 billion in privately owned assets in 1860 (perhaps more than $130 billion in 2022 values when adjusted for inflation, though the figures are so high that such calculations are effectively meaningless), a bewildering scale that contributed to the arguments that slavery was simply too capitalised, too privatised, to ever be abolished.[161] Slavery was the original 'too big to fail' industry. The Emancipation Proclamation was thus probably the largest single erasure of private property in global history, albeit an erasure of a very peculiar kind of property.[162]

Slaves were 'a speculative investment that had a tendency to increase in value over time, and they provided the capital basis for the southern credit system, stretching across the Atlantic Ocean'. Planters rented out their slaves during lean times, in another example of how these human commodities could be converted into 'liquid capital'.[163] Yet there remained an irresolvable tension here. Slaves – 'this troublesome property'[164] – were bought, sold and mortgaged like commodities, but they remained 'false-commodities ... insofar as human beings are not commodities even if people try to make them so'.¹⁶⁵ Slaves were 'a most unique product – a product that has the ability to emote, express, respond, reject, and liberate'.¹⁶⁶ Confounding one of Marx and Engels' most basic binary categories, slaves were at once labour *and* capital.¹⁶⁷ Slaves exhibited the standard attributes of private property; inheritable, alienable on the open market, a holding vessel for appreciating value. And yet they were a form of private property that could violently rebel against their own commodified situation, in turn damaging other forms of private property; such slave insurrections and their attendant attacks on private property were, indeed, one of the 'direst fears of settlers'.¹⁶⁸ Slaves can (and should) be placed in a history of the capitalist elite's fear of the mob.

In a different but important way, though, slavery made perfect coherent sense within capitalist conceptions of private ownership. Slave plantations were a logical conclusion to the Lockean conception of private property.¹⁶⁹ Slavery was a specific form of capitalist property ownership, but it also grew out of the type of capitalist land ownership that emerged in the vast 'empty' lands of the Americas. The *latifundias* and plantations of the New World were of such a size that they could not be worked by one individual, a point already recognised by Locke. Slavery was one solution to this 'problem' (though admittedly not the only one).¹⁷⁰ As one literary avatar of New World colonisation said of his and his fellow settlers' predicament in Brazil: 'they had all Plantations as well as I, and were straiten'd for nothing so much as Servants'.¹⁷¹ In other words, Robinson Crusoe had all the land he could imagine but lacked the slave labour to cultivate such a gigantic estate. In the Lockean framework, one individual man should only own as much landed property as he himself could work. But what if he owned a peculiar kind of property that in turn could work the land for him? Fitzhugh followed an unwittingly Lockean line of thinking when he wrote in 1862 that '[a]ppropriation of the lands by individual owners begets slavery; and slavery alone begets civilization'.¹⁷² Zach Sell has suggested that when W.E.B. du Bois wrote that '[n]o matter how degraded the factory hand, he is not real estate', he was getting at a truth inherent to slavery, that it was a system of capitalist property ownership simultaneously built on both Black corporeal property and land.¹⁷³ It was not at all a coincidence that as early as 1669 *The*

Fundamental Constitutions of Carolina (1669), which John Locke co-wrote, assigned 'absolute power' over enslaved Africans.[174]

Slaves played a major role in turning 'wilderness' into private property, in two simultaneous acts of privatisation: Africans were made into private property, and their coerced agricultural labour then converted American land into private property. Each process 'fed the other' and it was always presupposed that the 'expropriation of native lands' could not have occurred without 'exploitation of the enslaved'.[175] As with other forms of settler-colonialism, white American sovereignty 'was achieved at the cost of the absolute negation of the right to self-determination of those that were displaced', as well as of those who were enslaved.[176] Between the Louisiana Purchase in 1803 and the 1830s, via various wars on Native Americans in the 1810s, the Federal government acted as an official broker, 'selling public lands brutally stolen from southeastern Native Americans',[177] with the largest share of those lands being converted into plantations worked by slave labour.[178] Slavery was probably the only contemporary agrarian system that could have effected such a rapid privatisation of large, individually owned farms.[179] Thus, as a dense system of property ownership, slavery became *more entrenched* after the Louisiana Territory became available to American settler-colonialism.[180]

In her perspicacious study of the *Colonial lives of property*, Brenna Bhandar investigates how the ontological category 'property owner' in settler-colonies was defined by race and gender. This is of a piece with what Bhandar terms 'property law as a form of colonial domination'.[181] A 'racial regime of ownership' was constructed, in which to be Black was to be property (and thus not eligible for the kinds of property rights Locke accorded to active citizens), while to be white was to be the kind of active, property-owning citizen envisaged by Locke. Colonists in the Carolinas were forbidden from enslaving Native Americans, by temporary laws passed in December 1671 (and written in Locke's handwriting). This was based on the ontological assumption that the Native American 'natural man' could become 'civil man', a citizen, if given time and if not enslaved. Africans, however, were not afforded this privilege; they were placed outside this 'natural man' category, defined as not fully human and not fully male or sovereign; thus they could be enslaved and Locke could legitimise his ownership of shares in the slave-trading Royal African Company.[182] Slaves' very existence violated Lockean standards of sovereign possession – 'standards in which the first thing one owns is oneself' – and as such slaves had to be defined as existing outside civil society, even outside normative humanity.[183] 'The emergence of racial distinctions guaranteed the property rights of masters, while policing the boundary between slaves and liberty.'[184]

Between 1660 and 1710, 'virtually every English colony in the New World enacted laws defining slaves as conveyable property', i.e. property that could be bought, sold and freely transported. Defining slaves in these terms had the effect of cloaking chattel slavery with 'the sanctity of property rights', thus defanging any early abolitionist protests.[185] But it also had the effect of placing slaves outside the categories 'human' or 'citizen'; slaves were privately owned things, not people.[186] They were said to lack the 'rational self-control' necessary to be both property owners and citizens.[187] 'Distasteful as it may seem to modern readers, slave economies functioned through elaborate legal and financial channels, as fully developed and in some ways more fully developed than their counterparts in the free-labor states. In a word, they were systems of property rights.' Such a dense legal system could only work by fully dehumanising slaves, by depicting them as non-humans incapable of owning property.[188] And the dark skin of slaves allowed, in theory, for a clear demarcation between whites (legally capable of property ownership, even if only a minority ever did) and Black Africans, biologically marked as property-that-cannot-own-property.[189] Or as Fitzhugh stated in one of his few post-Civil War pieces: 'Savages always hold lands in common. Were they capable of originating and fully sustaining the institution of private property in lands, they would at once cease to be savages, and become civilized.'[190] Fitzhugh clearly shared the Burkean view that private property and civilisation are one and the same.

One recent study has claimed that slavery offered white men 'easy upward social mobility', the chance to be a secure property owner with their own retinue of unfree workers. Certainly, this understates the difficulties that poor whites faced in acquiring slaves or land; the consolidation of more and more southern land in fewer and fewer hands was a direct function of the propertied Lockean and capitalist logics that underpinned slavery. Nonetheless, the same study gives an accurate depiction of the romantic ideal that was being promised to white settlers:

> Southern slavery democratized the divine right of kings. No matter how poor a plantation owner might seem to a London merchant, on the grounds of his plantation he was the head of a royal family where his word was law. Every man of property was a little king, with the power to order sexual reproduction or summary execution.[191]

This was the propertied idyll – explicitly a utopia for white male slave owners, implicitly a dystopia for their commodified slaves – that Fitzhugh sought to defend, stating in *Cannibals all!* that '[i]n slaveholding countries all freemen should vote and govern, because their interests are conservative. In free states, the government should be in the hands of the landowners, who are also conservative.'[192] But in his apologia, Fitzhugh intentionally ignored the obvious brutalities inherent to slavery. Ultimately, his central argument was that a set of essentially capitalist practices and property-relations were not actually capitalist at all, but instead existed at a complete remove from any kind of profit-seeking or distasteful personal self-interest. This is, of course, a common move on the part of any number of capitalist ideologues; indeed, is there anything more ideologically capitalist than furiously denying you are a capitalist in the first place?

The manufactured connection between Black identity and a presumed incapacity to own property continued long after the 1860s. Across the expansive domains of Atlantic slavery, slaves had looked to property ownership as a means to control their own labour and lives, yet the promise that ex-slaves would enter a property-owning normality were not fulfilled: 'The postwar US South had large expanses of available farmland, but the authors and enforcers of the Jim Crow social order made sure that precious little of it could be owned by blacks'.[193] The (in)famous forty acres and a mule promised to ex-slaves 'melted quickly away' as du Bois later pointed out.[194] And the idea that communists sought to make all women public property, and as such were a threat to the basic civilisational order, remained a recurring allegation in the south well into the twentieth century.[195] The American property regime had acquired a racial essence that it would not easily lose. History in the United States continued to unfold 'at the juncture of racism and real estate'.[196] The next chapter jumps forward eighty years, to continue this history.

Notes

1. Grimball was a South Carolina plantation owner who recorded this observation in his diary in 1832. Quoted in Eugene D. Genovese. *Roll, Jordan, roll: the world the slaves made* (New York, 1972), 18.
2. This may have been the first book in English with the word 'sociology' in the title: Harvey Wish. *George Fitzhugh: propagandist of the old South* (Baton Rouge, LA, 1943), 82. Henry Hughes, a Mississippian, wrote *A treatise on sociology* in 1854, 'another pro-slavery book clad in sociological dress': *Propagandist of the old South*, 40.
3. Three years after *Sociology for the south* (Richmond, VA, 1854), Fitzhugh claimed that '[t]hat little work has met, every where, we believe, at the South, with a favorable reception. No one has denied its theory of Free Society, nor disputed the facts on which that theory rests': *Cannibals all! Or, slaves without masters* (Richmond, VA, 1857), xiii. Harvey Wish places *Cannibals all!* in the context of a post-election paranoia in the south in late 1856, when there were widespread fears of a slave insurrection: *Propagandist of the old South* (1943), 160.
4. *Cannibals all!* (1857), 69, 70. Harvey Wish provocatively points out the similarities between *Cannibals all!* and Thorsten Veblen's *Theory of the leisure class* (1899): *Propagandist of the old South* (1943), 175.
5. *Sociology for the south* (1854), 11–12, 13.
6. *Sociology for the south* (1854), 13–14. Fitzhugh had an especial interest in the Irish Famine of the previous decade, seeing it as at the natural result of the inherent flaws of free capitalist society: *Sociology for the south*, 42–3, 198. References to the Irish and their indigence run through his work. See also his comparisons of the fate of freed slaves in Jamaica with free labourers in Ireland: *Cannibals all!* (1857), 38–9.
7. *Sociology for the south* (1854), 15.
8. *Sociology for the south* (1854), 17.
9. *Sociology for the south* (1854), 87.

10 *Sociology for the south* (1854), 150–51. See also his claim that 'in merely agricultural countries all money not spent in living is carried off in some way from the country': *Sociology for the south*, 140; and his observation in *Cannibals all!* (1857), 75: 'As individuals possessing skill or capital exploitate [sic], or compel other individuals in the same community to work for them for nothing, or for undue consideration, precisely in the same way do nations possessed of those advantages exploitate other nations with whom they trade, who are without them.'
11 *Cannibals all!* (1857), 86.
12 *Cannibals all!* (1857), 87.
13 *Sociology for the south* (1854), 14–15.
14 *Sociology for the south* (1854), 20.
15 *Sociology for the south* (1854), 25. In *Cannibals all!* he further developed this: 'The moral philosophy of our age (which term we use generically to include Politics, Ethics, and Economy, domestic and national,) is deduced from the existing relations of men to each other in free society, and attempts to explain, to justify, to generalize and regulate those relations.' And he recognised slavery and freedom's binary relationship: 'No successful defence of slavery can be made, till we succeed in refuting or invalidating the principles on which free society rests for support or defence': *Cannibals all!* (1857), 79.
16 *Sociology for the south* (1854), 34.
17 *Cannibals all!* (1857), 31.
18 *Cf.* V.I. Lenin, 'Deception of the people with slogans of freedom and equality', in *Collected works*, Vol. 29, 4th English edition (Moscow, 1972), 377–81.
19 *Cannibals all!* (1857), 175. In his chapter on 'The working day' in *Capital*, Marx famously said that '[c]apital is dead labour, that, vampire-like, only lives by sucking living labour, and lives the more, the more labour it sucks': *Capital: a critique of political economy*, Vol. I: *The process of production of capital*, ed. Frederick Engels; ed., trans. Samuel Moore, Edward Aveling (London, 1954 [1887]), 224. Harvey Wish has it that Fitzhugh was probably familiar with 'the famous *Communist Manifesto* of 1848, either directly or indirectly, since he quoted its phraseology in *Cannibals all!*': *Propagandist of the old South* (1943), 182. It is, at most, only possible that Fitzhugh was 'indirectly' aware of Marx via his reading of the Northern abolitionist press; and perhaps he read Marx's columns in Horace Greeley's *New York Daily Tribune*. The first English edition of the *Manifesto* was published in 1850, but in the fairly obscure London-based *Red*

Republican newspaper. It would not be readily available as a text until the end of the century. It is not conceivable that Fitzhugh, who could not read German, would have had direct access. What is far more likely is that, as a reader of the radical abolitionist press, he was swimming in the same radical Atlantic currents as Marx, and there learning an identical vocabulary.

20 *Sociology for the south* (1854), 222.
21 *Sociology for the south* (1854), 22–3. See also his observation that: 'The complaint is universal that modern improvements, while they lessen the labor required to create wealth, and are vastly increasing its aggregate amount, beget continually its more unequal distribution. They are, as yet, but engines in the hands of the rich and the skillful to oppress the laboring class. The large towns are consuming the small ones, and the great capitalists eating up the lesser ones. Every day sends forth its new swarms of paupers, whilst every month begets its millionaires': George Fitzhugh. 'Centralization and socialism', *De Bow's Review*, June 1856, Vol. 20, No. 6.
22 *Sociology for the south* (1854), 33. He also held that there was an excess of crime in northern societies because of their *laissez-faire* social order: George Fitzhugh. 'Excess of population and increase of crime', *De Bow's Review*, February 1867, Vol. 3, No. 2 [new series]. In an 1859 article for *De Bow's Review*, Fitzhugh claimed that there was no murder, ignorance, starvation or unemployment in his home town of Port Royal and that this atmosphere bred true southern conservatism. Wish rightly says that 'this idyllic picture was retouched for the benefit of Northern readers': *Propagandist of the old South* (1943), 15.
23 *Sociology for the south* (1854), 38.
24 *Cannibals all!* (1857), 29–30.
25 *Cannibals all!* (1857), 36.
26 Fitzhugh, 'Excess of population and increase of crime' (1867).
27 *Cannibals all!* (1857), 51.
28 *Cannibals all!* (1857), 335.
29 *Sociology for the south* (1854), 92. See also his similar views of money: 'We do not doubt that its moderate use is essential to civilization and promotive of human happiness and well-being – and we entertain as little doubt, that its excessive use is the most potent of all causes of human inequality of condition, of excessive wealth and luxury with the few, and of great destitution and suffering with the many, and of general effeminacy and corruption of morals': *Cannibals all!* (1857), 303.

30 *Sociology for the south* (1854), 23–4.
31 Friedrich Engels; David McLellan, ed. *The condition of the working class in England* (Oxford, 1993 [1844]), 155.
32 Marx, *Capital*, Vol. 1 (1887), 661.
33 *Sociology for the south* (1854), 35–6. Amy Dru Stanley has observed the following of Fitzhugh: 'In *Sociology for the south* [Fitzhugh] wrote scathingly that freedom's defining social exchange was "hard dealing," its virtue "avarice," its only aspiration "to make the best bargains one can," and its watchword "*Caveat Emptor.*" Its "moral code" was expressed in the adage, "every man for himself, and the devil take the hindmost" ... Averring that "domestic affection cannot be calculated in dollars and cents," he held that free market relations eroded all paternalistic reciprocity between men and women as well as between masters and servants. As Fitzhugh saw it, marriage and prostitution were alike in free society, both representing commercial contracts that reduced sex to a market commodity': *From bondage to contract: wage labor, marriage, and the market in the age of slave emancipation* (Cambridge, 1998), 246–7.
34 *Sociology for the south* (1854), 164.
35 *Sociology for the south* (1854), 8, 51–2.
36 *Sociology for the south* (1854), 161.
37 *Sociology for the south* (1854), 39.
38 *Cannibals all!* (1857), 66.
39 *Sociology for the south* (1854), 165–6.
40 *Sociology for the south* (1854), 167.
41 *Sociology for the south* (1854), 167.
42 *Cannibals all!* (1857), 108.
43 *Sociology for the south* (1854), 28, 29.
44 *Sociology for the south* (1854), 67–8.
45 *Sociology for the south* (1854), 10–11.
46 'Civilization is no foreign hotbed exotic brought from distant climes, but a hardy plant of indigenous birth and growth. There never was yet found a nation of white savages; their wants and their wits combine to elevate them above the savage state. Nature that imposed more wants on them, has kindly endowed them with superior intelligence to supply those wants': *Sociology for the south* (1854), 20. Wish incorrectly claims that Fitzhugh rejected the notion of a racial hierarchy until 1861, when he read John H. Van Evrie's work *Negroes and negro 'slavery'* (1861): Wish, *Propagandist of the old South* (1943), 43. Racial hierarchies were present in Fitzhugh's writing from the start.

47 *Cannibals all!* (1857), 35.
48 *Sociology for the south* (1854), 204.
49 *Cannibals all!* (1857), 26.
50 *Cannibals all!* (1857), 29.
51 'Masters treat their sick, infant and helpless slaves well, not only from feeling and affection, but from motives of self-interest. Good treatment renders them more valuable': *Cannibals all!* (1857), 43.
52 *Cannibals all!* (1857), 29–30.
53 *Cannibals all!* (1857), 45–6. On the subject of morality, Fitzhugh says that slave society is more Christian than 'free competitive society' and 'Christian morality is practicable, to a great extent, in slave society – impracticable in free society': 47, 303–4.
54 *Cannibals all!* (1857), 317.
55 *Cannibals all!* (1857), 137.
56 *Sociology for the south* (1854), 222.
57 *Sociology for the south* (1854), 26.
58 *Sociology for the south* (1854), 37.
59 *Sociology for the south* (1854), 43.
60 *Cannibals all!* (1857), 302: 'the interests of master and slave are bound up together, and each in his appropriate sphere naturally endeavers to promote the happiness of the other'.
61 *Sociology for the south* (1854), 42.
62 *Sociology for the south* (1854), 48.
63 Wish says unambiguously, 'he came forward as a propagandist rather than as a scholar, reiterating a few well-chosen arguments which might be effective in the struggle to stem the critics of the South': *Propagandist of the old South* (1943), 15.
64 George Fitzhugh. 'Southern thought', *De Bow's Review*, October 1857, Vol. 23, No. 4. By 'Southern thought' he claimed to mean 'a Southern philosophy, not excuses, apologies, and palliations', though, of course, that is precisely what he developed.
65 Harvey Wish. *George Fitzhugh: conservative of the old South* (Charlottesville, VA, 1938), 3.
66 Wish, *Propagandist of the old South* (1943), 19. Indeed, Fitzhugh rarely traveled outside of the Virginian tidewater. Like 'most of his neighbors' his only regular trips were to Richmond, Fredericksburg and Washington, DC (but as I mention later he did take a trip to New Haven, CT in the mid-1850s): '*Propagandist of the old South*'.
67 *Sociology for the south* (1854), 81, 169.
68 Wish, *Propagandist of the old South* (1943), 174.
69 *Sociology for the south* (1854), 69.

70 *Sociology for the south* (1854), 70.
71 *Sociology for the south* (1854), iii.
72 Grace Elizabeth Hale. *Making whiteness: the culture of segregation in the south, 1890–1940* (New York, 1998), 48, 51. Hale also says that after slavery white southerners constructed 'a strangely other time and space within which first to deny and escape the present and then to reconstruct the foundations of racial difference': *Making whiteness*, 44. Again, as Fitzhugh shows, this predated Emancipation. Or, as Malcolm X once said, '[i]t's unbelievable how many black men and women have let the white man fool them into holding an almost romantic idea of what slave days were like': Malcolm X; Alex Haley. *The autobiography of Malcolm X* (New York, 1965), 212–13.
73 *Cannibals all!* (1857), x.
74 *Cannibals all!* (1857), xvii.
75 *Sociology for the south* (1854), 82.
76 *Cannibals all!* (1857), 332.
77 *Sociology for the south* (1854), 167–8.
78 'Within the family there is little room, opportunity or temptation to selfishness – and slavery leaves but little of the world without the family': *Cannibals all!* (1857), 55.
79 *Sociology for the south* (1854), 83.
80 *Cannibals all!* (1857), 116.
81 *Cannibals all!* (1857), 56.
82 *Sociology for the south* (1854), 29–30.
83 *Sociology for the south* (1854), 105–6.
84 Robin Blackburn. *The overthrow of colonial slavery, 1776–1848* (London, 1988), 90.
85 Quoted in Stephanie E. Jones-Rogers. *They were her property: white women as slave owners* (New Haven, CT, 2019), 14. This became a kind of self-fulfilling prophecy, since southern legislation not only defined slaves as unfree, but precluded the very idea of Black freedom. A law in Mississippi stipulated that freed slaves had to leave the state: Daina Ramey Berry. *The price for their pound of flesh: the value of the enslaved from womb to grave in the building of a nation* (Boston, MA, 2017), 139.
86 *Sociology for the south* (1854), 113.
87 *Sociology for the south* (1854), 171.
88 *Cannibals all!* (1857), 107. B.F. Stringfellow of St Louis claimed, in *Negro slavery, no evil* (1855), that northern abolitionism was an outcropping 'of religious infidelity and a challenge to all existing social institutions': Wish, *Propagandist of the old South* (1943), 41.

89 *Cannibals all!* (1857), 141.
90 Dorothy Roberts. *Killing the Black body: race, reproduction and the meaning of liberty* (New York, 1997), 34.
91 Caitlin Rosenthal. *Accounting for slavery: masters and management* (Cambridge, MA, 2018), 121.
92 W.E.B. du Bois; David Roediger, ed. *John Brown* (New York, 2001 [1909]), 41.
93 Rosenthal, *Accounting for slavery* (2018), 12.
94 Jones-Rogers, *They were her property* (2019), 8.
95 Rosenthal, *Accounting for slavery* (2018), 98–9.
96 Manning Marable. *How capitalism underdeveloped Black America: problems in race, political economy and society* (Boston, MA, 1983), 6–7. Marable's comments about whips as emblems of slavery are direct references to the work of Kenneth Stamp.
97 Quoted in David Roediger. *Class, race and Marxism* (London, 2017), 110.
98 Roberts, *Killing the Black body* (1997), 35.
99 Berry, *Price for their pound of flesh* (2017), 68.
100 Gwendolyn Wright. *Building the dream: a social history of housing in America* (Cambridge, MA, 1981), 47.
101 Wright, *Building the dream* (1981), 40, 44.
102 Roberts, *Killing the Black body* (1997), 34–5.
103 Angela Davis. *Women, race and class* (New York, 1981), 7.
104 Rosenthal, *Accounting for slavery* (2018), 115.
105 Jones-Rogers, *They were her property* (2019), 121.
106 Roberts, *Killing the Black body* (1997), 36, 49.
107 Jones-Rogers, *They were her property* (2019), 106. 'In the context of southern slave markets, enslaved mothers' breast milk was a commodity that could be bought and sold, and buyers and sellers recognized these women's ability to suckle as a form of largely invisible yet skilled labor': *They were her property*, 114.
108 Jones-Rogers, *They were her property* (2019), 83.
109 Rosenthal, *Accounting for slavery* (2018), 130–31; Ned Sublette, Constance Sublette. *The American slave coast: a history of the slave-breeding industry* (Chicago, 2016).
110 Jones-Rogers, *They were her property* (2019), 147. 'Slavery was, of course, not only racialized, but gendered. American slavery was unique in that it developed into a self-reproducing system, so that, even with the formal abolition of the slave trade, slavery could continue to expand south and west. Often slave women worked in the fields, the same as men, although in some cases their gender was

preferred for household tasks. And, as recorded in the story of Harriet Jacobs, female slaves were also regularly raped': James Parisot. *How America became capitalist: imperial expansion and the conquest of the West* (London, 2019), 120.

111 Jones-Rogers, *They were her property* (2019), 82.
112 Keri Leigh Merritt. *Masterless men: poor whites and slavery in the antebellum south* (Cambridge, 2017), 40.
113 Merritt, *Masterless men* (2017), 3–5, 7–9, 16, 40–2, 64. 'The price of slaves reached record highs on the eve of the Civil War – and with good reason: the harvest of 1860 had yielded large profits. But as political fortunes turned, prices plummeted and then ricocheted wildly. The Betts & Gregory price lists show this collapse ... in early January 1861, 'Extra Men' were bringing in $950–$1,000. Only five months earlier, in August 1860, another Betts & Gregory circular had priced the same category more than 50 percent higher, at $1,550–$1,625. Two months later, on a circular from March 1861, prices were back up. But this form was only partially completed, suggesting a breakdown in systematic pricing. Political uncertainty had turned the trade in enslaved people into a game of speculation': Rosenthal, *Accounting for slavery* (2018), 154.
114 Merritt, *Masterless men* (2017), 10–11. See also Honor Sachs. *Home rule: households, manhood and national expansion on the eighteenth-century Kentucky frontier* (New Haven, CT, 2015), 11, for a discussion of how elite land speculators consolidated property in Kentucky after 1776, reducing the majority of white settlers to the status of 'tenants, wage laborers, or itinerant "hirelings"'. And for a discussion of the process in pre-revolutionary Virginia, see Anthony S. Parent, Jr. *Foul means: the formation of a slave society in Virginia, 1660–1740* (Chapel Hill, NC, 2003). 3–4, 9.
115 *Cannibals all!* (1857), 98–9. By 'limited marriages', Fitzhugh presumably meant a marriage with a defined and finite life-span (something that no abolitionist actually advocated).
116 *Sociology for the south* (1854), 71.
117 *Cannibals all!* (1857), 202–3.
118 Gerald Horne. *The counter-revolution of 1776: slave resistance and the origins of the United States of America* (New York, 2014), 212–13. John C. Calhoun, one of the other archetypal apologists for slavery, regularly conflated defence of human chattel slavery with the defence of private property writ large. It is not a coincidence that Calhoun was also profoundly anti-democratic, fearful of mass politics and had recourse to imaginary depictions of an idealised south: Nancy

MacLean. *Democracy in chains: the deep history of the radical right's stealth plan for America* (New York, 2017), 9–11.
119 See also George Fitzhugh. 'The women of the south', *De Bow's Review*, August 1861, Vol. 31, No. 2, a fairly boring run-through of the standard ultra-conservative stereotypes about women (the helpmate of man, etc.).
120 Scott Henkel. *Direct democracy: collective power, the swarm and the literatures of the Americas* (Jackson, MS, 2017), 22.
121 *Cannibals all!* (1857), 282.
122 *Sociology for the south* (1854), 205–6.
123 *Sociology for the south* (1854), 195, 216. Marking a marriage by jumping over a broom was a common African American custom in the years immediately before the Civil War. The term 'jumping the broom' was also used as a synonym for a sham or fake marriage.
124 'Nothing in the signs of the times exhibits in strong relief the fact, that free society is in a state "of dissolution and thaw," of demoralization and transition, than the stir about woman's rights': *Sociology for the south* (1854), 213. For a further discussion of Fitzhugh's horror at the status of women in a free society, see Wish, *Conservative of the old South* (1938), 24.
125 *Sociology for the south* (1854), 215.
126 *Sociology for the south* (1854), 213.
127 Hidetka Hirota. *Expelling the poor: Atlantic seaboard states and the 19th century origins of American immigration policy* (Oxford, 2017), 52, 54.
128 Henkel, *Direct democracy* (2017), 83.
129 Wish, *Propagandist of the old South* (1943), throughout.
130 *Sociology for the south* (1854), 114. Like Burke, Fitzhugh advocated a 'prescriptive' politics, one that would be grounded in 'faith in the past': 'What's to be done with the negroes?' *De Bow's Review*, June 1866, Vol. 1, No. 6 [new series]. Fitzhugh also spoke of how he was influenced by Thomas Carlyle, another paragon of British conservative thought: *Cannibals all!* (1857), xix. He also drew on Disraeli, Young England and the Tory socialists, attracted to their vision of a harmonious social hierarchy: Wish, *Propagandist of the old South* (1943), 44.
131 *Sociology for the south* (1854), 128.
132 *Cannibals all!* (1857), 279; *Sociology for the south* (1854), 170.
133 Quoted in Eric Foner. *Free soil, free labor, free men: the ideology of the Republican Party before the Civil War* (New York, 1970), 66.
134 Quoted in MacLean, *Democracy in chains* (2017), 19.

The failure of free society   193

135 Eric Foner. *The fiery trial: Abraham Lincoln and American slavery* (New York, 2010), 97.
136 Quoted in Merritt, *Masterless men* (2017), 171–2, which also provides a useful overview of this inegalitarian sentiment's prevalence in southern society. In 1867, Fitzhugh half-heartedly advocated that America become a monarchy, but it seems that even he had given up on this idea by then: 'Monarchy in America', *De Bow's Review*, March 1867, Vol. 3, No. 3 [new series].
137 Wish, *Conservative of the old South* (1938), 4, 33. However genteel his family's origins, their social standing had since declined. Fitzhugh's father, also named George Fitzhugh, did own a plantation named Bellmount in King George County, VA, covering about 400–500 acres and presumably worked by slaves. The family had sold it, however, following the agricultural depression of 1825: Wish, *Propagandist of the old South* (1943), 7.
138 *Sociology for the south* (1854), 179–80.
139 *Sociology for the south* (1854), 189–90. Slave owners had long opposed the distribution of newly available Western lands to poor whites, out of a concern that such lands could not then be used for the large-scale, plantation-style farming they favoured; the Homestead Act could only be passed in 1862, when the opposition of slave owners had been removed from the political equation: Merritt, *Masterless men* (2017), 38; Heather Cox Richardson. *To Make men free: a history of the Republican Party* (New York, 2014), 33–4.
140 Fitzhugh also published a short pamphlet in 1850, 'Slavery justified, by a Southerner', 'a poorly printed, twelve-page article in small type, intended, he explained, for a few friends': *Propagandist of the old South* (1943), 54. This was his first work and was later folded into *Sociology for the south*.
141 In one of his last published pieces, for the Philadelphia-based *Lippincott's Magazine*, he argued for a system in which white landowners could seize further lands in the south, on condition that they provide non-voluntary labour for ex-slaves. 'When whites seize upon and appropriate the lands of savages, they deprive them of all means of living. It will be their duty to support them, but they can only do so by compelling them to labor. Savages are all vagrants but by being compelled to regular labor they would be cured of their vagrancy, and taught much of the useful arts of civilized life.' He admitted that this would be 'very like slavery', but still sought to deny that it would be so. 'Some will say I propose to reinstate slavery on a broader basis than ever. I propose no such thing, but that government shall

discharge its duty by compelling all men who have no visible means of support, to labor.' The article was accompanied by a disclaimer from the editor denying that the magazine supported Fitzhugh's views: George Fitzhugh, 'The freedman and his future', *Lippincott's Magazine*, 1 October 1869.

142 *Propagandist of the old South* (1943), 340.
143 Michael O'Brien. *Conjectures of order: intellectual life and the American south, 1810–1860*, Vol. II (Chapel Hill, NC, 2004), 948; Wish, *Propagandist of the old South* (1943), 168, 272.
144 Foner, *Free soil* (1970), 66, and *Fiery trial* (2010), 101, 113.
145 Wish, *Conservative of the old South* (1938), 11–12.
146 Wish, *Conservative of the old South* (1938), 8. William Lloyd Garrison's *Liberator* dismissed the book as 'crazy': *Conservative of the old South*, 11. The Washington-based abolitionist journal *National Era* did review *Sociology*, in a review that was unsurprisingly hostile. The *Era*'s editor Gamaliel Bailey was, Harvey Wish says, 'particularly angered' by the book (which reaction on the part of abolitionists was clearly one of Fitzhugh's intended goals). It is hard to gauge the influence of *Sociology*, but it did form part of an impactful shift in pro-slavery writing, which started to target the evils of northern society from the 1850s onwards. Moreover, *Sociology* sold well. 'The first edition was almost sold out within a few months': Wish, *Propagandist of the old South* (1943), 124–7.
147 Walter Johnson. *The broken heart of America: St Louis and the violent history of the United States* (New York, 2020), 169.
148 Wish, *Conservative of the old South* (1938), 10. The *Richmond Examiner*, the *Fredricksburg News* and the *Southern Literary Messenger* were all equally praising of *Cannibals all!*: *Conservative of the old South*, 10–11.
149 Wish points out that Fitzhugh 'seemed unaware of the true capitalistic spirit of such Southern cities as New Orleans, Richmond, Charleston, and Savannah. Only in London and Paris, in Manchester and Marseilles, and in their equivalents of the Northern cities could he recognize the specter of class antagonism': *Propagandist of the old South* (1943), 186. 'The debate over the question of slavery and capitalism has been long running and wide ranging. For some scholars, most influentially Eugene Genovese, southern slavery was not capitalist. Slaves were not "free to choose" to sell their labor power for a wage, and were not guided by the indirect coercion of the invisible hand, but by the direct violence of the whip … Yet other scholars have argued plantations were in fact capitalist institutions. Most

influentially and contentiously Fogel and Engerman, professional economists, argued that slavery was capitalist because slaveowners were rational profit calculators aiming to maximize their profits from slave labor. And many recent works of the "new" history of capitalism also emphasize the capitalist nature of the plantation south': Parisot, *How America became capitalist* (2019), 113. Peter Linebaugh argues that the slave trade worked in tandem with the enclosures of commonage in England to usher industrial capitalism into the modern world: *The Magna Carta manifesto: liberties and commons for all* (Berkeley, CA, 2008), 94. Paul Gilroy has called plantation slavery 'capitalism with its clothes off': *The Black Atlantic: modernity and double consciousness* (Cambridge, MA, 1993), 15.

150 Manisha Sinha. *The slave's cause: a history of abolition* (New Haven, CT, 2016), 3. It is unsurprising that after the Civil War Fitzhugh briefly attempted to reinvent himself as 'a "Chamber of Commerce booster"' of capitalist enterprise: Eric Foner. *Reconstruction: America's unfinished revolution, 1863–1877* (New York, 1988), 418.

151 Parisot, *How America became capitalist* (2019), 13; Rosenthal, *Accounting for slavery* (2018), throughout.

152 Edward Baptist. *The half has never been told: slavery and the making of American capitalism* (New York, 2014); Horne, *Counter-revolution of 1776* (2014), vii. Horne also shows how the vocabulary of capitalism has roots in slavery: 'The *deregulation* of the slave trade [after 1688] led to the mass entry into this dirty business of "separate" and "private" traders, which coincided with *free trade* in Africans and *capital flight* of this same valuable commodity: all of these italicized terms are part of today's jargon and should remind us of their less-than-glorious antecedents and their role as recurring building-blocks of today's capitalist society': *Counter-revolution of 1776*, xii–xiii.

153 Sven Beckert, *Empire of cotton: a new history of global capitalism* (London, 2014).

154 Rosenthal, *Accounting for slavery* (2018), 6.

155 Berry, *Price for their pound of flesh* (2017), 12, 45.

156 Berry, *Price for their pound of flesh* (2017), 97.

157 Foner, *Reconstruction*, 2.

158 'Although the industrial North had a very economically stratified society, it could not rival the extreme disparity pervading the slave South. Wherever the peculiar institution existed, inheritable slave property created a nonporous class barrier. In the year before the Civil War, 56 percent of the country's aggregate personal estate was concentrated in the South. Cotton was king, slave labor was profitable,

and slave prices were rising. Dixie had become the wealthiest region in America. Yet once again, the bulk of this wealth was concentrated in the hands of a very small group of slaveholders, while the pool of less affluent whites was growing larger by the day': Merritt, *Masterless men* (2017), 44.
159 Eric Williams. *Capitalism and slavery* (New York, 1966 [1944]), 36: 'in 1775 British West Indian plantations represented a valuation of fifty millions sterling, and the sugar planters themselves put the figure at seventy millions in 1788. In 1798 Pitt assessed the annual income from West Indian plantations at four million pounds as compared with one million from the rest of the world. As Adam Smith wrote: "The profits of a sugar plantation in any of our West Indian colonies are generally much greater than those of any other cultivation that is known either in Europe or America"': *Capitalism and slavery*, 53.
160 MacLean, *Democracy in chains* (2017), 2–3. It is not for nothing that MacLean calls plantation slavery 'the most profitable capitalist enterprise the world had yet seen': *Democracy in chains*, 8. Likewise, Huey P. Newton once said that 'slavery is capitalism in the extreme': quoted in Asad Haider. *Mistaken identity: race and class in the age of Trump* (London, 2018), 15.
161 Rosenthal, *Accounting for slavery* (2018), 156.
162 Lincoln's Proclamation pointedly did not discuss any form of remuneration (which slaveholders in the British Empire did receive after abolition in 1832): 'Final Emancipation Proclamation' (1 January, 1863), in Don E. Fehrenbacher, ed. *Lincoln: speeches, letters, miscellaneous writings, Presidential messages and proclamations, 1859–1865* (New York, 1989), 424–6. In Lincoln's thinking, slaves were the property of rebels and thus could be legally seized (and the slaves subsequently emancipated).
163 Parisot, *How America became capitalist* (2019), 115–16.
164 Horne, *Counter-revolution of 1776* (2014), 19. See also David Kazanjian's discussion of how African Americans were coded as 'raced property': *The colonizing trick: national culture and imperial citizenship in early America* (Minneapolis, MN, 2003), 38.
165 Daniel O. Sayers. *A desolate place for a defiant people: the archaeology of maroons, indigenous Americans and enslaved laborers in the Great Dismal Swamp* (Gainesville, FL, 2014), 57.
166 Berry, *Price for their pound of flesh* (2017), 5.
167 Rosenthal, *Accounting for slavery* (2018), 86. Rosenthal provides one of the most interesting investigations of slaves as a commodity-form, as well as the limits of that conceptualisation: 'How fully commodified

were enslaved people? The mark of full commodification in the sale of grain or cotton has always been the futures contract, an agreement to buy not a specific bushel or bale but any unit of a specified quality. There were no futures contracts for slaves; individual negotiations or auctions were the basis for most transactions. But the commodification of enslaved people advanced remarkably far considering the complexity and individuality of human assets. The genres of calculation described above all translated slaves into abstract units of value. Inventories rated their worth in dollars, price lists sorted them into categories, and the classification of fractional "hands" created a unit of human value that allowed a diverse array of people to be compared and combined': *Accounting for slavery*, 149.
168 Horne, *Counter-revolution of 1776* (2014), 30.
169 On Locke's ambiguous (but certainly not negative) views of slavery, see Holly Brewer. 'Slavery, sovereignty, and "inheritable blood": reconsidering John Locke and the origins of American slavery', *American Historical Review*, Vol. 122, No. 4 (2017), 1038–78; James Farr. '"So vile and miserable an estate": the problem of slavery in Locke's political thought', *Political Theory*, Vol. 14, No. 2 (1986), 263–89.
170 Williams, *Capitalism and slavery* (1966 [1944]), 5. 'Not many Englishmen were more knowledgeable – or less compassionate – than Locke about British colonialism and slavery. "You should feel nothing at all of others' misfortune," Locke advised a friend in 1670': Ibram X. Kendi. *Stamped from the beginning: the definitive history of racist ideas in America* (New York, 2016), 49.
171 Daniel Defoe; Thomas Keymer, ed. *Robinson Crusoe* (Oxford, 2007 [1719]), 35.
172 George Fitzhugh. 'Society, labor, capital, etc.', *De Bow's Review*, January–February 1862, Vol. 32, Nos. 1 and 2.
173 Zach Sell. *Trouble of the world: slavery and empire in the age of capital* (Chapel Hill, NC, 2021), 15.
174 Sell, *Trouble of the world* (2021), 42. On Lockean conceptions of slavery, see also Laura Brace. *The politics of property: labour, freedom and belonging* (Basingstoke, 2004), 161–3.
175 Horne, *Counter-revolution of 1776* (2014), 42, 164. In the words of Patrick Wolfe: 'As John Locke had provided, in texts that would profoundly influence Euroamerican colonial discourse, private property accrued from the admixture of labour and land. To put it very simply, Blacks provided the former and Indians the latter – the application of enslaved Black people's labour to evacuated Indian land produced the White man's property, a primitive accumulation if ever there was

one': 'Race and trace of history', in Lionel Bateman, Fiona Pilkington, eds. *Studies in settler colonialism: politics, identity, and culture* (New York, 2011), 275, quoted in Onur Ulas Ince. *Colonial capitalism and the dilemmas of liberalism* (Oxford, 2018), 69. And see Robinson Crusoe's words, in text relating to note 171.

176 Joe Cleary. *Literature, partition and the nation state: culture and conflict in Ireland, Israel and Palestine* (Cambridge, 2002), 40. On the brief existence of a free Black population in mid-seventeenth century Virginia, T.H. Breen and Stephen Innes make the following, enlightening comments: 'Freedom for such marginal figures was desperately insecure and many probably did not regard it as a significant improvement over slavery. Property made the difference. The black peasants of mid-century Northampton owned sizable tracts of land, competed with white neighbors in the marketplace, built up impressive herds of livestock, and from time to time, purchased dependent laborers. Property provided a livelihood as well as immunity from depredation. It gave the identity before the law and security in times of trouble.' As Breen and Innes later say (17), '[p]roperty, even a few cows or pigs, provided legal and social identity in this society; it confirmed individuality': *'Myne owne ground': race and freedom on Virginia's eastern shore, 1640–1676* (Oxford, 1980), 5–6, 17.

177 Merritt, *Masterless men* (2017), 43: 'In the early years of the Republic, public lands were purchased in bank notes, specie, or on credit. During this time, of course, land was always available for white settlers to purchase, due to the brutal elimination of Native Americans. In the Deep South, the removal of the Creek natives in Georgia began in the spring of 1816, and lasted until 1827. Between 1829 and 1832, the Cherokees were forced from their ancestral homelands in Appalachia and the foothills; by the early 1830s, the Choctaws and Chickasaws had been driven out of Mississippi; and the Florida Seminoles were completely removed from the state in 1842': *Masterless men*, 46.

178 The Federal government, as the ultimate arbiter of the land regime after the Louisiana Purchase, set the minimum price (in 1850) at $1.25 an acre (though actual prices hovered at a much higher rate), and 'specified a minimum number of acres for a single sale. This number was often set as high as 80 or 160 acres': Merritt, *Masterless men* (2017), 48. This had the dual effect of consolidating lands and of excluding poor whites from purchase.

179 Gavin Wright. *Slavery and American economic development* (Baton Rouge, LA, 2006), 50–51. Moreover, the types of commodity production that emerged often required slavery. The high mortality in

many sectors of the New World economies – sugar, most famously – precluded free labour. No free person would choose to work there: *Slavery and American economic development*, 15–16.
180 Johnson, *Broken heart* (2020), 81.
181 Brenna Bhandar. *Colonial lives of property: law, land and racial regimes of ownership* (Durham, NC, 2018), 5–6.
182 Barbara Arneil. *John Locke and America: the defence of English colonialism* (Oxford, 1996), 126–7. See also Susan Buck-Morss. *Hegel, Haiti and universal history* (Pittsburgh, PA, 2009), 28. Manisha Sinha points out that Locke found slavery to be 'abominable', except for the enslavement of Africans which he justified as being the legitimate condition for those taken in a just war. The 'racial slavery' and private property he thus helped to justify 'was the material basis for the growth of white republicanism in Virginia': *Slave's cause* (2016), 35.
183 Stephen M. Best. *The fugitive's properties: law and the poetics of possession* (Chicago, 2004), 2. On the other hand, nineteenth-century abolitionists condemned slavery precisely because it confused the Lockean boundaries between property and persons: *Fugitive's properties*, 8. Locke, of course, was a malleable thinker and both slavery and abolition are logical conclusions of his thought: cf. Brace, *Politics of property* (2004), 171.
184 Buck-Morss, *Hegel, Haiti and universal history* (2009), 91. 'Locke endorsed colonial slavery because he thought it an institution necessary to the productive exploitation of English colonies and because he saw in the planter-colonists a counterweight to royal power': Robin Blackburn. *The Making of New World slavery: from the baroque to the modern, 1492–1800* (London, 2010), 329.
185 Sean Wilentz. *No property in man: slavery and antislavery at the nation's founding* (Cambridge, MA, 2018), 27–8. See also Wright, *Slavery and American economic development* (2006), 6–7.
186 Daina Ramey Berry suggests that, in the United States, slave children understood that they were property by the time they were 10 years old: *Price for their pound of flesh* (2017), 35.
187 Julian B. Carter. *The heart of whiteness: normal sexuality and race in America, 1880–1940* (Durham, NC, 2007), 83.
188 Wright, *Slavery and American economic development* (2006), 12–13.
189 Blackburn, *Making of New World slavery* (2010), 586.
190 George Fitzhugh. 'Liberty and civilization', *De Bow's Review*, March 1866, Vol. 1, No. 3 [new series]. As with the bulk of his post-Emancipation output, this was a condemnation of Reconstruction and of any plans to apportion land to ex-slaves.

191 Sublette and Sublette, *American slave coast* (2016), 196, 305. On the processes of land consolidation and its effects on the poor white population, see Merritt, *Masterless men* (2017), 42.
192 *Cannibals all!* (1857), 358–9.
193 Johnhenry Gonzalez. *Maroon nation: a history of revolutionary Haiti* (New Haven, CT, 2019), 161, 162.
194 Sell, *Trouble of the world* (2021), 195.
195 Robin D.G. Kelley. *Hammer and hoe: Alabama communists during the Great Depression*, 2nd edition (Chapel Hill, NC, 2015), 78–91.
196 Johnson, *Broken heart* (2020), 9.

5

Privatised utopias

Property rights are human rights, too.

George Wallace[1]

The real enemy of the American home

On 5 January 1949, Harry S. Truman visited the Houses of Congress to deliver his annual State of the Union address, having won re-election at the end of the previous year in a famously close contest with his Republican challenger, Thomas Dewey. After succeeding from Franklin Delano Roosevelt in 1945, Truman had already begun to use his annual addresses to Congress to push for 'an all-out progressive philosophy and a sweeping liberal program of action', as his biographer calls his first address, one that would be far more rapidly expansive than the achievements of FDR.[2] Truman's 1948 address was 'an uncompromising reaffirmation of his liberal program' which greatly irked both the Republicans and the southern Democrats. He called for 'a national health insurance program, a massive housing program, increased support for education, increased support for farmers, the conservation of natural resources, and a raise in the minimum wage from 40 to 75 cents an hour'. He also announced then that 'he would be sending Congress a special message on civil rights'.[3]

Newly emboldened by his re-election, Truman used his 1949 State of the Union address to lay out his vision of how American politics had progressed since the Wall Street Crash of 1929, and where it might go in the future. Looking back at the previous sixteen years of Democratic rule, he observed that 'the American people have been creating a society which offers new opportunities for every man to enjoy his share of the satisfactions of life'. He said that this was a function of the American people's conservatism about the values and principles underpinning their politics, coupled with a progressive and 'forward-looking' mentality about the future. Under FDR and Truman, Americans had happily rejected the 'discredited theory' of elitism as well as 'trickle-down' economics. In place of this, a genuinely democratic socio-economic order was being built in which wealth was created 'for the benefit of all'. Truman's recent electoral victory was proof that this vision had majority support.

Truman censured the recently passed Taft–Hartley Act that weakened labour unions ('[a]t present, the working men and women of the Nation are unfairly discriminated against by a statute that abridges their rights, curtails their constructive efforts, and hampers our system of free collective bargaining') but also spoke in a language that suggested he favoured an economy defined by a harmony of labour and capital.

And then he came to the issue of housing and the need to promote property ownership:

> The housing shortage continues to be acute. As an immediate step, the Congress should enact the provisions for low-rent public housing, slum clearance, farm housing, and housing research which I have repeatedly recommended. The number of low-rent public housing units provided for in the legislation should be increased to one million units in the next seven years. Even this number will not begin to meet our need for new housing. Most of the houses we need will have to be built by private enterprise, without public subsidy. By producing too few rental units and too large a proportion of high-priced houses, the building industry is rapidly pricing itself out of the market. Building costs must be lowered. The Government is now engaged in a campaign to induce all segments of the building industry to concentrate on the production of lower priced housing. Additional legislation to encourage such housing will be submitted. The authority which I have requested, to allocate materials in short supply and to impose price ceilings on such materials, could be used, if found necessary, to channel more materials into homes large enough for family life at prices which wage earners can afford.

Truman's tone was measured but with a characteristic Missourian folksiness. And while there was also an aroma of the populism and radicalism that had often informed late-nineteenth- and early-twentieth-century progressivism – of which Truman was certainly a product – the ultimate vision was of a fraternal and well-ordered society, free of class struggle ('[t]he business cycle is man-made; and men of good will, working together, can smooth it out').[4]

Yet Truman could sometimes also be less guarded. When it came to identifying the root causes of housing problems in America, he not only saw specific culprits but could also be bluntly open in his views of them. A few months after his State of the Union address, Truman denounced the real estate lobby – a collective term for the National Association of Real Estate Boards (NAREB), the National Association of Home Builders, the American Savings and Loan League, the Mortgage Bankers Association and the American Bankers Association – as a 'little group of ruthless men' who spread 'lies' about his housing policies and engaged in 'misrepresentation and distortion against legislation of such crucial importance to the public welfare'. He was shocked that the lobby would so consistently and aggressively attack his policies, given that they stood to greatly benefit from a postwar housing boom.[5] The real estate lobby, he said, were 'the real enemy of the American home'.[6] There was a perennial tension here – between a desire to work with private industry and a need for the state to intervene in the private sector – that persisted throughout Truman's time as President and which sheds interesting light on the inner dynamics of American welfare-state politics and on Keynesian conceptions of private property more generally.

Intolerable conditions

It is difficult to overstate how profound a housing crisis there was in the United States during the Truman years.[7] The post-1945 housing shortage was 'the biggest housing shortage in history'.[8] There was a 'spectre' of homelessness immediately at the end of the war with 25,000 homeless in Washington, DC alone.[9] There were 100,000 homeless veterans in Chicago and the city was selling streetcars as emergency housing.[10] The Depression had had a serious and detrimental effect on housing:

> When the Democrats took over the reins of government in 1933, one of the most critical phases of the nationwide economic collapse which they had inherited from the Republicans was the prostration of home building and finance. Home construction was at a standstill, hundreds of thousands were losing their homes through foreclosure and lending institutions throughout the country were going into bankruptcy, taking with them the savings of families at the time when they were most needed ... The task of the Democratic Administration was to institute measures that would relieve distress and restore confidence in the American free-enterprise system, to revive housing construction, to rehabilitate and strengthen home finance so that the mistakes of the Republican 'boom-and-bust' era would not be repeated, and to improve the intolerable conditions under which millions of Americans were living.[11]

If America was supposed to be a Lockean paradise in which all men could own their own piece of real estate, and there be secure in their paternal status, the Depression had made such visions more unattainable for the masses than they had been before. With the American economy on a war footing after Pearl Harbor, construction of new homes shrank even further. At least 1 million families were living 'doubled up' with other families because of the 'acute housing shortage' during the war; the head of the Congress of Industrial Organizations said that more than 2 million families were in this situation and '[m]any more are homeless, living in tents, vacant stores, or public shelters'.[12] The looming return of postwar veterans in 1945 would exacerbate this even further. One high-ranking member of the Federal Housing Administration (FHA), John Blandford, estimated in June 1945 that 1.25 million new homes were needed, to replace dilapidated housing, make up for houses not built during the Depression and war, and to address the projected postwar boom in birthrates.[13] Blandford also spoke of the need to bring the USA back to 'normalcy' in terms of housing.[14] The director of information for the National Housing Agency, Howard Vickery, cited the same figure – 1.25 million – as the number of new houses that would be needed *every year*, for ten years, to solve the housing crisis, at an annual cost of $6- to $7 billion dollars requiring a workforce of 4 to

5 million.[15] In December 1945, the Federal government was estimating that a million veterans would be homeless within a year.[16] Those 12.5 million new homes that were said to be needed over ten years were probably a conservative estimate.[17]

Glen Taylor, a left-leaning senator from Idaho, travelled across the country in late 1946 and wrote to Truman of his impression that 'the greatest problem facing the United States this winter is the shortage of housing for veterans. It is acute everywhere. Every community feels it.'[18] Truman himself later spoke of the 'lack of adequate housing' as being 'certainly one of the country's most pressing domestic problems'.[19] And there were fears that 'the prolonged postwar housing shortage would have a damaging effect on the birthrate and on family stability'.[20] The threat to private property was a threat to familial reproduction and men's status as fathers. And while the tenor of the descriptions was muted, there was still a simmering fear here about the existence of a massive underclass of unhoused vagrants. Home ownership would assuage this fear, both in the obvious sense that it would end these people's homeless status, and also in the sense that they would be converted into stable homeowners with an economic stake in society.

Charles Abrams, a professor at the New School in New York and an expert on housing issues, was brutally frank in telling a meeting of the National Association of Housing Associations in December 1945 that '[p]rivate enterprise is not geared up to handle the housing shortage' and '[u]nless the Government sets up a positive program, designed to build low-cost dwellings, the present crisis may continue indefinitely with the situation growing more desperate than it is at present'.[21] Truman-era housing policy became a debate over the sanctity of private property and perceived threats to it. The subsequent fight between the Federal government and 'private enterprise' would reveal much of the inner tensions of postwar American Keynesianism.

The Housing Act of 1949

A radical shift in Federal housing policy had been instituted under the 1934 National Housing Act and the subsequent creation of the

FHA, 'the most prominent government agency to embody FDR's notion of an empowered, self-sufficient, homeowning public'.[22] The Banking Act of 1935 'created essential preconditions for postwar growth by revolutionizing the state's ability to manage the money supply and subsidize credit markets'.[23] The Federal government began to act as a guarantor for mortgages, thus making banks far more willing to issue loans. The repayments for such loans were now spread over several decades, rather than a single decade, reducing monthly mortgage repayments and making them more manageable. Rather than a deposit of 50 per cent of the house's value, home-buyers holding FHA mortgages were required to only pay a 10 per cent deposit, with the mortgage covering the other 90 per cent. Interest rates were around 4 per cent per annum and were tax-deductible, making this 'one of the most generous redistributions of wealth in American history'.[24] In these ways, the FHA revolutionised home-buying in the United States,[25] and noticeable levels of government intervention in the housing market continued as the war ended. The 1944 Servicemen's Readjustment Act, colloquially known as the GI Bill, offered subsidised housing to veterans, along with free education, vocational training and medical care.[26] The cumulative effect was to make private property more accessible to white working- and middle-class American men.

The Housing Act of 1949 – sometimes also called the Wagner–Ellender–Taft Act after its three co-sponsors in Congress – was the culminating moment of this longer legislative push to create a nation of white, male property owners. The 1949 Bill built on previous legislation for Federal mortgage insurance as well as financing research and slum clearance programmes. Most importantly, it allowed for 800,000 units to be built over six years (impressive, but still far below what was needed). 'Despite a frenzied campaign by the real estate lobby and even a fist fight on the House floor, the bill was eventually passed.'[27] Its language echoed Truman's State of the Union speech from earlier in the year:

> the general welfare and security of the Nation and the health and living standards of its people require housing production and related community development sufficient to remedy the serious housing shortage, the elimination of substandard and other inadequate housing through the clearance of slums and blighted areas, and the

realization as soon as feasible of the goal of a decent home and a suitable living environment for every American.²⁸

Additionally, the 1949 Housing Act had some remarkably conservative effects. The housing built under its auspices became a way to boost property taxes and was geared towards private investment (the Federal government never funded the houses built, it merely insured the mortgages on them). Families in receipt of public housing were liable to be evicted if their income rose above a threshold, contributing to the idea that public housing was temporary housing for the poor, racial minorities and the socially marginalised. In the Pruitt-Igoe housing projects in St Louis, which later became a convenient symbol of the supposed failures of public housing, residents were tacitly forbidden from owning TVs or phones, since this was taken to denote a level of personal wealth incompatible with living in public housing.²⁹ Even before the war, and far more after it, the FHA underwrote a housing boom in the suburbs, spurring an 'uneven development' in the American urban and suburban landscape. 'The essence of this "uneven development" was investment and development for suburbs, compared with extraction and deterioration in urban core communities.'³⁰ Nonetheless, there remained a profound tension between the Federal government and private-property owners in the midst of all this, with the latter regularly castigating the alleged 'socialism' of the former.

Give the poor property owner a break

A Federal-level rent control had been in place since 1941, initially justified as necessary for placing the economy on a war footing. Plans to extend this beyond the end of the war, when housing was still at an acute shortage, increased existing tensions. Such policies – indeed, Truman's policies on housing in general – prompted a vitriolic backlash from America's property-owning capitalist class.³¹ The Kansas Savings and Loan League described Truman's policies as an encroachment on free enterprise and on the sacred tenets of American political culture: 'Federal encroachment in the housing field is unreasonable and unnecessary and can lead only to paternalistic tendencies in the individual citizen's character and independence of thought that we, as Americans must certainly deplore and discourage'.[32] Fathers, secure in their private property, would be replaced by a paternalist state that undermined them. In 1944, representatives of the National Association of Home Builders of the US and NAREB wrote an open letter to John Blandford intimating that he was fully opposed to private enterprise.[33] The head of the North Jersey Savings and Loan Association said 'home financing institutions such as ours ... promote home ownership which is the back-bone of the American way of living'. A Federal housing authority, with rent control powers, would supposedly threaten all of this.[34] Where the Truman Administration feared what would happen if homelessness was allowed to persist, the real estate industry spoke with fear of what Truman portended for their work (and their profits).

The rhetoric that opponents of rent control or public housing used often slipped over into the extreme or the absurd. The real estate lobby condemned public housing as being equal parts socialist and improvident. 'Representatives of the lobby, based in Washington and Chicago, insisted that public housing would erode such noble virtues as individual dignity and self-sufficiency; their public education kits appealed to other sentiments such as racial prejudice.' A billboard in Georgia announced that 'PUBLIC HOUSING MEANS THE END OF RACIAL SEGREGATION IN SAVANNAH!'[35] The president of the First Federal Savings and Loan Association of Atlanta wrote to Truman to tell him the Wagner–Ellender–Taft Bill was 'the most dangerous piece of legislation ever proposed' for his industry.[36] Another letter-writer informed Truman he was a practitioner of 'socialized housing and Laski "Revolution by Consent"'.[37] The Commerce and Industry Association of New York published an accusatory pamphlet in March 1949 titled *Housing dictatorship and soft socialism*.[38] Truman was 'shocked' at the 'extraordinary propaganda campaign' which the real estate lobby orchestrated against his housing policies and in defence of their own specific conceptions of private property,[39] though, from another perspective, this was all quite unsurprising, since false accusations of socialism had been a central weapon of the American right since at least George Fitzhugh, and conservatives going back to Burke customarily imagined any restriction on property ownership to be a slippery slope to chaos. The spectre of Karl Marx continued to haunt the propertied imagination.

Various other letter-writers spoke of Truman's housing policies as 'the poison cup of communism' that would lead to a nationalisation of the entire economy; 'the most dangerous legislation ever proposed to our American way of life' that would eventually lead to 'a Socialistic or Welfare State'; 'hidious' [sic] and 'disreputable'; an 'injustice against landlords' and a 'great evil'; a 'cancer', an attack on 'all the fixed laws of the ages pertaining to property rights', an attack on 'the foundation of capitalistic government'; neither a New Deal nor a Fair Deal, but 'a Dirty Deal'.[40] NAREB demanded that Truman's administration 'clean house of all officials tainted with the philosophies of Socialism, Communism and controlled economies'.[41] This demand was echoed by the Construction League of Indianapolis: 'In war and in peace we have proven that there is no adequate substitute for free private enterprise. Persons who do not subscribe to the competitive system of private enterprise should not be permitted to hold responsible policy-making posts in government.'[42] Forecasting how southern voters in the 1960s would abandon the party over its embrace of civil rights, various other writers claimed that they would never again vote for the Democratic Party because of Truman's supposed assaults on private property and his purported crypto-socialism. And one writer beseeched Truman plaintively to 'at least give the poor property owner a break'.[43] All of this was a valuable line of political attack; while Truman had been portraying himself successfully as an anti-communist protector of the American people, in the 1948 midterm elections the Republicans turned this on him with accusations that Truman was soft on communism.[44]

As early as 1943, Ferd Kramer, vice-president of Draper & Kramer, a mortgage provider in Chicago, had alleged that the attitude of some builders, realtors and mortgage bankers towards the FHA was so unremittingly negative that they would rather see the war against the Nazis lost 'than see the Federal Government build houses'.[45] That Truman was willing to call them out, and sometimes with intemperate language, only added to the real estate lobby's jitters. Moreover, this intractable hostility to the government's housing proposals did not seem to have much popular support. An April 1948 editorial in the *Orlando Morning Sentinel* described claims that Truman supposedly had 'socialistic' tendencies as being 'slightly ridiculous'. The *Kansas City Star*, Truman's hometown newspaper, was equally dismissive.[46] Indeed, the vitriol against Truman appears to have been something of a Potemkin village.

Drew Pearson, a muck-raking journalist with a nationally syndicated column, claimed that 'an army of 3300 amateur lobbyists' had been recruited by the real estate lobby to 'diligently and secretly' work against public housing and rent control.[47] Raymond Foley, head of the FHA, similarly noted that builders' associations, realtors and others had worked together to create the appearance of a 'spontaneous flood of popular protests' against Truman.[48] Foley also observed that he himself was 'a champion of private enterprise' and it was 'plain nonsense' to say that the 1949 Housing Act would bring the government into the business of building houses directly.[49] Truman, echoing his views, agreed that 'good housing' would be supplied 'primarily through the private homebuilding industry', as he informed NAREB in his formal statement to their 1949 convention.[50] Indeed, John Blandford pointed out to two vociferous critics that the charged and often downright silly rhetoric of those who attacked Truman's administration as socialists and communists was completely at odds with the realities of Federal housing initiatives: 'public housing, as well as private, is built by private contractors'.[51] Incongruously, FHA actions after the war were being carried out in response to 'considerable pressure from the builders' lobby'[52] and NAREB leaders boasted that they placed 'hundreds' of 'their' people in government service, from where they exerted a direct influence over the execution of housing policy.[53]

> Despite their opposition to 'socialistic' public housing, American house builders and mortgage bankers wanted government support that would take the risk out of investments in conventional residential construction. After some initial disputes, there was little protest about government involvement in this 'private housing' field. The issue was how much authority government should have to regulate the products the builders constructed, the rates the bankers set, and the people who would live in the new housing.[54]

The goal of the real estate lobby seems to have been to discipline the government and to make sure that any Federal action *would not* infringe on the sanctity of private property.[55] All this 'public' housing was defined by a *privatised* way of thinking and seeing the world. The property regime that emerged from Truman's initiatives was one that reinforced private ownership as *the* normative economic ideal, and reinforced the single-family home as the most socially acceptable (perhaps the *only* truly acceptable) living arrangement. And as is well known, the suburbanisation that flowed from all this was defined by racial segregation.

A champion of private enterprise

On 3 May 1948, Raymond Foley appeared before the House Committee on Banking and Finance and outlined the 'philosophy' of the FHA and the Housing Bill. Much of that philosophy bordered on simplistic platitudes – '[t]he problem of housing ... is directly related to the general welfare of the entire people' – but Foley also tilted at deeper issues of race, gender and the social order and the long-standing assumption that a harmonious social order could only exist with and through private property: 'A supply of adequate housing, sufficient to meet the needs of all families, is essential to a sound and stable democracy, for the character of the home is a large factor in determining the character of family life, the conditions under which children grow up and assume the obligations of citizenship, and the general attitudes of people toward their community and their Government'. Yet, as much as this was a *public problem* or a *social problem*, Foley still grounded the solution in capitalist *private enterprise*:

> The bill [the 1949 Housing Act] would establish as the ultimate housing objective, the realization, as soon as feasible, of the goal of a decent home and a suitable living environment for every American family. The policy to be followed in seeking the provision of housing in the United States has been and will continue to be primarily and predominantly the function of private investment, private construction, and private ownership and management, and that Governmental

aids shall be designed to stimulate and supplement – not to impede or supplant – private enterprise operations.[56]

This would, in theory, be the final working out of the Lockean promise that all men would own their homestead in America. Foley elsewhere said that '[m]y whole experience in the field of housing convinces me that the main line of the government's efforts should be to expand the capacity of private enterprise to serve the housing needs of the people'.[57] Thus, the shortage of public housing would be solved through private means (and ultimately for private profits), in a cogent example of what Gregory Squires has called 'privatism', the long-standing attitude 'that government's job is to facilitate business development'.[58]

Foley also had a clear scepticism about housing built through cooperative and nonprofit organisations; he said government support for such initiatives should only be forthcoming as long as it did not discourage private enterprise and for-profit construction. Foley continued to believe a profit motive had to be central to house building and that single-family, privately owned homes would be especially preferable over all others.[59] A colleague of Foley's from his tenure as Michigan regional head of the FHA said he was 'personally unsympathetic' to housing directly funded by the government and that he was overly devoted to 'the accomplishments of private enterprise in the housing field'. She even claimed that Foley had sympathies for the (obviously anti-communist) ideas of Senator Joseph McCarthy as regards housing.[60] In 1948, Foley defined his own unchanging philosophy regarding homeownership thusly: 'a conviction, which I have retained, [is] that the task is primarily one for private enterprise and local community action'.[61] Indeed, when questioned about his track record during a radio interview on Christmas Eve, 1949, Foley spoke of how he had worked with private construction companies for fifteen years and 'I believe I am known as a champion of private enterprise'.[62] If the Truman Administration's housing policies had, indeed, been 'socialistic', Foley said he would not have supported them.[63]

This vigorous emphasis on private profits, actions and ownership defined the housing policies pursued in the Truman era. There was a belief within the Truman Administration that a federally backed private housing programme would halt the 'Threat of Reds or Socialists'.[64] In other words, Truman was not a puppet of the anti-private property mob, he was, in fact, seeking to curtail that communist mob through recruiting American men into private-property ownership! When John Blandford gave a speech in 1944 outlining the 'Next steps in our housing program', the seventh step he enumerated was 'We should work to improve methods of assistance to private enterprise'.[65] In general Blandford was not receptive to hostility towards capitalist builders and asked 'let us be optimistic and help private enterprise to do a better job'.[66]

> My own profound belief is that the government's housing role in our cities, in our states and in our Federal Government should be solely supplementary to the operations of private enterprise. I believe that government should step in only to the extent necessary to assist private enterprise in doing a fully adequate job, as measured by the housing needs of all the people.[67]

Nathaniel Keith, the Federal government's director of slum clearance and urban redevelopment, informed members of NAREB in January 1950 that there existed 'maximum opportunity for private enterprise to engage in the development or redevelopment' of slums and that those who took up this 'unprecedented opportunity' would be able to write off some of the costs accrued, thus making it 'generally competitive' to buy 'hitherto unavailable land' in slum redevelopment areas. According to Keith, there was a 'wide range of potential redevelopment activity for private enterprises, covering housing, commercial and industrial operations' in slum redevelopment areas. 'Private enterprise, then, can play the dominant role in redevelopment activity.'[68] Robert Taft, one of the main backers of the housing legislation in 1948, while recognising the limits of free-market capitalism, was unambiguous in his claim that the bill 'does not mean socialism; its major portion is devoted to encouraging private construction of homes'. Its actions would be carried out by the 'free-enterprise system'.[69] John Blandford told the Senate Subcommittee on Housing and Urban Development in April 1945 that his goal as national housing administrator was to 'encourage private capital to meet housing needs' and that through such an increase in 'privately-financed housing' there would be a gradual reduction in 'the need for public housing'.[70] From the very start of the organisation's existence, officials at the FHA publicly stated that their actions were *not* aimed at any dangerous undermining of private enterprise or of private property.[71] The perennial view that private property was a bulwark against (but also threatened by) an ill-defined rabble was at play here. But where Burke or Fitzhugh were remarkably candid about who this rabble exactly were, the counterposed binary opposite of the Truman imagination was never really specified or defined; it was a chaotic but blank void, a move that Geoff Mann has identified as paradigmatic of Keynesianism.[72]

The 'Statement of general housing policy' of the Truman Administration in February 1947 stated that the task of providing 'adequate, decent housing for all Americans' is one 'that must be assumed by private enterprise'. The Federal government would facilitate this by helping ease the provision of credit and as 'aid and assistance' to private enterprise, rather than competition with it.[73] 'Be smart for once', the Democratic politician Jesse H. Jones told the American Bankers Association in 1933, 'take the government in partnership with you'.[74] William Levitt, founder of Levittown in Pennsylvania and perhaps *the* paradigmatic property developer of the postwar era, candidly acknowledged in 1974 that '[w]e are 100 percent dependent on the government. Whether this is [morally] right or wrong, it is a fact.'[75]

Such frank observations were at odds with the claim of Herbert U. Nelson, executive vice-president of NAREB, who asserted that the Housing Act was 'an opening wedge for government ownership of homes and other property'.[76] But it is debatable whether leading capitalists actually believed this. The president of the US Chamber of Commerce, Eric Johnston, wrote to the housing administrator in 1944 to express his belief that 'widespread improvement in housing can only be accomplished through the building of homes in large numbers by the private home building industry'. He argued that the Federal government should forgo housing construction and instead restrict their activities to the encouragement of research, the development of standards for housing and 'by aid in the field of home finance'. In other words, the government should underwrite the finance while all housing and profits would remain privately owned,⁷⁷ which is more or less what the Housing Bill did eventually enact.

Truman's Council of Economic Advisers claimed in their 1948 report that 'American sentiment has always been firm in support of a system of free enterprise and in opposition to a planned economy'. (However, the Council did recognise how, notwithstanding this 'sentiment', American economic history was replete with examples of state intervention in the economy.)⁷⁸ A year later, one member of the Council, Edwin Nourse, used a speech to the Economic Club of Detroit to telegraph the desires of American businessmen 'to get back to conditions in which we show the world that free business under free government can keep resources used as steadily and fully as can authoritarianism and with much higher efficiency and fuller personal satisfactions'. These were desires with which Nourse clearly agreed.⁷⁹ The 'spat' between the Truman Administration and NAREB was a superficial and often performative one, constructed for public consumption as much as for any other reason. Behind the scenes, there was often an accord between government and business at odds with the public image of division and animosity. As one well-established banker said, Raymond Foley 'enjoys, and has enjoyed, the confidence of Mortgage Bankers and Portfolio Lenders alike'.⁸⁰ More broadly, American welfare provision had generally operated according to a 'natural affinity' with the 'basic American values' of private property, such that 'benefits' would only go to those who deserved them, never to the 'undeserving poor'.⁸¹ Sentiments such as these not only lurked behind the scenes, they played a defining role in the kinds of housing policies that emerged during the Truman era.

Homes are the foundation of a community

'Race' and 'property ownership' were already coterminous in the United States, with whiteness having a propertied nucleus since at least the early seventeenth century and then reinforced via both slavery and Jim Crow. Explicit racial zoning laws, which directly barred the sale of property to non-white buyers in specified districts, had been rapidly instituted in cities across the south between 1913 and 1917. These laws were invalidated in a Supreme Court decision in 1917, after which realtors began to refuse to sell homes to 'undesirables', generally agreed to be a thinly veiled code for African Americans, as well as, in certain times and places, Mexicans or Jews.[82] The Code of Ethics of NAREB had included an overtly racist clause stating that a realtor should never be instrumental in introducing into a neighbourhood 'members of any race or nationality' whose presence would depress property values; NAREB members could be expelled for violating this rule.[83] Attempting to justify such practices, a 1943 NAREB brochure, 'Fundamentals of real estate practice', outlined the supposed ill effects that newly arrived Black residents would bring to a previously all-white district:

> the prospective buyer might be a bootlegger who would cause considerable annoyance to his neighbors, a madame who had a number of Call Girls on her string, a gangster who wants a screen for his activities by living in a better neighborhood, a colored man of means who was giving his children a college education and thought they were entitled to live among whites ... No matter what the motive or character of the would-be purchaser, if the deal would institute a form of blight, then certainly the well-meaning broker must work against its consummation.[84]

According to this formulation, Black property ownership, and any related desire for upward social mobility, was on a par with criminality or deviant sexuality. In November 1949, the NAREB Code of Ethics was amended at the organisation's annual conference to a more anodyne (but still implicitly racist) formulation: 'A realtor should not be instrumental in introducing into a neighborhood a character of property or use which will clearly be detrimental to property values in that neighborhood'.[85] The racist effects of this remained largely the same.

The Depression-era and postwar housing crisis had hit Black Americans especially hard. Housing shortages for African American families were particularly acute and Black families were often confined to slum districts. Detroit, the 'Arsenal of Democracy', was an especially egregious wartime example, where an influx of Black migrant workers from the south found it next to impossible to find adequate housing; about 85,000 Black people (amounting to some

20,000 families) had arrived, with only 8,814 new housing units made available to them. The Detroit War Housing Center estimated a backlog of 4,000 eligible 'Negro war workers for whom no housing is now available' in June 1945, with those numbers expected to grow.[86] There was a quiet recognition within Truman's administration that housing policies were marred by 'avowedly discriminatory' practices on the part of mortgage-issuing institutions as well as 'the fear of the Negro population' evident among large swathes of white America.[87] Already in January 1945 John Blandford said 'Negro Housing' was a major concern for the government. But he also suggested that it was 'red', communist-sympathising, to say that no houses at all were built for Black families.[88] And in 1952 Raymond Foley informed the National Committee Against Discrimination in Housing that part of his job as head of the FHA was to make the housing stock of America more racially integrated.[89] Yet, along with racist landlords' refusal to rent to Black tenants in the midst of a general housing crisis, the root of the problem facing Black residents was indeed partly the fault of the Federal government.

Operating within a much older framework that always imagined private property and whiteness as coterminous, the Federal government was itself guilty of racial biases and practices. While figures in the Truman Administration may have denounced racial discrimination, it is simultaneously true that racial discrimination was entrenched into the very fabric of Federal policy. 'Red-lining' – labelling certain, mainly non-white, neighbourhoods as being in decline and decay and then strongly discouraging any investment into those areas – had already been a practice in the private real estate sector, pioneered by the Home Owners' Loan Corporation (HOLC). Both the FHA and, after 1944, the Veterans Administration (VA), 'adopted HOLC standards in their own massive loan programs to home builders and buyers'. The ostensible justification was to prevent Black residents from lowering the value of 'white' property. The academic and housing expert Charles Abrams observed, polemically but not unfairly, that the FHA was embracing 'a racial policy that could well have been culled from the Nuremburg Laws'.[90] He also called the FHA, in 1955, 'the protector of the all-white neighborhood'.[91]

Most infamously, the FHA's 1938 *Underwriting manual* issued to financial institutions that handled government-backed mortgages endorsed the 'prohibition of occupancy of properties except by the race for which they are intended' and offered specific examples of racial covenants to be utilised to 'protect' new sub-divisions. That prohibition was purged from the 1947 *Manual*, along with any mention of 'race', though the FHA would continue to engage in discriminatory lending until 'well into the 1960s'.[92] And indeed the ostensibly race-blind FHA seemed resigned to the fact that housing segregation 'is as prevalent in northern communities having heavy Negro populations as in the south, if not more so in many instances'.[93] As Stuart Schrader recently described it, post-1945 America became a country of 'racism without racists' in which 'persistent patterns of inequality [are] no longer legitimated by open avowals of bigotry'.[94] Truman-era Democrats were divided by many things, attitudes to race foremost among them. And yet, a certain rough consensus existed that property should remain defined by private ownership, and that racial segregation was to be accepted, if not outright promoted, in government actions related to private property.

An even more unified consensus existed on the issue of gender and housing, with government and private capital agreeing on a (white) woman's place in the American home. Again, this was operating within a long-existent framework, albeit with an immediate postwar context to it; while bourgeois white women had been recruited as workers for the war effort, and thus gained a degree of new-found financial independence, after 1945 they were forced back into the home and into an ecosystem of 'respectability and upward mobility'.[95] The 1950s was 'a pro-family period if there ever was one'; the birthrate rose from 18.4 per 1,000 women during the Depression to a high of 25.3 per 1,000 in 1957. The age for marriage and motherhood fell, divorce rates declined and women's educational parity with men dropped sharply.

> Popular commentators urged young families to adopt a 'modern' stance and strike out on their own, and with the return of prosperity, most did. By the early 1950s, newlyweds not only were establishing single-family homes at an earlier age and a more rapid rate than ever before but also were increasingly moving to the suburbs, away from

the close scrutiny of the elder generation ... The values of the 1950s families were also new. The emphasis on producing a whole world of satisfaction, amusement, and inventiveness within the nuclear family had no precedents.

Church attendance also tended to be higher in the propertied suburbs than in the renting cities.[96]

But this patriarchal and 'petty-bourgeois utopia'[97] was also part of an older discourse; if it was accepted that a man was sovereign in his own home, it followed that wives and children were his subjects. A 1922 NAREB pamphlet entitled 'A home of your own' had said that buying a home was not just a financial investment but 'A QUESTION OF LIFE ITSELF'. NAREB's pamphlet spoke of buying a home as a way of 'building moral muscle'. Becoming a homeowner 'puts the MAN back in MANHOOD'. Homeowners were 'completely self-reliant, and dominant' while renters were 'anti-family'. Children raised in a rented home were 'cheated' since they often did not have their own private yards or gardens in which to play. The pamphlet warned of 'rented homes in which many families of unknown habits lived'. Conversely, private homes avoided 'the unwholesome and not infrequently contaminating ideas of the floating classes that predominate in the close-in rental districts'. To a buy a home was a way to escape the urban proletarian mobs but also a way for a man to impress his wife: 'To install your wife in a home of her own is a convincing demonstration of your affection and consideration for her comfort and happiness'. A housewife in a home owned by her husband would know 'the joy of possession that relieves housework of its monotony'.[98] A privatised homeowning family would be a happy family.

The vocabulary with which the Truman government discussed housing was marked by a similar heteronormativity and an assumption that the privately owned single-family home was the only 'normal' home.[99] A primer on the government's legislation said that '[h]omes are the foundation of a community. A working-man [*sic*] spends one-third to two-thirds of his time there. A housewife spends 2/3's to 19/20's of her time there. A preschool child spends 2/3's to 19/20's of his time there. A school child spends half to 3/4's of his time there.'[100] Thus the privately owned home was the ideal site *for* the nuclear family, but it was also the site that *produced* (and *reproduced*) that normative family, of active working fathers and their obedient stay-at-home housewives. Raymond Foley showed how unquestioned these gender norms could be:

> I accept *in toto* the principle that our long-term objective cannot be less than the goal of a decent home and suitable living environment for every American family. The accomplishment of that objective is clearly a matter of national concern. It directly involves the stability of the community, family life, and the development of our children as healthy, loyal citizens.[101]

And yet there is a clearly an anxiety here, a fear of national *instability*. If Foley has to assert his support for this principle, there are clearly forces abroad in the land that threaten the ideal of the single family living in a one-family home. He elsewhere claimed that homes were the sites within which 'the attitudes and minds' of 'the children of today' were being formed. The lack of a proper housing programme for American families would have rippling social consequences, including 'increased disease, infant mortality, crime, juvenile delinquency, and broken homes'. A lack of housing was a 'threat to our way of life and our aspirations as a people and a democracy'.[102] Such claims subtly hearkened back to Burkean conservatism and the notion that a society without private property would, by definition, be chaotic and unnatural.

The postwar housing crisis was a crisis specifically because it threatened a man's ability to provide for his wife and children in the private family home. It was not just that veterans faced a problem, but also that 'the wives and babies of veterans, are having difficulty in finding housing accommodations'.[103] A lack of housing 'affects major aspects of family welfare', as well as, simultaneously, 'the security of the home-ownership structure'. These were problems that faced individual families but also portended something dangerous for 'the future well-being of American communities'.[104]

In a letter of October 1948, Foley apologised for 'sounding oratorical' in his pronouncement that 'housing is strikingly one of those areas where the activities of the government touch directly and intimately the lives and welfare of individual citizens and their families' (in a formulation suggesting that not all family members are 'citizens'). The availability and feasibility of home ownership, Foley said, 'play an important part in the stability of family relationships, the opportunities of children, and the wholesome growth and stability of neighborhoods and communities'. He concluded that the 'end result' of FHA work was 'a better chance for comfort and satisfaction for the average family'.[105] Addressing a Senate committee in early 1949, Foley said that the Housing Act of that year 'would establish as the ultimate housing objective the realization as soon as feasible, of the goal of a decent home and a suitable living environment for every American family'.[106] Such an objective clearly privileged 'the family' – and a specific kind of family at that – as the central object of both private property and of the government's welfare policy. Gender norms, like any other, have to be made and remade perpetually.

When Raymond Foley told the National Association of Home Builders that '[t]here is no single factor more basic to the preservation of our American Way of Life than the availability of a good home in a good neighborhood for all American families',[107] he was, in essence, summing up this specific ideology of stable, heteronormative families, implicitly white and living in privately owned homes in the arcadian and racially homogeneous harmony of a 'good neighbourhood'. There was a profound desire for 'stability' and 'normality' after the Depression and the war. But this was less of a return to an antebellum 'normality' and more of the construction of a new normality, albeit one in which existing conceptions of race, gender and private property would be central, as also would a vision of an American society emptied of ideological strife.[108]

Millions of working-class and lower-income white renters became homeowners thanks to the FHA.[109] Offering up an ideological justification for these massive shifts in housing, William Levitt said in 1948: 'No man who owns his own house and lot can be a Communist. He has too much to do.'[110] The idea that only those with a stake in society 'can be trusted to construct and maintain' society has always been a central idea of modern liberalism, 'one of the illiberal truths of liberalism'.[111] John Boughton has rightly called this line of thinking 'architectural determinism', the notion that 'an insurgent working class' would be placated through the provision of good-quality housing.[112]

Moreover, when public housing was built, the construction was underpinned by 'a peculiar attitude toward time'. The physical architectural edifices themselves were built to be visibly permanent, but the individual units were, in the main, small and spartan and thus not large enough for families; this was transient, short-term housing in which a person or persons were not expected to stay long. 'In contrast, a timeless quality lay over the suburbs. Everyone assumed that things would continue as they were here, with larger cars and more roads, newer houses, forever and ever.'[113] Suburban homes were built with traditional designs, colonial designs especially.[114] Such efforts to control the design of suburban homes were aimed at achieving 'neighborhood stability'. The FHA endorsed a host of zoning practices that prevented either multi-family dwellings or multiuse homes ('no single-family residence could have facilities that would allow it to be used as a shop, office, preschool, or rental unit'). And this ideal of neighbourhood stability was always understood in terms of racial homogeneity.[115] The Black mob would be kept out of this white utopia.

The new suburban frontier

The roots of homeownership as the preferred economic ideal for all (white) American families had roots in Lockean and Jeffersonian notions about independent yeoman farmers and of property ownership as the basis for full citizenship. But as late as the 1920s, slightly more than half of all American households did not own their own home.[116] It was only under Truman that 'homeownership bec[a]me the embodiment of the American dream'. Home ownership rates increased sharply after 1950, so that just over 60 per cent of Americans privately owned their homes by the start of the 1980s.[117] This supposedly democratised wealth, though, was still unequally shared. For all the hazy visions of suburban affluence, poverty remained widespread; a quarter of all Americans lived in poverty in the 1950s. A third of all children were classed as poor at the end of the decade and a third of the white population could not get by on the income of the household head.[118] The Lockean and Jeffersonian promises of self-reliant white male home ownership remained a vision that was always just over the horizon, always slightly out of reach.

While a Black middle class did start to emerge in the 1950s, fomented by the same Federal-backed policies as the suburban white middle class, the Black bourgeoisie remained systematically blocked from accessing suburban housing.[119] Black homeowners were thus, more or less, excluded from both the 11 million FHA-backed homes built before 1950 and the $119 billion in FHA-insured mortgages issued between the mid-1930s and mid-1970s.[120] The housing that was made available to African Americans was often of so low a standard that it could not become a capital asset.[121] The 2008 sub-prime mortgage crisis, which disproportionately affected Black mortgage-holders, exacerbated this, wiping out much of their wealth and probably wiping out any gains made since the passing of the Fair Housing Act of 1968.[122] As such, as of 2016, African Americans made up 13 per cent of the US population but only owned '2.7 percent of the nation's wealth'.[123]

By late 1949, the Federal government had authorised $1.5 billion 'to subsidize private builders in clearing the slums of American cities'.[124] By 1964, the FHA had facilitated the purchase of more than 12 million suburban homes, 'almost exclusively for whites'.[125] At the same time, postwar America became a noticeably suburban society. The FHA was itself an essentially suburban agency. Because of red-lining, one-half of Detroit and a third of Chicago were excluded from FHA insurance and not a single FHA-backed dwelling was built in Manhattan for the first twelve years of the organisation's existence.[126] From 1960 to 1970, 2.1 million white Americans moved to the suburbs. Over the same period, 2.6 million African Americans moved into the cities, 'becoming a disproportionately urban-based population',[127] so much so that 'urban' became a racialised code word.[128] Already in 1950, a quarter of all Americans lived in suburbs, rising to a third by the following decade. By 1990, the United States had a suburban majority. This postwar suburbanisation was 'fundamentally intertwined with the processes that reshaped postwar urban America, including capital flight, the concentration of African Americans in central cities, the hardening of racial divisions in housing markets, and the large-scale shift of governmental resources away from urban centers' and towards the white suburbs.[129] Suburbanisation both catalysed and resulted from changes in transportation, not least the building of a freeway system (also funded by the Federal government) and a decline in public transportation.[130]

Ultimately, a narrative was constructed by the Federal government that allowed white suburban homeowners to believe that they had acquired their home through the free market; those who did not acquire suburban homes were not the victims of racism but the side-effect of an impartial market. Thus there emerged a sense that the Federal government had no right to intervene in the private property market, despite the fact that this market had been remade by the government.[131] Suburbanisation contributed to a greater degree of social isolation and atomisation, as well as a creeping privatisation. Many of the seemingly 'public' spaces of American suburbia, in fact, are today privately owned. Also, suburban municipalities can legally impose lot sizes and can demand that the properties be used only for single-family dwellings, which reproduces class rigidities and heteronormativity. The general privatisation of services also contributes to a view of the city, town or municipality as a consumer product rather than a shared space in which all have equal rights to be present.[132]

This is *the* paradox of American Keynesianism; a massive, publicly funded housing programme not only steadfastly remained within a 'privatist' framework, but also contributed to a deepening of the same privatism, a privatism that has a long genealogy in American and Anglophone Atlantic history. Economic privatisation leads inexorably to the privatisation of the people who move through those spaces.[133]

Moving back across the Atlantic, Chapter 6 is a study of the decline of Keynesianism and of one of the most enthusiastic patrons of privatisation at the end of the twentieth century.

Notes

1 Quoted in Rick Perlstein. *Before the storm: Barry Goldwater and the unmaking of the American consensus* (New York, 2001), 317.

Privatised utopias   225

2 David McCullough. *Truman* (New York, 1992), 468.
3 McCullough, *Truman* (1992), 586.
4 State of the Union address, 1 January 1949, B.T. Fitzpatrick Papers, Box 1, Correspondence, Harry S. Truman Presidential Library [Truman Library]. In a 1950 address to Congress, Truman said '[t]he basis of our policy has always been fairness to both the landlord and the tenant': open address to Congress from Harry S. Truman, 21 April, Official Files (OF), Box 373, OF 63-A, Papers of Harry S. Truman, Truman Library.
5 'Truman blasts "lies" of housing foes', Associated Press press cutting, June 1949, Box 1, Scrapbook 2: 1948–1949, B.T. Fitzpatrick Papers, Truman Library.
6 'Truman blasts "trouble makers", again disclaims Congress feud; excoriates "real estate lobby"', *Washington Star*, 21 March 1949. Truman's comments echo the stance FDR had taken in a famous 1936 electoral speech at Madison Square Garden: 'For nearly four years you have had an Administration which instead of twirling its thumbs has rolled up its sleeves. We will keep our sleeves rolled up. We had to struggle with the old enemies of peace – business and financial monopoly, speculation, reckless banking, class antagonism, sectionalism, war profiteering … Never before in all our history have these forces been so united against one candidate as they stand today. They are unanimous in their hate for me – and I welcome their hatred': Franklin Roosevelt, address announcing the second New Deal, 31 October 1936, available at http://docs.fdrlibrary.marist.edu/od2ndst.html, accessed 9 July 2022.
7 As the Second World War ended there were also widespread fears that an economic depression would ensue due to winding down of the war industries: 'what was to be done with the millions of workers and newcomers? … Harry Truman presided over a vast demobilisation of the military and the wartime military-industrial complex': Bruce Cumings. *Dominion from sea to sea: Pacific ascendancy and American power* (New Haven, CT, 2009), 339.
8 McCullough, *Truman* (1992), 470. McCullough probably means American history, not global history, but the situation was nonetheless grave.
9 Michael Harloe. *The people's home: social rented housing in Europe and America* (Oxford, 1995) 269.
10 McCullough, *Truman* (1992), 470.
11 'Housing: the Democratic record, 1933–1947', Box 2, Folder 2 (Legislation – Voting Records on Housing – General), Nathaniel S.

Keith Papers, Truman Library. And even predating the Wall Street Crash, that American housing was of a generally poor quality was a recurring complaint in the Reform era of 1900–1914: Robert J. Gordon. *The rise and fall of American growth: the US standard of living since the Civil War* (Princeton, NJ, 2016), 102. FDR was motivated to support Federal housing partly because one-third of the jobless worked in the building trades: Gwendolyn Wright. *Building the dream: a social history of housing in America* (Cambridge, MA, 1981), 220.

12 'Report on housing: memorandum for the President', John W. Snyder, director of war mobilization and reconversion, 8 December 1945, OF, Box 360, OF 63 December 1945, Papers of Harry S. Truman, Truman Library; letter from R.J. Thomas, chairman, Congress of Industrial Organizations' Committee on Housing and Community Development, to Harry S. Truman, 30 November 1945, OF, Box 360, OF 63 December 1945, Papers of Harry S. Truman, Truman Library.

13 The University of Chicago Roundtable – 'Housing: today and tomorrow', a radio discussion by John Blandford, Herbert Emmerich and Fred Kramer, 10 June 1945, Box 12, Folder 5, John B. Blandford Papers, Truman Library.

14 'Outlines plan for "normalcy"', *Newark News*, 27 October 1945.

15 Letter from Howard F. Vickery, director of information, National Housing Agency, to Charles G. Ross, secretary to the President, 31 May 1945, OF, Box 360, OF 63 April–August 1945, Papers of Harry S. Truman, Truman Library.

16 'US will call labor-industry conference on lack of housing', *St Louis Post Dispatch*, 2 December 1945. See also memorandum by Leon H. Keyserling, 30 December 1946, Box 8, White House Contacts – Clark M. Clifford, 1946–1952 [1 of 2], Leon H. Keyserling Papers, Truman Library.

17 Wright, *Building the dream* (1981), 242.

18 Letter from Sen. Glen E. Taylor to Harry S. Truman, 26 November 1946, OF, Box 361, OF 63 November 1946, Papers of Harry S. Truman, Truman Library.

19 Draft letter from Harry S. Truman to Gardner Cowles, associate editor, *Look* magazine, n.d. [April/May 1948], OF, Box 369, OF 63 Miscellaneous January–May 1948, Papers of Harry S. Truman, Truman Library.

20 Wright, *Building the dream* (1981), 243.

21 'US must act in housing crisis, research expert tells conferees', *AC [Atlantic City?] World*, 15 December 1945, Box 2, Folder 3 (Newspaper clippings), Nathaniel S. Keith Papers, Truman Library.

22 Thomas Sugrue. *The origins of the urban crisis: race and inequality in postwar Detroit* (Princeton, NJ, 1996), 60.
23 David M.P. Freund, 'Marketing the free market: state intervention and the politics of prosperity in metropolitan America' in Kevin M. Kruse, Thomas J. Sugrue, eds. *The new suburban history* (Chicago, 2006), 15.
24 Perlstein, *Before the storm* (2001), 110.
25 Keeanga-Yamahtta Taylor. *Race for profit: how banks and the real estate industry undermined Black homeownership* (Chapel Hill, NC, 2019), 31–2.
26 Harloe, *People's home* (1995), 230.
27 The Bill required those moved out of slums to be rehoused, but that instead became a means to move 'racially undesirable groups', leading to a belief that 'urban renewal is negro removal': Harloe, *People's home* (1995), 271.
28 Quoted in David Madden, Peter Marcuse. *In defence of housing: the politics of crisis* (London, 2016), 191.
29 Walter Johnson. *The broken heart of America: St Louis and the history of American violence* (New York, 2020), 356.
30 Taylor, *Race for profit* (2019), 32.
31 The backlash against housing was itself part of a larger hostility and anger against FDR's New Deal and Truman's Fair Deal: 'right-wing American businessmen [who were] still smarting from the loss of time-honored prerogatives of the propertied class … were told that they had to negotiate with unions and meet new regulatory agency rules and standards. To them, the reforms of the Depression and World War II constituted an illegitimate "revolution." The New Deal was "nothing more or less than the Socialistic doctrine called by another name," in the summary of one of the men who founded the American Liberty League to combat it … Their arguments were so crude and self-interested that their mobilization redounded to the president's [FDR's] advantage, enabling him to denounce the millionaires as "economic royalists" bent on keeping others down': Nancy MacLean. *Democracy in chains: the deep history of the radical right's stealth plan for America* (New York, 2017), 39, 46. As C. Wright Mills wrote a decade after Truman's presidency: 'The political aim of the petty right formed among the new upper classes of the small cities is the destruction of the legislative achievements of the New and Fair Deals': *The power elite* (New York, 1956), 36.
32 Resolution adopted by the Kansas Savings and Loan League, 23 November 1945, OF, Box 360, OF 63 December 1945, Papers of Harry S. Truman, Truman Library.

33 Letter from Frank W. Cortwright and Herbert U. Nelson to John B. Blandford, 4 November 1944. Box 1, Folder 2 (Blandford, John B.), Nathaniel S. Keith Papers, Truman Library. As Blandford pointed out in his response: 'public housing, as well as private, is built by private contractors ... a good part of the housing payroll represents agencies which serve only private enterprise and such groups as your own [National Association of Home Builders of US and National Association of Real Estate Boards]'. And the private sector was already well behind schedule on H-1 housing contracted 'for migrating war workers'. Letter from John B. Blandford to Frank W. Cortwright and Herbert U. Nelson, 7 November 1944, Box 1, Folder 2 (Blandford, John B.), Nathaniel S. Keith Papers, Truman Library.
34 Letter from Bertram F. Holden, president, North Jersey Savings and Loan Association, to Harry S. Truman, 21 February 1946, OF, Box 360, OF 63 February 1946, Papers of Harry S. Truman, Truman Library.
35 Wright, *Building the dream* (1981), 220–21.
36 Letter from George W. West, president, First Federal Savings and Loan Association, Atlanta, to Harry S. Truman, 10 December 1945, OF, Box 360, OF 63 December 1945, Papers of Harry S. Truman, Truman Library.
37 Brief by Zach Lamar Cobb, n.d., OF, Box 360, OF 63 December 1945, Papers of Harry S. Truman, Truman Library.
38 'On the other hand: New York financier has discovered frightening name for public housing', *Washington Star*, 30 March 1949.
39 Letter from Harry S. Truman to the Speaker of the House, 17 June 1949, Presidential Secretary File (PSF), Box 126, Housing File, Papers of Harry S. Truman, Truman Library.
40 Letter from Joseph D. Henderson, national managing director, American Association of Small Business, to Harry S. Truman, 27 June 1949, OF, Box 370, OF 63 Miscellaneous June–July 1949, Papers of Harry S. Truman, Truman Library; letter from W.W. Bowerman, Jackson, Michigan, to Harry S. Truman, 24 June 1949, OF, Box 370, OF 63 Miscellaneous June–July 1949, Papers of Harry S. Truman, Truman Library; 'Landlords' strike program to be detailed', press release from Greater Detroit Property Owners Inc., 12 February 1946, OF, Box 371, OF 63-A 1945–October 1946, Papers of Harry S. Truman, Truman Library; letter from the Publicity Committee of the Greater Miami Apartment House Association to members of the US Senate and House of Representatives, 1 March 1949, OF, Box 373, OF 63-A January–April 1949, Papers of Harry S. Truman, Truman Library.

41 Statement of policy of the National Association of Real Estate Boards, November 1946, OF, Box 362, OF 63 December 1946 [2 of 3], Papers of Harry S. Truman, Truman Library.
42 Resolution from the Construction League of Indianapolis, 4 October 1946 OF, Box 361, OF 63 October 1946, Papers of Harry S. Truman, Truman Library.
43 Letter from Carl Yanow, Los Angeles, to Harry S. Truman, 2 August 1950 OF, Box 375, OF 63-A Miscellaneous 'X-Y-Z', Papers of Harry S. Truman, Truman Library.
44 Vincent Bevins. *The Jakarta method: Washington's anticommunist crusade and the mass murder program that shaped our world* (New York, 2020), 15.
45 Letter from Ferd Kramer to Harold G. Woodruff [president of the Mortgage Bankers Association], 27 September, 1943, Box 12, Folder 5, John B. Blandford Papers, Truman Library.
46 *Orlando Morning Sentinel*, 28 April 1948, *Kansas City Star*, 23 April 1948. See also 'Are the objections to s.1942 valid?', notes for a pamphlet by Sen. Allen Ellender, Louisiana, 30 January 1946, Box 1, Folder 7 (Legislation, 1946 – Res. S 1592 – Housing Bill), Nathaniel S. Keith Papers, Truman Library.
47 'The Washington merry-go-round: real estate lobby set for action', press cutting (n.d.), Box 1, Scrapbook 2: 1948–1949, B.T. Fitzpatrick Papers, Truman Library.
48 Memorandum from Raymond M. Foley to Charles S. Murphy, administrative assistant to the President, 14 June 1949, Box 9, Chronological File II 1949, Raymond M. Foley Papers, Truman Library.
49 Letter from Raymond M. Foley to J.B. Haverstick, Haverstick Builders, Dayton, OH, 31 March 1949, Box 1, Chronological File 1949, Raymond M. Foley Papers, Truman Library; radio interview of Raymond Foley by Bert Andrews, transcript, 24 December 1949, Box 3, Press and Radio Statements 1948–52, Raymond M. Foley Papers, Truman Library.
50 Statement by Harry S. Truman to the National Association of Real Estate Brokers and National Builders Convention, Detroit, 22 August 1949, Box 1, Chronological File 1949, Raymond M. Foley Papers, Truman Library.
51 Letter from Blandford to Cortwright and Nelson, 7 November 1944.
52 Freund, 'Marketing the free market' in Kruse and Sugrue, *New suburban history* (2006), 27. Freund, though, does not pick up on the tensions between the public and private sectors.

53 Arnold R. Hirsch. 'With or without Jim Crow: Black residential segregation in the United States' in Arnold R. Hirsch, Raymond A. Mohl, eds. *Urban policy in twentieth century America* (New Brunswick, NJ, 1993), 85.
54 Wright, *Building the dream* (1981), 240.
55 Gregory D. Squires. *Capital and communities in Black and white: the intersections of race, class, and uneven development* (Albany, NY, 1994), 51.
56 Statement of Raymond M. Foley, housing and home finance administrator before the House Committee on Banking and Currency on S. 866, 3 May 1948, Box 1, Folder 11 (Legislation, 1948 – Statements and Testimony (Housing) – House of Representatives), Nathaniel S. Keith Papers, Truman Library.
57 Letter from Raymond M. Foley to James K. Pollock, Commission on Organization of the Executive Branch of the Government, 5 October 1948, Box 1, Chronological File 1946–1947–1948, Raymond M. Foley Papers, Truman Library.
58 Squires, *Capital and communities* (1994), 10. For a further discussion of privatism, see Taylor, *Race for profit* (2019), 14.
59 'Direct Federal loans for non-profit housing cooperatives', memorandum from Raymond M. Foley to Charles S. Murphy, 25 March 1949, Box 1, Chronological File 1949, Raymond M. Foley Papers, Truman Library.
60 Letter from Mrs R. Louis Gomon, Detroit, to Harry S. Truman, 19 January 1948, OF, Box 1757, OF 1282 (Miscellaneous), Papers of Harry S. Truman, Truman Library.
61 Letter from Foley to Pollock, 5 October 1948.
62 Radio interview, Foley by Andrews, 1949. In a letter of March 1949, Foley declared '… I am a champion of private enterprise, as you know. So, I am sure, is the President': letter from Foley to Haverstick.
63 Radio interview for the Arrowhead Network, March 1950, Box 3, Legislative Notes, Raymond M. Foley Papers, Truman Library. In the midst of controversies surrounding the Wagner–Ellender–Taft Bill, Truman had indeed turned to Foley as a way to rebuild links with the real estate industry: Harloe *People's home* (1995), 270.
64 'Housing program called a bulwark', *New York Times*, 8 April 1949.
65 'Next steps in our housing program', speech by John B. Blandford, Jr, National Association of Housing Officials, Chicago, 3 May 1944, Box 3, Folder 4, Nathaniel S. Keith Papers, Truman Library.

66 UChicago Roundtable – 'Housing: today and tomorrow'.
67 John B. Blandford, Jr, 'The housing industry's post-war job', *American Savings and Loan News*, Vol. 65, No.1 (1945).
68 Address by Nathaniel S. Keith, director of slum clearance and urban redevelopment, Housing and Home Finance Agency, before members of Home Builders Association and Realty Board, 27 March 1950, Box 3, Folder 6, Nathaniel S. Keith Papers, Truman Library; address by Nathaniel S. Keith, director of slum clearance and urban redevelopment, Housing and Home Finance Agency, before members of the National Association of Real Estate Boards, 12 January 1950, Box 3, Folder 6, Nathaniel S. Keith Papers, Truman Library.
69 'Should industry support the Wagner–Ellender–Taft Bill?', undated press transcription, Box 1, Folder 4 (Debates and Statements Concerning Housing Legislation), Nathaniel S. Keith Papers, Truman Library.
70 Statement of John B. Blandford, Jr, national housing administrator, at the executive session before the Senate Subcommittee on Housing and Urban Development, 10 April 1945, Box 12, Folder 5, National Housing Agency 1945 [1 of 3], John B. Blandford Papers, Truman Library.
71 Freund, 'Marketing the free market' in Kruse and Sugrue, *New suburban history* (2006), 20.
72 'As Keynes's theory of civilisation makes clear, because the bourgeoisie cannot imagine a nonbourgeois society, it cannot conceive of its own end as anything other than the end of the world. The spectre behind its fear, therefore, is neither the multitude, nor the 99 per cent as the-truth-of-the-working-class, nor the-people-as-historically-"autonomous" force striving to overthrow the existing order to free itself or take power. Rather, the multitude or the 99 per cent represents the potential destruction of the social stability that keeps disorder at bay. Liberalism has little fear of the masses' historical mission. On the contrary, the core premise of liberalism is that the masses, by definition, have no mission – only conservatives think the multitude are actually trying to achieve something "positive". For liberals, the multitude is either a contented populace or the rabble, the people or the anti people that always lurks within it': Geoff Mann. *In the long run we are all dead: Keynesianism, political economy, and revolution* (London, 2017), 23. This definitely seems to be true of the post-1945, Keynesian-variant liberalism; though it would require major reformulation for discussion of earlier forms of 'liberalism', which was definitely amenable to defining the 'rabble'.

73 Statement of general housing policy of Federal Government, 17 February 1947, PSF, Box 126, Housing File, Papers of Harry S. Truman, Truman Library.
74 Quoted in Bethany Moreton. *To serve God and Wal-Mart: the making of Christian free enterprise* (Cambridge, MA, 2009), 32. Jones later served as Secretary of Commerce under FDR; his conservatism was legendary, so much so that he was often referred to as 'Jesus H. Jones'.
75 Quoted in Taylor, *Race for profit* (2019), 46.
76 'Should industry support the Wagner–Ellender–Taft bill?'
77 Letter from Eric A. Johnston (Chamber of Commerce) to John B. Blandford, 4 November 1944, Box 1, Folder 2 (Blandford, John B.), Nathaniel S. Keith Papers, Truman Library.
78 Council of Economic Advisers: *Third annual report to the President*, December 1948, Box 2, Leon H. Keyserling Papers, Truman Library.
79 Edwin G. Nourse. 'Private enterprise and public enterprise', speech to the Economic Club of Detroit, 21 March 1949, Box 5, Leon H. Keyserling Papers, Truman Library.
80 Introduction of Raymond M. Foley at the Mortgage Bankers Association of America Convention, New York, by Milton T. Mac Donald, vice-president of the Trust Company of New Jersey, 22 September 1948, Box 9, Chronological File II 1948, Raymond M. Foley Papers, Truman Library.
81 George Klosko. *The transformation of American liberalism* (Oxford, 2017), 32.
82 Hirsch, 'With or without Jim Crow' in Hirsch and Mohl, *Urban policy* (1993), 73–4. The contracts for a home purchase in the interwar period would generally include a 'racial covenant' in which the homeowner would legally agree not to resell the house to an 'undesirable', almost always defined as an African American. In *Corrigan v. Buckley* (1926), the Supreme Court gave its tacit approval to lower court rulings that upheld the validity of racial covenants. *Shelley v. Kraemer* (1948) 'ruled that restrictive covenants violated the Fourteenth Amendment's due process clause, invalidating their use across the country and shaking the legal foundation of segregated neighborhoods': David McAllister. 'Realtors and racism in working-class Philadelphia, 1945–1970' in Kenneth L. Kusmer, Joe W. Trotter, eds. *African American urban history since World War II* (Chicago, 2009), 126–7.
83 Taylor, *Race for profit* (2019), 10. 'A realtor who violated the guidelines [the pre-1948 guidelines on selling to Black buyers] faced penalties or expulsion from the Real Estate Board, and was denied access

to the board's cross-listing service ... Offended white customers often harassed and boycotted real estate companies that breached racial barriers': Sugrue, *Urban crisis* (1996), 46.
84 Kevin M. Kruse. *White flight: Atlanta and the making of modern conservatism* (Princeton, NJ, 2005), 60–61; Hirsch, 'With or without Jim Crow' in Hirsch and Mohl, *Urban policy* (1993), 75.
85 'Realtors may drop clause; FHA ban false alarm recalled', *New York Tribune*, 20 August 1949.
86 Letter from John B. Blandford to Rep. John Lesinski, 18 June 1945, OF, Box 360, OF 63 April–August 1945, Papers of Harry S. Truman, Truman Library.
87 'Racial implications of Title I of the Housing Act of 1949', memo from Frank S. Horne to Raymond Foley, 3 June 1949, Box 1, Folder 3 (Correspondence), Nathaniel S. Keith Papers, Truman Library.
88 UChicago Roundtable – 'Housing: today and tomorrow'.
89 'Integrated approaches to community housing problems', statement by Raymond M. Foley to the National Committee Against Discrimination in Housing, New York, 20 May 1952, Box 6, Addresses 1952, Raymond M. Foley Papers, Truman Library.
90 Kruse, *White flight* (2005), 60–61.
91 McAllister, 'Realtors and racism' in Kusmer and Trotter, *African American urban history* (2009), 126–7.
92 Freund, 'Marketing the free market' in Kruse and Sugrue, *New suburban history* (2006), 16. 'In the suburbs, the FHA encouraged the use of restrictive covenants to ensure neighborhood homogeneity and to prevent any future problems of racial violence or declining property values. The 1947 manual openly stated: "If a mixture of user groups is found to exist, it must be determined whether the mixture will render the neighborhood less desirable to present and prospective occupants. Protective covenants are essential to the sound development of proposed residential areas, since they regulate the use of the land and provide a basis for the development of harmonious, attractive neighborhoods."' Raymond Foley waited for two years after the 1948 Supreme Court decision outlawing racial covenants before saying that the FHA would no longer issue mortgages for properties in restricted neighborhoods. And until 1968, 'FHA officials still accepted unwritten agreements and existing "traditions" of segregation': Wright, *Building the dream* (1981), 247–8.
93 'Racial implications of Title I'.
94 Stuart Schrader. *Badges without borders: how global counterinsurgency transformed American policing* (Berkeley, CA, 2019), 30. For

a broad overview of racial discrimination as a recurring factor within New Deal liberalism, see Ira Katznelson. *When affirmative action was white: an untold history of racial inequality in twentieth-century America* (New York, 2005).

95 Shulamith Firestone. *The dialectic of sex: the case for feminist revolution* (New York, 2003 [1970]), 25–6. Firestone goes on to say that, as a result of these actions, '[t]he fifties was the bleakest decade of all, perhaps the bleakest in some centuries for women'. She has an obvious racial blind spot here; it is hard to think that the 1950s were worse for Black women than the 1850s. And for working class women, home ownership was a definite step up from the Depression years. But Firestone's observations are certainly valid for white bourgeois women.

96 Stephanie Koontz. *The way we never were: American families and the nostalgia trap*, 2nd edition (New York, 2016), 23, 25, 27, 37. Koontz goes on to evocatively describe the mood of this new society: 'All women, even seemingly docile ones, were deeply mistrusted. They were frequently denied the right to serve on juries, convey property, make contracts, take out credit cards in their own name, or establish residence. A 1954 article in *Esquire* called working wives a "menace"; a *Life* author termed married women's employment a "disease." Women were excluded from several professions, and some states even gave some husbands total control over family finances. There were not many permissible alternatives to baking brownies, experimenting with new canned soups, and getting rid of stains around the collar. Men were also pressured into acceptable family roles, since lack of a suitable wife could mean the loss of a job or promotion for a middle-class man': Koontz, *The way we never were* (2016), 35.

97 This was the specific term Engels used to describe the dream of workers all owning their own homes: Frederick Engels; C.P. Dutt, ed. *The housing question* (Moscow/Leningrad, 1935 [1872]), 17.

98 Lawrence J. Vale. 'The ideological origins of affordable homeownership efforts' in William M. Rohe, Harry L. Watson, eds. *Chasing the American dream: new perspectives on affordable homeownership* (Ithaca, NY, 2007), 24–6.

99 'In its administrative and institutional form ... the New Deal set forth a series of abstract category distinctions that subtly served to reinforce the privilege of the white male breadwinner family.' This is a result of what Melinda Cooper identifies as 'the paternal function of the state': *Family values: between neoliberalism and the new social conservatism* (New York, 2017), 33.

100 'Reference and source material on housing and housing needs', Public Housing Administration, May 1949, Box 3, Folder 2, Nathaniel S. Keith Papers, Truman Library. Another administration document spoke of how, with private sector assistance, 'the Government must see that every family has a minimum standard or decent shelter along with subsistence, medical care, and education'. See 'Should industry support the Wagner-Ellender-Taft Bill?'
101 Testimony of Raymond M. Foley, national housing administrator and Federal Housing Commissioner on S. 866 at hearings before the Senate Banking and Currency Committee, 18 March 1947, OF, Box 362, OF 63 April–May 1947, Papers of Harry S. Truman, Truman Library.
102 Statement by Raymond M. Foley, housing and home finance administrator, before the Senate Committee on Banking and Currency, on S. 138 and S. 712, 3 February 1949, Box 3, Housing Act of 1949 Folder, Raymond M. Foley Papers, Truman Library.
103 Brief by Cobb, n.d.
104 Memorandum to the President from the National Housing Conference, 20 February 1952, OF, Box 371, OF 63 Miscellaneous 1952–53 Folder 1, Papers of Harry S. Truman, Truman Library.
105 Letter from Foley to Pollock, 5 October 1948.
106 Statement by Foley before the Senate Committee on Banking and Currency, 3 February 1949.
107 'National Home Week', suggested statement for the President drafted by Raymond Foley, HHFA administrator, 9 May 1949, Box 1, Chronological File 1949, Raymond M. Foley Papers, Truman Library.
108 'While in 1918 the dominant social forces had favoured a "return to normality", in 1945 the disastrous political and economic consequences of this choice were widely recognized. The mass unemployment, social unrest and political disintegration of the interwar years had served the interests of neither labour nor capital. So there was little nostalgia for the past': Harloe, *People's home* (1995), 210.
109 Taylor, *Race for profit* (2019), 32.
110 Quoted in Squires, *Capital and communities* (1994), 39. Communist groups came under direct FBI surveillance in 1947 as the Bureau abandoned its monitoring of Nazi and fascist groups, 'an abrupt shift from the US wartime alliance with the left against the right': Greg Grandin. *The last colonial massacre: Latin America and the cold war* (Chicago, 2004), 8. There were also prevalent fears at the time, primarily (but not exclusively) manufactured by conservative politicians, that communism and homosexuality would go hand-in-hand,

and would progressively weaken the virility of the nation: David K. Johnson. *The lavender scare: the cold war persecution of gays and lesbians in the Federal government* (Chicago, 2004), 94–6. 'Normality' was a multifaceted dream of gendered, racialised, ideological and sexual order.
111 Mann, *In the long run we are all dead* (2017), 114.
112 John Boughton. *Municipal dreams: the rise and fall of council housing* (London, 2018), 34, 76, 183.
113 Wright, *Building the dream* (1981), 218–19.
114 Wright, *Building the dream* (1981), 242.
115 Wright, *Building the dream* (1981), 247.
116 Vale, 'Ideological origins' in Rohe and Watson, *Chasing the American dream* (2007), 17.
117 Madden and Marcuse, *In defence of housing* (2016), 25–6. Under Eisenhower, the administration of the various Federal agencies was handed over to former members of the real estate lobby, a more direct indication of the priorities of the new government: Harloe, *People's home* (1995), 271–3, though it could be pointed out that some in the Truman Administration had form with this too. After retiring from the FHA, Raymond Foley was named president of the Colonial Federal Savings and Loan Association in Grosse Pointe Woods, Michigan. See Detroit Public Library, Burton Historical Collection, Raymond Foley Reading Room File, press cutting: *Detroit News*, 'Former FHA chief to head S&L', undated [1953?].
118 Koontz, *Way we never were* (2016), 31.
119 Andrew Wiese, '"The house I live in": race, class, and African American suburban dreams in the postwar United States', in Kruse and Sugrue, *New suburban history* (2006), 99–119. Sugrue points out that a singular narrative of Black 'ghettoization' after 1945 simplifies a more complex reality; class divisions were never absent within the Black community, and wealthier Black families had better chances to purchase property, though this did mean that these families were often on the direct receiving end of white backlash as they moved into predominantly white neighbourhoods: 'class segregation took place within the confines of systematic discrimination in housing': *Urban crisis* (1996), 188. The Black urban uprisings of the later 1960s were a direct response to the lack of decent housing for Black populations: Keeanga-Yamahtta Taylor. *From #BlackLivesMatter to Black liberation* (Chicago, 2016), 46.
120 Hirsch, 'With or without Jim Crow' in Hirsch and Mohl, *Urban policy* (1993), 87.

Privatised utopias

121 Taylor, *Race for profit* (2019), 141.
122 Taylor, *From #BlackLivesMatter* (2016), 12; Johnson, *Broken heart* (2020), 416.
123 Ibram X. Kendi. *Stamped from the beginning: the definitive history of racist ideas in America* (New York, 2016), 2.
124 'Housing plan caution urged under new plan', *New York Tribune*, 14 November 1949.
125 Freund, 'Marketing the free market' in Kruse and Sugrue, *New suburban history* (2006), 17.
126 Hirsch, 'With or without Jim Crow' in Hirsch and Mohl, *Urban policy* (1993), 87.
127 Taylor, *Race for profit* (2019), 106.
128 By the time of the 1980 census, there were fourteen major American cities with Black populations of 200,000 or higher: New York, Chicago, Detroit, Philadelphia, Cleveland, Houston, New Orleans, Memphis, Atlanta, Dallas, Washington DC, Baltimore, St Louis and Los Angeles. All were defined by 'consistently high levels of segregation': Hirsch, 'With or without Jim Crow' in Hirsch and Mohl, *Urban policy* (1993), 79.
129 Kevin M. Kruse, Thomas J. Sugrue, 'The new suburban history' in Kruse and Sugrue, *New suburban history* (2006), 1, 2.
130 Gordon, *Rise and fall of American growth* (2016), 12–13, 18, 366; Cotten Seiler. *Republic of drivers: a cultural history of automobility in America* (Chicago, 2008). The Federal Highway Act of 1956 provided for the construction of 41,000 miles of highways: see Wright, *Building the dream* (1981), 248.
131 Freund, 'Marketing the free market' in Kruse and Sugrue, *New suburban history* (2006), 11–12.
132 David M.P. Freund. *Colored property: state policy and white racial politics in suburban America* (Chicago, 2007), 8; Gerald Frug, 'The legal technology of exclusion in metropolitan America', in Kruse and Sugrue, *New suburban history* (2006), 205–19.
133 Madden and Marcuse, *In defence of housing* (2016), 98.

6

The Iron Lady's imaginary childhood

> There is no better course for understanding free-market economics than life in a corner shop.
>
> Margaret Thatcher[1]

The subtle art of Conservative biography

Margaret Thatcher's first memories were of sun, excitement, traffic, 'the bustle of Grantham' and a public park in her Lincolnshire market town.[2] Such recollections, foregrounding the public and the social, were cracks in an otherwise carefully constructed façade. Her memoirs are filled with bucolic visions of lower-middle-class middle England, of her family's grocery store and a pious Methodism; in the earliest chapters of her memoirs of her early life, Thatcher builds up an image of a childhood already dedicated to the virtues of what she would later term a 'property-owning democracy'.[3] She might have been born Margaret Roberts, but *Margaret Thatcher*, the defender of a privatised politics, always existed.[4] Indeed, as she told an audience in Korea in 1992, she never invented 'Thatcherism', she and her colleagues merely 'rediscovered it'. Thatcherism was a politics of common sense that had always existed, a product of a timeless England ruled over by sensible property owners: 'The values, ideas and beliefs which I was privileged to be able to put into effect in Britain in the eleven-and-a-half years of my Prime Ministership were rooted in the experience of the past and reinforced by events in my lifetime'.[5] How Thatcher chose to remember her own childhood reveals these propertied and privatised political concerns.[6]

This was a familiar tack for late-twentieth-century conservative autobiographers.[7] The reminiscences of Barry Goldwater, in *With no apologies* (1979), 'reflected more than a quaint past; they represented a political ideology'. In his childhood, '[t]here was no Federal welfare system, no federally mandated employment insurance, no Federal agency to monitor the purity of the air, the food we ate, or the water we drank ... Everything that was done, we did it ourselves.'[8] *With no apologies* was dedicated to Goldwater's parents and their parents, 'whose courage and strength in helping to settle the Far West have been an inspiration to me over the years'. The vision is implicitly libertarian and white; the state is absent other than in its violent role of the US Cavalry ending 'the attacks of hostile Indians on white pioneers'.[9] Ronald Reagan – who often told contradictory and fanciful stories in his two memoirs, *Where's the rest of me?* (1965) and *An American life* (1990) – painted his Illinois childhood in similar, if more subtly politicised, terms. His childhood memories are often melodramatic and end usually with some form of redemption, even if only of a minor kind. 'Ronald Reagan was an athlete of the imagination, a master at turning complexity and confusion and doubt into simplicity and stout-hearted certainty.' The tales of his childhood were thus of a 'Huck Finn-Tom Sawyer' type, depicting a rugged, stoic and more socially harmonious America (while conveniently covering up his father's business failures and alcoholism).[10] As Bruce Cumings has said, conservatives 'are usually angry about something from their childhood that got lost along the way'. Both Goldwater and Reagan constructed their ideal future society in the past, thus suggesting that the ideals of the past have been forgotten in the present (but will be regained in the future). They would probably have agreed with Newt Gingrich's assessment that 1955 was the apotheosis of the American Dream – the calm before the horrors of Vietnam, the counterculture, the civil rights movement, Black Power, Watergate and second-wave feminism, when privatised suburbanism was in the ascendant.[11] Thatcher also used her childhood in these ways, constructing a romantic image of the propertied stolidity that existed before leftist chaos took hold.

Foreshadowing their daughter's politics, Thatcher's parents were, she said, thrifty savers, committed patriots and, above all, striving entrepreneurs:[12] 'I was born into a home which was practical, serious, and intensely religious' and '[i]n my family we were never idle – partly because idleness was a sin, partly because there was so much work to be done, and partly no doubt because we were just that sort of people'. Though, hinting at a darker side of her childhood, she does admit that she came 'from a family where the relationship between cleanliness and Godliness was no laughing matter'.[13] Hers was a childhood of idealised *petit-bourgeois* values, with the frivolous games of other children replaced, in Roberts/Thatcher's case, with right-leaning activities that presaged her later political career: board games based on the Chicago Mercantile Exchange and visits to see films that taught the follies of communism and revolutions. She remembered Grantham as a place where duty and work formed a seamless whole. It was an allegedly classless society, defined by strongly felt imperial sentiment, in which the proletariat were only the most pro-monarchical element.[14] However, Thatcher also showed herself to have been all too aware of the actual existence of class barriers in her childhood: 'I recall that it was the street with some of the poorest families in the worst housing, Vere Court, which was most attractively turned out' for George V's silver jubilee.[15] For sure the Labour Party had a presence, but presented as one emptied of any politics or serious ideological differences; '[p]olitics was a matter of civic duty and party was of secondary importance. The Labour councillors we knew were respected and friendly and, whatever the battles in the council chamber or at election time, they came to our shop and there was no partisan bitterness.' There is a suspiciously selective memory at work here. Eric J. Evans, for instance, points out that Thatcher's father was more of a one-nation Tory and with little of the moral censoriousness of his daughter.[16] Additionally, Thatcher's pedestrian prose style and simplistic philosophical maxims mask the complexities of this politico-literary project: she is constructing her own mythology, an idealised vision of her own childhood and ultimately a vision of a seemingly depoliticised (but actually highly ideological), propertied, English arcadia.[17]

Belying her own fond claim that she was 'never happier than in children's company', surprisingly few children are mentioned in her childhood memories.[18] Outside her own siblings, none are mentioned by name (not even 'my closest friend'). In their place, though, are the various authority figures of her schooling, who *are* mentioned by name: Miss Williams, a headmistress fond of imparting housewifely wisdom to her charges, Miss Harding, 'a particularly inspiring History teacher', and Miss Kay, Thatcher's influential chemistry teacher. The focus on childhood authority figures is of a piece with a focus on authority and order in her adult life. Indeed, Thatcher's memory of her teachers – 'a genuine sense of vocation' and 'highly respected by the whole community' – acts as an implicit counterpoint to her views of public sector workers decades later: grasping, no sense of vocation, disrespectful and (rightfully) disrespected, a mob.

Against any modish notions that childhood could be a time of experimentation, Thatcher described her childhood in static terms; she was always respectful of proper authority and she always knew the central truths of Conservatism: privatism and due respect for authority figures.[19] She described the passion for politics she shared from a young age with her father, a greengrocer, preacher and one-time mayor of Grantham. Her father's trips to the local library, and the books he picked out for her, meant that 'I found myself reading books which girls of my age would not generally read'. The inference built up is that she was less a child and more a smaller version of her later adult self. She unabashedly claimed that the 1935 general election, when she was a mere 10 years old, was 'the contest in which I cut my teeth politically'. Pushing this trope further, she attempted to narrate her father's political career as a precursor to her own, his own loss of elected office in 1952 being 'something not too dissimilar' to Thatcher's fall in 1992. And as a recurring motif of her memoirs, Thatcher recalled prophetic moments that point to her future: a fortune-teller at a Conservative fête early in her career who promised great things ['as great as Churchill']; John Buchan's political novel *The gap in the curtain*, in the tea-leaves of which Thatcher read her own future. The tone borders on the mystical, yet there is a deeper imperative at work here.

The image of Thatcher (and of her provincial background) were part of a broader media project. Prior to becoming Tory leader, Thatcher was '[i]n some respects a semi-comic figure to the British public'.[20] A sustained media campaign was a necessary step in her path to power. Alongside Diana Spencer, Thatcher would become one of the two most photographed women in 1980s Britain, and she hired image consultants and a voice coach to help her control the narrative constructed around these proliferating images of the Iron Lady.[21] Where she had earlier downplayed her father's politics and her *petit-bourgeois* roots in the hopes of 'acquiring the poise and accent of the Tory *grande dame*', by the 1970s she rediscovered Grantham. 'The image of Thatcher as "the grocer's daughter", the defender of small property owners, was partly a media construction, fashioned by interviewers and eager political journalists. Yet it was keenly embraced as a creation myth by Thatcher herself, allowing her to refashion her public profile in the image of the privatised society she hoped to lead.'[22] As a political symbol, she merged the public with her own private and personal narratives:

> The narrative was unmistakably one of upward mobility, akin to the nineteenth-century *Bildungsroman*, and was used as evidence that Britain was now controlled by meritocracy rather than aristocracy – a useful Conservative fiction. Thatcher often sought to identify herself with the electorate by reminding them that her values were those passed down by her Victorian grandmother and working-class father. Correspondingly, the domestic and financial security she received from her marriage to the wealthy Denis Thatcher in 1951 was played down. Mapped onto the nation, this narrative of Thatcher's life was particularly seductive to her electoral demographic.[23]

This was a carefully constructed narrative of British social harmony built on a foundation of private property, simultaneously looking backwards to idealised Victorian times and forwards to a better future after the domestic dismantling of socialism (and its hostility to private property) and the global dismantling of communism. As the journalist and labour activist Andrew Murray once observed, it is a mistake to think that Britain's ruling class does not also have its precious folk memories.[24] Thatcher's memories of her childhood served to construct her own personal folktale:[25] a propertied folktale in which she was somehow always a right-wing campaigner, one that could never be dissuaded: 'both by instinct and upbringing I was always a "true blue" Conservative. No matter how many left-wing books I read or left-wing commentaries I heard, I never doubted where my political loyalties lay ... though of course it would take many years before I came to understand the philosophical background to what I believed, I always knew my mind.' As a child in wartime Britain, she claims to have already known that Nazism and communism were just two sides of the same collectivist coin.[26] Even after four years at Oxford, her character and her beliefs allegedly remained unchanged. And Thatcher's vision of the Grantham of her childhood – hard-working, harmonious, filled with independent people and their private holdings – stood in contrast to her vision of post-1945 Britain.

Make Great Britain great again

Already in 1950, early in both her own career and the history of the welfare state, Margaret Thatcher had spoken of the need to abandon the 'Socialist election manifesto' of the Labour Party and instead, with a Trumpian flourish, to 'make Great Britain great again'.[27] That a statist economics which did not place private property at the centre of the nation had somehow unmade Britain was a recurring theme in her political world-view. Thatcher claimed that thirty-five years of the Keynesian consensus had resulted in the 'distorting' of 'British society'.[28] She spoke of how socialism engaged in 'high-minded rhetoric' while simultaneously playing on 'the worst aspects of human nature'. The rule of the welfare state, which ostensibly decentred and desanctified private property, 'had literally demoralized communities and families, offering dependency in place of independence as well as subjecting traditional values to sustained derision'.[29] A mob had taken power and had made Britain a mob society. Perhaps showing the influence of the Austrian economist Friedrich Hayek, she said that the project of transitioning to a state-run economy would easily slip into a dictatorial regime of surveillance and control and would promote a culture of 'petty jealousies, minor tyrannies, ill-neighbourliness and sheer sourness',[30] all of which is in diametric opposition to the 'idealism and equality' which socialism promises. Channeling Burkean conceptions of propertied social stability, young people in this new Britain had become rootless and 'lacked both the authority which had been imposed on their predecessors in the 1950s and the discipline which the need to qualify for a good job would place on students in the eighties'.[31] They were the product of 'the bleak years of socialist supremacy in the 1960s and '70s'.[32] All of this this was, of course, a gross exaggeration:

> As in other western European countries, socialists came and went from power in Britain, introduced a Welfare State and took control of large swathes of the economy without democracy and individual freedoms being threatened. The NHS was set up, council houses were built, social security was established, state education was expanded, coal, rail and steel nationalised, yet despite all the planning this required, millions of private businesses, small, medium and large, carried on merrily competing (or co-operating) with each other, flourishing or going to the wall as the market determined. Private doctors kept their clinics on Harley Street, young aristos still ruggered their way across the playing fields of Eton, the private shop windows of Harrods still blazed forth at Christmas time. Bankers and stockbrokers thronged the City, and the farmers owned their land.[33]

The assumption that private property was being degraded or even desecrated was always overblown. What was real, though, was a capitalist economic crisis in the 1970s as well as an attendant set of popular sentiments that Thatcher was able to mine and to push in an avowedly anti-socialist, pro-private property direction. The British economy had never really recovered from a recession in 1966–7, and in the years since then Britain alternated between periods of stagnation and of more or less acute depression, without again achieving stable growth.[34] On the eve of Thatcher coming to power 1.5 million British workers were unemployed.[35] In the four years of Edward Heath's premiership (1970–74), five national emergencies were declared (compared to only two in the high Keynesian period from 1950 to 1970).[36] In British popular memory, the Heath years were defined by strikes, industrial action and the rationed electricity consumption of the government-imposed three-day week.[37] The 1971 bankruptcy of Rolls-Royce – 'the talisman of British manufacturing excellence' – symbolised the country's economic humiliation.[38] The 'string of trade union victories from 1971 to 1974', not least the National Union of Mineworkers strike that ultimately brought down the Heath government, fomented a sense of 'defeatism and pessimism' in a 'frightened and demoralised'

Conservative Party.[39] A new bloc formed, with Thatcher and her ally Keith Joseph at its centre, who were aggressive towards organised labour and looked to dispense with the idea of 'one-nation Conservatism', preferring instead to speak only for the propertied sections of the nation.[40] The Thatcher-Joseph bloc, with its harsh focus on British decline, its authoritarianism and its confrontational style, found a receptive audience in 'the backwoods of the party'.[41] Britain's post-1945 decline as a world power – 'imperialists reduced to the dole queue'[42] as one leftist wit put it – was also particularly galling for the Tories.[43] The intervention by the International Monetary Fund into the British economy in 1976 exemplified the economic aspect of a broader decline in Britain's global status.[44]

Moreover, as the historians Jon Lawrence and Florence Sutcliffe-Braithwaite have shown, there was a pervasive anxiety about 'class struggle' in mid-1970s Britain; one poll found that almost two-thirds of Britons believed there was 'a class struggle in this country' and that the middle classes were being squeezed out. Any leftward turn by the Labour Party – such as the February 1974 declaration by Denis Healey that a Labour government would 'squeeze property speculators until the pips squeak' – was just further fuel to this.[45] The 1970s came to be seen as 'the most dreadful [decade] of the postwar era, a litany of racial conflict in England, nationalist discontent in Scotland and Wales, war in Ireland and perpetual strikes everywhere'.[46] The 'winter of discontent' of 1978–9 was the high water mark of this mood, when labour unrest seemed to be at its peak: 'Images of rubbish piled up in Leicester Square, striking gravediggers, and picketed hospitals eventually became trenchant symbols that would embody the chaos of an entire decade'.[47] Under Thatcher, the Tories offered a simple, even simplistic, explanation for the state of the country, exemplified in their succinct slogan used for the 1979 general election campaign: 'Labour isn't working'.[48]

In a 1978 essay, Stuart Hall noted how, even prior to Thatcher coming to power, the popular right-wing reaction to this narrative of 'decline' was heavily imbued with authoritarianism and racism as well as an inchoate anger against innovations in the educational system, the end of corporal punishment, feminism and changes in family values. 'Race is only one of the elements in this wider ideological crusade to "clean up" Britain, to roll up the map of progressive liberalism and to turn the clock of history back to the times when the world was "safe for ordinary Englishmen".[49] Indeed, this was how Hall continuously understood 'Thatcherism' – a word he helped coin; as a reaction to a constructed moral panic.[50] Intimately bound up with this 'return' to a white Britain was the rhetorical use of private property as a return to normality and greatness, not all that different from the valorisation of suburban housing and nuclear families in the USA after 1945.

It is certainly the case that Thatcher successfully channelled the general sense of outrage and humiliation existing across the political spectrum of 1970s and 1980s Britain, offering up a politics of uncomplicated moral pieties, a reactionary world-view and money-supply simplifications.[51] A 1979 Conservative internal paper on 'Themes' to be emphasised in electioneering argued that '[f]ear is more potent than hope', and that the Conservative Party should start by making 'clear the threat', identifying an ensemble of mobbish enemies: 'Labour', 'the criminal', 'violent criminals and thugs', 'hooligans at junior and senior levels', 'immigrants', 'the young unemployed in the ethnic communities', 'the government', 'strike committees and pickets', 'terrorism' and 'convicted terrorists'. Many of these were barely cloaked codewords for racial and ethnic minorities, and all these people apparently had their part to play in the decline of 1970s Britain, even if the connections between such disparate groups remained diplomatically unstated.[52] In a speech in July 1979, two months after her election, Thatcher declared:

> The extent of our decline compared with other countries may show up most clearly in economic statistics. But that does not mean that the remedy lies only in economics. The mission of this Government is much more than the promotion of economic progress. It is to renew the spirit and solidarity of the nation ... At the heart of a new mood in the nation must be a recovery of our self-confidence and our self-respect.

And she explicitly recognised that Britain's decline had taken place in a postcolonial context, phrasing her conception of the national 'mission' in suitable neoimperial terms:

> It will not be given to this generation of our countrymen to create a great Empire. But it is given to us to demand an end to decline and

to make a stand against what Churchill described as the 'long dismal drawling tides of drift and surrender, of wrong measurements and feeble impulses'. Though less powerful than once we were, we have friends in every quarter of the globe, who will rejoice at our recovery, welcome the revival of our influence, and benefit from the message and from the example of our renewal.[53]

John Medhurst has labeled these 'political prejudices dressed up as sound economic doctrine',[54] which proved hugely attractive to 'Thatcher's specific constituency of propertied voters, including the aspirant "middle class" of "shopkeepers, foremen, and the small self-employed businessmen – the *petit bourgeois*" for whom Thatcher's values of thrift, self-responsibility and economic independence specifically appealed'.[55]

Socialism, for Thatcher, was more than just a *bad* economic philosophy. It was a pernicious source of contemporary social breakdown. Thatcher spoke of 'unchecked expenditure on welfare benefits' in the same breath with 'family breakdown'; 'the growing welfare dependency will demotivate and demoralize young men and women on whose contributions in the workforce industrial expansion and advance depend'.[56] This ideology of social solidarity in fact encourages 'anti-social behaviour'. Like Burke two centuries earlier, Thatcher saw private property as the keystone of social stability; if it disappeared, so would everything else. In her vision of socialist Britain, once private property had been dethroned school misbehaviour and truanting would become rampant. The social safety net had made it 'financially advantageous to have children outside marriage' and '[t]hose with the shortest time-horizons and the least self-discipline or support from their families have responded all too readily to this new framework and have begun to form ... an "underclass"'.[57] The incentive to work fostered in a society of private property and competition had been replaced by 'perverse encouragement for idleness and cheating'. Britain was a diseased land and 'the prevailing social mood was one of snarling envy and motiveless hostility' yet Thatcher looked askance at her Parliamentary colleagues and their plans for even more of the socialism she believed had caused this disease. 'To cure the British disease with socialism was like trying to cure leukaemia with leeches.'[58]

As she recalled her time as leader of the Opposition from 1975 to 1979, '[t]he economy had gone wrong because something else had gone wrong spiritually and philosophically. The economic crisis was a crisis of the spirit of the nation.'[59] She claimed that the Labour government of James Callaghan was running advertising campaigns 'to persuade people of the virtues of dependence'.[60] She later accused Labour politicians of being motivated by 'something coarse and brutal in their imagination'.[61] Socialism had effected a 'poisonous legacy', which she saw at work in 'nationalization, trade union power, a deeply rooted anti-enterprise culture' that now prevailed in Britain.[62] In Thatcher's imagination, the *wrong* leaders and the *wrong* policies, with an insufficient regard for private property, had turned Britain into the *wrong* kind of society. Thus, 'it would take more than tactics to transform Britain'.[63] In a speech in Cardiff during the 1979 general election campaign she described 'how socialism had debilitated Britain'.[64] In the same campaign, she spoke of 'sweeping away the cobwebs' and 'applying a new broom' in the country and at a speech in Birmingham, 'I pledged to "place a barrier of steel" against the socialist path to lawlessness'.[65] Britain was a country in need of 'medicine'.[66] Where Burke used a vocabulary of natural private property and unnatural Jacobins, Thatcher spoke in medical terms: private property equals health while socialism is a disease.

A starkly different ideology would be needed to remedy all this. She was dismissive of Conservatives who might treat capitalism as a kind of 'lucky dip' from which one could pick or choose without recognising the deeper social and moral significance of *laissez-faire* and a regime in which private property was sanctified. It was not enough to merely accept the efficiency of privatised capitalism, which must also be allowed to sink its 'deep roots' into society.[67] Conservatives, she said, would have to win 'the battle of ideas in social as in economic policy'.[68] There could be no compromise with the socialist mob. As she said in a 1996 speech:

> Our weaknesses are not inevitable. Our errors are not irreparable. Our sickness is not terminal. It is a crisis of the spirit, not a depletion of resources, that cripples us. Ours is the superior system, the victorious creed, the best, indeed the only, hope for a free and just, peaceful and prosperous world. Let us recall our principles – and live up to them.[69]

Her language suggests that there *is* a cure for socialism, and yet the movement to undo socialism will be a permanent revolution. There can never be any compromising with socialists or with weak-willed Conservatives given to back-sliding (the so-called Tory 'wets'). Thatcher had little time for those Tories who favoured a compromise with Labour: 'the one thing you never get from parties which deliberately seek the middle way between left and right is new ideas and radical initiatives. We were the mould breakers, they the mould.'[70]

In a curious and almost erotic phrase, she claimed that once in power 'the Tories loosened the corset of socialism'.[71] And '[i]t was not just that we had won an election: we had also won a new kind of mandate for change.' Thatcher spoke of 'break[ing] free in a new direction'.[72] Continuing her medical language, she talked about how reversing the 'decline of Britain' would require 'painful measures'.[73] In October 1980 she proclaimed that '[w]ithout a healthy economy we cannot have a healthy society. Without a healthy society the economy will not stay healthy for long.' And at the end of the decade, as *perestroika* was in full flight, she alleged that 'Labour's real prescription for Britain is the disease half the world is struggling to cure'.[74] Thatcher's use of health and disease metaphors brought negative and positive valences into a single framework, 'with her tendency to simplify issues by emphasising the contrast between two positions'.[75] Indeed, as one analyst of her rhetoric has observed, Thatcherism operated according to a series of moralised and simplistic binaries:

Conservative policy is a life force	Labour/socialism is a death force
Conservative policies are a medicine	Labour/socialist policies are a disease
Conservative policies are unimpeded movements	Labour policies are impeded movements
Conservatism is moral/honest	Labour/socialism is sinful/duplicitous
The state is a servant	The state is a master[76]

In one of her most famous speeches, she quoted St Francis of Assisi as she entered 10 Downing Street in 1979, and set up a binary opposition between the positive markers of private property and the free market and the wholly negative aspects of socialism: 'where there is discord, may we bring harmony ... Where there is error, may we bring truth. Where there is doubt, may we bring faith. And where there is despair, may we bring hope.' As Thatcher recalled, somewhat undercutting this message of harmony: 'The forces of error, doubt and despair were so firmly entrenched in British society, as the "winter of discontent" had just powerfully illustrated, that overcoming them would not be possible without some measure of discord'.[77] In 1984 she claimed 'I have always regarded it part of my job ... to kill socialism in Britain'.[78]

Thatcher's view that socialism did major damage to the spiritual fabric of a propertied society extended beyond her views of post-1945 England. Notwithstanding her support for the state of Israel, she said that *kibbutzim* 'were a rather unnerving and unnatural collectivist social experiment'.[79] She spoke of communism as being 'ultimately a system of slavery imposed by imprisoning whole populations'. Indeed, the Bolshevik revolution had had 'no constructive results whatever'.[80] It was purely *destructive*. She 'never had any doubt that the communist system was doomed to fail' since it was a system that 'ran against the grain of human nature';[81] she shared Burkean conservative notions about the naturalness of private property, and the inherent unnaturalness of anyone who acted against private property. Communism and socialism were not just *bad* ideologies, they were pernicious forces that destroyed the 'orderly freedom' of capitalist society.[82] Communism 'impoverished not just souls but society'.[83] In an uncharacteristically ecological speech to the Conservative Central Council in March 1990 she stated: 'as we peel back the squalor of the socialist regimes in Eastern Europe we discover the natural and physical squalor underneath. They exploited nature every bit as ruthlessly as they exploited the people. In their departure, they have left her [nature] choking amidst effluent, acid rain and industrial waste.'[84] She claimed that there was 'a pervasive lack of trust and civility' in the Soviet Union, as well as a 'breakdown of civil society in matters large and small'. The USSR was a society defined by 'petty corruption, inefficiency, bad service, ill manners, the loss of every social grace, and a society pervaded by rampant egoism'.[85]

Private property was not just an economic nicety. As a good Burkean conservative, Thatcher believed private property was a necessary ingredient for defending orderly freedom, along with a 'sense of personal responsibility and of the quintessential value of the individual human being'.[86] Private property was *the* necessary condition for free-enterprise capitalism to work; it was the 'first fundamental condition ... essential because it brings stability and confidence'.[87] A lack of private property would cut off the possibility of progress, would cause stagnation in any society; 'closed totalitarian systems are so sluggish and mediocre'.[88] Thus the Cold War was 'a life-and-death struggle' and she was proud that 'we anti-communists' had won it.[89] And in opposition to unnatural communism stood, of course, the 'natural' social order of private property and capitalism: 'Free-enterprise capitalism is at one level a system so simple that we might be tempted not to describe it as a system at all. It is, in truth, just about the most natural thing in the world.'[90] In Thatcher's mind, the fight to end socialism in Britain was one part of the broader twentieth-century fight to defend natural, propertied 'freedom' from both communism *and* Nazism. Thatcher described the twentieth century in terms of 'two world wars, concentration camps, the *gulag*, and totalitarian enslavement' but also said that it was 'the time when freedom fought back so that our own way of life – a law-governed liberty – should prevail'.[91] Indeed, her views of communism could take on a civilisational and almost racial tinge. She saw 'traditional Balkan despotism' as being embodied in Ceausescu and spoke of 'that stilted formal courtesy that communists adopted as a substitute for genuine civilization'. Communism was 'a primitive ideology'.[92]

The reconstitution of Powellism

That Thatcher would think of race in terms of economics (and vice versa) was not surprising, since private property and a subtly stated sense of racial superiority were both central to how she perceived the world; indeed, race has been central to all modern notions of private property in the Anglophone Atlantic world. She certainly believed that some racial groupings had innate tendencies to capitalism. She spoke of 'the Chinese people's cultural predisposition to trading and commerce', believing that 'the spirit of entrepreneurship comes more easily to some people than to others'.[93] She spoke of Jews as 'clever, energetic people' who shared her fears of state-run charity: 'My old constituency of Finchley has a large Jewish population. In the thirty-three years I represented it I never had a Jew come in poverty and desperation to one of my constituency surgeries. They had always been looked after by their own community.' She goes on to discuss 'the Jewish emphasis on self-help and acceptance of personal responsibility', two classically Thatcherite tropes. Her claim that 'I have enormous admiration for the Jewish people' notwithstanding,[94] she here rehearsed stereotypes that merged the philosemitic with the antisemitic.[95]

Thatcher openly avowed her imperial sentiments and her nostalgia for a time when Britain ruled over a hierarchy of lesser nations and races. In *The path to power* she touched on her own family's pro-imperial politics and the legitimacy of imperial control over ostensibly inferior nations: 'my family like most others was immensely proud of the Empire. We felt that it had brought law, good administration and order to lands which would never otherwise have known them ... Later, I seriously considered going into the Indian Civil Service, for to me the Indian Empire represented one of Britain's greatest achievements.'[96] She added to this: 'Looking back at the reports in the local newspapers of what I said at the time [1945], there is little with which I would disagree now ... The British Empire, the most important community of peoples that the world has ever known, must never be dismembered.'[97] Indeed, she claimed that 'there are parts of Africa and Asia where order cannot be provided locally' and for which the international community have no remedies, 'certainly no remedy as effective as colonial rule was a century ago'.[98] She was also ambiguous in her views of the white supremacist regimes in Rhodesia and *apartheid*-era South Africa, refusing to condemn them out of hand.[99]

Against a certain contempt for non-Western peoples, Thatcher presented Anglo-American societies as the pinnacle of civilisation, defining 'civilisation' in terms of individualism and private property: 'The very essence of Western culture – and the heart of both the strengths and weaknesses of Western policy during the Cold War years – was recognition of the unique value of the individual human being'.[100] She saw 'the Western inheritance of freedom' as being the best of all possible political economies, even if it was always in need of 'defense, entrenchment, and extension'.[101] Referencing the work of the conservative political scientist James Q. Wilson, Thatcher pinpointed the interconnected factors that shaped British notions of freedom: 'physical isolation (which helped protect us from invasion); a deep-rooted and widespread commitment to private property; ethnic homogeneity (which helped create a common culture) and a tradition of respect for legality and the rights it guaranteed'. Americans inherited this freedom, mixing it with 'the risk-taking, the enterprise and the courage which endured every danger, natural and man-made, to bring virgin forests and open prairies into productive use',[102] ignoring the large number of unfree victims of this Lockean American settler-colonial liberty.

Elsewhere, Thatcher nodded towards a vaguely defined 'Judaeo-Christian tradition' and the ways in which it supposedly valued individualism and imagination as well as 'the value of work'. Far less instrumental in her views of religion than Burke, who was willing to see non-Western religions as a tool for maintaining private property, she accused the 'great Asian religious traditions' – by which she seems to mean Buddhism and Hinduism – of not valuing free will, a charge she also levels at the religious traditions of Africa, 'insofar as we know about them'.[103] 'The West' was clearly the superior space and force in the world and Thatcher had little time for post-1989 suggestions that 'the West was essentially a Cold War construct'. Rather, she said, 'the distinctive features of the Western political, social, and economic system existed long before communism and will continue after it. Those features are: the long-standing historic commitment to human rights, the rule of law, representative democracy, limited government, private property, and tolerance.'[104]

This sense of Western superiority, which conceived history and the world from afar, found an echo in Thatcher's approach to racial questions at home in contemporary Britain, so much so that Paul Gilroy has defined Thatcherism as a 'reconstitution of Powellism', in reference to the notorious race-baiter Enoch Powell.[105] A one-time member of the Conservative Party, Powell began to fall foul of the party with his 'Rivers of Blood' speech in April 1968, when he warned that Britain was entering a period of dangerous multiculturalism during which 'the black man will have the whip hand over the white man'.[106] He would ultimately find a political home in the Ulster Unionist Party.[107] Thatcher, though, talked about Powell as being the Conservative Party's 'finest intellect – classicist, historian, economist and Biblical scholar' and displaying 'remorseless logic and controlled passion'.[108] And '[a]bove all, as a West Midlands MP witnessing the effect of large-scale immigration into his constituency he was frustrated by the Party's failure to take a tougher stance on the question.'[109] Thatcher said of the notorious Rivers of Blood speech that it was 'strong meat' and she even confessed that there was 'a sinister ring' to certain portions. But she still saw much with which she was comfortable:

> I strongly sympathized with the *gravamen* of his argument about the scale of New Commonwealth immigration into Britain. I too thought this threatened not just public order but also the way of life of some communities, themselves already beginning to be demoralized by insensitive housing policies, Social Security dependence and the onset of the 'permissive society'. I was also quite convinced that, however selective quotations from his speech may have sounded, Enoch was no racist.[110]

Note how her apologia for Powell mixes racial anxieties with an unease about the sexual cultures of the 'permissive society' and a perceived need to defend private property from 'insensitive housing policies'. For Thatcher, Powell was right to identify the dangers to the propertied social order. She regretted the harsh reaction to his speech, albeit for the specific reason that the backlash against it *prevented* the Tories being harsher on immigration. Yet she also looked longingly at the freedoms Powell enjoyed once he split from a Conservative Party still dominated by 'wets': 'He was free to develop a philosophical approach to a range of policies ... This spanned both economic and foreign affairs and embraced what would come to be called "monetarism", deregulation, denationalization, an end to regional policy, and culminated in his opposition to British membership of the Common Market.' She saw Enoch Powell as Thatcherism's John the Baptist: 'Having Enoch preaching to such effect in the wilderness ... shifted the basis of the political argument to the right and so made it easier to advance sound doctrines without being accused of taking an extreme position.'[111] Like Powell, Thatcher's racism was also a 'careful choice of symbols and metaphors' suggestive of 'precise calculation'.[112] Like Powell, Thatcher advocated a 'guilt-free British nationalism'[113] in which 'the Empire' is always present but insulated from any criticisms or negative commentary. And for both, private property had to be defended from a socialist state and racial outsiders.

As Prime Minister, Thatcher would regularly strike a Powellian pose, identifying racial outsiders as a threat to the social order and the property order. In the aftermath of the Toxteth riots in 1981, caused by long-standing tensions between the Black community in Liverpool and an institutionally racist police force, she laid the blame on the 'high animal spirits' of young men who had no authority figures in this welfare state world; immigration, which had destroyed existing communities, and a broader culture that undermined the traditional, conservative values of ethnic minorities; welfare arrangements that fed a culture of dependency; and a television culture that undermined traditional morals.[114] Vron Ware has observed how, across the 1980s, 'racist ideology fixed the idea that the inner cities were unsafe because that was where most blacks lived, and the phrase "the inner city" became shorthand for "the race problem"'.[115]

> Press reports of the 1981 riots emphasised, with voyeuristic fascination, the image of the unruly crowd. The tabloid papers in particular laid bare the mix of horror and fear that has informed public narratives about youthful spontaneity and lack of discipline since at least the 1950s. The fears expressed were racial and also generational: readers were presented with nightmare images of 'black youth' rejecting social control and acting out their dreadful potential. The urban and commercial setting was significant. 'Black youth' on the streets, or silhouetted against huge bonfires as they looted smashed shop windows, became stock images whether of Brixton, Wood Green or Toxteth.[116]

Thatcher herself was instrumental in this urban-focused 'New Racism'[117] of the 1980s, in which Black mobs were construed as a brooding threat to Britain's commercial and property-owning stability. Her memoirs discuss 'the real problems that immigration sometimes caused', which had been glossed over by a foolish left who relished 'the "multi-cultural", "multi-racial" nature of modern British society'.[118] In January 1978, she spoke of Britain being 'swamped by people with a different culture',[119] for which she was heavily criticised by Labour opponents. Nonetheless, the Tories gained an eleven-point lead in polls, 'a large and welcome boost at an extremely difficult time', showing the value of this propertied race-baiting.[120] As with her sense that socialism had caused the degradation of Britain so also she had a foreboding sense that cultural relativism and the rapid changes caused by mass immigration had impacted adversely on the country. And there was a unified solution to both problems: private property and capitalism. 'Nothing is more colour-blind than the capitalism in which I placed my faith for Britain's revival … the whole purpose of the political and economic system I favoured was to liberate the talents of those individuals for the benefit of society.' She also claimed that the 'rabble rousers' of the far right National Front, for which she had 'no sympathy', were part of the same statist, anti-private property problem: 'I found it deeply significant that such groups, both now and in the past, were just as much socialist as they were nationalist. All collectivism is always conducive to oppression: it is only the victims who differ.'[121]

In addition, what Thatcher saw as a racial crisis and a decline in socio-economic order was paralleled by a degradation in gender and sexual *mores*. Something had gone wrong in Britons' sex lives under socialism.

What is right for the family is right for Britain

While being somewhat progressive on issues like divorce, homosexuality and abortion, Thatcher clearly felt that the wholesome family life exemplified by places like pre-war/pre-welfare state Grantham had been replaced by a degenerate attitude to human sexuality. This sexual conservatism was reflective of a wider backlash against 'the permissive society' in 1970s Britain, with Thatcher appointing herself as a 'populist' and as an ordinary woman 'taking on an effete or decadent establishment'.[122] In the context of the pervasive unemployment of the 1970s and early 1980s, the notion that women should be confined to the domestic sphere, rather than taking up otherwise scarce paid employment, 'appear[ed] to make sense'.[123] These anxieties around sex and the sexual revolution of the 1960s were just one expression of the ways in which 'the spectre of revolution', of the mob, 'continued to haunt' liberals and conservatives in the later twentieth century, a set of fears on which Thatcher would capitalise.[124]

The feminist writers Michèle Barrett and Mary McIntosh have shown how 'families' in Thatcherism often functioned as a code for women, with the assumption that the privatised family 'should be a self-sufficient enterprise needing little support from the state', since women can take up any shortfall from welfare cuts. However, 'the continual evocation of the family in Thatcher's pronouncements does not mean that the government is pursuing a straightforward policy of "getting women back into the home"'. Low-paid female workers are too necessary, 'especially in a situation of deskilling and erosion of wage levels', for that to take place. Nonetheless, there is a rhetorical familism here, one that holds up the male-led privatised household as British society's normative ideal.[125] Paul Gilroy called this the 'masculinism' and 'family-oriented populist ideology' essential to Thatcherite conservatism and its visions of a property-owning democracy.[126] Contemporaries in the Conservative Party certainly saw a normative gender order as a key ingredient for the successful maintenance of private property. Ivor Stanbrook, a London MP, told the House of Commons that it was 'part of the British way of life for the father to provide a home for the family'; for the homestead to not be male-owned is unnatural and 'contrary to all common sense'. Ian Gilmour, a Tory MP who served in Thatcher's government, said in 1977 that '[t]he family is the citadel of individual freedom, but that citadel needs its moat of private property'.[127] Moats, of course, are a protection from dangerous medieval attackers.

Yet there can be a certain fuzziness to Thatcher's views on gender and gender roles and how they pertain to private property. It is interesting to note, for example, that in Thatcher's memoirs her mother, Beatrice Roberts, is practically non-existent, pointing to the relative values Thatcher assigned to the entrepreneurial small-trading of her father *versus* female homemaking.[128] In a 1982 speech entitled 'Women in a changing world' she sketched out the history of women's employment, noting the long history of female employment outside the home (rather than any idealised housewifely vision) and changes in women's access to private property (a 'reasonable measure, which stopped the married woman from being a mere chattel of her husband'). But she also took aim at the 'permissive society' and its false promises of female liberation. In contrast, she argued for a society 'founded on dignity, reticence and discipline'. Women, she said, 'know instinctively that the disintegration of society begins with the death of idealism and convention. We know that [for] our society as a whole and especially for the children, much depends upon the family unit remaining secure and respected.' In the same speech, she observed that '[t]he battle for women's rights has been largely won. The days when they were demanded and discussed in strident tones should be gone for ever. And I hope they are. I hated those strident tones that you still hear from some Women's Libbers.'[129] She once said she 'owed nothing to women's lib' and, in constructing her public persona, she not only drew on her position as a housewife and a mother but also reinforced conventional stereotypes surrounding both roles within a private property imaginary. And it is worth mentioning that she only ever appointed one other woman to her cabinet.[130] Thatcher's anti-feminism led many commentators to point out how little she did for women; she 'smashed the glass ceiling only to reinforce it with concrete'.[131] On one hand, she spoke wryly of how '[w]omen have plenty of roles in which they can serve with distinction: some of us even run countries' and at the same time she felt that 'generally we are better at wielding the handbag than the bayonet'.[132] Gender roles, for Thatcher, were fluid but always with one eye on making sure they were not too fluid. And a nostalgia for a lost heteronormative family, always tacitly assumed to be living in their own privately owned home, recurred in her writings and speeches. She believed that it 'is now generally agreed to be commonsense' that 'the growth of single parenthood is bad for the children growing up without a father, and imposes heavy costs on society'.[133] As leader of the opposition, she had stated that '[w]hat is right for the family is right for Britain'.[134] Her 1986 speech to the Conservative Women's

Conference defined the family home as 'heaven on earth', a safe haven from the interventionist state.[135] As Heather Nunn describes, Thatcher and her fellow-travellers 'singled out one imaginary form of "family" as a privileged site of authentic community'. This was 'nostalgia for an imaginary pure, uncomplicated and implicitly white community in which women stayed [in the privately owned family] home and received consumer gifts while men brought home the wages and children were loved but not heard'.[136]

Thus the decline of the supposedly traditional family, and all its positive valences, could only have negative social repercussions: 'Not only in such circumstances do children grow up without the guidance of a father: there are no involved, responsible men around to protect those who are vulnerable, exercise informal social control or provide examples of responsible fatherhood. Graffiti, drug trafficking, vandalism and youth gangs are the result and the police find it impossible to cope.' In other words, a heteronormative and patriarchal familial discipline, all carried out in the private space of the family home, is needed for a broader social discipline.[137] Thatcher built on this idea of discipline and families, linking both to the privatized, capitalist, social order:

> Contrary to what the liberal-left would like to think, most children still grow up in a traditional family; most people marry; and most of these have children. In fact, no amount of philosophy, theology or social theory can provide stronger support for the argument that the family is the natural and fundamental unit of society than its resilience in the adverse climate of opinion and perverse financial incentives of the last thirty years. But this is no ground for complacency ... It is far from clear that a capitalist economy and a free society can continue to function if substantial minorities flout the moral, legal and administrative rules and conventions under which everyone else operates. What is clear is that at present we are moving rapidly in the wrong direction.[138]

Again, Thatcher's conception of contemporary Britain is built on the assumption that something terrible has happened or is potentially happening, that terrible people are massing against 'us'.[139] There is an ever-present tension here; the dangers of social breakdown are real and always just around the corner. But so also is the solution consistently at hand, to be found in the resolve of an idealised British nation.

Under the regime of the welfare state, a community of hard-working shopkeepers, dignified property owners, responsible housewives and contented workers was on the point of degenerating into dependency, sloth and decay. A cast of gendered and propertied political subjects – 'mother', 'working woman', 'homeowner', 'concerned parent', 'law-abiding citizen', 'proud Britisher', 'responsible father', 'taxpayer' and 'entrepreneur', all carrying racialised attributes – were beset by a series of violent enemies: 'the miners, Marxists, "loony Lefties", trade unionists, unruly children, hooligans, muggers, and "trendy" teachers that littered Thatcher's speeches'.[140] Families had cracked under the weight. A once homogeneous and bucolic society, built on private property, had been 'swamped' by 'different culture[s]'. This was the potential end result of the welfare state, at least in Thatcher's mind. And this extreme chaos would require a stringent set of reforms to make Britain great again; Great Britain would defeat these dangerous mobs and rebuild its lost past through privatisation and a mass expansion in property ownership.

A property-owning democracy

The idea of a 'property-owning democracy' had been a part of Tory rhetoric since at least Anthony Eden in the 1950s.[141] In 1976, a policy document outlining Thatcher's first statement of the new Conservative doctrine, aptly titled *The right approach*, targeted 'the traditional Socialist vendetta against the private sector' with a particular stress on housing.[142] The 1977 Ridley Report, produced by the hard-right Selsdon Group within the Conservative Party, promised to make 'every man [sic] a capitalist' by extending and popularising share ownership.[143] The 1979 Conservative election manifesto contained a pledge to help people own their own homes.[144] This pledge was certainly met. In Thatcher's first year in office, 55,000 publicly owned houses were sold to their occupants, rising to a peak of 204,000 houses in 1982/3. In the decade after 1979, owner-occupation (as opposed to rental or public council tenancies) increased from 55 to 63 per cent of the country's housing stock, 'one of the highest figures in the industrialized world'.[145] The historian of council housing, John Boughton, has described those who bought their council homes as the 'fifth column' of Thatcherism, such working-class voters often becoming ardent supporters.[146] In 1975, Thatcher told the politically sympathetic *Daily Telegraph* that 'if a Tory does not believe that private property is one of the main bulwarks of individual freedom, then he had better become a socialist and have done with it'.[147] Writing in 1993, she claimed that 'the heart of the Conservative mission is something more than economics – however important economics might be: there is a commitment to strengthen, or at least not undermine, the traditional virtues which enable people to live fulfilling lives without being a threat or a burden to others'.[148] For Thatcher, the proper social order would be achieved by returning to a nostalgic and privatised vision of the traditional British past.

Thatcher personally disliked the word 'privatise', 'a dreadful bit of jargon to inflict on the language of Shakespeare'. Nonetheless, she relished 'how much hope it offers, and how great [are] the benefits it brings'. She characterised privatisation as integral to the creation of 'popular capitalism', which she extolled as 'a crusade: a crusade to enfranchise the many in the economic life of Britain'. Privatisation would 'give power and responsibility back to people', it would 'restore to individuals and families the sense and feeling of independence' and 'the freedom and the dignity which come from having something they can call their own'.[149] And indeed, the scale of privatisation that took place during her twelve years in power is staggering.[150] James Meek provides an itemised list of how much of the British economy was state-owned prior to 1979, and thus targeted for privatisation:

> The health service, most schools, the armed forces, prisons, roads, bridges and streets, water, sewers, the National Grid, power stations, the phone and postal system, gas supply, coal mines, the railways, refuse collections, the airports, many of the ports, local and long-distance buses, freight lorries, nuclear fuel reprocessing, air traffic control, much of the car-, ship- and aircraft-building industry, most of the steel factories, British Airways, oil companies, Cable & Wireless, the aircraft engine makers Rolls-Royce, the arms makers Royal Ordnance, the ferry company Sealink, the Trustee Savings Bank, Girobank, technology companies Ferranti and Inmos, medical technology firm Amersham International ...

Much of this was a legacy of the post-1945 Labour government of Clement Attlee, as well as of the 'Keynesian consensus' that had defined post-war British politics. By the time Thatcher left office in 1990, 60 per cent of the old state industries had been privatised.[151]

The privatisation of publicly owned housing was 'by far the largest single privatisation of public goods' under Thatcher,[152] amounting to £22 billion of state assets by 1997. Brett Christophers has calculated that £40 billion of housing stock was sold off between 1983 and 2008. In his estimation, 2 million hectares of public land – 10% of the entire British land mass – was privatised from 1979 onwards, a total of £400 billion in previously state-owned assets (twelve times the cost of nationalising the Royal Bank of Scotland during the credit crisis of 2008, according to Christophers).[153] Satnam Virdee argues, quite reasonably, that the Conservatives could pursue privatisation 'comfortable in the knowledge that they had secured the consent of a stratum of the working class – one that was atomized, individualistically oriented, and averse to socialist politics'.[154]

To encourage their purchase, and contradicting her own free marketeer rhetoric, houses were often sold below market prices (sometimes at discounts up to 50 per cent) and with government subsidies.[155] Flats, less conducive to family life and valued less highly than conventional suburban homes, were particularly slow to sell. Familism here clashed with privatism! 'This was a problem recognised by the government when it increased the minimum discount on flat purchases to 44 per cent and the maximum to 70 per cent in 1986.'[156] Likewise, when British Telecom was privatised in 1984, the price of the shares was deliberately set low, to encourage new shareholders to buy in.[157] Thatcher stressed the moral dimensions of privatisation, seeing public ownership as inherently inferior and a dangerous slippery slope to socialism.[158] Conversely, privatisation would give birth to the 'generation of risk-taking, wealth-enhancing popular capitalists of Thatcher's dream'.[159]

In a 1979 speech in Cardiff, in which she claimed Britain had become debilitated by socialism, she hinted at her solution to this debility. The country must return 'to principles from which we had mistakenly departed'. In the speech, Thatcher played with time in her vision of a perfected British future: 'Away with the recent bleak and dismal past. Away with defeatism. Under the twin banners, choice and freedom, a new and exciting future beckons the British people.'[160] Britain was thus laying down a path away from socialism that would later be copied across Europe. A new/old privatised society was being built; 'the popular mood was moving away from remote bureaucracies and towards historically rooted local and national identities'.[161] The private Britain of her idyllic childhood would be rebuilt in the future, once the diseased 'socialism' of the present tense had been dismantled.

Private property was Thatcher's solution to the degradation of Britain. And she held up the Grantham of her childhood as the ideal society, one whose lessons should be applied across Britain. Thatcher reminisced about growing up in pre-welfare state Britain and how '[s]mall provincial towns in those days had their own networks of private charity'.[162] She claimed the Grantham of her childhood was a model of this private charity that did not need a state-run safety net and thus avoided the dependency it supposedly engendered.[163] Indeed, she said that '[m]y "Bloomsbury" was Grantham – Methodism, the grocer's shop, Rotary and all the serious, sober virtues cultivated and esteemed in that environment'.[164] Grantham made her impervious to socialism and its assault on private property: 'What I learned in Grantham ensured that abstract criticisms I would hear of capitalism came up against the reality of my own experience: I was thus *inoculated* [another medical metaphor!] against the conventional economic wisdom of post-war Britain'.[165] She claimed that upon taking power in 1979, 'I felt that the experiences I had lived through had fitted me curiously well for the coming struggle'.[166] Private property and capitalism together represented the best of all possible worlds. Capitalism's tendency towards crises was, she alleged, a myth propagated in the 'hefty, unreadable tomes of the Marxist pseudo-economists'.[167] Rather, capitalism was a crisis-proof social system and capitalism and private property would redeem the country. Interviewed by the *Weekend World* TV programme in January 1983, she waxed nostalgic about going 'back to Victorian times' and that a Britain would be built in which all citizens are property owners and the nation becomes 'strong and independent of government'.[168] Indeed, Thatcherism tended to conflate the ontologies of 'citizen' and 'property owner', suggesting that those who lacked property did not deserve to be citizens.[169] Racialised and gendered conceptions nestled comfortably within these Thatcherite ontologies.

In one of her most notorious utterances, Thatcher told the editor of *Woman's Own* magazine in 1987 that '[t]here is no such thing' as society. Instead, there are just 'individual men and women and there are families'.[170] The anti-social individualism of this has been taken as emblematic of the Thatcherite project; the emphasis on 'families' has been less commented on. Thatcher's 'property-owning democracy' privileged a discretely defined ideal of normative families, ones that were implicitly white and British.[171] Thatcher offered up a vision of a 'family romance' peopled by 'a strong Britain of strong British subjects'.[172] Her normative family required their own private property; when Labour voted against Thatcher's 'right-to-buy' programme in October 1986, she charged them with 'kill[ing] the hopes and dreams of so many families'.[173] Heather Nunn has spoken of how these gendered fantasies served as a 'defence' against social disorder.[174] In Anna Marie Smith's estimation, Thatcherism operated by claiming that there is 'nothing beyond the boundaries of the hegemonic project except total political chaos'.[175] The suburban, privatised, Thatcherite home, and the nuclear family living there, were refuges from the perceived chaos of multiracial cities and their socialist local governments, just as private property has long been seen as both a bulwark against mobs and perennially beset by those dangerous mobs.[176]

Thatcher would continue to steadfastly believe that 'there was still too much socialism in Britain'. Socialism had dug itself into 'the institutions and mentality of Britain' and could therefore survive, even though Thatcher's government 'had sold thousands of council homes', which is to say that previously publicly owned homes had been converted into private property. Thatcher herself was upset that toward the end of her tenure as Prime Minister, '29 per cent of the housing stock remained in the public sector', unions still held sway in much of the economy, and not all agreed with her desires for a radical restructuring of the economy; '[i]n all this, my problem was simple. There was a revolution still to be made, but too few revolutionaries.'[177] Thatcher did believe, though, that the 1980s 'saw the rebirth in Britain of an enterprise economy'.[178] And privatisation was the 'fundamental' plank of this renaissance, 'it was one of the central means of reversing the corrosive and corrupting effects of socialism'. Where ownership by the state is impersonal and has negative social effects, Thatcher promoted 'the kind of privatization which leads to the widest possible share ownership by members of the public'. Private home ownership promotes personal responsibility and gives more of the citizenry a share in the economy; it generates more liberty and equality than the false promises of socialism. Thatcher was 'reclaiming territory for freedom'.[179]

As one historian points out, though, the initially low share prices of newly privatised companies quickly became a temptation to sell once the market set the price. Most shares 'quickly found their way back to the large financial institutions. The long-term beneficiaries of privatisation were pension-fund managers.' Public support for privatisation declined, particularly as the promised improvements in services never materialised and as Tory MPs engaged in 'downright squalid' practices, often becoming the heads of the companies they had helped privatise.[180] Newly minted owner-occupiers also tended to (re-)sell their homes at a higher price. In London, slightly over a third of all previously public housing is now rented through private landlords and in some areas that figure is above half.[181] The sell-off of council housing also meant that such homes were no longer available to younger tenants; privatisation was paralleled by a sharp drop in the construction of new public housing. Across the 1980s homelessness rose by 76,342 persons to 178,867, part of a general rise in inequality in the Thatcher years.[182] And James Meek has outlined the gap between Thatcher's dream and the reality she created:

> Many people who bought their council houses sold them on to private landlords, who rented them to people on housing benefit who couldn't get a council house, at double or triple the levels of council rent. Right to Buy thus created an astonishing leak of state money – taxpayers' money if you like to think of it that way – into the hands of a *rentier* class.[183]

The result has been a nation of market-bound renters, rather than the liberatory, property-owning democracy promised by Thatcher.[184]

Thatcher the neoconservative

Thatcher's economic project is conventionally seen as the start of a neoliberal turn in global politics. Yet it would be more accurate to state that Thatcher shows both the blurred boundaries that separate neoliberalism from neoconservatism, and the soft authoritarianism that always exists within neoliberalism (and which neoliberal cant about 'liberty' and 'freedom' obfuscates). Her obsession with history and defence of the British past, her overt espousal of absolute truths and, more than all this, her Burke-style emphasis on social order and the duties and responsibilities of citizens are at odds with standard definitions of neoliberalism.[185] Where neoliberalism is often assumed to privilege a perpetual present tense and a contempt for history or tradition, Thatcher showed a keen interest in heritage, passing National Heritage Acts in 1980 and 1983 and thus envoking ideal (and archly propertied) images of the British past.[186] Indeed at times she could even be suspicious of the dangers of an impersonal capitalist society.[187] Thatcher also talked of the military as a state of exception, a space partitioned off from the rules of *laissez-faire* capitalist society, where rules of discipline prevail and yet a state presumably key to maintaining the order of capitalist society.[188] For all her talk of privatisation and cutbacks, one of her first acts as Prime Minister was to raise pay for police and the armed forces, the thin blue line of private property.[189] Police staff numbers were increased by 20 per cent between 1980 and 1989.[190]

Thatcher's obsessions with families and gender roles fits a recent observation of Melinda Cooper's that '[n]eoliberalism and neoconservatism may be diametrically opposed on many issues, but on the question of family values, they reveal a surprising affinity'.[191] Likewise, Adam Kotsko's perceptive unpacking of neoliberal ideologies shows how neoliberalism has a regular recourse to nationalism and racism, at odds with any silly claims of being post-national or post-racial.[192] I would argue that Thatcher's focus on a property-owning democracy *required* this focus on families and a racialised image of the British past, since these have long been inherent to the propertied imagination.

Highlighting the complex nature of her ideology of 'Liberty', Thatcher described herself as someone who believed in 'sound finance' and 'the creative potential of free enterprise'; both standard neoliberal concerns. Yet she also supported the promotion of 'social discipline'. What she meant by this 'social discipline' was shown by her professed support for legislation that would introduce 'birching or caning for young violent offenders'.[193] She continued to hold out a pronounced role for the state – and an overtly coercive role at that. Thatcher saw the law as a means for social engineering, in which laws 'are signposts to the way society is developing – and the way the legislators of society envisage that it should develop'.[194] She talked of how '[a] functioning free society cannot be value-free'[195] and said that 'even a well-established system of free government is vulnerable to any profound changes in the outlook and mentality of the populace in general and the political class in particular'. To protect against such undue changes, Thatcher urged 'a return to those traditional virtues – for example, thrift, self-discipline, responsibility, pride in and obligation to one's community, what are sometimes called the "Victorian virtues"' and wrote 'I find it difficult to imagine that anything other than Christianity is likely to resupply most people in the West with the virtues necessary to remoralize society in the very practical ways which the solution of many present problems requires'.[196] Indeed, Thatcher spoke of a 'providential harmony between the kind of political economy I favour and the insights of Christianity'.[197] As we saw with people as diverse as Burke, Locke, Fitzhugh and Foley, private property is always unstable and always in need of consistent, robust defence.

Her vision of freedom was bound up with a vision of order:

> you cannot have freedom without order, and order is essential for justice, the rule of law, and moral and social responsibility. We must reestablish the balance between freedom and order and strengthen the institutions of the family, the courts of law, and democratic and traditional forms of government out of which legitimate authority flows. We must again create a climate in which people have to live up to and apply in daily life the standards and values that are the foundations of our civilization.[198]

Indeed, she claimed that '[t]heorists and practical men alike have generally agreed that the primary purpose of the state is to maintain order'.[199] Words like 'order' and 'civilisation', for Thatcher, always referred, simultaneously, to a stable regime of private property, a white racial order and a family-led society of relatively strict gender norms. Her goal was less the expansion of freedom, and more the top-down enforcement of all this. As she said in *The path to power*, with a consciously Burkean flourish, '[a] perfect democracy is the most shameless thing in the world'.[200]

Notes

1 Margaret Thatcher. *The path to power* (New York, 1995), 566.
2 *Path to power* (1995), 3.
3 Hansard, *House of Commons Debate*, 22 November 1990, Vol. 181, cols 439–518. This speech was Thatcher's last as Prime Minister.
4 This point is satirically made by Sue Townsend in 'The secret diary of Margaret Hilda Roberts aged 14¼', included as an appendix in *The true confessions of Adrian Albert Mole* (London, 1989).
5 Margaret Thatcher. 'The principles of Thatcherism', speech in Korea, 3 September 1992, available at www.margaretthatcher.org/document/108302, accessed 11 July 2022. James Meek has observed that '[r]eading Margaret Thatcher's autobiography the impression grows that she believed the transformational effect of privatisation was such as to turn executives into self-consciously moral, patriotic, civically minded entrepreneurs like her father; as if a monopoly on water supply for several million people were a local grocery shop in a small English town in the 1940s': *Private island: why Britain now belongs to someone else* (London, 2014), 18.
6 Reinforcing the idea that her memories were consciously constructed, Thatcher claims she 'never kept a diary' – Margaret Thatcher. *The Downing Street years* (New York, 1993), xiv, 33 – and so presumably both of her memoirs drew on how she *wanted* to remember her own past, rather than any genuinely contemporary recording.
7 For a brief comparative discussion of how Thatcher's imagined childhood compares with that of the French populist Pierre Poujade, see Ellen Meiksins Wood. *The pristine culture of capitalism: a historical essay on old regimes and modern states*, 2nd edition (London, 2015), 40.

8 Heather Cox-Richardson. *To make men free: a history of the Republican Party* (New York, 2014), 255; Barry Goldwater. *With no apologies* (New York, 1979), 5. The reality of Goldwater's youth was, of course, far less ruggedly heroic: 'Goldwater grew up the wealthy son of a wealthy son, with a nurse, chauffeur, and live-in maid. He never carried cash in Phoenix because he could charge anything he wanted to his father, who had long since handed the day-to-day operations of the business to a professional manager. Goldwater chose to quit college after only a year because he didn't like it. When he married, he married an heiress': Cox-Richardson, *To make men free* (2014), 255. Goldwater's family's wealth was made through their eponymous department store, which itself relied on Federal subsidies and assistance.
9 Goldwater, *With no apologies* (1979), 5.
10 Rick Perlstein. *The invisible bridge: the fall of Nixon and the rise of Reagan* (New York, 2014), 24–5, 26, 31.
11 Bruce Cumings. *Dominion from sea to sea: Pacific ascendancy and American power* (New Haven, CT, 2009), 295–6.
12 'Thatcher's tendency to make public stories of her personal past ... often legitimated, through self-example, a moral economy in which the enterprising individual's hard work and self-sufficiency earned the right breaks to success': Heather Nunn. *Thatcher, politics and fantasy: the political culture of gender and nation* (London, 2002), 28.
13 *Path to power* (1995), 36.
14 On the role of monarchism in these imaginary visions of the British past, see David Cannadine's claim that '[j]ust as many late Victorians began their autobiographies with recollections of the Diamond Jubilee of the Great White Queen, so I suspect that many of my contemporaries will begin theirs with their recollections of the coronation of Queen Elizabeth II in 1953, and the extraordinary feelings of hope and euphoria it generated': *Ornamentalism: how the British saw their empire* (Oxford, 2001), 183.
15 *Path to power* (1995), 20. She later claimed that she and Denis Thatcher were 'passionate devotees of the monarchy': *Path to power*, 78.
16 Eric J. Evans. *Thatcher and Thatcherism*, 3rd edition (London, 2013), 6.
17 Heather Cox-Richardson has said that post-Goldwater American conservatism's 'anti-intellectualism became a strength. That their rhetoric did not address reality mattered less than that it seemed to offer a

comforting route to bring back the prosperity and security voters associated with an idyllic American past': *To make men free* (2014), 274. '"Mastery", "control", "curb", "calculate", "order", "discipline" are the watchwords throughout [Thatcher's] memoir and are values intimately related to "capitalism", her "creed for the common man". Interviewed by Pete Murray on *The Late Show* in March 1982, she told the radio audience that her childhood was "rich in the right values" which overrode material scarcity ... Throughout her memoir, the utterances of the political opposition are constructed as immoderate: "shameless", "immoral", "a stream of crude invective"': Nunn, *Thatcher, politics and fantasy* (2002), 90–91.

18 In Thatcher's account of her childhood, 'no glimpse of the spontaneous, the private or domestic is allowed': Nunn, *Thatcher, politics and fantasy* (2002), 79. Some of Nunn's Freudian analyses are overly personal, though, getting lost in the weeds of Thatcher the person, and losing sight of the broader politics.

19 'Thatcher envisaged a "privatization" of the child that symbolised a broader extraction of Thatcherite subjects from the dependency of the Welfare State and into consumer self-sufficiency ... adult fears about the undisciplined or politically indoctrinated child tapped into and stirred up unconscious anxieties about subjective fragmentation and desires for authority and control': Nunn, *Thatcher, politics and fantasy* (2002), 21.

20 John Medhurst. *That option no longer exists: Britain, 1974–76* (London, 2014), 119.

21 Louisa Hadley. *Responding to Margaret Thatcher's death* (London, 2014), 65, 74. The sculpting of Thatcher's media image was handled by Gordon Reece, the party's director of publicity, who later received a knighthood for his work: Evans, *Thatcher and Thatcherism* (2013), 18. Thatcher's hiring of the Saatchi & Saatchi firm in 1979 perhaps represented the first example of commercial political campaigning in Europe. Tim Bell, the man who ran Thatcher's 1979 campaign, 'later worked for the National Coal Board against the striking miners in 1984, and for the Pinochetista Presidential candidate Hernán Büchi – who lost in 1989 – as well as for the Pinochet Foundation. In 1996, he was the Saatchi & Saatchi man organizing Yeltsin's electoral victory in Russia': Göran Therborn. *Inequality and the labyrinths of democracy* (London, 2020), 35.

22 Ben Jackson, Robert Saunders, 'Introduction: varieties of Thatcherism' in Ben Jackson, Robert Saunders, eds. *Making Thatcher's Britain* (Cambridge, 2012), 3–4.

23 Louisa Hadley, Elizabeth Ho. '"The lady's not for turning": new cultural perspectives on Thatcher and Thatcherism' in Louisa Hadley, Elizabeth Ho, eds. *Thatcher and after: Margaret Thatcher and her afterlife in contemporary culture* (London, 2010), 4. See also Nunn, *Thatcher, politics and fantasy* (2002), 28.
24 *Morning Star*, 19 March 1984. Quoted in Seumas Milne. *The enemy within: the secret war against the miners* (London, 2004), 6.
25 Or as Anna Marie Smith said: 'Every political era is remembered in terms of its defining myth, and Thatcherism is no exception': *New Right discourse on race and sexuality: Britain, 1968–1990* (Cambridge, 1994), 1.
26 *Path to power* (1995), 28–9.
27 Margaret Thatcher. 1950 general election address, 3 February 1950, available at http://www.margaretthatcher.org/document/100858, accessed 11 July 2022. 'Make Britain great again' was the Tories' slogan for the 1950 general election. The racialised meaning nestled within this phrase was more overt in a slogan proposed (but ultimately rejected) for the 1955 general election: 'Keep Britain white': Paul Gilroy. *'There ain't no black in the Union Jack': the cultural politics of race and nation* (Chicago, 1991), 46. Simon Peplow calls this the proposed 'keep England white' campaign slogan in 1955, noting that it had the active support of Churchill: *Race and riots in Thatcher's Britain* (Manchester, 2019), 19. The Tories' 1987 electoral slogan was 'Britain's great again, don't let Labour wreck it': Evans, *Thatcher and Thatcherism* (2013), 27. David Cameron would later say of Thatcher: 'she made our country great again': Hadley, *Responding to Margaret Thatcher's death* (2014), 40. It is worth considering how racialised this sentiment has always been, where national 'greatness', for Conservatives, cannot be imagined absent of whiteness.
28 *Path to power* (1995), 46.
29 *Downing Street years* (1993), 625.
30 *Downing Street years* (1993), 12.
31 *Path to power* (1995), 186.
32 *Downing Street years* (1993), 12.
33 Meek, *Private island* (2014), 12.
34 Henk Overbeek. *Global capitalism and national decline: the Thatcher decade in perspective* (London, 1990), 1. Overbeek also makes the important point that the economic anxieties to which Thatcherism gave voice had their analogue in the rise of the New Right in the USA.

35 Andrew Gamble. 'Thatcherism and Conservative politics', in Stuart Hall, Martin Jacques, eds. *The politics of Thatcherism* (London, 1983), 109.
36 Fintan O'Toole. *Heroic failure: Brexit and the politics of pain* (London, 2018), 16.
37 Nunn, *Thatcher, politics and fantasy* (2002), 49. Gallas describes the 1970s as a period of 'catastrophic equilibrium', a term he borrows from Gramsci. In terms of labour–capital relations, 'both sides are strong enough to launch attacks, but neither side is capable of defeating the other … the fierce class struggles in 1970s Britain followed this pattern': Alexander Gallas. *The Thatcherite offensive: a neo-Poultanzasian analysis* (Chicago, 2016), 75.
38 Evans, *Thatcher and Thatcherism* (2013), 12.
39 Medhurst, *That option no longer exists* (2014), 44.
40 Gallas, *Thatcherite offensive* (2016), 81.
41 Stuart Hall, Martin Jacques. 'Introduction' in Hall and Jacques, *Politics of Thatcherism* (1983), 10; Gallas, *Thatcherite offensive* (2016), 93.
42 Tom Nairn. 'Britain's living legacy', in Hall and Jacques, *Politics of Thatcherism* (1983), 282.
43 Gamble, 'Thatcherism and Conservative politics', 110–11.
44 Britain had an annual growth rate of 2.2% from 1962–72, compared to 4.7% in France. In the 1950s, Britain had the ninth highest gross domestic product per capita in the world, falling to fifteenth in 1971 and eighteenth by 1976. Labour productivity was also a source of shame; the USA had a rate 50% higher than the UK, and West Germany had a rate 25% higher: Evans, *Thatcher and Thatcherism* (2013), 11.
45 Jon Lawrence and Florence Sutcliffe-Braithwaite. 'Margaret Thatcher and the decline of class politics', in Jackson and Saunders, *Making Thatcher's Britain* (2012), 132, 133. 'One of the most notable right-wing groups to gain momentum in the 1970s was the National Association for Freedom (NAFF), launched in the [*sic*] 1975. Their Charter of Rights and Liberties included: Freedom to withdraw one's labour, other than contrary to public safety. Freedom to belong or not to belong to a trade union … The right to private ownership. Like the Socialist Workers' Party, they sold papers on the streets in London. John Gouriet, the director of NAFF in the 1970s, was part of a Right wing that, as the journalist Andy Beckett puts it, had a "sense that the world was tilting dangerously towards Leftism and anarchy"': Tara Martin López. *The winter of discontent: myth, memory and history* (Liverpool, 2014), 35.

46 Richard Wright's *Patriots: national identity in Britain, 1940–2000* (London, 2002), quoted in O'Toole, *Heroic failure* (2018), 15.
47 Martin López, *Winter of discontent* (2014), 9. 'The Winter of Discontent has cast a pall over British collective memory; this is nowhere more apparent than in the dirge-like vocabulary evoked to describe it … "hangover", "violent", "hues of the blackest black", "evil ogre", "revenge", "self-interest", and even "hara-kiri".' Though even then, López discusses how this image of pre-Thatcherite Britain was itself the product of savvy post-1979 media manipulation by the Tories: *Winter of discontent*, 11, 23–4. Anti-Left sentiment – a 'widespread fear of the domestic radical left and Soviet-style authoritarian socialism' in Britain – was already strong prior to the winter of discontent. Anti-union feeling became so strong that even Labour leader Jim Callaghan and Trades Union Congress leader Len Murray turned on striking workers that winter: Gallas, *Thatcherite offensive* (2016), 116, 117.
48 Gallas, *Thatcherite offensive* (2016), 116.
49 Stuart Hall. 'Racism and reaction' (1978) in Stuart Hall; Sally Davison et al., eds. *Selected political writings: The great moving right show and other essays* (Durham, NC, 2017), 153, 155. See also Stuart Hall. 'The great moving right show' (1983) in *Selected political writings*, 172–86.
50 Stuart Hall, Chas Critcher, Tony Jefferson, John Clarke, Brian Roberts. *Policing the crisis: mugging, the state, and law and order* (London, 1978). Key to this moral panic was the idea that Britain was beset by a series of interchangeable internal threats, 'the enemy within', a term used by Angus Maude, in the *Sunday Express* on 2 May 1971, to describe American-style street criminals: *Policing the crisis*, 26. Enoch Powell had used the phrase 'the enemy within' at a speech in Northfield during the 1970 election to describe student radicals and Irish terrorists: Hall, 'Racism and reaction' (1978), 153. Famously, Thatcher would later call the National Union of Mineworkers 'the enemy within': Milne, *Enemy within* (2004).
51 Hall and Jacques, 'Introduction' (1983), 13. The phrase 'general sense of outrage and humiliation' was how the Marxist historian Eric Hobsbawm remembered the immediate pre-Thatcher period: Richard J. Evans. *Eric Hobsbawm: a life in history* (London, 2019), 515. Indeed, the anxiety about moral decline was shared by much of the political left. 'The Thatcherites share with the left the view that something is deeply wrong with the British economy and that fundamental changes are needed': Bob Rowthorn, 'The past strikes back' in Hall and Jacques, *Politics of Thatcherism* (1983), 71.

52 Gallas, *Thatcherite offensive* (2016), 121.
53 Smith, *New Right discourse on race and sexuality* (1994), 4.
54 Medhurst, *That option no longer exists* (2014), 3.
55 Nunn, *Thatcher, politics and fantasy* (2002), 52. Heather Nunn, in unpacking the rhetoric of Thatcherism, argued that a nostalgia for a glorious British past, whether of the Second World War or of the Victorian era, served as a defence against the present, as well as a defiance of that present: *Thatcher, politics and fantasy*, 23.
56 *Path to power* (1995), 538–9.
57 *Path to power* (1995), 544.
58 *Downing Street years* (1993), 8.
59 *Path to power* (1995), 395.
60 *Downing Street years* (1993), 7.
61 *Downing Street years* (1993), 301. As if to reinforce the idea that all her opponents were evil, she wrote of supposed contacts between the NUM and the Libyan government as 'a preternatural alliance between these different forces of disorder'. She also spoke of 'the devious ruthlessness of the NUM leaders' and called them 'the Fascist Left': *Downing Street years*, 351, 364, 378.
62 *Downing Street years* (1993), 157. 'For Thatcher, trade unions were the "enemy" of enterprise culture, "much more difficult to fight, [and] just as dangerous to liberty", and she was determined to take a firm and unwavering approach to handling them': Hadley and Ho, 'The lady's not for turning', 7–8.
63 *Path to power* (1995), 422.
64 *Path to power* (1995), 448.
65 *Path to power* (1995), 449, 452. The speeches at Cardiff and Birmingham became 'the standard speech I made to audiences around the country' and were also used as the basis for press releases: *Path to power*, 455.
66 *Downing Street years* (1993), 160. Thatcher did admit, though, that Thatcherism was never as popular in Scotland where socialism allegedly continued to cause 'new strains of social and economic disease': *Downing Street years*, 618.
67 Margaret Thatcher. *Statecraft: strategies for a changing world* (New York, 2002), 412.
68 *Path to power* (1995), 557.
69 Margaret Thatcher. 'Managing conflict – the role of international intervention', in 'Managing conflict in the post-cold war world: the role of intervention', Report of the Aspen Institute Conference, 2–6 August 1995 (Queenstown, MD, 1996), 53.

70 *Downing Street years* (1993), 264–5.
71 *Downing Street years* (1993), 7.
72 *Path to power* (1995), 461.
73 *Downing Street years* (1993), 10. Thatcher's lieutenant Keith Joseph saw unions as a 'malignancy' in Britain, which, as Alexander Gallas points out, 'evokes the image of a cancerous body' that must be aggressively treated, through excision if necessary: *Thatcherite offensive* (2016), 91.
74 Jonathan Charteris-Black. *Politicians and rhetoric: the persuasive power of metaphor* (London, 2005), 101, 102.
75 Charteris-Black, *Politicians and rhetoric* (2005), 101.
76 Charteris-Black, *Politicians and rhetoric* (2005), 114.
77 *Downing Street years* (1993), 19.
78 Hadley, *Responding to Margaret Thatcher's death* (2014), 8. The 'kill socialism in Britain' promise is also quoted in Gallas, *Thatcherite offensive* (2016), 6 and 140. In October 1977 she made the prediction 'I look to the day when we throw off the Socialist yoke and together turn to the task of setting our country on the road to a real and lasting recovery': Charteris-Black, *Politicians and rhetoric* (2005), 99.
79 *Path to power* (1995), 373.
80 *Statecraft* (2002), 23.
81 *Statecraft* (2002), 69.
82 *Statecraft* (2002), 21.
83 *Statecraft* (2002), 69.
84 Andrew S. Crines, Timothy Heppell, Peter Dorey. *The political rhetoric and oratory of Margaret Thatcher* (London, 2016), 97.
85 Margaret Thatcher. 'The common crisis: Atlantic solutions', in Gerald Frost, William E. Odom, eds. *The Congress of Prague: revitalizing the Atlantic alliance* (Washington, DC, 1997), 88.
86 *Statecraft* (2002), 21.
87 *Statecraft* (2002), 416.
88 *Downing Street years* (1993), 451.
89 *Statecraft* (2002), 1–2, 9.
90 *Statecraft* (2002), 413. She talked of the fall of communism as 'The World Turned Right Side Up', with 'Right' presumably being a pun. And '[a]s that old order crumbled … its people emerged blinking into the light': *Downing Street years* (1993), 768, 813.
91 Margaret Thatcher. 'Liberty and responsibility', in David L. Boren, Edward J. Perkins, eds. *Democracy, morality, and the search for peace in American foreign policy* (Norman, OK, 2002), 25. 'The end of the Cold War was the significant *political* event of my lifetime: but it did

not mean the end of conflict. There will *always* be conflict: it is part of human nature, part of the eternal battle between good and evil': 'Managing conflict' (1996), 45. Emphases added.
92 *Path to power* (1995), 355–6.
93 *Path to power* (1995), 386.
94 *Downing Street years* (1993), 509–10.
95 For the history of claims of Jewish superior intelligence, and how easily 'Smart Jews' can become cunning or scheming Jews, see Sander Gilman. *Smart Jews: the construction of the image of Jewish superior intelligence* (Lincoln, NE, 1996). The philosemitic claim that Jews look after their own is a warmed-over version of the antisemitic claim that Jews are clannish and self-regarding.
96 *Path to power* (1995), 24. She later says of Neville Chamberlain's appeasement of Hitler: 'British foreign policy is at its worst when it is engaged in giving away other people's territory', though she says nothing about Britain *taking* other people's territory: *Path to power*, 27.
97 *Path to power* (1995), 45. In an observation that ignores how much British rule had fomented the root causes of violence and communalism in India and across much of the Empire, Thatcher approvingly spoke of 'the role of Britain, not just as guarantor of sound administration and humane justice in our Imperial territories, but rather as a kind of midwife for their birth, growth and maturity as responsible member of the international community ... In a tragic sense the civil war which now broke out [in India], in which a million people died, showed the degree to which British rule had been the guarantee of Indian unity and peace': *Path to power*, 54–5.
98 *Path to power* (1995), 56. Writing in 1982, Stuart Hall made the following perceptive comment: 'Empires come and go. But the imagery of the British Empire seems destined to go on forever ... As the country drifts deeper into recession, we seem to possess no other viable vocabulary in which to cast our sense of who the British people are and where they are going, except one drawn from the inventory of a lost imperial greatness': 'The empire strikes back' (1982) in Hall; Davison et al., *Selected political writings* (2017), 200.
99 *Path to power* (1995), 368.
100 *Statecraft* (2002), 16.
101 'The common crisis: Atlantic solutions', 85.
102 *Statecraft* (2002), 21–2.
103 *Statecraft* (2002), 416. Like many who employ the post-Holocaust construct of 'the Judaeo-Christian tradition', Thatcher has little to say about how Islam fits into their schema.

104 'The common crisis: Atlantic solutions', 91.
105 Gilroy, *Ain't no black in the Union Jack* (1991), 47. Gallas also sees Powell as a forerunner of Thatcher: 'Many of his themes were to reappear in the Thatcherite discourse, not least because some of his followers became leading Thatcherites, and because he found an admirer in Thatcher': Gallas, *Thatcherite offensive* (2016), 81–2.
106 For a full text of the speech, see www.telegraph.co.uk/comment/3643823/Enoch-Powells-Rivers-of-Blood-speech.html, accessed 11 July 2022. A Gallup poll conducted just after the speech was given found that 25 per cent of respondents wanted Powell to be the next head of the Conservative Party. At the time London dock-workers demonstrated in his support: Gallas, *Thatcherite offensive* (2016), 82–3.
107 The Anglo-Pakistani leftist, Tariq Ali, offers a succinct summary of Powell's politics, seeing him as part of the cadre of lower-middle-class Britons who had seen the empire as a path to social advancement, only to have that path closed off firmly by decolonisation: Tariq Ali. *Street fighting years: an autobiography of the sixties* (London, 2005), 107–8. The parallels to Thatcher's own background are provocative!
108 Eric Evans' sarcastic appraisal is probably closer to the mark: Enoch Powell was 'probably the twentieth-century politician with the largest brain and the smallest amount of common-sense': *Thatcher and Thatcherism* (2013), 9.
109 *Path to power* (1995), 144–5.
110 *Path to power* (1995), 146.
111 *Path to power* (1995), 147.
112 Gilroy, *Ain't no black in the Union Jack* (1991), 45. Thatcher's embrace of Enoch Powell was a major reason why she continued to be seen as a threat within immigrant communities: Hadley *Responding to Margaret Thatcher's death* (2014), 70.
113 Smith, *New Right discourse on race and sexuality* (1994), 7.
114 *Downing Street years* (1993), 146.
115 Vron Ware. *Beyond the pale: white women, racism and history* (London, 2015), 7–8. The idea that racial strife in American cities was the future facing British cities was an 'emergent trope' on the British far right in the 1970s: Paul Jackson, 'Accumulative extremism: the post-war tradition of Anglo-American neo-Nazi activism' in Paul Jackson, Anton Shekhovtsov, eds. *The post-war Anglo-American far right: a special relationship of hate* (London, 2014), 18.
116 Nunn, *Thatcher, politics and fantasy* (2002), 116.

117 Gilroy, *Ain't no black in the Union Jack* (1991), 43, 77. Gilroy investigates how 'Englishness' as a national/racial category in Thatcherism was synomous with being law-abiding, which had the obvious effect of branding all non-English, non-white people as potential or actual criminals. See also Martin Kettle, 'The drift to law and order' in Hall and Jacques, *Politics of Thatcherism* (1983), 216–34.

118 *Path to power* (1995), 405–6. For the broader history of race, racism and belonging in post-imperial Britain, see Kennetta Hammond Perry. *London is the place for me: Black Britons, citizenship, and the politics of race* (Oxford, 2015).

119 The statement was made as part of a TV interview, in which the fuller statement was: 'If we went on as we are then by the end of the century there would be 4 million people of the new Commonwealth or Pakistan here. Now, that is an awful lot and I think it means that people are really rather afraid that this country might be rather swamped by people with a different culture and, you know, the British character has done so much for democracy, for law and order, and so much throughout the world, that if there is any fear that it might be swamped, people are going to react and be rather hostile to those coming in': Kevin A. Morrison, 'There's no place like home: Margaret Thatcher at Number 10 Downing Street' in Hadley and Ho, *Thatcher and after* (2010), 116. In April 1979, five days before the general election, a Black listener to a phone-in discussion on BBC Radio 4 challenged Thatcher to retract the 'swamped' statement. She refused, and instead asserted that '[s]ome people do feel swamped if streets they had lived in for the whole of their lives are now really quite different': Martin Barker. *The new racism: conservatives and the ideology of the tribe* (Frederick, MD, 1981), 1.

120 *Path to power* (1995), 408–9. Anna Marie Smith gives the slightly less impressive figure of a nine-point jump in polls: *New Right discourse on race and sexuality* (1994), 5. Either way, it is clear that Thatcher's rhetoric was politically useful.

121 *Path to power* (1995), 405–6. That the National Front were 'socialists' is, of course, absurd. It is also almost diametrically opposed to the truth; Ware argues that from the late 1970s onwards, 'the support for the tiny fascist parties that was expressed both during elections and on the street shifted towards the right wing of the Conservative Party, encouraged by the popular racism being voiced in "respectable" circles': Ware, *Beyond the pale* (2015), 24. Likewise, Peplow has shown the connections between the Tories' 'tough stance on immigration', their 1979 electoral victory and 'the visible popularity of the

NF [National Front] promoting racist views': Peplow, *Race and riots* (2019), 31. Thatcher was closer to the National Front than she would have liked to accept.
122 Matthew Grimley. 'Thatcherism, morality and religion' in Jackson and Saunders, *Making Thatcher's Britain* (2012), 78.
123 Jean Gardiner. 'Women, recession and the Tories' in Hall and Jacques, *Politics of Thatcherism* (1983), 195.
124 Joe Cleary, *Outrageous fortune: capital and culture in modern Ireland* (Dublin, 2006), 64.
125 Michèle Barrett, Mary McIntosh. *The anti-social family*, 2nd edition (London, 2015), 12–13. Race is noticeable by its absence from their otherwise perceptive accounting, particularly in their discussion of 'law-and-order' and making women safe on the streets, both of which have an undisguised racial register for Thatcherism.
126 Gilroy, *Ain't no black in the Union Jack* (1991), 18.
127 Barker, *New racism* (1981), 23, 49.
128 Nunn, *Thatcher, politics and fantasy* (2002), 80.
129 Margaret Thatcher. Speech on 'Women in a changing world' (1st Dame Margery Corbett-Ashby Memorial Lecture), 26 July 1982, available at www.margaretthatcher.org/document/105007, accessed 11 July 2022. For a further discussion of this speech, see Lynne Segal. 'The heat in the kitchen', in Hall and Jacques, *Politics of Thatcherism* (1983), 207–15.
130 Hadley and Ho, 'The lady's not for turning', 4; Hadley, *Responding to Margaret Thatcher's death* (2014), 17, 64. Hadley says Thatcher constructed herself as an 'ordinary working mother' and 'played' on her gender so much that it is impossible to consider her politics without noting this deliberate use of gender: *Responding to Margaret Thatcher's death,* 18, 28. 'Again and again throughout her premiership, Thatcher emphasised that she was Mrs Thatcher first and foremost, a housewife and a mother, and that as a wife and mother she was able to understand the concerns of ordinary women': Laura Beers, 'Thatcher and the women's vote' in Jackson and Saunders, *Making Thatcher's Britain* (2012), 118. 'Throughout her political career, Thatcher worked to valorise housewives in British society, and to facilitate, as she perceived it, a woman's ability to balance work and family. She appealed to women primarily through media seen as outside the purview of politics – such as *Cosmopolitan*, or *Woman's Own*' and '[t]hroughout Margaret Thatcher's term as Prime Minister, women continued to prefer the Conservative Party to Labour in greater numbers than their male counterparts. This fact in itself was

not surprising. While the differentials between male and female voting had varied as long as polling data had been available, the so-called "gender gap" had always favoured the Conservatives. Only in 2005 did women begin to show a stronger preference than men for the Labour Party': Beers, 'Thatcher and the women's vote', 113, 119.
131 Hadley, *Responding to Margaret Thatcher's death* (2014), 54.
132 *Statecraft* (2002), 45.
133 *Path to power* (1995), 539.
134 Margaret Thatcher. 'Speech to Shipley Conservatives', 28 June 1975, available at www.margaretthatcher.org/document/102726, accessed 19 July 2022.
135 Nunn, *Thatcher, politics and fantasy* (2002), 105, 106. 'The smallest and the largest components of national life are interlinked. Thatcher disavowed dependency, powerlessness and passivity in both the private and the public spheres. The private space of the family was not only the model for public behaviour but also the utopia to be strive for and the "Heaven" to be protected against the hostility and destruction that characterised her vision of the public political world': *Thatcher, politics and fantasy*, 134.
136 Nunn, *Thatcher, politics and fantasy* (2002), 112.
137 *Path to power* (1995), 549.
138 *Path to power* (1995), 550.
139 The junior education minister Rhodes Boyson blamed social unrest on the dissolution of 'stable families' and the lingering effects of 1960s permissiveness, a sentiment Thatcher shared: Nunn, *Thatcher, politics and fantasy* (2002), 119.
140 Nunn, *Thatcher, politics and fantasy* (2002), 21.
141 Peter Riddell. *The Thatcher decade: how Britain has changed during the 1980s* (Oxford, 1989), 114–15; Matthew Francis. '"A crusade to enfranchise the many": Thatcherism and the "property-owning democracy"', *Twentieth Century British History*, Vol. 23, No. 2 (2012), 275–97.
142 Joel Krieger. *Reagan, Thatcher and the politics of decline* (Oxford, 1986), 73–4. Krieger also points to the politicking value of this; the council estates were bedrocks of Labour support; converting them to private ownership was intended to convert them to bastions of Conservative support.
143 Gallas, *Thatcherite offensive* (2016), 105.
144 Evans, *Thatcher and Thatcherism* (2013), 18. Working-class home ownership had already risen from 51 per cent of households in 1971 to 58 per cent in 1981; Labour were in support of this. Thatcher was

thus, in one sense, a function of an already progressing change, rather than its initial catalyst: John Boughton. *Municipal dreams: the rise and fall of council housing* (London, 2018), 144.
145 Evans, *Thatcher and Thatcherism* (2013), 35; Riddell, *Thatcher decade* (1989), 114–15.
146 Boughton, *Municipal dreams* (2018), 169. This was accompanied by a drastic drop in the popularity of council housing; '[e]ven in 1966, two-thirds of the population gave owner occupation as their tenure of choice but still over one in five said they would prefer to rent from the council. By 1989, only 12 per cent gave council housing as their preferred form of tenure': *Municipal dreams*, 173.
147 *Daily Telegraph*, 30 January 1975, quoted in *Path to power* (1995), 275.
148 *Downing Street years* (1993), 278–9.
149 Crines, Heppell and Dorey, *Political rhetoric and oratory of Margaret Thatcher* (2016), 95–6.
150 As part of her project of privatisation, Thatcher's first Chancellor of the Exchequer, Geoffrey Howe, cut the top rate of income tax from 83% to 60%, and cut the basic rate from 33% to 30%: Jackson and Saunders, 'Introduction: varieties of Thatcherism', 5. 'While cutting income tax and public spending, Thatcher raised VAT. It was 8% when she came to power; today [2014] it is 20%. This regressive tax affects the poorest far more than it does the richest; the richest 20% pay 4% extra tax in VAT today while the poorest fifth pay an extra 8.7%': Meek, *Private island* (2014), 22.
151 Meek, *Private island* (2014), 8–9. In his generally sympathetic account of the Thatcher era, Peter Riddell identifies the underlying presumption that 'everything than can be sold should be': *Thatcher decade* (1989), 87.
152 Boughton, *Municipal dreams* (2018), 169.
153 Brett Christophers. *The new enclosure: the appropriation of public land in neoliberal Britain* (London, 2018), 1–2.
154 Satnam Virdee. *Racism, class and the racialized outsider* (London, 2014), 147.
155 'According to Hugo Young, Thatcher had to be talked into Right to Buy by a desperate Edward Heath, then her leader, who'd been persuaded by his friend Pierre Trudeau after his electoral defeat in February 1974 that he needed a fistful of populist policies. No wonder Thatcher baulked. Right to Buy violated basic Thatcherite values: that self-reliance was good, state handouts bad. Right to Buy was a massive handout to people who weren't supposed to need handouts. In fact

that was why they got the handout – because they were the kind of people who didn't need handouts': Meek, *Private island* (2014), 191.
156 Boughton, *Municipal dreams* (2018), 170–71, 174, 175.
157 Evans, *Thatcher and Thatcherism* (2013), 36.
158 Evans, *Thatcher and Thatcherism* (2013), 36.
159 Evans, *Thatcher and Thatcherism* (2013), 37.
160 *Path to power* (1995), 448.
161 *Path to power* (1995), 474.
162 *Path to power* (1995), 12–13. Grantham's private charity echoed the approach Thatcher saw being taken in the United States, 'the richest and freest country on earth; and, not surprisingly, it is also the most generous. Each year Americans give over $200 billion to good causes. Britain too shares in this tradition, where individual freedom and individual responsibility are assumed to go together – hence the country's inspiring history of charitable foundations and voluntary effort. The more we rely on remote public authorities to cope with the tragedies of life, the less we will do ourselves – and the more the unpleasing canker of self-materialism will grow': *Statecraft* (2002), 425.
163 *Path to power* (1995), 546.
164 *Path to power* (1995), 565. Thatcher was not unaware of the nature of her constructed vision of an ideal Britain. As she wrote in 2002, '[t]o have an idea of a country is not necessarily to have a distorted view of it. It is, if the idea is a true one, to gain an insight into the mystery of a nation's identity': *Statecraft* (2002), 19–20.
165 *Path to power* (1995), 566. Emphasis added.
166 *Downing Street years* (1993), 10.
167 'The common crisis: Atlantic solutions', 88.
168 Riddell, *Thatcher decade* (1989), 10.
169 Gallas, *Thatcherite offensive* (2016), 145, 201.
170 Margaret Thatcher. Interviewed by *Woman's Own*, 23 September 1987, available at www.margaretthatcher.org/document/106689, accessed 11 July 2022. She later repudiated this comment, and indeed it is at odds with the fact that 'society' plays a major role in her vision of the proper social order. In her autobiographies, she talks fondly of how the Rotary Club's motto, 'service above self', was so much a part of her father's outlook that it 'was engraved on his heart': *Path to power* (1995), 16. She also observed that '"extreme" individualism at the expense of society or community was the left's principal charge against me'. In an effort to correct the record, she stated that 'on that score I plead not guilty: for me duties precede rights, and though charity begins, it does not end at home': *Statecraft* (2002), 248.

171 'In contemporary [1980s] Britain, statements about nation are invariably also statements about "race". The Conservatives appear to recognize this and seek to play with the ambiguities which this situation creates. Their recent statements on the theme of Britishness betray a sophisticated grasp of the interface between "race" and nation created in the post-"rivers of blood" era': Gilroy, *Ain't no black in the Union Jack* (1991), 57.
172 Nunn, *Thatcher, politics and fantasy* (2002), 22.
173 Charteris-Black, *Politicians and rhetoric* (2005), 108.
174 Nunn, *Thatcher, politics and fantasy* (2002), 23.
175 Smith, *New Right discourse on race and sexuality* (1994), 37.
176 Smith, for example, shows how Tory MPs fused opposition to local government with homophobia by constructing an image of local councils controlled by militant gay activists: Smith, *New Right discourse on race and sexuality* (1994), 16.
177 *Downing Street years* (1993), 306.
178 *Downing Street years* (1993), 668.
179 *Downing Street years* (1993), 676.
180 Evans, *Thatcher and Thatcherism* (2013), 37. The expansion of shareholding 'has not been deep'. Most shareholders only invested in one company. Of the 5.4 million 'new shareholders', 800,000 bought between four and nine shares and only 300,000 'have what can reasonably be described as a portfolio of over ten shares'. Most holdings of shares were worth 'no more than £2,500 per investor', with even this value dropping in the October 1987 stock market crash: Riddell, *Thatcher decade* (1989), 119.
181 David Madden, Peter Marcuse. *In defence of housing: the politics of crisis* (London, 2016), 41. Madden and Marcuse tell of one particular estate in London, in which 'more than forty ex-public housing units are owned by the son of the government minister who presided over the privatization of public housing in the 1980s'. This is a familiar refrain in the history of neoliberal privatisations. Note the similarities in Tony Wood's description of post-1989 Russia: 'The privatizations of the early 1990s hadn't created a nationwide mass of shareholders, but rather an oligarchy that proceeded to pile up wealth on a scale previously unimaginable. For the bulk of population, ownership of assets remained out of reach. Housing was one partial and substantial exception to this trend, but even here outcomes were ambiguous and uneven. Starting in 1992, the majority of the country's housing stock was divested to municipalities, who were then supposed to oversee its sale to households. In practice, about half of

housing was sold in this way, mainly because legal title to an apartment brought increased costs – maintenance services – that few were able to take on. While a large number of city-dwellers came to own apartments they could then sell (this was an especially lucrative move in Moscow), across most of Russia, there was only the most tentative kind of real estate market': *Russia without Putin: money, power and the myths of the new cold war* (London, 2018), 66.

182 Boughton, *Municipal dreams* (2018), 175. 'If an unofficial "poverty line" is drawn at half the average national income, the numbers in poverty increased from 5 million in 1979 to 14.1 million in 1992': Evans, *Thatcher and Thatcherism* (2013), 156. By 2014, 'the share of the nation's wealth owned by the top 1% is once again back at 1918 levels and heading towards Victorian levels of inequality': Medhurst, *That option no longer exists* (2014), 7.

183 Meek, *Private island* (2014), 193–4.

184 As house prices rose across late Thatcherism, internal migration within the UK became increasingly difficult; northern homeowners lacked the equity needed to cash in their property investment and buy a house in the south: Riddell, *Thatcher decade* (1989), 165.

185 Being middle class, she said in an interview with the *Evening Standard* in 1974, 'has never been simply a matter of income, but a whole attitude to life, a will to take responsibility for oneself': *Path to power* (1995), 263.

186 Hadley and Ho, 'The lady's not for turning', 12.

187 'My experience of college life contributed to my later conviction that if you wish to bring the best out of people they should be encouraged to be part of smaller, human-scale communities rather than be left to drift on a sea of impersonality': *Path to power* (1995), 36–7.

188 *Statecraft* (2002), 44, 46.

189 *Downing Street years* (1993), 32. Thatcher claimed the police were not 'properly paid' and that she hoped to avoid a 'crisis of morale'.

190 Gallas, *Thatcherite offensive* (2016), 141.

191 Melinda Cooper. *Family values: between neoliberalism and the new social conservatism* (New York, 2017), 33. See also Florence Sutcliffe-Braithwaite. 'Neo-liberalism and morality in the making of Thatcherite social policy', *The Historical Journal*, Vol. 55, No. 2 (2012), 497–520.

192 Adam Kotsko. *Neoliberalism's demons: on the political theology of late capital* (Stanford, CA, 2018), 21 and throughout. It is, indeed, tempting to not just pinpoint the authoritarianism inherent to neoliberalism, but also look ahead from Thatcher to Brexit and Trump,

which thus appear less like aberrations in the twenty-first century and more like the culmination of certain racist, nationalist and misogynist strands of neoliberalism that were there all along. Is Trumpism what happens when the normalising claims of neoliberalism are abandoned?

193 *Path to power* (1995), 116.
194 *Path to power* (1995), 153.
195 *Path to power* (1995), 553.
196 *Path to power* (1995), 554.
197 *Path to power* (1995), 555.
198 'Liberty and responsibility', 30.
199 *Path to power* (1995), 542.
200 *Path to power* (1995), 46. She directly adapted this line of thinking from Burke: 'For me as a British Conservative, with Edmund Burke the father of Conservatism and first great perceptive critic of the Revolution as my ideological mentor, the events of 1789 represent a perennial illusion in politics. The French Revolution was a Utopian attempt to overthrow a traditional order – one with many imperfections, certainly – in the name of abstract ideas, formulated by vain intellectuals, which lapsed, not by chance but through weakness and wickedness, into purges, mass murder and war. In so many ways it anticipated the still more terrible Bolshevik Revolution of 1917. The English tradition of liberty, however, grew over the centuries; its most marked features are continuity, respect for law and a sense of balance, as demonstrated by the Glorious Revolution of 1688': *Downing Street years* (1993), 753.

Epilogue
Interplanetary settler-colonialism

> ... witness Katrina in black and white neighbourhoods of New Orleans, Sandy in Haiti and in Manhattan, sea level rise in Bangladesh and in the Netherlands ... For the foreseeable future – indeed, as long as there are class societies on earth – there *will* be lifeboats for the rich and privileged, and there will *not* be any shared sense of catastrophe. More than ever, class divisions will become matters of life and death: who gets to drive out of the city when the hurricane approaches; who can pay for seawalls or homes solid enough to withstand the coming flood. The capitalist class is evidently not very worried. Quite a few fractions of it are rather gathering up for some sweet profits ...
>
> Andreas Malm[1]

The updated comic-book superhero

There is an instructive moment about one-third of the way through the 2010 movie *Iron Man 2*. The eponymous Iron Man/Tony Stark is attending the Monaco Grand Prix and as he walks across the floor of an exclusive restaurant perched high above the race track, he bumps into an old friend, Elon Musk, and exchanges some overly scripted pleasantries about their shared plans to build electric jets. The cameo is presumably intended to have a 'meta' feel to it; Tony Stark, the fictional tech genius rubs shoulders with Musk, the ostensibly real-life one. The comparisons between the two are not necessarily as forced as this. Both Musk and Stark arguably embody fantasies of a particular variant of early-twenty-first-century capitalism; both present themselves as independent, maverick geniuses. Both valorise the private sector (in an early scene in *Iron Man 2*, Stark proudly boasts 'I've successfully privatised world peace')[2] while politely ignoring their dependency on the state. Stark Industries seems to have no actual non-executive employees and all their cool gadgets are apparently made by Stark in his workshop, in a kind of updated version of Thomas Edison. Elon Musk is not known for showing respect for his employees, as evidenced by the working conditions at his Tesla Motors.[3] Much of the PR surrounding Musk has exploited his appearance in *Iron Man 2*, pitching him as a real-life Tony Stark.[4] When Musk was featured in *Foreign Policy*'s 'Top 100 global thinkers', the write-up on him – presumably based on company press releases – specifically mentioned the Iron Man connection, romanticising Musk as 'the real-life model for Robert Downey Jr's update of the comic-book superhero'.[5] Likewise, *The Guardian* called him the 'apparent inspiration' for Iron Man (even though that character was originally invented in 1963, eight years before Musk was born) and 'a god-like figure for engineers'.[6] Such encomia almost certainly have their origins in the PR departments of Musk's companies, as is common practice in Silicon Valley.[7]

This is a far-reaching act of capitalist myth-making, in which we are all, to paraphrase Mark Fisher, living through *someone else's* dream coming true.[8] Musk himself has a penchant for media stunts and for crafting his own fastidious self-image:[9] he has claimed that his tunneling firm, The Boring Company, could end the notorious traffic-gridlock of Los Angeles by building a complex network of subterranean tunnels.[10] He has a tendency to arrive uninvited at important news events or natural disasters, asserting that his tech can solve whatever problem or crisis is at hand.[11] In July 2017, Musk claimed to have received 'verbal [government] approval' to build a 'hyperloop', a hypothetical transport system that would send capsules through frictionless high-pressure tubes, to connect New York City, Philadelphia, Baltimore and Washington, DC; this was promptly denied by the municipal authorities concerned.[12]

While Elon Musk's actual engineering or managerial skills are probably overrated, he is certainly adept at public relations. The proof of that is surely in the fact that he is so successful at getting the media to accept his self-image as a business genius: 'Through these repeated acts of petty propaganda, Musk has developed a reputation as a Tony Stark-like man of action – rather than, say, an endlessly self-aggrandizing, union-busting executive whose empire rests on billions in government subsidies and canny acts of self-dealing'.[13] But perhaps his biggest act of capitalist fantasy is his propertied vision of Martian exploration and colonisation.

It'll be, like, really fun to go … You're gonna have a great time

Musk has long spoken of a planned colonisation of Mars, promising in 2017 that he would begin an agricultural settlement by 2024, with ten volunteers as farm labourers, and would add groups of twenty regularly after that.[14] Within a vaguely delineated '40–100 years', 1 million people would be living in the colony.[15] His company, SpaceX, has built links with NASA as it provides commercial satellite services and refuelling to the International Space Station alongside these claims to be planning a new world on Mars.[16] In a September 2016 speech at the International Astronautical Congress in Guadalajara, Musk bombastically announced the BFR and BFS (respectively, Big Fucking Rocket and Big Fucking Spaceship), centrepieces of his Interplanetary Transportation System. He claimed to be working on plans to begin expeditions to Mars while also admitting that he's 'not the best' at meeting timelines.[17]

The media coverage of SpaceX has vacillated between the hyperbolic and the superficial, with the press tending to repeat his bold claims without criticism while ignoring his perennially missed deadlines; 2019 was a proposed departure date in 2018 and he has also promised manned flights by 2024.[18] In 2016 he said he would start 'as soon as 2022'.[19] Breezy assertions that his spaceship design 'is not that complicated' and a desire to 'not get bogged down in technical detail' are given an easy pass. How Mars can be made habitable is also left unexamined.[20] Rather than engaging in sober analyses of how far-fetched and difficult all this will be, Musk has merely said 'It'll be, like, really fun to go … You're gonna have a great time',[21] with little in the way of critical media probing of all that. At other times, journalists have praised SpaceX's 'sleek white spacesuit[s]', launched on Instagram,[22] or have seemingly been overawed by the publicity stunt of launching into space a $100,000 Tesla Roadster car (made by one of Musk's other, equally troubled companies).[23] One of Musk's first extra-terrestrial initiatives was a 'P.T. Barnum-like stunt' in which he would send a rocket to Mars with a greenhouse and seeds; live images of 'a leafy green plant rising against the lifeless, red landscape' would be beamed home. He called it 'Mars Oasis' and said it could be done for $15–30 million. In an early meeting with experts, he was apparently told it could not be done for less than $180 million.[24] Musk is here following in the footsteps of his fellow space-privatiser, Richard Branson. Branson promised that Virgin Galactic would become the first commercial spaceline, with flights starting in 2007 and flying 3,000 people in the first five years. All of this has yet to happen and it is worth asking if this was always a PR stunt. 'Branson wasn't the first to try to sell the allure of space. During the 1960s, Pan Am started promoting trips to the Moon as a way to cash in on the surging interest the Apollo program generated. So, it created a waiting list of passengers who wanted to go to the Moon.' None of that happened either. In the mock-up of Virgin Galactic's spaceship, '[t]he seats were ergonomic, the windows numerous, and the first flights safe and sublime'. The 'large windows' are a give-away that this rocket would never exist; spaceships require tiny windows as a heat-saving mechanism.[25]

Yet the SpaceX fantasies of Martian colonisation also draw on harsh realities. Musk's vision of the future seems to be of a depleted Planet Earth, where all resources have been consumed and a relocation to Mars is the only means to escape extinction.[26] Becoming 'a multi-planetary species' is the only way to avoid 'an inevitable extinction event'.[27] With the election of Donald Trump, Musk pitched Mars as an escape hatch during a possible Third World War.[28] The Red Planet will be a 'backup drive' for humanity.[29] Yet his claim that 'history is going bifurcate along two directions'[30] points to a recognition that only a select few will be able to leave (or more accurately, be able *to afford* to leave). Travel costs could be around $10 billion per passenger,[31] though Musk has said this can eventually be brought down to 'only' $100,000. As one critical observer accurately described it, Musk's

Martian endeavour 'looks a lot like joining a country club or gated community – or any other model of private access to space for those who can afford it'.[32] Outer space is an extreme way to avoid the dangerous mobs at home. Mars might indeed be the ultimate gated community.[33] Or an off-planet version of Baghdad's Green Zone.[34]

Space exploration is the ultimate status symbol

Musk's vision of colonies on Mars is arguably part of a broader phenomenon in contemporary capitalist culture. Jeff Bezos, the founder of Amazon, has deployed a similar rhetoric and propertied and privatised imaginary to Musk's; his childhood dream was 'to colonise space' and as an 18-year-old, allegedly he was already fantasising about evacuating Earth via 'space hotels, amusement parks and colonies'.[35] His Blue Origin 'space tourism and exploration' company has a barely concealed rivalry with SpaceX as well as a shared propensity for publicity stunts. In 2018, Bezos offered Donald Trump an invitation on one of their future manned flights and the chance to fly to space for eleven minutes with Bezos in 2021 was auctioned for $28 million.[36] Writing for *The Guardian*, a prime source for uncritical echoing of these capitalist fantasies, the tech journalist Dan Tynan stated '[f]orget gilded mansions and super yachts; among the tech elite, space exploration is the ultimate status symbol'.[37]

In this, Bezos, like Musk, continues the echoing of Richard Branson. Tom Hanks, Leonardo DiCaprio and Ashton Kutcher are among the 700 passengers who each paid $250,000 for advance seats on Branson's Virgin Galactic SpaceShip Two; despite charging this remarkable amount, Branson's 'Galactic' ship had not yet been launched.[38] As with Bezos, Branson is presumably able to fund all this with a fortune that would, in an earlier time, have been taxed at a higher (read: more equitable) rate.[39] The space fantasies of tech billionaires operate within the low-tax and pro-privatisation regimes of neoliberalism. In a perceptive study of seasteading – the libertarian dream of creating floating cities, a first cousin of space colonisation – China Miéville has shown how much these fantasies derive from a simple hatred of taxes and a desire to escape the states that demand taxation. Such extra-national cities would also escape 'pesky labor and environmental laws', while simultaneously (if paradoxically) acting as vehicles for concerns about the environment. In these floating cities, citizenship would be bought; it is hard to imagine how illegal immigration could occur, though who exactly will do the menial tasks on board these libertarian floating cities is left unexamined.[40] It is also worth remembering that Musk's dreams of Martian colonisation probably find their fullest meaning within an America increasingly defined by Mitch McConnell's suppression of Black voters and manufactured hysteria about 'critical race theory' and 'cultural Marxism'. For both Musk and McConnell, we could imagine the goal being a society of, by and for white, male, property owners. But unlike the GOP's more unguarded sentiments, Elon Musk never explicitly says who exactly will not be invited. Whether we are talking about a seemingly backward-looking Trumpian nostalgia for Jim Crow America or fantasies that only play out in a futuristic register, the goal still appears to be some kind of white American *embourgeoisement* and an attempt to stave off the fear of having to live in a genuinely multiracial polity.

What is on display here is arguably just a postmodern working out of a propertied anxiety that has haunted liberalism since at least John Locke. As Madden and Marcuse have pointed out, '[a] city where the dangerous classes have been removed does not rebel'.[41] There will be no 'masterless men' on board. Libertarian fantasies of seasteading or Martian colonisation seek to achieve this from the opposite direction; rather than removing the rebels through gentrification, these plans promise to build cities that contain no rebels or dangerous classes to begin with.[42] The Asgardia satellite project of Azerbaijani businessman Igor Ashurbeyli promises to house a new orbiting nation, 'free from the constraint of a land-based country's laws'.[43] In fantasy/vanity projects such as this, there is a strong dose of what Miéville calls libertarianism's 'philosophy of venal *petite-bourgeois* dissidence'.[44] The 'constitution' on Asgardia's website describes it not as a libertarian nation-state, but as a 'space kingdom', suggesting certain old hierarchies will be recreated in space.[45] Locke's vision of the New World, remember, included chiefs and margraves, using a hereditary title carried over from feudalism.

The broader uptick in interest in Martian settler-colonialism, artificial islands and orbiting libertarian satellites draws on the same climatological anxieties as Musk's SpaceX, coupling a desire to 'avert environmental disaster' with an impetus to 'possibly mint fortunes in the process'.[46] And the privatisation of outer space has powerful supporters. In October 2016 Barack Obama spoke of sending manned flights to Mars by the 2030s, in a project that 'will require continued cooperation between government and private innovators'.[47] SpaceX's liaison with NASA is Liam Sarsfield, 'a huge proponent of the commercialization of space'.[48] Michael Griffin, the NASA administrator from 2005 to 2009, wanted to jump-start a private sector of rockets and spacecraft.[49] The far-right senator Ted Cruz predicted in June 2018 that the first trillionaire 'will be made in space'. At the time of this pronouncement, Cruz was chairman of the US Senate's Space, Science, and Competitiveness Subcommittee and was pushing for the creation of 'a regulatory environment that is conducive for major expansions of the commercial space sector', which is to say a deregulation that would facilitate resource extraction off-planet.[50] It was presumably in pursuit of such extreme profits that Peter Thiel, the particularly zealous libertarian and founder of PayPal, gave $100,000 to an 18-year-old named John Burnham, as an investment in his asteroid mining company.[51] Google founders Larry Page and Eric Schmidt have also invested in asteroid mining via the Planetary Resources company, and Goldman Sachs has similarly given some attention to extra-terrestrial mining.[52] The 'Mars Foundation' of Dennis Tito, a wonkish finance capitalist, has sought private donations to fund a flight around Mars. Mars One, a Dutch nonprofit, aims to fund a Martian colony through 'merchandise sales, ads on video content, brand partnerships, speaking engagements, [b]roadcasting rights, intellectual property rights, games & apps, and events'.[53] Companies like Planetary Resources and Deep Space Industries 'intend to mine rare earth minerals and ice asteroids'.[54] This emerging sector of the economy promotes rights to own off-planet real estate 'in accordance with current international law where possible, by modifying international law if feasible, or by destroying the international treaty regime if necessary'.[55] The companies that have emerged from this oscillate between 'feasibility and harebrained-ness';[56] those devoted to asteroid mining, like Planetary Resources, have a short shelf-life, generally pivoting to things like satellite production as the impossibility (even absurdity) of their plans becomes apparent.

In addition, it is rarely clear how a totally privatised space colonisation could enforce private property. As one legal scholar has said, while outer space was initially seen as *res communis*, common space, it is increasingly claimed to be *res nullius*, empty space awaiting privatisation. But therein lies a knotty problem:

> A property right must be recognized by a sovereign government for that right to have legal force. As a practical matter, a property right cannot exist in the absence of a controlling legal regime. Outside such a regime, where a state of anarchy prevails, any claim to property must be defended by the force of arms; it is not a right, but a physical act of occupation.[57]

A privatised libertarian space colonisation that has slipped the bonds of both Earth and the state is a mess of contradictions. When Musk founded SpaceX in 2002, his stated goal was 'to privatize space'.[58] But privatised extra-terrestrial resource extraction itself violates two current international agreements: the 1967 Treaty on Principles Governing the Activities of States in the Exploration and Use of Outer Space, including the Moon and Other Celestial Bodies, and The Moon Agreement of 1979.[59] While both predominantly focus on the use of military arms in space, they also place the extra-planetary beyond nation-states, and probably also beyond private property and capitalism. The 1979 agreement bans any private or governmental ownership of the Moon.[60] But more recently HR 5063, the American Space Technology for Exploring Resource Opportunities In Deep Space (ASTEROIDS) Act, allows for private ownership of mining rights on asteroids.[61] Scratch the surface of these new space fantasies and there is just old-fashioned, privatised, capitalist, resource extraction. Indeed, there are many underlying hints that labour shortages and labour exploitation could be rife on Musk's hypothetical colony:[62]

One can imagine the grueling labor required to make an inhospitable planet habitable. On Mars, employees would exhaust themselves for a corporation under the guise of 'survival.' After all, regardless of whether a foundation or a corporation spearheads the colonization effort, they will be incentivized, even forty million miles away, to squeeze as much labor out of their workers at the lowest cost.[63]

It is worth remembering that the (often equally utopian) colonisation of the Virginia Territory quickly ran into labour shortages, 'solved' through indentured labour and, ultimately, racial slavery. Moreover, who would actually own the land of Mars (or an asteroid's surface)? For reasons of life-support and absent any major technological breakthrough in terraforming, it could not be divided up into discrete family farms like seventeenth-century Virginia. Musk's colony would, at best, be a kind of sci-fi *kibbutz*; more likely it would be a company town that controls its residents' oxygen supply.[64]

Don't be evil

In any case, Musk, Bezos and their fellow travellers have a pronounced tendency to ignore the harsh realities of conditions on Mars. The surface of the planet is covered with a 'toxic cocktail' of chemicals that would wipe out living organisms. The ultraviolet light that hits Mars would have the effect of 'sterilising the upper layers' of any soil development. Carcinogenic radiation would be an inescapable, perhaps fatal, problem.[65] The lighter gravity on Mars would also have large-scale, probably detrimental, effects on the bone structure of long-term residents. Calcium degradation and muscle loss would be highly likely, as would a swelling of the optic nerve that already affects astronauts on the International Space Station. There is a risk of infection from as yet undiscovered Martian micro-organisms. It could take fifteen to twenty years for any food production systems to be viable and Martian dust-storms, which regularly reach up to seventy miles per hour, would prove hazardous for any construction efforts. Likewise, the absence of water on Mars would cause obvious problems, probably only solvable through 'the recycling of urine'. Human faeces would be the primary (perhaps only) source of fertiliser. At a large remove from Musk's attractive fantasies of a fun life on Mars, settlers would almost certainly have to 'eat their own shit' (which perhaps answers why, for all his boosting, Musk never seems to want to go there himself!). And all this is aside from the basic fact that no technology yet exists that would allow manned flights to Mars.[66]

But in Silicon Valley – with the emphasis generally placed on upbeat ideals of 'disruption'[67] and a tech-innovation that can solve all problems – realistic concerns like this are dismissed as grim or petty or missing the point. Much of Musk's hype is based on a Whig-like faith in the ever-increasing potential of capitalist technology. Neuralink, one of his many startups, is dedicated to merging human brains with computers.[68] At his most pop-philosophical, Musk has claimed that reality itself is a *Matrix*-like computer simulation.[69] This silliness is depressingly common in Silicon Valley where, as of October 2016, at least two active, billionaire-backed, projects were dedicated to 'breaking us out of the simulation'. Musk has asserted that there is only 'a billion to one chance' that reality is actually real rather than being computer-generated, the ultimate expression of his faith in capitalism's claim to never-ending improvement and perfection.[70]

Silicon Valley tech utopianism is often heavily reliant on popular science fiction.[71] Jeff Bezos' space company initially operated through front companies 'named for explorers who had opened up frontiers' or for characters from *Star Trek*; his space capitalism imagined as a mixture of settler-colonialism and sci-fi.[72] An early SpaceX rocket was called *Falcon*, after the *Millennium Falcon* from *Star Wars*.[73] SpaceX's offices are designed within a sci-fi register, made to look like Cyberdyne Systems in the *Terminator* movies. There is a life-size Iron Man figure at the elevators, apparently placed there by Musk himself.[74] Musk is an avid sci-fi fan, with a 'feeling of dismay' that the sci-fi visions of his youth have not been realised in the twenty-first century.[75] Even Musk's rarer criticisms of modern technology – killer robots, mass layoffs because of automation – derive from a belief in its astonishing power.[76] Such fantasies are of particular interest to libertarians, who have found a receptive home in Silicon Valley, which shares their opposition to government intervention or taxation.[77]

The obvious literary analogue here is the character John Galt from Ayn Rand's *Atlas Shrugged*: 'The Randian ethos of the heroic individual entrepreneur as alpha white male (and sometimes female) genius fits the self-mythologizing self-image of Silicon Valley tech startups particularly well'.[78] Even so, the libertarian image of Silicon Valley belies how reliant it is on government funding – from the initial development of the internet via the Pentagon's Advanced Research Projects Agency (ARPA) to the onoing funding of research and design[79] – a criticism of which Musk seems particularly sensitive.[80] For all of Musk's libertarian posturing, SpaceX is highly dependent on government actions and investments. The company's early test flights took place at Edwards Air Force Base in southern California and Musk has also regularly used Air Force satellites for communications purposes.[81] The Pentagon's DARPA ('Defense ARPA') invested 'a few million dollars' in SpaceX in 2004, and when SpaceX moved to a government launch site in the Marshall Islands in 2006 'DARPA helped with the transition'.[82] After their Marshall Islands launch, SpaceX received a $278 million government contract followed, at the end of 2008, by a $1.6 billion NASA contract.[83] As the business journalist Ashlee Vance pointed out, that latter contract probably saved the company from an otherwise imminent bankruptcy, as indeed 'big-ticket contracts' from the Federal government were what 'kept SpaceX alive during its leanest years'.[84] And yet Musk and the staff at SpaceX still held to a view that the company was acting alone. Musk 'wasn't high on government help', according to one observer.[85] Privatised rhetoric (with public funds) is *de rigeur* in this sector. Yet the chances of sending a manned flight to Mars are probably lower today, with privatised space companies, than during the era of large-scale Federal investment in the 1970s.[86]

It is also rarely apparent that Musk is the technological wizard that the Tony Stark PR claims him to be. His first planned rocket had 'a real thermal problem', because of its giant windows. His plans to plant seeds in Martian soil seemed to ignore how toxic that soil is. It is hard to escape the conclusion that as he set out on this venture – for all his posturing with old Soviet rocket manuals – he did not actually understand what he was trying to do.[87] The engineers at SpaceX were reportedly infuriated by Musk's claims to have designed the *Falcon* single-handedly.[88] Nor is it clear whether he understands the computer code used in his companies.[89] Even a sympathetic observer of SpaceX has seen that it was the employees, not Musk, who 'were doing [the] real work, building engines and hardware'.[90] Similarly, when Richard Branson 'flew' across the Atlantic in a balloon in 1987, he did it with a pilot named Per Lindstrad. Branson himself 'hardly knew how to fly'.[91] When Blue Origin had its first successful launch, Jeff Bezos joked (quite accurately) that his only job was to pop the champagne cork.[92]

Instead of solving hard problems, contemporary Silicon Valley capitalism makes bold claims of innovation as a veneer on top of conventionally run-of-the-mill capitalist enterprises with conventional – even quite old-fashioned – attitudes towards private property and gender.[93] Under the Iron Man hype, Elon Musk appears to be a fairly conventional capitalist, with the usual hostility to unionisation or to criticism from his employees.[94] Likewise, for all the noise about radically new work practices, the culture of Silicon Valley is remarkably old-fashioned when it comes to attitudes towards gender, race and the poor.[95] There have been credible accusations that Musk's female employees suffer from 'pervasive harassment' at their workplace.[96] There have also been accusations that Musk's Tesla Motors is a hostile work environment for gay and Black employees.[97] It should not therefore be a surprise that Donald Trump found so quick an audience among the Tech Bros.[98] And it is perhaps worth asking whether capitalism has simply run out of new ideas.

Those who cannot remember the past are condemned to have it resold to them forever

If we have reached the global limits of capitalism, it is little wonder, then, that capitalists now look beyond the planet for new ways to revivify capitalism. The promise offered by both capitalism in general and Lockeanism in particular (as well as Marxism) is that the future will be better than the past. By the twenty-first century that promise seems to have been cancelled on Earth only to be reopened off-planet. What is surprising, though, is how old-fashioned this can sound, as capitalism reverts to old myths. Ted Cruz has claimed that the 'desire to explore', by which he presumably means the desire to find new territories to privatise, 'has fueled much of the achievement of mankind', from the 'exploration of the New World that led to the colonization of America' to 'Neil Armstrong walking on the Moon' and 'exploration in space'.[99] Jeff Bezos is sceptical of Martian colonisation, but does think all heavy industry could and should be moved to space, claiming that a cargo route to space will be built that would be similar to the railroads that opened up the American West.[100] Martian explorers-as-early-Americans has become something of a meme, part of what journalist Caroline Haskins polemically, but reasonably, calls 'the racist language of space exploration'.[101] Corey Pein has observed how online alt-rightists

> saw in the miraculous futuristic designs of men such as a [sic] Peter Thiel and Elon Musk a vision that was entirely compatible with their notions of racial supremacy, and they expected to personally benefit in the tech titans' new order. To certain devotees, Musk's dream of human settlements on Mars offered an escape from this benighted earth, where their wretched enemies would be left behind, in a final act of vengeance by the tech-savvy master race.[102]

Mike Gold, legal representative of Bigelow Aerospace, a company that seeks to privatise lunar real estate, 'is fond of comparing the current state of human space activity to the settling of the American West: first comes government exploration (NASA, Lewis and Clark), but the most important work is done by the next wave of arrivals, the private individuals and enterprises seeking their fortunes'. Gold has argued for an updated version of the Homestead Act (1862) to give legitimacy to this postmodern land-grab.[103] Peter Diamondis, a medical doctor and aerospace engineer, and founder of Planetary Resources, believes that '[i]n the same way that we Europeans looked upon the New World to colonize for resources, we as humanity can look toward space as the ultimate supply of resources'. He displayed, as Corey Pein points out, an 'ahistorical and romantic view of conquest'.[104] And indeed, as early as 1962, John F. Kennedy compared a future Moon landing to the career of William Bradford, governor of the Plymouth Bay Company in the mid-seventeenth-century and instigator of anti-Indian massacres.[105] Musk talks about a 'Mars Colonial Fleet' departing *en masse* for the Red Planet. SpaceX presentations depict the future colonised Mars as 'a promised land with an atmosphere glowing around it like a halo'.[106] Ashlee Vance quotes Musk as imagining Mars would be 'like people coming to America back in the New World days. You move, get a job there, and make things work',[107] thus simultaneously ignoring both the brutalities of the American settler-colonial past and the extreme difficulties of his own projected future. Private property continues to be tethered to implicitly racialised visons.

Jonathan Crary has stressed that fantasies of sci-fi capitalism are, on one level, absurd and unrealisable, but they still serve to shape and regulate our contemporary imagination.[108] Fredric Jameson has famously warned that it is easier to imagine the end of the world than the end of capitalism.[109] That we cannot imagine a form of custodial ownership outside of private property is a cause both of the climate crisis and of the weak response to it. Visions of a better future have largely dropped out of popular culture, the utopia of *Star Trek* replaced by various apocalyptic imagery in which we are all under siege from ultra-violent zombified mobs.[110] As Mark Fisher observed, '[i]t doesn't feel like the future. Or, alternatively, it doesn't feel as if the 21st century has started yet. We remain trapped in the 20th century.'[111] It is certainly easy to think that we live in an interregnum between a zombie twentieth century that will not die off, and a stillborn twenty-first. Fisher's idea of a delayed future, though, is based on a myth of ever-improving progress, one that has stalled for the moment. Is our current predicament that we are living in a period between 'good' times? Maybe this is just the norm for capitalism (though it appears extra-upsetting in the long shadow of Keynesianism). Perhaps we are still trapped in early modern Lockean fears of mobs.

Elon Musk's sci-fi fantasies read like a despondent attempt to retain a vision of a better future. But in his depictions of space exploration, the Final Frontier reveals itself not as a place where we can imagine a better, more utopian, perfected world, but a boundary that is already assumed to be within capitalism's web of life.[112] It is just another space to be privatised in capitalism's never-ending self-perpetuation.[113] And so we end up back where we began; with the problems of a crowded capitalist ecology being solved by an act of imagination, by imagining an empty space in which a new world can be created, freed from some evils of the old, but still replicating real evils of the old world – greed, privatisation, rigid hierarchies, exploitation of the commons and of other human beings. Colonisation remains a safety valve for a society beset by supposedly dangerous mobs who threaten the property order; and behind all that, is a vision of a world in which white men are the only natural rulers. The history of private property is a circle.[114]

Notes

1. Andreas Malm. *Fossil capital: the rise of steam power and the roots of global warming* (London, 2016), 391.
2. It surely says something that the self-absorbed neoliberal Stark is always far less likeable than Steve Rogers/Captain America, an avatar of New Deal-era Keynesianism and its focus on the shared common good.
3. 'Black Tesla employees describe a culture of racism', *Los Angeles Times*, 25 March 2022; 'Tesla workers reveal pain, injury and stress', *The Guardian*, 18 May 2017.
4. Robert Downey Jr appears to have sought out Musk as an inspiration for Tony Stark, and the film's director Jon Favreau played up the comparison. Discussed further in Ashlee Vance. *Elon Musk: Tesla, SpaceX and the quest for a fantastic future*, 2nd edition (New York, 2017), 181.
5. 'Elon Musk: for putting his money where his mouth is', *Foreign Policy*, 26 November 2012.
6. 'Rocket men: why tech's biggest billionaires want their place in space', *The Guardian*, 5 December 2016.
7. The tech journalist Corey Pein has made the harsh but fair comment that '[w]ith rare exception, the tech press – by which I mean both the trade press focused exclusively on the tech industry and the tech sections of general-interest news organisations – functions as an appendage of the Silicon Valley marketing machine': *Live work work work die: a journey into the savage heart of Silicon Valley* (New York, 2017), 107.
8. Mark Fisher. *Capitalist realism: is there no alternative?* (London, 2009), 56.

9 See, for example, his June 2018 stunt involving selling flame-throwers: '"A great item to have": flamethrowers sell like hot cakes at Elon Musk sale', *The Guardian*, 9 June 2018.
10 Jacob Silverman, 'The Musk of success, choking our cities', *Baffler*, 23 May 2017.
11 'Elon Musk floats solar overhaul of Puerto Rico power grid, governor says "let's talk"', *Huffington Post*, 6 October 2017; 'Elon Musk says he has a green light to build a NY–Philly–Baltimore–DC hyperloop', *The Verge*, 20 July 2017. Though the most embarrassing version of this tendency was his infamous intervention in Thailand in July 2018, when he arrived hoping to use a mini-submarine to save boys trapped in an underground cave and left, accusing the actual rescuer of paedophilia: 'Elon Musk and the Thai cave rescue: a tale of good intentions and bad tweets', *Vox*, 18 July 2018.
12 'Green light to build hyperloop', *The Verge*; 'Elon Musk: I got "government approval" for New York–DC hyperloop. Officials: no he didn't', *The Guardian*, 20 July 2017.
13 Silverman, 'Musk of success' (2017).
14 'Elon Musk: SpaceX can colonise Mars and build Moon base', *The Guardian*, 29 September 2017.
15 'Life on Mars: Elon Musk reveals details of his colonisation vision', *The Guardian*, 16 June 2017.
16 'Has spacesuit, will travel: former SpaceX employee is among NASA's new recruits', *The Guardian*, 27 August 2017.
17 'Elon Musk wants to send you to Mars – here's how he plans to do it', *Vice News*, 27 September 2016.
18 'Elon Musk: we must colonise Mars to preserve our species in a third world war', *The Guardian*, 11 March 2018; 'SpaceX can colonise Mars', *The Guardian*.
19 'Rocket men', *The Guardian*.
20 'Elon Musk wants to send you to Mars', *Vice News*.
21 Keith A. Spencer. 'Keep the red planet red', *Jacobin*, February 2017.
22 'Elon Musk reveals sleek SpaceX spacesuit for crewed flights in 2018', *The Guardian*, 24 August 2017.
23 'SpaceX oddity: how Elon Musk sent a car towards Mars', *The Guardian*, 7 February 2018. The Roadster had the message 'Don't panic!' stamped on its dashboard and David Bowie playing on the speakers – to cruise through high-energy radiation belts that circuit Earth towards deep space, its projected path will bring it close to Mars, though there is only a slim chance it will make its destination. More likely it will simply drift in space.

24 Christian Davenport. *The space barons: Elon Musk, Jeff Bezos and the quest to colonize the cosmos* (New York, 2018), 20, 39–40.
25 Davenport, *Space barons* (2018), 109, 111. A place on the waiting list for Virgin Galactic cost $200,000 and by early 2006 the company had raised $13 million in deposits. Eventually Virgin Galactic stopped providing a date for their launch: *Space barons*, 112. Christian Davenport's elegiac commentary is that 'Branson, and his Virgin brand, had never been in the business of "disillusionment", but of making the illusory real'. Branson 'provided the vision, not the technical specifications': *Space barons*, 233. A less generous analysis would see Branson as a fantasist who leaves the actual work to others.
26 'Elon Musk wants to send you to Mars', *Vice News*.
27 'Rocket men', *The Guardian*.
28 'Elon Musk: third world war', *The Guardian*.
29 'Life on Mars', *The Guardian*.
30 'Elon Musk wants to send you to Mars', *Vice News*.
31 'Life on Mars', *The Guardian*.
32 Spencer, 'Keep the red planet red' (2017). Or as Raj Patel and Jason Moore have perceived it: 'We may all be in the same boat when it comes to climate change, but most of us are in steerage': *A history of the world in seven cheap things: a guide to capitalism, nature, and the future of the planet* (Berkeley, CA, 2017), 24.
33 'Across the world, the rich are demonstrating their desire to escape from the rest of us … infrared sensors, facial recognition technologies, and defensive systems that spray noxious smoke or pepper spray. All this for people who, although rich, are largely anonymous and hardly prominent targets for would-be attackers. Paranoid though they may seem, large numbers of the economic elite appear to regard themselves as a set-upon minority, at war with the rest of society. Silicon Valley is a hotbed of such sentiments, plutocrats talking openly about "secession"': Peter Frase. *Four futures: life after capitalism* (London, 2016), 130.
34 Mike Davis has described how the ultra-rich playground of Dubai functions as both gated community and Green Zone: 'Sand, fear, and money in Dubai' in Mike Davis, Daniel Bertrand Monk, eds. *Evil paradises: dreamworlds of neoliberalism* (New York, 2007), 60. Julia Bodnár has similarly observed 'bourgeois utopias of isolation' in her discussion of Budapest: 'Becoming bourgeois: (postsocialist) utopias of isolation and civilization' in Davis and Monk, *Evil paradises* (2007), 141. Göran Therborn has said that 'the 1 per cent in the US has broken off contact not only with the national middle class but with all the other Western upper classes, and has retreated into a

caste of its own'. This is perhaps an overblown comment – it would not be hard to find counter-examples – but it does correctly identify a real trend: *Inequality and the labyrinths of democracy* (London, 2020), 45.
35 'Jeff Bezos: the boy who wanted to colonise space', *The Guardian*, 25 April 2018.
36 'Jeff Bezos', *The Guardian*; 'Who paid $28 million for 11 minutes in heaven with Jeff Bezos?', *Forbes*, 14 June 2021.
37 'Rocket men', *The Guardian*.
38 'Rocket men', *The Guardian*.
39 Quoting the journalist Mark Ames, David Golumbia says 'Big Tech's larger political goals are in alignment with the old extraction industry's: undermining the countervailing power of government and public politics to weaken its ability to impede their growing dominance over their portions of the economy, and to tax their obscene stores of cash': David Golumbia. *The politics of Bitcoin: software as right-wing extremism* (Minneapolis, MN, 2016), 8.
40 China Miéville, 'Floating utopias: freedom and unfreedom of the seas', in Davis and Monk, *Evil paradises* (2007), 251–61. Seasteading also seems to be an attempt to privatise the oceans, one of the last commonage spaces on the planet (and the majority of the Earth's surface). The dream of privatising the seas was animating Hugo Grotius as early as the seventeenth century.
41 David Madden, Peter Marcuse. *In defence of housing: the politics of crisis* (London, 2016), 94.
42 '[T]he spatial logic of neoliberalism (*cum* plutonomy) revives the most extreme colonial patterns of residential segregation and zoned consumption. Everywhere, the rich and near rich are retreating into sumptuary compounds, leisure cities, and gated replicas of imaginary California suburbs ... The "Off Worlds" advertised in the apocalyptic skies of *Blade Runner*'s Los Angeles are now open and ready for occupancy from Montana to China. Meanwhile, a demonized criminal underclass ... stands outside the gate (although sometimes as little more than symbolic lawn jockeys), providing a self-serving justification for the withdrawal and fortification of luxury lifestyles. This unprecedented spatial and moral secession of the wealthy from the rest of humanity also expresses itself in current fads for high-end monasticism ... floating city-states ... space tourism, private islands, restored monarchies, and techo-murder [*sic*] at a distance': Mike Davis, Daniel Bertrand Monk, 'Introduction' in Davis and Monk, *Evil paradises* (2007), xiii–xiv.

43 'Will you become a citizen of Asgardia, the first nation state in space?' *The Guardian*, 12 October 2016.
44 Miéville, 'Floating utopias' (2007), 252.
45 https://asgardia.space/constitution/, accessed 12 July 2022.
46 '"Grow food on Mars": LA startups tackle climate change with inventive solutions', *The Guardian*, 18 May 2018.
47 'Barack Obama: America will take the giant leap to Mars', CNN, 11 October 2016.
48 Davenport, *Space barons* (2018), 45.
49 Davenport, *Space barons* (2018), 133.
50 'Ted Cruz: the first trillionaire will be made in space', *Politico*, 1 June 2018.
51 Pein, *Live work work work die* (2017), 228.
52 'We believe space mining is still a long way from commercial viability, but it has the potential to further ease access to space and facilitate an in-space manufacturing economy,' an analyst for Goldman Sachs wrote in a note to investors. 'Space mining could be more realistic than perceived ... a single asteroid the size of a football field could contain $25 billion to $50 billion worth of platinum': Davenport, *Space barons* (2018), 249. This ignores market forces and basic laws of supply and demand; if the platinum market was flooded with new ore, prices would drop exponentially; in other words, the extraterrestrial platinum is only worth $50 billion provided it is brought to Earth gradually and the market could be persuaded to accept an adequate risk premium; otherwise it would be worth much less.
53 Spencer, 'Keep the red planet red' (2017).
54 Rachel Riederer. 'Whose moon is it anyway?', *Dissent*, Fall 2014.
55 Thomas Gangale. *The development of outer space: sovereignty and property rights in international space law* (Santa Barbara, CA, 2009), 5.
56 Spencer, 'Keep the red planet red' (2017).
57 Gangale, *Development of outer space* (2009), 10, 15–16.
58 Davenport, *Space barons* (2018), 237.
59 For the text of the 1967 Treaty, see Appendix 3: Treaty on Principles governing the Activities of States in the Exploration and Use of Outer Space, including the Moon and Other Celestial Bodies (27 January 1967) in Gangale, *Development of outer space* (2009), 273–9.
60 'An accident on the Moon, young lawyers to the rescue', NPR, 22 September 2017; Riederer, 'Whose moon is it anyway?' (2014).
61 Riederer, 'Whose moon is it anyway?' (2014).

62 'Life on Mars', *The Guardian*. 'When Musk sets unrealistic goals, verbally abuses employees, and works them to the bone, it's understood to be – on some level – part of the Mars agenda. Some employees love him for this. Others loathe him but remain oddly loyal out of respect for his drive and mission': Vance, *Elon Musk* (2017), 17.

63 Spencer, 'Keep the red planet red' (2017).

64 Musk once said 'I could go and buy one of the islands in the Bahamas and turn it into my personal fiefdom, but I am much more interested in trying to build and create a new company': Vance, *Elon Musk* (2017), 79. In this, he elides how much of a 'personal fiefdom' his Mars colony would be. Wendy Liu has pointed out that Google's corporate motto – 'don't be evil' – is a tacit recognition that such companies (and their CEOs) have considerable power to do evil in the world: *Abolish Silicon Valley: how to liberate technology from capitalism* (London, 2020), 37.

65 Musk tends to ignore the problem of radiation. Radiation, he thinks, 'is not too big of a deal': Davenport, *Space barons* (2018), 244.

66 'Why we can't send humans to Mars yet (and how we'll fix that)', *Wired*, 21 May 2013; 'The strange, deadly effects Mars would have on your body', *Wired*, 11 February 2014; 'The mysterious syndrome impairing astronauts' sight', *Washington Post*, 9 July 2016; 'Mars covered in toxic chemicals that can wipe out living organisms, tests reveal', *The Guardian*, 7 July 2017.

67 Mark Fisher has illustrated that 'disruption' is just a synonym for 'permanent structural instability', the effect of which is the 'cancellation of the long term' and 'invariably stagnation and conservatism, not innovation': *Capitalist realism* (2009), 76. From the opposite end of the political spectrum, Robert J. Gordon has highlighted how little the supposedly innovative tech sector has been able to reverse the slow decline of American economic growth: *The rise and fall of American growth: the US standard of living since the Civil War* (Princeton, NJ, 2016), 23 and throughout.

68 'Elon Musk wants to connect brains to computers with new company', *The Guardian*, 28 March 2017; 'Neurotechnology, Elon Musk and the goal of human enhancement', *The Guardian*, 1 January 2018. See also 'Elon Musk says humans must become cyborgs to stay relevant. Is he right?' *The Guardian*, 15 February 2017.

69 'Is our world a simulation? Why some scientists say it's more likely than not', *The Guardian*, 11 October 2016.

70 'Is our world a simulation?' *The Guardian*. Musk has also claimed that his own brain is a type of computer: Vance, *Elon Musk* (2017), 32.

71 See, for example, 'NASA invests in a fuel-free thruster and 21 other *Star Trek*-like inventions', *Huffington Post*, 10 April 2017.
72 Davenport, *Space barons* (2018), 20. There is a model of the Starship *Enterprise* in the lobby of Bezos' Blue Origin company and Bezos had a cameo in *Star Trek Beyond* (2016): Davenport, *Space barons* (2018), 251, 254.
73 Davenport, *Space barons* (2018), 42.
74 Vance, *Elon Musk* (2017), 225–6.
75 Davenport, *Space barons* (2018), 38.
76 'Elon Musk: automation will force governments to introduce universal basic income', *Futurism*, 14 February 2017; 'Elon Musk: regulate AI to combat "existential threat" before it's too late', *The Guardian*, 17 July 2017; 'Elon Musk leads 116 experts calling for outright ban on killer robots', *The Guardian*, 20 August 2017; 'Elon Musk says AI could lead to third world war', *The Guardian*, 4 September 2017.
77 Frase, *Four futures*, 31; Golumbia, *Politics of Bitcoin*, 4, 8, 21. Corey Pein calls this 'free-market techie futurism': *Live work work work die* (2017), 214.
78 Lisa Duggan. *Mean girl: Ayn Rand and the culture of greed* (Berkeley, CA, 2019), 88.
79 Bruce Cumings. *Dominion from sea to sea: Pacific ascendancy and American power* (New Haven, CT, 2009), 430–3.
80 'Elon Musk hits back at coal baron who called him a "fraud" over green subsidies', *The Guardian*, 11 October 2016. As Adam Kotsko has written: 'It does not take much critical acumen to see through the vulgar libertarianism with which neoliberal ideologues seek to veil a regime in which state action is absolutely pervasive': Adam Kotsko. *Neoliberalism's demons: on the political theology of late capital* (Stanford, CA, 2018), 65.
81 Vance, *Elon Musk* (2017), 121; Davenport, *Space barons* (2018), 178.
82 Davenport, *Space barons* (2018), 130–1.
83 Davenport, *Space barons* (2018), 139, 144. Musk was irked by what he saw as government interference in 'his' rocket and its failed launch from the Marshall Islands, not seeming to recognise that a rocket taking off from a government facility on a mission funded by the government is a government affair: *Space barons*, 136.
84 Vance, *Elon Musk* (2017), 207, 246. Likewise, Tesla Motors is heavily reliant on tax credits from the Department of Energy and in January 2010 made a $465 million loan agreement with that Department: *Elon Musk*, 287–9.

85 Davenport, *Space barons* (2018), 132.
86 Gangale, *Development of outer space* (2009), 2.
87 Vance, *Elon Musk* (2017), 98, 104. A similar tilt at mythology is the idea that Musk was 'a man who arrived in the United States with nothing': *Elon Musk*, 211. In actuality, his wealthy father funded his first company.
88 Vance, *Elon Musk* (2017), 133. Musk, though, was conveniently willing to share blame for technical faults.
89 Vance, *Elon Musk* (2017), 67–8, 73.
90 Davenport, *Space barons* (2018), 45.
91 Davenport, *Space barons* (2018), 101–2.
92 Davenport, *Space barons* (2018), 146.
93 The company Juicero, for example, was packaged as a cutting-edge way to make fruit juice. Their automatic juicer cost $400, until one journalist noticed that consumers could just cut open the pre-sold packets of fruit and vegetables and squeeze them into a glass for exactly the same result: 'America has become so anti-innovation – it's economic suicide', *The Guardian*, 11 May 2017. Moreover, Adam Greenfield has noted 'the ways in which these allegedly disruptive technologies leave existing modes of domination mostly intact': Adam Greenfield. *Radical technologies: the design of everyday life* (London, 2017), 8.
94 'Elon Musk decries UAW union, promises employees frozen yogurt and rollercoaster machine', SF Gate, 28 February 2017; 'Elon Musk in union spat after wrongly calling Tesla worker a paid agitator', *The Guardian*, 11 February 2017; Ronnie Shows. 'Opinion: Elon Musk is not the answer for Democrats', *The Hill*, 9 December, 2016; 'The NLRB just issued a complaint to Tesla for labor law violations', *Vice News*, 31 August 2017.
95 '"Elitist den of hate": Silicon Valley pastor decries hypocrisy of area's rich liberals', *The Guardian*, 22 May 2018; 'Why is Silicon Valley so awful to women?', *The Atlantic*, April 2017; 'From Elon Musk to Tim Cook, tech leaders hardly follow women on Twitter', *The Guardian*, 4 October 2016.
96 'Female engineer sues Tesla, describing a culture of "pervasive harassment"', *The Guardian*, 28 February 2017; 'Tesla fires female engineer who alleged sexual harassment', *The Guardian*, 1 June 2017.
97 'Tesla workers claim anti-LGBT threats, taunts, and racial abuse in lawsuits', *The Guardian*, 19 October 2017; 'Black workers accused Tesla of racism for years. Now California is stepping in', *The Guardian*, 19 February 2022.

98 Ben Tarnoff. 'Donald Trump, Peter Thiel and the death of democracy', *The Guardian*, 21 July 2016; Jathan Sadowski. 'Silicon Valley for Trump', *Jacobin*, December 2016; Liu, *Abolish Silicon Valley* (2020), 116.
99 'Ted Cruz: the first trillionaire', *Politico*.
100 Davenport, *Space barons* (2018), 258–60.
101 'Unlike the first European settlers who came to America – a land rich with soil for farming, lumber, minerals, people, and trade opportunities – Mars is a barren, lifeless, cold deadly place': 'Why *The Martian* author won't join Elon Musk's Mars mission', *Vice Motherboard*, 29 September 2016.
102 Pein, *Live work work work die* (2017), 233. Bezos sees Neil Armstrong as a hero, and likewise Wernher von Braun, 'the German-born chief architect of the Apollo-era Saturn V rocket', conveniently ignoring his Nazi past: Davenport, *Space barons* (2018), 255.
103 Riederer, 'Whose moon is it anyway?' (2014).
104 Pein, *Live work work work die* (2017), 253.
105 Caroline Haskins, 'The racist language of space exploration', *The Outline*, 14 August 2018.
106 Davenport, *Space barons* (2018), 242.
107 Vance, *Elon Musk* (2017), 333.
108 Jonathan Crary. *24/7: late capitalism and the ends of sleep* (London, 2013), 97. 'The stated ambitions of America's tech oligarchs are almost comically solipsistic – endless lifespans, superhuman powers, personal hyper-speed transport. They truly imagine themselves as a superior race. And while it is unlikely that they will attain everything they imagine, it is unfortunately true that this hyper-elite class will reap the benefits of any new technologies society develops, while the costs will fall, as ever, on the rest of us. This will not be a situation without precedent. It's exactly how things were with the rotten kings of yore. But if history teaches us one thing, it's that complex problems often have simple solutions. Off with their heads': Pein, *Live work work work die* (2017), 292.
109 Fredric Jameson. *Postmodernism, or, the cultural logic of late capitalism* (Durham, NC, 1991).
110 David Graeber. 'Of flying cars and the declining rate of profit' in *The utopia of rules: on technology, stupidity and the secret joys of bureaucracy* (New York, 2015), 105–47; Dora Apel. *Beautiful terrible ruins: Detroit and the anxiety of decline* (New Brunswick, NJ, 2015), 132–52. *World War Z* (2013) provides the most blatant evidence that 'zombies' serve as a stand-in for fears about non-white mobs; in

a central plot development in the film, the Israeli government initially escapes the zombie apocalypse by building a large wall – 'they sealed off their entire country days before the undead attacked' – in an obvious reference to the 708 km wall through the West Bank designed to keep Palestinians out of sight.

111 Mark Fisher. *Ghosts of my life: writings on depression, hauntology and lost futures* (London, 2014), 8.

112 Jason Moore. *Capitalism in the web of life: ecology and the accumulation of capital* (London, 2015).

113 'In the 1960s and 1970s, capitalism had to face the problem of how to contain and absorb energies from outside. It now [post-1989], in fact, has the opposite problem; having all-too successfully incorporated externality, how can it function without an outside it can colonize and appropriate?' Fisher, *Capitalist realism* (2009), 8. Mars is one new space to colonise. The other 'space' is debt: 'In a world where there is increasingly no outside to colonize, no significant territory that has yet to be incorporated into the capitalist order, we can view the explosion of debt as a form of temporal colonization, using the future itself as a site of primitive accumulation': Kotsko, *Neoliberalism's demons* (2018), 122. Jason Moore understands the switch from industrial capitalism to 'neoliberal financialization' as a switch from 'the appropriation of space to the colonization of time' caused by a contracting of 'opportunities for accumulation by appropriation': *Capitalism in the web of life* (2015), 304. This is no doubt accurate, but what people like Elon Musk are trying to do is create new frontiers of resource extraction off-planet. And while their plans may be ludicrous, they still point to a nagging problem in late capitalism: capitalism has run out of places to exploit, the very problem Moore has so deftly unpacked.

114 'It hardly needs to be pointed out that the current environmental predicament of the planet is the consequence of the development of an understanding of property in terms of the exploitation of nature, combined with the globalisation of the consequences of that understanding through its link to European expansion': Andrew Fitzmaurice. *Sovereignty, property and empire, 1500–2000* (Cambridge, 2014), 4. In the words of the late Mark Fisher: 'those who can't remember the past are condemned to have it resold to them forever': *Ghosts of my life* (2014), 25.

Bibliography

Archival sources

Detroit Public Library
 – Burton Historical Collection
Margaret Thatcher Foundation (Online)
Truman Library
 – John B. Blandford Papers
 – B.T. Fitzpatrick Papers
 – Raymond M. Foley Papers
 – Nathaniel S. Keith Papers
 – Leon H. Keyserling Papers
 – Papers of Harry S. Truman

Newspapers and online news sources

American Savings and Loan News
The Atlantic
Baffler
CNN
Daily Telegraph
De Bow's Review
Detroit News
Dissent
Foreign Policy
Futurism
The Guardian
The Hill
Huffington Post
Jacobin
Kansas City Star

Bibliography 311

Lippincott's Magazine
Newark News
New York Daily Tribune
New York Times
New York Tribune
NPR
Orlando Morning Sentinel
The Outline
Politico
Der Schweizerische Republikaner
SF Gate
The Verge
Vice Motherboard
Vice News
Vox
Washington Star
Wired

Printed primary sources

Ali, Tariq. *Street fighting years: an autobiography of the sixties* (London, 2005)
Arendt, Hannah. *The origins of totalitarianism*, 2nd edition (New York, 1968)
Bevan, Aneurin. *In place of fear* (London, 1952)
Burke, Edmund. *A philosophical enquiry into the origin of our ideas of the sublime and beautiful, and other pre-revolutionary writings*, David Womersley, ed., 2nd edition (London, 2004 [1757])
— *Reflections on the Revolution in France and on the proceedings in certain societies in London relative to that event*, Conor Cruise O'Brien, ed. (London, 1986 [1790])
— *The correspondence of Edmund Burke*: Vol. I, April 1744–June 1768, Thomas W. Copeland, ed. (Chicago, 1958)
— *The correspondence of Edmund Burke*: Vol. II, June 1768–June 1774, Lucy S. Sutherland, ed. (Chicago, 1960)
— *The correspondence of Edmund Burke*: Vol. III, July 1774–June 1778, George H. Guttridge, ed. (Chicago, 1961)
— *The correspondence of Edmund Burke*: Vol. VI, July 1789–December 1791, Alfred Cobban, Robert A. Smith, eds. (Chicago, 1967)
— *The correspondence of Edmund Burke*: Vol. VII, January 1792–August 1794, P.J. Marshall, John A. Woods, eds. (Chicago, 1968)
— *The correspondence of Edmund Burke*: Vol. VIII, September 1794–April 1796, R.B. McDowell, ed. (Chicago, 1969)

— *The works: twelve volumes in six*, Vol. V (Hildesheim, 1975 [1887])
— *Further reflections on the Revolution in France*, Daniel Ritchie, ed. (Indianapolis, 1992)
Connolly, James. *Collected works*, Vol.1 (Dublin, 1987)
Davitt, Michael. *The fall of feudalism in Ireland, or the story of the Land League revolution* (London, 1904)
Defoe, Daniel; Thomas Keymer, ed. *Robinson Crusoe* (Oxford, 2007 [1719])
Du Bois, W.E.B. *John Brown*, David Roediger, ed. (New York, 2001 [1909])
— *Darkwater: voices from within the veil* (New York, 1969 [1920])
— *Black reconstruction in America, 1860–1880* (New York, 1992 [1935])
Engels, Friedrich. *The condition of the working class in England*, ed. David McLellan (Oxford, 1993 [1844])
— *The housing question*, C.P. Dutt, ed. (Moscow/Leningrad, 1935 [1872])
— *The origin of the family, private property and the state* (Chicago, 1909 [1884])
Fitzhugh, George. *Sociology for the south* (Richmond, VA, 1854)
— *Cannibals all! Or, slaves without masters* (Richmond, VA, 1857)
— 'Centralization and socialism', *De Bow's Review*, June 1856, Vol. 20, No. 6
— 'Excess of population and increase of crime'. *De Bow's Review*, February 1867, Vol. 3, No. 2 [new series]
Hansard, House of Commons Debates
Hegel, G.W.F. *The philosophy of history* (New York, 1991 [1837])
Goldman, Emma. *Living my life*, Vol. II (New York, 1970 [1931])
Goldwater, Barry. *With no apologies* (New York, 1979)
Joyce, James. *Ulysses* (New York, 1986 [1922])
Kautsky, Karl; Henry F. Mins, trans. *Foundations of Christianity* (New York, 1953 [1908])
Locke, John; E.S. De Beer, ed. *The correspondence of John Locke*, Vol. I (Oxford, 1976)
— *Two treatises of government*, Peter Laslett, ed. (Cambridge, 1988)
— *The correspondence of John Locke*, Vol. VIII (Oxford, 1989)
— *Locke on money*, Vol. I, Patrick Hyde Kelly, ed. (Oxford, 1991)
Kramnick, Isaac, ed. *American political thought: a Norton anthology* (New York, 2009)
Lenin, V.I. 'Deception of the people with slogans of freedom and equality', in *Collected works*, Vol. 29, 4th English edition (Moscow, 1972)
Lincoln, Abraham. *Lincoln: speeches, letters, miscellaneous writings, Presidential messages and proclamations, 1859–1865*, Don E. Fehrenbacher, ed. (New York, 1989)

Marx, Karl. *Capital: a critique of political economy*, Vol. I: *The process of production of capital*, ed. Frederick Engels, ed., trans. Samuel Moore, Edward Aveling (London, 1954 [1887])
— 'Economic and philosophic manuscripts of 1844', in *Collected works*, Vol 3: 1843–1844 (London, 1975)
— *A contribution to the critique of political economy*, ed. Maurice Dobb (New York, 1970 [1859])
— *Critique of Hegel's 'Philosophy of right'*, ed. Joseph O'Malley, trans. Annette Jolin, Joseph O'Malley (Cambridge, 1970)
— *Eighteenth Brumaire of Louis Napoleon* (New York, 1963 [1852])
— *Grundrisse: foundations of the critique of political economy*, trans. Martin Nicolaus (London, 1973)
Marx, Karl, Friedrich Engels; A.J.P. Taylor, ed. *The communist manifesto* (London, 1985 [1848])
— *Ireland and the Irish question*, I.L. Golman, V.E. Kunina, eds. (Moscow, 1971)
McGuinness, Frank. *Plays Two* (London, 2002)
Mill, John Stuart; Elizabeth Rapaport, ed. *On liberty* (Indianapolis, IN, [1859])
Mills, C. Wright. *The power elite* (New York, 1956)
O'Donnell, Peadar. *There will be another day* (Dublin, 1963)
Price, Richard. *A discourse on the love of our country* (London, 1789)
Rousseau, Jean-Jacques; Christopher Betts, trans. *The social contract* (Oxford, 1994 [1762])
Sartre, Jean-Paul; George J. Becker, trans. *Anti-semite and Jew* (New York, 1948)
Thatcher, Margaret. *The Downing Street years* (New York, 1993)
— *The path to power* (New York, 1995)
— *Statecraft: strategies for a changing world* (New York, 2002)
— 'Managing conflict – the role of international intervention', in 'Managing conflict in the post-cold war world: the role of intervention', report of the Aspen Institute Conference, 2–6 August 1995 (Queenstown, MD, 1996)
— 'The common crisis: Atlantic solutions', in Gerald Frost, William E. Odom, eds. *The Congress of Prague: revitalizing the Atlantic alliance* (Washington, DC, 1997)
— 'Liberty and responsibility', in David L. Boren, Edward J. Perkins, eds. *Democracy, morality, and the search for peace in American foreign policy* (Norman, OK, 2002)
Townsend, Sue. *The True Confessions of Adrian Albert Mole* (London, 1989)
X, Malcolm; Alex Haley. *The autobiography of Malcolm X* (New York, 1965)

Secondary sources

Agamben, Giorgio; Daniel Heller-Roazen, trans. *Homo sacer: sovereign power and bare life* (Stanford, CA, 1998 [1995])

Alatas, Syed Hussein. *The myth of the lazy native: a study of the image of the Malays, Filipinos and Javanese from the 16th to the 20th century and its function in the ideology of colonial capitalism* (London, 1977)

Albritton Jonsson, Fredrik. *Enlightenment's frontier: the Scottish Highlands and the origins of environmentalism* (New Haven, CT, 2013)

Alexander, Michelle. *The new Jim Crow: mass incarceration in the age of colorblindness* (New York, 2010)

Allen, Theodore. *The invention of the white race*, Vol. 1: *Racial oppression and social control*, 2nd edition (London, 2012)

Anderson, Kevin. *Marx at the margins: on nationalism, ethnicity, and non-Western societies* (Chicago, 2010)

Anderson, Perry. *Lineages of the absolutist state* (London, 1979)

— *Considerations on Western Marxism* (London, 1984)

— *The Indian ideology* (London, 2013)

Apel, Dora. *Beautiful terrible ruins: Detroit and the anxiety of decline* (New Brunswick, NJ, 2015)

Arneil, Barbara. *John Locke and America: the defence of English colonialism* (Oxford, 1996)

Ascher, Ivan. *Portfolio society: on the capitalist mode of prediction* (New York, 2016)

Auslander, Leora. *Cultural revolutions: everyday life and politics in Britain, North America and France* (Oxford, 2008)

Avineri, Shlomo. *The social and political thought of Karl Marx* (Cambridge, 1968)

Baker, Keith Michael, ed. *The French Revolution and the creation of modern political culture*, Vol. 4: *The Terror* (Oxford, 1994)

Barker, Martin. *The new racism: conservatives and the ideology of the tribe* (Frederick, MD, 1981)

Bannerjee, Sikata. *Muscular nationalism: gender, violence, and empire in India and Ireland, 1914–2004* (New York, 2012)

Baptist, Edward. *The half has never been told: slavery and the making of American capitalism* (New York, 2014)

Barrett, Michèle, Mary McIntosh. *The anti-social family*, 2nd edition (London, 2015)

Beatty, Aidan. *Masculinity and power in Irish nationalism, 1884–1938* (London, 2016)

— 'An Irish revolution without a revolution', *Journal of World-Systems Research* Vol. 22, No. 1 (2016), 54–96

— 'The Gaelic League and the spatial logics of Irish nationalism', *Irish Historical Studies*, Vol. 43, No. 163 (2019), 55–72
— 'Marx and Engels, Ireland, and the racial history of capitalism', *Journal of Modern History*, Vol. 94, No. 4 (2019), 815–47
— 'Where does the state end and the church begin? The strange career of Richard S. Devane', *Studi Irlandesi: A Journal of Irish Studies* 9 (2019), 443–64
— 'The two Irish wives of Friedrich Engels: recovering the narratives of Mary and Lizzie Burns', *Socialist History*, 60 (2021), 5–22
Beckert, Sven. *Empire of cotton: a new history of global capitalism* (London, 2014)
Belew, Kathleen. *Bring the war home: the white power movement and paramilitary America* (Cambridge, MA, 2018)
Berkhofer, Robert F., Jr. *The white man's Indian: images of the American Indian from Columbus to the present* (New York, 1978)
Berman, Marshall. *All that is solid melts into air* (New York, 1988)
Berry, Daina Ramey. *The price for their pound of flesh: the value of the enslaved from womb to grave in the building of a nation* (Boston, MA, 2017)
Best, Stephen M. *The fugitive's properties: law and the poetics of possession* (Chicago, 2004)
Bevins, Vincent. *The Jakarta method: Washington's anticommunist crusade and the mass murder program that shaped our world* (New York, 2020)
Bhandar, Brenna. *Colonial lives of property: law, land and racial regimes of ownership* (Durham, NC, 2018)
Blackburn, Robin. *The overthrow of colonial slavery, 1776–1848* (London, 1988)
— *The making of New World slavery: from the baroque to the modern, 1492–1800* (London, 2010)
Boughton, John. *Municipal dreams: the rise and fall of council housing* (London, 2018)
Boulton, David. *Gerrard Winstanley and the republic of heaven* (Dent, Cumbria, 1999)
Bourke, Joanna. *What it means to be human: reflections from 1791 to the present* (Berkeley, CA, 2011)
Bourke, Richard. *Empire and revolution: the political life of Edmund Burke* (Princeton, NJ, 2015)
Brace, Laura. *The politics of property: labour, freedom and belonging* (Basingstoke, 2004)
Bradstock, Andrew. *Radical religion in Cromwell's England: a concise history from the English Civil War to the end of the Commonwealth* (London, 2011)

Breen, T.H., Stephen Innes. *'Myne owne ground': race and freedom on Virginia's eastern shore, 1640–1676* (Oxford, 1980)

Brenner, Robert. *Merchants and revolution: commercial change, political conflict, and London's overseas traders, 1550–1653* (Princeton, NJ, 1993)

Brewer, Holly. 'Slavery, sovereignty, and "inheritable blood": reconsidering John Locke and the origins of American slavery', *American Historical Review*, Vol. 122, No. 4 (2017), 1038–78

Briggs, Laura. *Taking children: a history of American terror* (Berkeley, CA, 2020)

Brown, Wendy. *Undoing the demos: neoliberalism's stealth revolution* (New York, 2015)

Buck-Morss, Susan. *Hegel, Haiti and universal history* (Pittsburgh, PA, 2009)

Burt, Richard, John Michael Archer, eds. *Enclosure Acts: sexuality, property, and culture in early modern England* (Ithaca, NY, 1994)

Butler, Judith. *Gender trouble: feminism and the subversion of identity*, 2nd edition (London, 2006)

Campbell, Fergus. *Land and revolution: nationalist politics in the west of Ireland, 1891–1921* (Oxford, 2005)

— *The Irish establishment, 1879–1914* (Oxford, 2009)

Cannadine, David. *Ornamentalism: how the British saw their empire* (Oxford, 2001)

Canny, Nicholas P. 'The ideology of English colonization: from Ireland to America', *William and Mary Quarterly*, Vol. 30, No. 4 (1973), 575–98

Carter, Julian B. *The heart of whiteness: normal sexuality and race in America, 1880–1940* (Durham, NC, 2007)

Charteris-Black, Jonathan. *Politicians and rhetoric: the persuasive power of metaphor* (London, 2005)

Chakrabarty, Dipesh. *Provincializing Europe: postcolonial thought and historical difference*, 2nd edition (Princeton, NJ, 2007)

Chibber, Vivek. *Postcolonial theory and the spectre of capital* (London, 2013)

Christophers, Brett. *The new enclosure: the appropriation of public land in neoliberal Britain* (London, 2018)

Clark, Gregory, Anthony Clark. 'Common rights to land in England, 1475–1839', *The Journal of Economic History*, Vol. 61, No. 4 (2002), 1009–36

Cleary, Joe. *Literature, partition and the nation state: culture and conflict in Ireland, Israel and Palestine* (Cambridge, 2002)

— *Outrageous fortune: capital and culture in modern Ireland* (Dublin, 2006)

Colletti, Lucio; Lawrence Garner, trans. *Marxism and Hegel* (London, 1973)
Conrad, Kathryn. *Locked in the family cell: gender, sexuality and political agency in Irish national discourse* (Madison, WI, 2004)
Cooper, Melinda. *Family values: between neoliberalism and the new social conservatism* (New York, 2017)
Crary, Jonathan. *24/7: late capitalism and the ends of sleep* (London, 2013)
Crenshaw, Kimberlé. 'Demarginalizing the intersection of race and sex: a Black feminist critique of antidiscrimination doctrine, feminist theory and antiracist politics', *University of Chicago Legal Forum* (1989), 139–67
Crines, Andrew S., Timothy Heppell, Peter Dorey. *The political rhetoric and oratory of Margaret Thatcher* (London, 2016)
Cronon, William. *Changes in the land: Indians, colonists and the ecology of New England* (New York, 1983)
Crotty, Raymond. *Ireland in crisis: a study in capitalist colonial undevelopment* (Dingle, 1986)
Crispin, Jessa. *Why I am not a feminist: a feminist manifesto* (New York, 2017)
Cumings, Bruce. *Dominion from sea to sea: Pacific ascendancy and American power* (New Haven, CT, 2009)
Curry, Tommy. *The man-not: race, class, genre and the dilemmas of Black manhood* (Philadelphia, PA, 2017)
Curtis, L. Perry. *Apes and angels: the Irishman in Victorian culture*, 2nd edition (Washington, DC, 1997)
Daftary, Farhad. 'The "Order of the Assassins": J. von Hammer and the orientalist misrepresentations of the Nizari Ismailis', *Iranian Studies*, Vol. 39, No. 1 (2006), 71–81
Dailey, Jane. *White fright: the sexual panic at the heart of America's racist history* (New York, 2020)
Darwin, John. *After Tamerlane: the rise and fall of global empires, 1400–2000* (New York, 2008)
Davenport, Christian. *The space barons: Elon Musk, Jeff Bezos and the quest to colonize the cosmos* (New York, 2018)
Davidson, Neil. 'Marx and Engels on the Scottish Highlands', *Science & Society*, Vol. 65, No. 3 (2011), 286–326
Davis, Angela Y. *Women, race and class* (New York, 1981)
Davis, Mike. *Old gods, new enigmas: Marx's lost theory* (London, 2018)
Davis, Mike, Daniel Bertrand Monk, eds. *Evil paradises: dreamworlds of neoliberalism* (New York, 2007)
de Baecque, Antoine; Charlotte Mandell, trans. *The body politic: corporeal metaphor in revolutionary France, 1770–1800* (Stanford, CA, 1993)

de Barra, Caomhín. *The coming of the Celts, AD 1860: Celtic nationalism in Ireland and Wales* (Notre Dame, IN, 2018)

de Nie, Michael. *The eternal Paddy: Irish identity and the British press, 1798–1882* (Madison, WI, 2004)

Devine, T.M. *The Scottish clearances: a history of the dispossessed, 1600–1900* (London, 2018)

Donnelly, James S., Jr. *Captain Rock: the Irish agrarian rebellion of 1821–1824* (Madison, WI, 2009)

Dooley, Terence. *The land for the people: the land question in independent Ireland* (Dublin, 2004)

Douglas, R.M. *Architects of the revolution: Ailtirí na hAiséirghe and the fascist 'new order' in Ireland* (Manchester, 2009)

Duggan, Lisa. *Mean girl: Ayn Rand and the culture of greed* (Berkeley, CA, 2019)

Dwan, David, Christopher J. Insole, eds. *The Cambridge companion to Edmund Burke* (Cambridge, 2012)

Eley, Geoff, William Hunt, eds. *Reviving the English Revolution: reflections and elaborations on the work of Christopher Hill* (London, 1988)

Evans, Eric. *Thatcher and Thatcherism*, 3rd edition (London, 2013)

Evans, Richard J. *Eric Hobsbawm: a life in history* (London, 2019)

Farr, James. '"So vile and miserable an estate": the problem of slavery in Locke's political thought', *Political Theory*, Vol. 14, No. 2 (1986), 263–89

Federici, Silvia. *Caliban and the witch: women, the body and primitive accumulation* (New York, 2014)

— *Beyond the periphery of the skin: rethinking, remaking and reclaiming the body in contemporary capitalism* (Oakland, CA, 2020)

Firestone, Shulamith. *The dialectic of sex: the case for feminist revolution* (New York, 2003 [1970])

Fisher, Mark. *Capitalist realism: is there no alternative?* (London, 2009)

— *Ghosts of my life: writings on depression, hauntology and lost futures* (London, 2014)

Fitz-Gibbon, Desmond. *Marketable values: inventing the property market in modern Britain* (Chicago, 2018)

Fitzmaurice, Andrew. *Humanism and America: an intellectual history of English colonisation, 1500–1625* (Cambridge, 2003)

— *Sovereignty, property and empire, 1500–2000* (Cambridge, 2014)

Fennessy, R.R. *Burke, Paine and the rights of man: a difference of political opinion* (The Hague, 1963)

Foner, Eric. *Free soil, free labor, free men: the ideology of the Republican Party before the Civil War* (New York, 1970)

— *Reconstruction: America's unfinished revolution, 1863–1877* (New York, 1988)
— *The fiery trial: Abraham Lincoln and American slavery* (New York, 2010)
Francis, Matthew. '"A crusade to enfranchise the many": Thatcherism and the "property-owning democracy"', *Twentieth Century British History*, Vol. 23, No. 2 (2012), 275–97
Frase, Peter. *Four futures: life after capitalism* (London, 2016)
Fraser, Steve. *The age of acquiescence: the life and death of American resistance to organized wealth and power* (New York, 2015)
Freund, David M.P. *Colored property: state policy and white racial politics in suburban America* (Chicago, 2007)
Furet, François, Mona Ozouf, eds. *The French Revolution and the creation of modern political culture*, Vol. 3: *The transformation of political culture, 1789–1848* (Oxford, 1989)
Gallas, Alexander. *The Thatcherite offensive: a neo-Poultanzasian analysis* (Chicago, 2016)
Gangale, Thomas. *The development of outer space: sovereignty and property rights in international space law* (Santa Barbara, CA, 2009)
Garrigan Mattar, Sinead. *Primitivism, science, and the Irish revival* (Oxford, 2004)
Garvin, Tom. *The evolution of Irish nationalist politics* (Dublin, 2005)
Genovese, Eugene D. *Roll, Jordan, roll: the world the slaves made* (New York, 1972)
Ghodsee, Kristen R. *Why women have better sex under socialism, and other arguments for economic independence* (New York, 2018)
Gilman, Sander. *Smart Jews: the construction of the image of Jewish superior intelligence* (Lincoln, NE, 1996)
Gilroy, Paul. *'There ain't no black in the Union Jack': the cultural politics of race and nation* (Chicago, 1991)
— *The Black Atlantic: modernity and double consciousness* (Cambridge, MA, 1993)
Golumbia, David. *The politics of Bitcoin: software as right-wing extremism* (Minneapolis, MN, 2016)
Gonzalez, Johnhenry. *Maroon nation: a history of revolutionary Haiti* (New Haven, CT, 2019)
Goode, Mike. *Sentimental masculinity and the rise of history, 1790–1890* (Cambridge, 2009)
Goodwin, Albert. *The friends of liberty: the English democratic movement in the age of the French Revolution* (Cambridge, MA, 1979)
Gordon, Robert J. *The rise and fall of American growth: the US standard of living since the Civil War* (Princeton, NJ, 2016)

Graeber, David. *The utopia of rules: on technology, stupidity and the secret joys of bureaucracy* (New York, 2015)
Gramsci, Antonio; David Forgacs, ed. *The Antonio Gramsci reader: selected writings, 1916–1935* (London, 1988)
Grandin, Greg. *The last colonial massacre: Latin America and the cold war* (Chicago, 2004)
Greenfield, Adam. *Radical technologies: the design of everyday life* (London, 2017)
Grossman, James R., ed. *The frontier in American culture* (Berkeley, CA, 1994)
Gurney, John. *Brave community: the Digger movement in the English Revolution* (Manchester, 2007)
Hadley, Louisa. *Responding to Margaret Thatcher's death* (London, 2014)
Hadley, Louisa, Elizabeth Ho, eds. *Thatcher and after: Margaret Thatcher and her afterlife in contemporary culture* (London, 2010)
Haider, Asad. *Mistaken identity: race and class in the age of Trump* (London, 2018)
Hale, Grace Elizabeth. *Making whiteness: the culture of segregation in the south, 1890–1940* (New York, 1998)
Hall, Catherine. *Civilising subjects: metropole and colony in the English imagination, 1830–1867* (Chicago, 2002)
Hall, Stuart; Jennifer Daryl Slack, Lawrence Grossberg, eds. *Cultural studies 1983: a theoretical history* (Durham, NC, 2016)
— *Selected political writings: The great moving right show and other essays*, Sally Davison et al., eds (Durham, NC, 2017)
— *Essential essays*, Vol. 1: *Foundations of cultural studies*, David Morley, ed. (Durham, NC, 2019)
Hall, Stuart, Martin Jacques, eds. *The politics of Thatcherism* (London, 1983)
Hall, Stuart, Chas Critcher, Tony Jefferson, John Clarke, Brian Roberts. *Policing the crisis: mugging, the state, and law and order* (London, 1978)
Hämäläinen, Pekka. *The Comanche empire* (New Haven, CT, 2008)
Hancock, Ange-Marie. *Intersectionality: an intellectual history* (Oxford, 2016)
Hanley, Brian, Scott Millar. *The lost revolution: the story of the Official IRA and the Worker's Party* (Dublin, 2009)
Harloe, Michael. *The people's home: social rented housing in Europe and America* (Oxford, 1995)
Harris, Cheryl I. 'Whiteness as property', *Harvard Law Review*, Vol. 106, No. 8 (1993), 1707–91
Harvey, David. *Spaces of capital: towards a critical geography* (New York, 2001)
— *A companion to Marx's Capital* (London, 2010)

Hatherley, Owen. *The ministry of nostalgia* (London, 2016)
Hazan, Eric; David Fernbach, trans. *A people's history of the French Revolution* (London, 2014)
Helsinger, Elizabeth K. *Rural scenes and national representation: Britain, 1815–1850* (Princeton, NJ, 1997)
Henkel, Scot. *Direct democracy: collective power, the swarm and the literatures of the Americas* (Jackson, MS, 2017)
Herzog, Don. *Poisoning the minds of the lower orders* (Princeton, NJ, 1998)
Hiers, Richard H. 'Transfer of property by inheritance and bequest in Biblical law and tradition', *Journal of Law and Religion*, Vol. 10, No. 121 (1993), 121–55
Higonnet, Patrice. *Goodness beyond virtue: Jacobins during the French Revolution* (Cambridge, MA, 1998)
Hill, Christopher. *The world turned upside down: radical ideas during the English Revolution* (London, 1975)
— *The century of revolution, 1603–1714*, 2nd edition (New York, 1980)
— *The collected essays of Christopher Hill* (Amherst, MA, 1986)
Hirsch; Arnold R., Raymond A. Mohl, eds. *Urban policy in twentieth century America* (New Brunswick, NJ, 1993)
Hirota, Hidetka. *Expelling the poor: Atlantic seaboard states and the 19th century origins of American immigration policy* (Oxford, 2017)
Holt, Thomas C. *The problem of freedom: race, labor, and politics in Jamaica and Britain, 1832–1938* (Baltimore, MD, 1992)
Hogan, Sarah. *Other Englands: utopia, capital and empire in an age of transition* (Stanford, CA, 2018)
Hooper, Glenn. *Travel writing and Ireland, 1760–1860: culture, history, politics* (London, 2005)
Horne, Gerald. *The counter-revolution of 1776: slave resistance and the origins of the United States of America* (New York, 2014)
Horning, Audrey. *Ireland in the Virginia sea: colonialism in the British Atlantic* (Chapel Hill, NC, 2013)
Horowitz, Elliot. *Reckless rites: Purim and the legacy of Jewish violence* (Princeton, NJ, 2006)
Hunt, Lynn. *Politics, culture and class in the French Revolution* (Berkeley, CA, 1984)
Hunt, Tristram. *Marx's general: the revolutionary life of Friedrich Engels* (New York, 2009)
Huyler, Jerome. *Locke in America: the moral philosophy of the founding era* (Lawrence, KS, 1995)
Ignatiev, Noel. *How the Irish Became white* (New York, 2008)
Ince, Onur Ulas. *Colonial capitalism and the dilemmas of liberalism* (Oxford, 2018)

Inglis, Tom. *Moral monopoly: the rise and fall of the Catholic church in modern Ireland*, 2nd edition (Dublin, 1998)
Isenberg, Nancy. *White trash: the 400-year untold history of class in America* (New York, 2016)
Jackson, Ben, Robert Saunders, eds. *Making Thatcher's Britain* (Cambridge, 2012)
Jackson, Paul, Anton Shekhovtsov, eds. *The post-war Anglo-American far right: a special relationship of hate* (London, 2014)
James, Stanlie M., Abena P.A. Busia, eds. *Theorizing Black feminisms: the visionary pragmatism of Black women* (London, 1993)
Jameson, Fredric. *Postmodernism, or, the cultural logic of late capitalism* (Durham, NC, 1991)
Johnson, David K. *The lavender scare: the cold war persecution of gays and lesbians in the Federal government* (Chicago, 2004)
Johnson, Walter. *The broken heart of America: St Louis and the history of American violence* (New York, 2020)
Jones, Emily. *Edmund Burke and the invention of modern conservatism, 1830–1914: an intellectual history* (Oxford, 2017)
Jones-Rogers, Stephanie E. *They were her property: white women as slave owners* (New Haven, CT, 2019)
Kane, Anne. *Constructing Irish national identity: discourse and ritual during the land war, 1879–1882* (New York, 2011)
Kapp, Yvonne. *Eleanor Marx*, Vol. 1: *Family life (1855–1883)* (New York, 1972)
— *Eleanor Marx*, Vol. 2: *The crowded years, 1884–1898* (New York, 1976)
Karuka, Manu. *Empire's tracks: indigenous nations, Chinese workers, and the transcontinental railroad* (Berkeley, CA, 2019)
Katznelson, Ira. *When affirmative action was white: an untold history of racial inequality in twentieth-century America* (New York, 2005)
Kavanagh, Declan. *Effeminate years: literature politics and aesthetics in mid-eighteenth-century Britain* (Lewisburg, PA, 2017)
Kazanjian, David. *The colonizing trick: national culture and imperial citizenship in early America* (Minneapolis, MN, 2003)
Kelley, Robin D.G. *Hammer and hoe: Alabama communists during the Great Depression*, 2nd edition (Chapel Hill, NC, 2015)
Kendi, Ibram X. *Stamped from the beginning: the definitive history of racist ideas in America* (New York, 2016)
Kimmerling, Baruch. *Zionism and territory: the socio-territorial dimensions of Zionist politics* (Berkeley, CA, 1983)
Klosko, George. *The transformation of American liberalism* (Oxford, 2017)
Koontz, Stephanie. *The way we never were: American families and the nostalgia trap*, 2nd edition (New York, 2016)

Kostick, Conor. *Revolution in Ireland: popular militancy, 1917–1923*, 2nd edition (Cork, 2009)
Kotsko, Adam. *Neoliberalism's demons: on the political theology of late capital* (Stanford, CA, 2018)
Kramnick, Isaac. *The rage of Edmund Burke: portrait of an ambivalent conservative* (New York, 1977)
Krieger, Joel. *Reagan, Thatcher and the politics of decline* (Oxford, 1986)
Kruse, Kevin M. *White flight: Atlanta and the making of modern conservatism* (Princeton, NJ, 2005)
Kruse, Kevin M., Thomas J. Sugrue, eds. *The new suburban history* (Chicago, 2006)
Kupperman, Karen Ordahl. *Indians and English: facing off in early America* (Ithaca, NY, 2000)
Kusmer, Kenneth L., Joe W. Trotter, eds. *African American urban history since World War II* (Chicago, 2009)
Laffan, Michael. *The partition of Ireland, 1911–1925* (Dundalk, 1983)
Landes, Joan D., ed. *Feminism, the public and the private* (Oxford, 1998)
Lebowitz, Michael. 'The politics of assumption, the assumption of politics', *Historical Materialism*, Vol. 14, No. 2 (2006), 29–47
Lee, J.J. *The modernisation of Irish society, 1848–1918* (Oxford, 1973)
Lee, Robert. 'Accounting for conquest: the price of the Louisiana Purchase of Indian country', *Journal of American History*, Vol. 103, No. 4 (2017), 921–42
Leerssen, Joep. *Mere Irish and Fíor-Ghael: studies in the idea of Irish nationality, its development and literary expression prior to the nineteenth century* (Notre Dame, IN, 1997)
Lefebvre, Georges; Elizabeth Moss Evanson, trans. *The French Revolution: from its origins to 1793* (London, 1962 [1957])
Levin, Yuval. *The great debate: Edmund Burke, Thomas Paine, and the birth of right and left* (New York, 2014)
Levine, Norman. *The tragic deception: Marx contra Engels* (Oxford, 1975)
Linebaugh, Peter. *The Magna Carta manifesto: liberties and commons for all* (Berkeley, CA, 2008)
Linebaugh, Peter, Marcus Rediker. *The many-headed hydra: sailors, slaves, commoners, and the hidden history of the revolutionary Atlantic*, 2nd edition (Boston, MA, 2013)
Liu, Wendy. *Abolish Silicon Valley: how to liberate technology from capitalism* (London, 2020)
López, Tara Martin. *The winter of discontent: myth, memory and history* (Liverpool, 2014)
Lorde, Audre. 'Learning from the '60s'. In *Sister outsider: essays and speeches* (New York, 1984)

Maciag, Drew. *Edmund Burke in America: the contested career of the father of modern conservatism* (Ithaca, NY, 2013)

Mac Laughlin, Jim. 'Emigration and the peripheralization of Ireland in the global economy', *Review (Fernand Braudel Center)* Vol. 17, No. 2 (1994), 243–73

MacLean, Nancy. *Democracy in chains: the deep history of the radical right's stealth plan for America* (New York, 2017)

Macpherson, C.B. *The political theory of possessive individualism: Hobbes to Locke* (Oxford, 1962)

Mac Suibhne, Breandán. *The end of outrage: post-Famine adjustment in rural Ireland* (Oxford, 2017)

Madden, David, Peter Marcuse. *In defence of housing: the politics of crisis* (London, 2016)

Makdisi, Saree. *Making England Western: occidentalism, race and imperial culture* (Chicago, 2014)

Malm, Andreas. *Fossil capital: the rise of steam power and the roots of global warming* (London, 2016)

Mandel, Ernest. *Late capitalism* (London, 1978)

Mann, Geoff. *In the long run we are all dead: Keynesianism, political economy, and revolution* (London, 2017)

Marable, Manning. *How capitalism underdeveloped Black America: problems in race, political economy and society* (Boston, MA, 1983)

Martin, Amy. 'Blood transfusions: constructions of Irish racial difference, the English working class, and revolutionary possibility in the work of Carlyle and Engels', *Victorian Literature and Culture*, Vol. 32, No. 1 (2004), 83–102

— *Alter-nations: nationalisms, terror, and the state in nineteenth-century Britain and Ireland* (Columbus, OH, 2012)

Matthiessen, Peter. *In the spirit of Crazy Horse: the story of Leonard Peltier and the FBI's war on the American Indian Movement* (New York, 1992)

McCullough, David. *Truman* (New York, 1992)

Medhurst, John. *That option no longer exists: Britain, 1974–76* (London, 2014)

Meek, James. *Private island: why Britain now belongs to someone else* (London, 2014)

Merritt, Keri Leigh. *Masterless men: poor whites and slavery in the antebellum south* (Cambridge, 2017)

Mies, Maria. *Patriarchy and accumulation on a world scale: women in the international division of labour*, 2nd edition (London, 1998)

Miller, Kerby. *Emigrants and exiles: Ireland and the Irish exodus to North America* (Oxford, 1985)

Milne, Seumas. *The enemy within: the secret war against the miners* (London, 2004)

Minsky, Hyman P. *Stabilizing an unstable economy* (New Haven, CT, 1986)
Moore, Jason. *Capitalism in the web of life: ecology and the accumulation of capital* (London, 2015)
Moore, Jason, Raj Patel. *A history of the world in seven cheap things: a guide to capitalism, nature, and the future of the planet* (Berkeley, CA, 2017)
Moreton, Bethany. *To serve God and Wal-Mart: the making of Christian free enterprise* (Cambridge, MA, 2009)
Moreton-Robinson, Aileen. *The white possessive: property, power, and indigenous sovereignty* (Minneapolis, MN, 2015)
Morgan, Edmund S. *American slavery, American freedom: the ordeal of colonial Virginia* (New York, 1975)
Morrissey, Conor. *Protestant nationalists in Ireland, 1900–1923* (Cambridge, 2019)
Moyn, Samuel. 'The secret history of constitutional dignity', *Yale Human Rights and Development Journal*, Vol. 17, No. 1 (2014), 39–73
Mulder, David W. *The alchemy of revolution: Gerrard Winstanley's occultism and seventeenth-century English communism* (New York, 1990)
Naarden, Bruno. 'Marx and Russia', *History of European Ideas*, Vol. 12, No. 6 (1990), 783–97
Nelson, Bruce. *Irish nationalists and the making of the Irish race* (Princeton, NJ, 2013)
Neocleous, Mark. *A critical theory of police power*, 2nd edition (London, 2021)
Nirenberg, David. *Anti-Judaism: the Western tradition* (New York, 2013)
Nunn, Heather. *Thatcher, politics and fantasy: the political culture of gender and nation* (London, 2002)
O'Brien, Michael. *Conjectures of order: intellectual life and the American south, 1810–1860*, Vol. II (Chapel Hill, NC, 2004)
Ó Conchubhair, Brian. *Fin de siècle na Gaeilge: Darwin, an athbheochan agus smaointearacht na hEorpa* [*Irish-language Fin de Siècle: Darwin, the Gaelic revival and European intellectual thought*] (Indreabhán, 2009)
Ó Grada, Cormac. 'The population of Ireland, 1700–1900: a survey', *Annales de Démographie Historique* (1979), 281–99
O'Neill, Daniel I. *The Burke–Wollstonecraft debate: savagery, civilization, and democracy* (University Park, PA, 2007)
— *Edmund Burke and the conservative logic of empire* (Berkeley, CA, 2016)
O'Neill, Peter. *Famine Irish and the American racial state* (New York, 2017)
O'Toole, Fintan. *Heroic failure: Brexit and the politics of pain* (London, 2018)

Overbeek, Henk. *Global capitalism and national decline: the Thatcher decade in perspective* (London, 1990)
Parent, Anthony S., Jr. *Foul means: the formation of a slave society in Virginia, 1660–1740* (Chapel Hill, NC, 2003)
Parisot, James. *How America became capitalist: imperial expansion and the conquest of the West* (London, 2019)
Pearl, Sharrona. *About faces: physiognomy in nineteenth-century Britain* (Cambridge, MA, 2010)
Pein, Corey. *Live work work work die: a journey into the savage heart of Silicon Valley* (New York, 2017)
Peplow, Simon. *Race and riots in Thatcher's Britain* (Manchester, 2019)
Perlstein, Rick. *Before the storm: Barry Goldwater and the unmaking of the American consensus* (New York, 2001)
— *Nixonland: the rise of a President and the fracturing of America* (New York, 2008)
— *The invisible bridge: the fall of Nixon and the rise of Reagan* (New York, 2014)
Perry, Kennetta Hammond. *London is the place for me: Black Britons, citizenship, and the politics of race* (Oxford, 2015)
Petegorsky, David W. *Left-wing democracy in the English Civil War: a study of the social philosophy of Gerrard Winstanley* (New York, 1972)
Pierson, Christopher. *Just property, a history in the Latin West*, Vol. 1: *Wealth, virtue and the law* (Oxford, 2013)
— *Just property, a history in the Latin West*, Vol. 2: *Enlightenment, revolution, and history* (Oxford, 2016)
Pincus, Steven. *1688: the first modern revolution* (New Haven, CT, 2011)
Prashad, Vijay. *The darker nations: a people's history of the Third World* (New York, 2007)
Rees, John. *The Leveller revolution: radical political organisation in England, 1640–1650* (London, 2016)
Richardson, Heather Cox. *To make men free: a history of the Republican Party* (New York, 2014)
Riddell, Peter. *Thatcher decade: how Britain has changed during the 1980s* (Oxford, 1989)
Roberts, Dorothy. *Killing the Black body: race, reproduction and the meaning of liberty* (New York, 1997)
Roberts, William Clare. 'Marx in Hell: the critique of political economy as katabasis', *Critical Sociology* Vol. 31, Nos 1, 2 (2005)
— *Marx's inferno: the political theory of capital* (Princeton, NJ, 2017)
Robin, Corey. *The reactionary mind: conservatism from Edmund Burke* (Oxford, 2011)
Robinson, Cedric J. *Black Marxism: the making of the Black radical tradition*, 2nd edition (Chapel Hill, NC, 2000)

Roediger, David. *The wages of whiteness: race and the making of the American working class* (London, 1991)
— *Class, race, and Marxism* (London, 2017)
Rogers, G.A.J., ed. *Locke's philosophy: content and context* (Oxford, 1994)
Rohe, William M., Harry L. Watson, eds. *Chasing the American dream: new perspectives on affordable homeownership* (Ithaca, NY, 2007)
Rose, R.B. *Gracchus Babeuf: the first revolutionary communist* (Stanford, CA, 1978),
Rosenthal, Caitlin. *Accounting for slavery: masters and management* (Cambridge, MA, 2018)
Ross, Kristin. *Communal luxury: the political imaginary of the Paris Commune* (London, 2015)
Sachs, Honor. *Home rule: households, manhood and national expansion on the eighteenth-century Kentucky frontier* (New Haven, CT, 2015)
Saito, Kohei. *Karl Marx's ecosocialism: Capital, nature, and the unfinished Critique of political economy* (New York, 2017)
Saxton, Alexander. *The rise and fall of the white republic: class politics and mass culture in nineteenth-century America* (London, 1990)
Sayers, Daniel O. *A desolate place for a defiant people: the archaeology of Maroons, indigenous Americans and enslaved laborers in the Great Dismal Swamp* (Gainesville, FL, 2014)
Schechter, Ronald. *Obstinate Hebrews: representations of Jews in France, 1715–1815* (Berkeley, CA, 2003)
Schrader, Stuart. *Badges without borders: how global counterinsurgency transformed American policing* (Berkeley, CA, 2019)
Schwab, Gail M., John R. Jeanneney, eds. *The French Revolution of 1789 and its impact* (Westport, CT, 1995)
Scott, Joan Wallach. *Gender and the politics of history*, revised edition (New York, 1999)
Scott, Julius S. *The common wind: Afro-American currents in the age of the Haitian revolution* (London, 2018)
Seiler, Cotten. *Republic of drivers: a cultural history of automobility in America* (Chicago, 2008)
Sell, Zach. *Trouble of the world: slavery and empire in the age of capital* (Chapel Hill, NC, 2021)
Shanin, Teodor. *Late Marx and the Russian road: Marx and the peripheries of capitalism* (New York, 1983)
Sharman, Frank A. 'An introduction to the Enclosure Acts', *Legal History*, Vol. 10, No. 1 (1989), 45–70
Sinha, Manisha. *The slave's cause: a history of abolition* (New Haven, CT, 2016)

Sinha, Mrinalini. *Colonial masculinity: the 'manly Englishman' and the 'effeminate Bengali' in the late nineteenth century* (Manchester, 1995)

Slater, Eamonn. 'Engels on Ireland's dialectics of nature', *Capitalism, Socialism, Nature*, Vol. 29, No. 4 (2018), 31–50

Smith, Anna Marie. *New Right discourse on race and sexuality: Britain, 1968–1990* (Cambridge, 1994)

Sperber, Jonathan. *The European revolutions, 1848–1851* (Cambridge, 1984)

— *Karl Marx: a nineteenth century life* (New York, 2014)

Squires, Gregory D. *Capital and communities in Black and white: the intersections of race, class, and uneven development* (Albany, NY, 1994)

Stalybrass, Peter, Allon White. *Politics and poetics of transgression* (Ithaca, NY, 1986)

Stanley, Amy Dru. *From bondage to contract: wage labor, marriage, and the market in the age of slave emancipation* (Cambridge, 1998)

Stannard, David. *American holocaust: the conquest of the New World* (Oxford, 1992)

Sublette, Ned, Constance Sublette. *The American slave coast: a history of the slave-breeding industry* (Chicago, 2016)

Sufian, Sandra M. *Healing the land and the nation: malaria and the Zionist project in Palestine, 1920–1947* (Chicago, 2007)

Sugrue, Thomas. *The origins of the urban crisis: race and inequality in postwar Detroit* (Princeton, NJ, 1996)

Sutcliffe-Braithwaite, Florence. 'Neo-liberalism and morality in the making of Thatcherite social policy', *The Historical Journal*, Vol. 55, No. 2 (2012), 497–520

Takaki, Ronald. *Iron cages: race and culture in nineteenth-century America* (Oxford, 2000)

Talbot, Ann. *'The Great Ocean of Knowledge': the influence of travel literature on the work of John Locke* (Leiden, 2010)

Taylor, Keeanga-Yamahtta. *From #BlackLivesMatter to Black liberation* (Chicago, 2016)

— *Race for profit: how banks and the real estate industry undermined Black homeownership* (Chapel Hill, NC, 2019)

Therborn, Göran. *Inequality and the labyrinths of democracy* (London, 2020)

Thompson, E.P. *The making of the English working class* (New York, 1966)

Valente, Joseph. *The myth of manliness in Irish national culture* (Champaign, IL, 2011)

Vance, Ashlee. *Elon Musk: Tesla, SpaceX and the quest for a fantastic future*, 2nd edition (New York, 2017)

Vaughan, W.E. *Landlords and tenants in mid-Victorian Ireland* (Oxford, 1994)
Virdee, Satnam. *Racism, class and the racialized outsider* (London, 2014)
Vitale, Alex. *The end of policing* (London, 2017)
Wahnich, Sophie; David Fernbach, trans. *In defence of the Terror: liberty or death in the French Revolution* (London, 2012)
Walkowitz, Judith. *City of dreadful delight: narratives of sexual danger in late-Victorian London* (Chicago, 1992)
Wallerstein, Immanuel. *The modern world-system*, Vol. I: *Capitalist agriculture and the European world economy in the sixteenth century*, 2nd edition (Berkeley, CA, 2011)
— *The modern world-system*, Vol. III: *The second era of great expansion of the capitalist world-economy*, 2nd edition (Berkeley, CA, 2011)
— *The modern world-system*, Vol. IV: *Centrist liberalism triumphant, 1789–1914* (Berkeley, CA, 2011)
Walter, John. *Understanding popular violence in the English Revolution: the Colchester plunderers* (Cambridge, 1999)
Ware, Vron. *Beyond the pale: white women, racism and history* (London, 2015)
Webster, Charles, ed. *The intellectual revolution of the seventeenth century* (London, 1974)
Weinbaum, Alys Eve. *Wayward reproductions: genealogies of race and nation in transatlantic modern thought* (Durham, NC, 2004)
Whyte, J.H. *Church and state in modern Ireland, 1923–1970* (Dublin, 1971)
Wilentz, Sean. *No property in man: slavery and antislavery at the nation's founding* (Cambridge, MA, 2018)
Williams, Eric. *Capitalism and slavery* (New York, 1966 [1944])
Williams, Raymond. *Culture and society* (London, 1958)
— *The country and the city* (Oxford, 1973)
Williams, William H.A. *Tourism, landscape and the Irish character: British travel writers in pre-Famine Ireland* (Madison, WI, 2008)
Winter, Alison. *Mesmerized: powers of mind in Victorian Britain* (Chicago, 1998)
Wish, Harvey. *George Fitzhugh: conservative of the old South* (Charlottesville, VA, 1938)
— *George Fitzhugh: propagandist of the old South* (Baton Rouge, LA, 1943)
Wood, Ellen Meiksins. *Citizens to lords: a social history of Western political thought from antiquity to the Middle Ages* (London, 2008)
— *The pristine culture of capitalism: a historical essay on old regimes and modern states*, 2nd edition (London, 2015)

Wood, Neal. *John Locke and agrarian capitalism* (Berkeley, CA, 1984)
— *Tyranny in America: capitalism and national decay* (London, 2004)
Wood, Tony. *Russia without Putin: money, power and the myths of the new cold war* (London, 2018)
Worster, Donald. *Rivers of empire: water, aridity, and the growth of the American West* (New York, 1985)
— *Shrinking the Earth: the rise and decline of American abundance* (Oxford, 2016)
Wright, Gavin. *Slavery and American economic development* (Baton Rouge, LA, 2006)
Wright, Gwendolyn. *Building the dream: a social history of housing in America* (Cambridge, MA, 1981)
Yablon, Nick. *Untimely ruins: an archaeology of American urban modernity* (Chicago, 2009)
Zamoyski, Adam. *Phantom terror: political paranoia and the creation of the modern state* (New York, 2015)

Index

Abrams, Charles 205
Adams, John 8, 41
Alien Land Acts (California, 1913 and 1920) 42–3
American Space Technology for Exploring Resource Opportunities In Deep Space (ASTEROIDS) Act 293
Anti-Jacobin 95
Armstrong, Neil 298
Attlee, Clement 262

Bacon, Francis 32
Bacon's Rebellion 176
Ben-Gurion, David 43
Berkeley, William 46, 176
Bezos, Jeff 290, 294, 295, 297, 298
Blackstone, William 3
Blandford, John 204, 213
Boone, Daniel 40
Boswell, James 91–2
Branson, Richard 289, 290, 297
Brexit 284
Burke, Edmund 5, 8, 12, 13, 164
 anti-Jewish attitudes of 69, 79–81, 84, 87
 belief in social hierarchies of 79
 and conservatism 95–6, 112
 and Ireland 115

and prescriptive property rights 71
Reflections on the Revolution in France (1790) 67, 70
unmarked grave of 99
xenophobia and/or racism of 68–9, 82, 87, 91
Burns, Lydia ("Lizzie") 114, 137, 141–2
Burns, Mary 114, 141–2

Calhoun, John C. 176, 191–2
Canning, George 95
Chamberlain, Neville 276
Change Alley (London) 81
Chartism 95
Cherokee 42
Cicero 50, 72, 101
Cobbett, William 78
Coercion Bill (1833) 95
Columbus, Christopher 37
Connolly, James 154
Corrigan v. Buckley (1926) 232
Cromwell, Oliver 4
Cruz, Ted 292
Cuba 37
Cushman, Robert 45

Daily Picayune 172
Dawes Severalty Act (1887) 58

De Bow, James D.B. 178
De Bow's Review 178, 186
de Sepúlveda, Juan Ginés 38
Depont, Charles-Jean-François 68, 73, 89
Dewey, Thomas 201
Downey Jr, Robert 286–7
Drayton, Michael 35
du Bois, W.E.B. 1, 9, 167, 169–70, 180, 183

East India Company 93, 98
Eden, Anthony 260
Eisenhower, Dwight D. 236
Enclosures 2–3
Engels, Friedrich 12, 13
  1856 visit to Ireland 113–14, 130
  1869 visit to Ireland 137
  and *Conditions of the Working Class in England* 116, 120
  and *Origins of the Family* 136
  and Thomas Carlyle 149

Fair Housing Act (1968) 223
Federal Housing Administration (FHA) 204, 206, 207, 210, 211, 214, 217, 221–3, 233
  Underwriting Manual (1938) issued by 217
Filmer, Robert 23, 24, 26
Fitzhugh, George 8, 13–14
  compared to Edmund Burke 175–6, 178, 182, 208
  gender politics of 168–9, 174–5
  interest in Ireland of 184
  and Karl Marx 159, 162, 185–6
  and socialism 166, 168, 173
Fitzhugh, William 176
Foley, Raymond 211–12, 215, 217, 220, 230, 233, 236
Fox, Charles James 66
Francis, Philip 102

Garat, Dominique 77
Garrison, William Lloyd 177
Gingrich, Newt 239
Glorious Revolution, the (1688) 65, 285
  and French Revolution 70, 72, 74
Goldman, Emma 154
Goldwater, Barry 14, 239
Gordon, George 80
Gramsci, Antonio 76
Gray, Robert 35
Greeley, Horace 177, 185
Grégoire, Henri 77
Grotius, Hugo 55
Guadalupe Hidalgo, Treaty of (1848) 42

Haitian Revolution 175
Hakluyt, Richard 32, 51
Hammond, James 176
Hastings, Warren 95
Hayek, Friedrich 243
Heath, Edward 244, 281
Hegel, G.W.F. 145, 148
Hispaniola 37
Homestead Act (1862) 45, 298
Howe, Geoffrey 281
Hume, David 70
Hussein, Saddam 112

Illustrated London News 177
International Working Man's Association 124, 145

Jacobins, Jacobinism 12, 63, 66, 67, 77, 83, 87, 99, 102, 248
  ideological diversity of 77
Jamestown, Virginia 32, 44
Jefferson, Thomas 40, 47
  and Edmund Burke 95
Jim Crow 167, 183, 215, 291
Johnson, Andrew 172–3

Johnson v. M'Intosh (1823) 41
Joseph, Keith 245, 275

Kautsky, Karl 154
Keith, Nathaniel 213
Keynes, John Maynard 231

'Land of Cockaygne' 35
La Salle, René-Robert 56
Levitt, William 214, 221
Lincoln, Abraham 171, 177, 196
Locke, John 5, 8, 11, 13, 27, 35,
    43, 47, 77, 133, 164, 291–2
  and Edmund Burke 92
  and the enclosures 35
  'First treatise' 23, 25, 28
  and Native Americans 28, 30, 48
  and race 25, 197–8
  'Second treatise' 23, 26, 31
  as settler-colonial thinker 43, 46
  and slavery 180–1, 182, 199
  views of the Irish of 30, 33, 115
  work for the Board of Trade of
    32, 34
London Corresponding Society 63
Louisiana Purchase 41, 58
Luther, Martin 38

McCarthy, Joseph 212
McConnell, Mitch 291
Mackay, Charles 177
Malcolm X 189
Marie Antoinette 80, 82, 84
Marx, Eleanor 137
Marx, Karl 1, 11, 12, 13
  and *18th Brumaire* 134
  and 1844 Manuscripts 122
  and *Capital* 121, 122, 131, 140
  conservatives' fears of 209
  compared to Locke and Burke
    135–6, 138–40
  and views of Jews 153
Mather, Cotton 39

Mill, John Stuart 55, 93–4
Mix, Charles E. 42
Moon Agreement (1979) 293
Morgan, Lewis 136
More, Thomas 32
Mormonism 166
Morton, Thomas 45
Musk, Elon 15
  and government funding received
    by 296
  and Iron Man 286–7
  and Martian fantasies 294
  and race 291

National Housing Act (1934)
National Housing Agency 204
National Union of Mineworkers
    244, 274
New York Daily Tribune 124, 185
New Yorker Volkszeitung 137

Obama, Barack 292
Ochs, Phil 111
O'Connell, Daniel 94, 120
O'Connor, Fergus 6
O'Donnell, Peadar 126
Old Jewry (London) 12, 64, 68,
    69

Paine, Thomas 83
Pamunkey 39
Paradise Lost (1667) 89
Patriarcha 23
Penal Laws 115
Phillips, Wendell 177
Pitt, William (the Younger) 87, 95
Polanyi, Karl 161
Powell, Enoch 253–5, 277
Powell, J.W. 42
Powhatan Confederacy 39, 44
Price, Richard 12, 64–6
  Edmund Burke's views of 68–9
Purchas, Samuel 51

Raleigh, Walter 51
real estate lobby 203, 206, 208, 209, 210, 211, 229, 236
  promotion of gender roles by 219
Reagan, Ronald 7, 14, 15,
  nostalgic childhood memories of 239
Reconstruction 7
Red Republican 185–6
Ricardo, David 129
Rich, Robert 35
Richey, Alexander 116
Robespierrre, Maximilien 77
Robinson Crusoe (1719) 38, 180
Roosevelt, Franklin Delano 201, 202, 206, 227
Royal African Company 182
Ross, John 42
Seymour, Horatio 42
Rousseau, Jean-Jacques 92–3
rundale 43, 60

Sartre, Jean-Paul 63
Schweizerische Republikaner, Der 120, 125
Selsdon Group 260
Servicemen's Readjustment Act [GI Bill] (1944) 206
Seymour, Horatio 42
Shelley v. Kraemer (1948) 232
Sieyès, Emmanuel-Joseph (Abbé Sieyès) 76
Smith, Adam 129
Smith, John 39
Society for Commemorating the Revolution in Great Britain 63, 64
Society for Constitutional Information 63
Southern Rose 168
Specie Circular Act (1836) 172

Spencer, Diana 242
Spenser, Edmund 114
State v. Will (1834) 170

Taft–Hartley Act (1947) 202
Taylor, Frederick 178
Taylor, Glen 205
Thatcher, Denis 269
Thatcher, Margaret 7, 8, 15, 161
  childhood 238
  and Enoch Powell 253–5
  ethnic stereotypes of 252, 276
  and gender politics of 256–9, 266, 279–80
  and privatisation 261–2
  religious beliefs of 253
Treaty on Principles Governing the Activities of States in the Exploration and Use of Outer Space, including the Moon and Other Celestial Bodies (1967) 293
Trudeau, Pierre 281
Truman, Harry 14
  allegations of crypto-socialism against 209–10, 212
  Council of Economic Advisors of 215
  State of the Union addresses of 201, 206
Trump, Donald 284–5, 289, 290
  and Silicon Valley 297
Turner, Nat 175

United Irishmen 5, 95

Vesey, Denmark 175
Vespucci, Amerigo 37
Vickery, Howard 204
Virginia Company 35
von Westphalen, Jenny 142

Wagner–Ellender–Taft Act (1949)
  206, 207, 211, 221, 230
Wallace, George 201
War of 1812 41
Waitingi, Treaty of (1840) 43
Wayne, John 23
Winstanley, Gerrard 4

Winthrop, John 38
Wollstonecraft, Mary 95, 106

X, Malcolm *see* Malcolm X

Young, Arthur 104

EU authorised representative for GPSR:
Easy Access System Europe, Mustamäe tee 50,
10621 Tallinn, Estonia
gpsr.requests@easproject.com

www.ingramcontent.com/pod-product-compliance
Lightning Source LLC
Chambersburg PA
CBHW051557230426
43668CB00013B/1886